BUILDING SEAGRAM

BUILDING SEAGRAM

PHYLLIS LAMBERT

FOREWORD BY BARRY BERGDOLL

YALE UNIVERSITY PRESS
NEW HAVEN AND LONDON

Publication of *Building Seagram* is supported by grants from the Graham Foundation for Advanced Studies in the Fine Arts and Furthermore: a program of the J. M. Kaplan Fund.

Copyright © 2013 by Yale University.

All rights reserved.

This book may not be reproduced, in whole or in part, including illustrations, in any form (beyond that copying permitted by Sections 107 and 108 of the U.S. Copyright Law and except by reviewers for the public press), without written permission from the publishers.

yalebooks.com/art

Designed by Jeff Wincapaw
Set in Minion Pro and Verlag
Printed in China.

ISBN 978-0-300-16767-2
Library of Congress Control Number: 2012948915

A catalogue record for this book is available from the British Library.

Frontispiece: Philip Johnson, Ludwig Mies van der Rohe, and Phyllis Lambert in front of an image of the model for the Seagram building, New York, 1955. Gelatin silver print, 7½ × 9⅜ in. Photographer unknown.

This paper meets the requirements of ANSI/NISO Z39.48–1992 (Permanence of Paper).

10 9 8 7 6 5 4 3 2

CONTENTS

	vii	Foreword *Barry Bergdoll*
	xi	Acknowledgments
PROLOGUE	1	Unlikely Convergences
CHAPTER 1	13	A Site and an Architect for Seagram
CHAPTER 2	38	Mies van der Rohe's Ur-Building
PORTFOLIO	88	Richard Pare: Plaza Studies, 2000 and 2010
CHAPTER 3	102	Union of Building and Plaza in the Urban Landscape
CHAPTER 4	122	Light: Philip Johnson's *Stimmung*
CHAPTER 5	150	Architecture and Art Allied
CHAPTER 6	194	Ironies in the Public Life of Architecture: Regulation and the Modern Metropolis
CHAPTER 7	210	Sustaining Architectural Culture
EPILOGUE	231	Changing Hands
APPENDIXES	240	1. Phyllis Lambert to Samuel Bronfman, June 28, 1954
	248	2. Seagram Plaza Installations and Seagram Gallery Exhibitions
	251	3. Some Conservation Issues as Remembered by Arvid Klein and Tom Stetz of Pasanella + Klein
	254	Notes
	295	Index
	304	Illustration Credits

FOREWORD *Barry Bergdoll*

Mies van der Rohe's quest for universality sustained the architect's lifelong project of "working on architecture as a language" even as it undergirded his determination to create an architecture that engaged so profoundly with the cultural stakes of the present that it could find resonance on a much longer historical horizon. Yet for decades that quest also fostered a critical reception of his work as self-referential, divorced from topographic and historic specificity—frequent refrains in the critiques of Mies in the postmodern decades of the 1970s and 1980s—to such an extent that these central issues with which Mies grappled from his earliest houses on the outskirts of Berlin to his final works in Chicago were largely obscured from view. These are among the myriad of frames deployed by Phyllis Lambert in this critical history/memoir of the architect's only New York City project, the seminal Seagram building, to reopen eyes and discussion. Lambert grounds her interpretation of this masterwork of Mies's American career in its consummate mastery of a formal language of materials, proportion, and tectonic expression in an exquisitely conceived and detailed office building, to be sure. But equally she broadens the aperture to encompass the set of urban and landscape strategies and attitudes that were integral parts of the design from its inception. These are precisely features of Mies's practice to which critics have been all but blind before the recent renaissance of evaluation of Mies's seminal and still relevant contributions to place making. In the decade since the dual 2001 exhibitions *Mies in Berlin* and *Mies in America* (Terence Riley and I worked in tandem on the German Mies, Phyllis Lambert on the North American Mies), Mies's work has been increasingly reconnected to the stakes of architectural practice first in modernizing interwar Berlin and then in the postwar North American city. His search for a language of expression that could address both material realities and higher aspirations had been reaffirmed in 1950 a few years before the Seagram commission. "Wherever technology reaches its real fulfillment, it transcends into architecture. . . . Architecture has nothing to do with the invention of forms. It is not the playground for children, young or old. Architecture is the real battleground of the spirit," he wrote in "Architecture and Technology." Mies in his studies of glass in 1920s Berlin and in 1950s North America took that material not simply as a transparent or neutral field to celebrate the glory of the steel or concrete frame. Rather, he was keenly interested in exploring a haptic approach to architecture and opening up new relationships to nature, to the city, to landscapes, and to awareness, or consciousness, as many of the philosophical texts that engaged Mies's reading and research framed it. Mies's deep interest in exploring a formal language was not an autonomous quest for an abstract language of building divorced from experience but rather a quest for the very frame for experience, for dialectic between change and constancy, which he took to be one of the key challenges of modern consciousness.

If the Seagram building today seems to have the repose of a resolved work of art, it was in fact the culmination of lengthy research as well as the product of a singular set of collaborations. Settling in Chicago in 1937, a somewhat reluctant émigré from Hitler's Germany, Mies was forced to begin a career anew against the background of the worldwide economic depression and the beginnings of a second war. The war and the postwar American economic boom would radically alter the social, political, and psychic framework of the very present that Mies embraced as a prelude to design. Having explored a wide array of architectural expressions in the heady atmosphere of the Berlin avant-garde in which he sought to find a place in the 1920s as well as directed the experimental Bauhaus through the traumatic years of its gradual demise, 1930–33, Mies declared famously in America that he did not want to invent a new architecture every Monday morning, even as he set out to adjust to a new daily language and a new culture. Yet in the 1940s and 1950s he did invent a new language of structural and spatial expression, one that was rapidly to become paradigmatic for at least two generations. This he pursued as well in his role as an educator at the Illinois Institute of Technology, where he also forged an ethos of how architecture might function in the postwar North American city, and through his creation of an architectural office in which key collaborators, including Myron Goldsmith, Peter Carter, Gene Summers, and Phyllis Lambert herself, worked on elaborating that language. Embracing the unadorned reality of American milled steel with its factory-set dimensions as well as the challenges of North American cities undergoing enormous social and economic changes and torn between discourses of growth and decay, Mies and his office developed a set of types that would become tools for intervening in existing urban fabrics. These not only provided the laboratories of the office's work for several decades but were so frequently emulated that it has often been forgotten how the complex stakes of key works were lost in the countless imitations of the Miesian idiom, an idiom that by the 1960s had found followers worldwide. Having been disparaged by a generation of postmodernists, these very stakes have in the past fifteen years revealed themselves to sustain a whole series of creative projects in artistic as well as architectural practice that have reciprocally opened new lines of understanding of the architect's major designs.

The Seagram building is at once emblematic of Mies van der Rohe's work on the American skyscraper and a wholly singular building. So serene is its presence on Park Avenue that few critics, historians, or casual tourists consider the complexity of its composition of plazas, subsidiary connected buildings of different heights, and intertwined circulation paths for visitors to its offices, restaurants, and plazas and gardens, even though countless people enjoy this veritable urban-district-as-monument daily. So seemingly timeless is it in its stately demeanor that few imagine that a skyscraper of uncommon poise could have a complex, and even troubled, biography. What might have been a fairly standard American urban story of the mid-twentieth century—a CEO client and an architect, Samuel Bronfman of the Montreal-based Distillers Corporation–Seagrams Limited and the corporate firm of Pereira & Luckman—became a complex story involving a group of people who were not only to create a singular building but to have a profound influence on architectural culture: Mies van der Rohe, Philip Johnson, and Bronfman's daughter, Phyllis. Charles Luckman, the likely first choice of architect, ironically had begun his designing career only in 1950 after having been president of Lever Brothers and therefore client for Skidmore, Owings & Merrill's Lever House diagonally across Park Avenue. A radically different approach to the same brief—a corporate headquarters that would set architectural standards and create amenities for users and public alike—was to take shape in the late 1950s on the east side of the avenue. Lambert was to be a lynchpin to the story, first provoking her father to reconsider the company's initial assumptions, next setting out to select the best possible architect as a first act of curating the scene of contemporary practice, and then, as director of planning for Seagram, working side by side with the team of designers who would conceive everything from the building and plaza to the remarkable interior design of the Four Seasons Restaurant. Lambert was also to be the force behind new directions in Seagram's art collecting, as well as the selection of works of art that became an integral part of the building—notably the Picasso theater curtain for the ballet *Le Tricorne* (1919) and the majestic but gossamer Richard Lippold sculpture hung above the Four Seasons bar. One might even say that the Canadian Centre for Architecture, Lambert's most comprehensive and—along with the landmarked Seagram building—most enduring contribution to the culture of architecture was born in part at Seagram in the photography project *Court House* (undertaken for the Bicentennial of United States Independence), which she directed with the photographer Richard Pare.

In her commitment to architectural excellence and to defending and enhancing the public realm Lambert has long been skilled at juggling many roles—architect, preservationist, curator, scholar, artist, patron, citizen activist—so it is not surprising that she should invent a virtually unprecedented type of architectural study to take stock of her role not only in the creation of the Seagram building but in its stewardship as a work of civic art. Subject and author, diarist and critical historian: these are perspectives that might seem, at first glance, in conflict. But in fact the chapters of this book—at once scholarly and page-turning—bring together information available only in Lambert's personal archives, notes, and memories, with an almost uncanny propensity to consider even her own lived experience from the vantage point of a later moment. *Building Seagram* offers a model of a building monograph in which the traditional art historical enterprise of tracing a limited arc from commission and design intent through construction and delivery of the building is extended well beyond to give equal importance to the controversies and debates this singular tower activated, notably its role as a protagonist in debates over building taxation, zoning, and landmark preservation protection for recent works of "the building art."

It has long been a cliché that the Seagram building is a kind of perfection of a type—the American tall office building first theorized by Louis Sullivan, Mies van der Rohe's forerunner in late nineteenth-century Chicago—and that as such it could be almost taken as a sculptural perfection that might be admired in its own right. Karl Friedrich Schinkel— the early nineteenth-century Berlin architect from whom Mies asserted one could learn everything there is to know about architecture—claimed that architects should seek at once designs that are "complete in and of themselves" and take on the social and political role of being "the ennobler of all human relations." Here perfection and progressive change are set in a dialectical relationship. Mies, for all his determination to perfect the technology of American steel frame construction, created here—as in his other favorite buildings of his American career, Crown Hall at the Illinois Institute of Technology in Chicago and the twin apartment houses at 860 and 880 Lakeshore Drive—at once a type and a work so site specific that Seagram can be understood only in its place in the grid of midtown Manhattan and in the context of the postwar architectural, cultural, political, and business culture. For the Seagram building creates at once a monument and an interlocked landscape, a building on a podium and a podium that connects in complex ways with the avenue and side streets at slightly different levels. It creates a rich processional approach to a transparent lobby, a set of gardens that are at once part of the street composition of the building, and an unexpected filter through which the spectacle of the city on Park Avenue can be watched at a contemplative distance from the bar and tables of the Pool and Grill Rooms of the Four Seasons, along with a plaza that is at once the epitome of urban dignity and a prototype of a new place of daily urban occupation. Here is an experience at once quotidian and transcendent that gives concrete meaning to a goal Mies gave himself in 1938 on taking up the directorship of the architecture program at the future Illinois (then Armour) Institute of Technology: "In its simplest form architecture is entirely rooted in practical considerations, but can reach up through all degrees of value to the highest realm of spiritual existence, into the realm of the sensuously apprehendable, and into the pure sphere of art." At Seagram, Mies created a building that transforms not only the city but the view and the experience of a key part of the city. Lambert reminds us that at the Seagram building, as with true masterworks, the work of understanding, interpreting, and extending is never finished.

ACKNOWLEDGMENTS

Building Seagram derives from my firsthand involvement in the realization of the Seagram building and plaza and many associated programs. From the summer of 1954 this involved research to identify the architect, my engagement as director of planning from the design process through to completion of construction in 1959, and, subsequently, my work as consultant to the company through 2000, assuring maintenance of the building in its entirety as well as the Seagram Company offices, supervising the curation of collections and exhibitions and the process of landmarking. Documents held in various archives and libraries sustained my memory and augmented my knowledge of associated events.

Archival holdings have been indispensable in writing this book. I wish to acknowledge and warmly thank committed individuals in institutions who searched for and shared documents in their collections. Germane to this study, the Canadian Centre for Architecture (CCA) holds my own archives. Cataloguing Seagram-related correspondence and documents in my fonds was begun by Robert Michel, making accessible a vast array of records. I am immensely grateful to him and especially to Glenn Brown, who continued this huge task and extended it to specific topics as well as to my professional papers and those donated to the CCA by the Seagram Curator's Office.

The CCA was exceedingly supportive in reference and research. Renata Guttman, Head, Collection Reference, invariably found texts within the library and translated others on interlibrary loan; I wish also to acknowledge the help of Judy Silverman, Head of Collection Cataloguing, librarian Paul Chenier, and library support staff Pierre Boisvert, Suzie Quintal, and Colin MacWhirter, as well as Elspeth Cowell, Head of Collection and Programs Services, and Marc Pitre, Senior Copyright Officer. CCA photographers Michel Boulet and Michel Legendre made digital images of works from the institution's collection.

The CCA also provided offices and the institutional resources to my research assistants for more than a decade.

Throughout the length of this study from 2002 to 2011, Marjorie McNinch, Reference Archivist, Hagley Museum and Library, Archives Department, Wilmington, Delaware, most generously responded to countless requests relating to the Seagram Company administrative files, which Hagley holds. Lynn Catanese, Chief Curator, Library Collections at Hagley, was of great assistance during the process of editing this book, and Jon M. Williams, Andrew W. Mellon Curator of Prints, helped with Seagram photographic resources.

Support by many at the Museum of Modern Art (MoMA), New York, was very much appreciated. I wish to thank Terry Riley and Barry Bergdoll, respectively the former and current Philip Johnson Chief Curator of Architecture and Design, for the courtesy extended by members of the department, including Paul Galloway, Study Center Supervisor, and Christian Larsen, Curatorial Assistant; Michelle Harvey, Associate Archivist, Museum Archives, who gave access to correspondence of Alfred Barr, Léonide Massine, and John Szarkowski; Megan Feingold, Assistant, Department of Photography; Samantha Friedman, Curatorial Assistant, Department of Drawings, who helped with *Le Tricorne* conservation reports; and Jenny Tobias in MoMA's library, who provided access to various textual records and to MoMA's Photographic Archive.

I owe a debt of gratitude to curators in other institutions who kindly gave access to specific material: Conrad Graham, Curator of Decorative Arts, McCord Museum, Montreal; Janet S. Parks, Curator of Drawings and Archives, Avery Architectural and Fine Arts Library, Columbia University; Laura Tatum, Architectural Records Archivist, Manuscripts and Archives, Yale University Library; and Dean M. Rogers, Special Collections Assistant, Vassar College Library. At the John Soane Museum, Tim Knox, Director, and Stephanie Coane, Librarian, clarified the history of Soane's guide to his house and collections. In addition to those mentioned below relating to Picasso's *Le Tricorne,* telephonic discussions with art historian and Picasso biographer John Richardson were a rare privilege. Also deserving of my thanks are Marisa Bourgoin, Richard Manoogian Chief of Reference Services, Archives of American Art, Smithsonian Institution, who provided documents from the Klaus Perls Galleries records, and Joy Weiner, Archives Specialist in the Smithsonian's Archives of American Art, who provided copies of selected documents from the Alfred Barr Papers.

The fastidious work of reading the briefs on the Seagram tax issue was initiated by Felicity Scott, who provided me with a copy of the New York State Court of Appeals 1964 *amici curiae* brief; Sheldon Wein and Barbara Massago of the New York State Library scanned and sent numerous other related briefs from the Seagram court cases. George E. Bushnell III, Senior Vice President and Deputy General Counsel, Vivendi S.A., with Stuart Chessman, Director, Taxes, Vivendi S.A., searched the Seagram company files for tax issues and, with Gail Sargent, located documents relating to Seagram's lease at 380 Madison Avenue. Bushnell also searched for information on various subjects including the Seagram corporate seal and the 1970s sale of the Seagram building. Adrienne Ascencio of the Landmarks Preservation Commission of New York most kindly gave access to photographs and letters submitted during the Four Seasons landmarking court proceedings.

Individual scholars generously helped: as a graduate student Margaret Maile Petty provided information on Richard Kelly before his archives were deposited at Yale, while Philip G. Cialdella, Regional Vice President of Sales, Louis Poulsen Lighting, New York, provided a copy of a Kelly exhibition brochure. Wallis Miller was instrumental in identifying the status of the Schinkel rooms at Charlotenhof in the 1920s and 1930s. The design date of

Frank Lloyd Wright's Mile High project was discussed with the late H. Allen Brooks and with Bruce Brooks Pfeiffer of the Frank Lloyd Wright Archives. The late Professor Donald Harleman of MIT, who was consulted on the design of fountains for the Seagram plaza, generously lent me William B. Davis's 1958 S.M. thesis on water flow, "Transition Phenomena in Radial Free Surface Flow," with which he had assisted.

Beginning in 1993 Sandra Coley Byron, assistant to me for special projects when I was director of the Canadian Centre for Architecture, established a bibliographic database on the Seagram building, which now numbers nearly twelve hundred entries. My gratitude goes to her and to Roberta Prevost, research assistant, who not only augmented this file over the next years but also sought out and obtained, classified and maintained, archival material from various institutions and individuals. I have depended on Prevost's meticulous record keeping, rigorous copyediting, and coordination. I would not have been able to complete this book without her devoted attention. In addition, Prevost, with the effective help of Catherine Bella, identified and located copyright holders of images used in this book and pursued the onerous work of obtaining copyright permission and refining license agreements. Thanks also go to Catherine Bella for the drawings she made for this publication. Stefan Zebrowski-Rubin researched data on New York buildings and building codes, as well as on landmarking the Seagram building and Four Seasons Restaurant, and located images of *Le Tricorne* at the New York Public Library for the Performing Arts at Lincoln Center. Anya Domlesky undertook research on the curtain's provenance and connected material at MoMA and the Archives of American Art with published sources.

David Thompson, Producer, Arts & Classical Music, BBC, provided Sidney Janis correspondence regarding the Rothko Four Seasons mural commission, and Christopher Rothko generously provided a scan of his father's manuscript notes on the commission. Alex von Bidder, general manager and co-owner of the Four Seasons Restaurant, answered queries about the restaurant's ownership history, and members of my family, Edgar M. Bronfman and Edgar Bronfman, Jr., and Charles de Gunzburg, were of substantial help in verifying numerous facts. I am equally grateful to Claude Michaud for ongoing technical support, and to Mary Delmonico and Lars Müller for insights regarding design and publishing. Hubert Damisch suggested the title of this book; I thank him, Teri Wehn-Damisch, as well as Irving Lavin and Marilyn Aronberg Lavin, for general discussion and moral support. I must also mention the enchanting walks with Barry Bergdoll in Potsdam observing Karl Friedrich Schinkel's work at Glienicke Park and Charlottenhof and the particularly revealing tour of the Society of Architectural Historians, led by Barry and Dietrich Neumann, to study Mies's work in and around Berlin.

The photographs in this volume are primarily archival, contemporaneous with the events they represent. The Seagram plaza, however, has never been a subject of visual analysis, and to this end Richard Pare created a portfolio of fine images identifying the parts and the whole within the site and the immediate environment of the city. I am grateful to Pare and thank Steve Morrows, Frank J. Farella, and Evelyn Alvarez, RFR Realty LLC, and Eliza R. Carmona, Boston Properties, for permission to photograph. I wish to thank Ada Louise and Garth Huxtable for the very fine service and tableware they designed for the Four Seasons Restaurant, which is ever present.

Most of the chapters were initially given as lectures, which established the book's initial framework. I benefited by questions from the audience and from their comments. While the locus of later lectures is acknowledged in chapters 3, 4, 6, and 7, I wish to thank the institutions at which I delivered my first lectures concerning the building in 2002–3: Bryn Mawr College, Bryn Mawr, Pennsylvania; Technion–Israel Institute of Technology, Haifa;

the Royal Ontario Museum, Toronto; and Brown University, Providence, Rhode Island. I owe a debt of gratitude to readers who contributed to developing this manuscript at various stages. Over the years, Denise Bratton insightfully edited the lectures I prepared as well as the book chapters as they took shape. Geoffrey Smedley commented on the early chapters, and the input of the late Gene Summers and Carla Ash to discussions of the subjects with which they were involved is very much appreciated. Chapter 5 of this book attests to Ash's enormous contribution to the Seagram art programs, and Barry Winiker, her assistant, should also be mentioned. I am indebted to Timothy More whose knowledge of real estate law, his patience in helping me understand its particular language and his close reading of the chapters in which this litigation occurs were invaluable. Thank you to Pierre-André Themens of Davies Ward Phillips & Vineberg LLP, who helped clarify other legal issues. I am grateful to Dietrich Neumann for his comments enhancing my discussion of the architectural history of artificial illumination and of Richard Kelly's contribution to the field. My thanks go to author Ann Charney, who kindly read the first full draft for continuity. Later drafts were read by Mirko Zardini, Mario Carpo, and the readers for Yale University Press, all of whom I thank for their encouragement and suggestions. I am most grateful to Mary Christian, who edited the final version of the text, immeasurably improving the flow. Great thanks go to the very fine editing process of the Yale University Press: Michelle Komie, senior editor, art and architecture, who with Mary Mayer, production manager, and Katherine Boller, assistant editor, wisely shepherded the process from manuscript to printed volume. I also extend my thanks to Laura Jones Dooley, manuscript editor, and Enid Zafran, indexer. Finally I wish to thank Jeff Wincapaw for his finely wrought and elegant design of *Building Seagram*.

Ultimately, I wish to thank my mother, my father, and Mies.

PROLOGUE
UNLIKELY CONVERGENCES

Looking at the past through the eyes of the present, it might be assumed that the commissioning, design, and construction of Ludwig Mies van der Rohe's Seagram building were politically driven by the world of power and intrigue. In fact, *Building Seagram* is not a story of architectural or corporate power plays but rather one of unlikely convergences, extraordinary coincidences, and ironic turns. In 1951, when the building project got under way, my father, Samuel Bronfman, whom I shall refer to as SB, the "client," de jure, was still effectively an outsider in New York, Mies was living in Chicago, and I was working as an artist in Paris. Only Philip Johnson, through his longtime position as director of the Department of Architecture and Design at the Museum of Modern Art, was any sort of powerful figure in New York City at the time. Real estate development, on the threshold of a postwar boom, did not yet wield the influence that it would eventually assume. Though it is difficult to comprehend today, architecture itself was generally considered to be little more than a commercial product at the beginning of the 1950s.

This book is based on my involvement with the Seagram building from its beginnings—identifying the architect, serving as director of planning and, in effect, as "client" from 1954 to 1959, building the company's collections, and continuing to be involved with the maintenance and stewardship of the building as well as the artworks and programs through the end of the twentieth century. It is a personal account of how Mies designed the Seagram building as well as Philip Johnson's role, both as I experienced the process at the time and as I see it now, some fifty years later. Ultimately, it is very much about the life of the building in the city. This post–World War II phenomenon is seen against and within the coming of age of architecture and the arts in New York, transformations from war technology to building construction, the first real changes in zoning regulations in New York City,

1 David Jerome Spence, architect, Distillers Corporation–Seagrams Limited building, 1430 Peel Street, Montreal, 1928, with 1931 addition. Photographer unknown.

the evolution of real estate from individual practices to a highly structured and influential industry in the city, and the onset of legislation aimed at sustaining the urban fabric.

The story begins with Samuel Bronfman, president of the Canadian holding company Distillers Corporation–Seagrams Limited, or DC-SL. Brought to the Canadian prairies from Bessarabia as an infant, he was raised in poverty.[1] Through his family's management of small hotels, he repositioned himself to trade in distilled spirits, and learned to manufacture whisky when he moved from Winnipeg to Montreal in 1924. There he built his first distillery in Ville LaSalle, choosing a site on the south shore of the island of Montreal at the head of the Lachine Rapids, seven miles west of the city. In that same decisive year, SB created Distillers Corporation Limited (DCL) to run the new venture. Only eighteen months later, after contracting with a top distiller from Kentucky to build the new plant (but also to learn from him),[2] he had the temerity to travel to Scotland to meet the directors of the most powerful whisky company in the world, Distillers Company Limited, with the aim of forming a partnership.[3] An agreement between the Scottish and Canadian companies was signed the month and year that I was born, January 1927. On March 2, 1928, DCL became Distillers Corporation–Seagrams Limited with the acquisition of Joseph E. Seagram & Sons, Ltd., of Waterloo, Ontario.[4]

In 1928 the company's office building, a small, turreted stone castle, was completed at 1430 Peel Street, in a former residential area that was being transformed into Montreal's rapidly developing commercial downtown. Three years later it was cleverly doubled in size—its facade replicated—by MIT-trained architect David J. Spence (fig. 1).[5] It stood opposite the largest hotel in the British Empire, the eleven-hundred-room Beaux-Arts Mount Royal Hotel, built between 1920 and 1922 during a decade of nationwide economic surge.[6]

Against the new large, sober structures, the little Scottish "Tudor-Gothic" baronial castle held its own. Its street facade was intricately articulated in Montreal limestone, surmounted by battlements, crenellations, corbeled turrets, a central tower with a steep slate roof between stepped gables and carved emblems, together with a portcullis raised under a low, arched recess to protect, symbolically, the main entrance. Inside the double-height entrance hall were displayed crossbows, swords, Highland daggers, and circular shields, as well as sporrans and tartans on the mezzanine railing. As a child, I was captivated by this space, where the telephone operator plugged cables into the switchboard and a full suit of armor stood halfway down the stairs leading to the reception hall. This little baronial castle was SB's homage to the world's preeminent aristocratic Scottish distillers, whom the shy but brilliant and tough prairie boy had boldly sought out and with whom he had entered into partnership. On trips to Scotland, he studied the DCL distilling process as well as its bottling, labeling, and advertising traditions.

SB valued quality in all things, an abiding concern that was echoed in the corporate emblem he had designed for Seagram, with rampant maned horses flanking an oval shield wreathed in sheaves of grain and mounted on a compartment of oak leaves and a single acorn. The shield bears the letter "S" in Old English script. Above the shield, following Scottish tradition, is an elaborate floral banner (surmounted by a third rampant horse shown in half-torso) carrying the name of The House of Seagram; below, a riband supporting the two flanking horses carried the motto my father tried to live by: Integrity—Tradition—Craftsmanship.[7]

Shortly before Prohibition was repealed on December 5, 1933,[8] the parent company DC-SL established a subsidiary, Joseph E. Seagram & Sons, Inc., in the United States,[9]

acquiring distilleries and moving into offices in the recently completed Chrysler building in New York City in 1934. The company was in full operation by June 1934. That same year SB began to translate his compulsion for quality into newspaper and magazine advertising campaigns. With its first print advertisement of October 1934, the House of Seagram sought to educate potential customers, asserting: "We who make whiskey say: 'Drink Moderately.'"[10] The ad compared the "rawness and harshness" of poor and unknown whisky brands produced cheaply during Prohibition with the pleasure of the aroma, flavor, and mellowness found only in "whiskey that has been properly distilled and then brought to . . . full wholesomeness, by aging." Most notable were ads that appeared each year on Father's Day, beginning in June 1938, arguing that "the coming generation will be less apt to use liquor intemperately if older people will regard it as a luxury and treat it as a contribution to gracious living—to be enjoyed in moderation." SB's biographer, Michael Marrus, points to the enormous marketing successes of the post-repeal era, when Seagram identified its products with high quality and great prestige.[11] Marrus connected this to SB's craving for "the status and gentility associated with 'the best,'" but Marrus also understood SB's alertness to common ambitions: "He . . . sensed that millions of North Americans had similar aspirations; in the depths of the Depression, ordinary people would also respond to the appeals of quality."[12]

Intent on developing the distilling industry, SB divided his life between two cities, riding the train every Friday to see his family in Montreal (though he spent most of the time meeting with business associates) and returning by train to New York every Sunday or Monday night. The alliance of whisky and science was also a route to self-respect. He envisaged Seagram's new distillery in Louisville, Kentucky, as "the show-piece of the industry" and "a seat of learning, a laboratory. People will come to it from all over the world to study the art of making and blending whiskies. . . . Research. . . . The industry needs more of it."[13] The building was to be a cloistered "campus" set in the idyllic countryside surrounded by oaks and elms. In 1936, he hired H. Frederick Willkie away from Hiram Walker. Brother of the presidential candidate Wendell Willkie, with broad experience in production, science, and technology, Willkie was made head of Seagram production in the United States and given a free hand in research. *Fortune* claimed in 1948 that he put a "social-religious" emphasis on advancing whisky blends. To this end, emphasis was placed on scientific research at the new Louisville plant, where the atmosphere of a university was found— "Ph.D.'s studiously operating mash tubs, and fermenters with automatic controls, holding classes for foreign students and conducting psychology tests on the intricacies of taste."[14]

The need to ally spirits with scientific research and product quality were essential in order to bring prestige to an industry battered by the scandals of the Prohibition era. The company also undertook cultural projects to elevate its image and status. At SB's request, in 1941 Stephen Leacock's *Canada: The Foundations of Its Future* was written and freely distributed in order to bolster morale during wartime.[15] Rather than putting forward the company's profile, it was a positive history of Canada's industrial capacity. In his foreword, SB emphasized the role of business organizations in building the country: "The horizon of industry, surely, does not terminate at the boundary-line of its plants; it has a broader horizon, a farther view, and that view embraces the entire Dominion."[16] While the book was praised in *La Presse* in tolerant Catholic Quebec, it was criticized as institutional advertising in the Anglo-Protestant West. In 1959 Seagram was ordered to stop distributing the book in British Columbia with the claim that it contravened the anti-advertising section of the province's Liquor Act.[17]

An exhibition of fifty paintings and sketches of twenty-two Canadian cities commissioned by the House of Seagram in 1951 and launched in the spring of 1953 was a more forthright form of institutional advertising.[18] *The Cities of Canada* traveled to fifteen cities in South America and Europe, as well as to the twenty-two Canadian cities depicted. In his foreword to its brochure, SB wrote that his intention was to "bring to the peoples of the world some glimpses of the Canadian landscape and sky-line . . . [and] in this fashion to establish abroad a familiarity with our urban life, and so evoke a deeper understanding, a closer rapport between ourselves and peoples of the world."[19]

Striking parallels emerge between the operations and personalities involved in establishing Seagram's headquarters in Montreal in the 1920s and in New York in the 1950s. In both cities, the new company headquarters were located in prestigious residential areas that were on the cusp of transformation into major new centers of commerce. The project to build in New York arose from Seagram's need for considerably more space than what was provided by its elegant quarters on the fifteenth floor of the Art Deco Chrysler building—symbol of machine-age technology, and the world's tallest steel-supported brick building. The company had occupied this space since 1934, when the Chrysler building was four years old, and gradually expanded to other areas in the building. The spirit of British Gothic was carried from the baronial castle in Montreal to New York City in the quarter-cut oak linenfold paneled offices Seagram installed (fig. 2). The designer of these offices was never mentioned, and only recently did I discover, to my astonishment, that they were not the anodyne work of an interior decorator but rather of an architect who later became

2 Morris Lapidus, architect, Ross-Frankel, Inc., entrance to the chief executive offices of Joseph E. Seagram & Sons, Inc., Chrysler building, 405 Lexington Avenue, New York, 1934. Photographer unknown.

3 Morris Lapidus, architect, Ross-Frankel, Inc., executive bar, Joseph E. Seagram & Sons, Inc., in the Chrysler building, 405 Lexington Avenue, New York, 1934. Photograph: Gottscho-Schleisner, Inc., August 25, 1939.

infamous for his flamboyant hotels in Miami Beach, Morris Lapidus.[20] The completion of his first and most notorious hotel, the Fontainebleau (about which the mildest comment in the architectural press stated that it was "too far off the mainstream of architecture to warrant publication"),[21] at the end of 1954 coincided with Mies van der Rohe's commission as architect of the Seagram building. Incongruous things happen. It is droll, but accurate, to say that Mies van der Rohe succeeded Morris Lapidus as architect to the Seagram Company. The divergence is breathtaking.

Lapidus designed Seagram's New York offices in what he described as "an authentic Tudor Style."[22] Seemingly strange was Lapidus's insertion into this Gothicizing décor what he called a "sampling room," generally known as the Seagram Executive Bar, a small room deep in the great Art Deco Chrysler Building, designed in a modern manner, with what he characterized as "my 'cheese holes,' the undulating wall with a mural, and a sweeping curving bar" (fig. 3).[23] These "cheese holes"—which displayed Seagram's products—and the curving mirrored bar that multiplied the effect, were Lapidus trademarks honed while designing small interior spaces for Ross-Frankel, Inc., beginning in 1928, shortly after graduating from Columbia.[24] Lapidus would explore a similar entreaty to the luxurious seduction of distilled beverages for his design for the exhibits and interiors of the Distilled Spirits Institute Pavilion for the 1939 New York World's Fair.[25] And in 1941, no doubt at his urging, Seagram had considered building its own headquarters; Lapidus prepared sketches for a proposed Seagram, Calvert, Carstairs building in New York City (fig. 4). The location was to be midblock, between Fifty-Seventh and Fifty-Eighth Streets, west of Fifth Avenue, where a six-story U-shaped building would wrap around a courtyard garden.[26] But a set of more propitious though unlikely convergences was instead destined to take its course.

For Samuel Bronfman, the client, as well as for Mies van der Rohe, the future architect of the Seagram building, the decade of the 1920s had been auspicious: SB burst upon the scene as an exceptional industrialist and strategist, while Mies gained recognition as a major figure in architecture with the publication of the drawings and models for his epoch-changing glass towers of 1920–22. SB's love of fine materials found resonance in Mies's careful deployment of onyx, travertine, *verde* antique marble, and tinted glass in his Barcelona Pavilion of 1928–29 and Tugendhat house of 1928–30. Both men had a pervasive sense of quality, and both understood the need to spend money to obtain it. They were each also autodidacts and absorbed entirely in their work. Neither gave praise nor was a good parent: my father was for all intents and purposes physically absent; his strong personality and fierce temper terrified his children; Mies merely neglected his.

I see now that the driving force in my father's life, his genuine and passionate love affair with what he called the "romance of business," was also the essential generator of the building in New York. The Seagram building was to be more than a company headquarters: I believe he came to see it as a monument to the opportunities business afforded in the New World, a monument to his company, which was his own doing, and therefore, ultimately, a monument to himself. But these desires were latent and needed to be articulated. Even though my motivation for building Seagram came from a very different place, I was able to catalyze my father's vision.

My contact with my father up to 1954 had been minimal. He considered only his sons to be in the line of business succession, and as a child with a strong aversion to all talk about business and money, I was a self-imposed outsider, immersed in art, committed to sculpture by the age of nine, constantly daydreaming about becoming an independent artist. As a child, I learned to look at my work objectively from my sculpture teacher, Herbert McCrae Miller, who would have me leave the room and return as "Mrs. Smith," who would critique Phyllis's work. Miller both read to me (no one else did) and treated me as an adult and friend, recounting his experiences. The two afternoons a week I spent in his studio were the most continuous, concentrated time I would spend with anyone as a child or adolescent. Working with him over seven years was highly pleasurable and developed in me a sense of craft and a devotion to art. I loved the adventure of building a work, from making an armature with crossed wood "butterflies" on a metal pipe to building up the form with the heavy, malleable clay. I loved the fetid odor of the clay that was kept moist

4 Morris Lapidus, architect, Ross-Frankel, Inc., perspective rendering of project for Seagram, Calvert, Carstairs building (unbuilt), Fifty-Seventh Street, New York, c. 1941. Draftsman unknown.

in bins. From 1940 to 1944, when I left Montreal to attend university, my dedication to art had been reinforced by the fact that my work was accepted in numerous juried exhibitions of the Royal Canadian Academy at the Montreal Museum of Fine Arts and The Art Gallery of Ontario in Toronto.[27] However, working as an artist did not seem to be an option for me. My parents vetoed all my attempts to attend summer art courses in Maine and to enroll at the Cranbrook Academy in Michigan. Yet clearly my immersion in the exploration of form in sculpture became the basis for a response to architecture.

The 1948 Arts Conference that took place during my last year at Vassar College was a crucial experience, giving me an opportunity to learn about contemporary architecture against the backdrop of my coursework in art history. With my fellow student Eve Borsook, as part of the conference I prepared an exhibition on the theme of the interrelationship of art and architecture in the twentieth century, learning in the process about the art and architectural revolution of the 1920s, whose leading figures were still alive and working, many in the United States.[28] In the early 1950s, I attended courses at the Institute of Fine Arts, New York University, where Richard Krautheimer's lectures on architecture, particularly of the Renaissance, had a profound influence on the development of my thinking.[29] After living between New York and Paris for a few years, I settled in Paris in 1952 and set up a studio where I worked as an artist and put some distance between myself and my family. Knowing of my father's intention to build in New York, I used my camera to study architecture in Rome and Tuscany, and in London I studied Modernism, particularly the work of the Dutch architects Willem Dudok and J. J. P. Oud in the library of the Royal Institute of British Architects.

Not until I returned to New York did I learn about Mies van der Rohe's visionary proposals for glass skyscrapers and his Barcelona Pavilion built for the 1929 International Exhibition, which had transformed the paradigm of contemporary architecture and made him a major figure of the European avant-garde. His silent, solid, statuesque being, coupled with an inner assuredness, a sense of the dramatic gesture, and great organizational capacity brought him to the foreground as the organizer of the 1927 Weissenhof Siedlung in Stuttgart, the foremost housing manifesto of the modern movement. In the foreword to the official catalogue of the exhibition, Mies decried the slogans of the time: "The problem of rationalization and typification . . . are only the means, they must never be the goal." For Mies, "the problem of the new housing [was] basically a spiritual problem, and the struggle for new housing . . . only an element of the larger struggle for new forms of living."[30]

This problem, like all other problems of building, was for him always part of a larger whole. The "battle of the spirit" was always present.[31] No longer able to build in Hitler's Germany, where Modernism was condemned as "degenerate art," Mies emigrated to Chicago in 1939 to chair the Department of Architecture at the Armour Institute of Technology (AIT), which became the Illinois Institute of Technology (IIT) in 1940. Whereas European technology of the 1920s and 1930s was not developed to the level that his visionary glass towers required, Mies was able to achieve his ideas in the heartland of the American steel industry. Step by step, he experimented with low-rise buildings for the IIT campus in Chicago until he could build his glass and steel towers at 860 and 880 Lake Shore Drive between 1949 and 1952. It was then only a few steps to the Seagram building.

In 1954 Philip Johnson was already a significant figure in the cultural ambit of New York, having founded the Department of Architecture at the Museum of Modern Art (MoMA) in 1932.[32] It was Philip who introduced Mies to America with other avant-garde European architects in his and Henry-Russell Hitchcock's groundbreaking 1932 exhibition

Modern Architecture: International Exhibition, putting Mies's Tugendhat house on the cover of the catalogue, and it was Philip who canonized Mies with a one-man show at MoMA in 1947. Johnson then became an architect himself. Relations between the two were strained when Johnson built his Glass House in Connecticut in 1949, a work directly inspired by studies for the glass house Mies conceptualized for Dr. Edith Farnsworth near Chicago in 1945 but completed only in 1951.[33] That he would come to be associated with Mies to build Seagram just a few years later was certainly not preordained. I was present the infamous time Mies blew up at Philip, angrily leaving the Glass House late at night in the fall of 1954—an event which, like so many parts of the Seagram story, has been variously told. Certainly the tension surrounding the Glass House underlay the quarrel, as did perhaps a fair amount of drinking. Ironically, however, Mies's explosion was triggered by Philip's flippant dismissal of the Dutch architect Hendrik Petrus Berlage's 1903 brick Amsterdam Commodity Exchange, which Mies admired for its honesty, fine craftsmanship, and clarity of construction. Mies later told me that for Philip to condemn the Berlage in front of me, the client, was wrong, but he clearly must have sensed that Philip was veering away from the principles of the modern movement. Still, Philip's personality enlivened the office and fueled social exchanges. Although Mies was unquestionably the architect of Seagram, Philip's interest in what one can best call "atmospheric lighting" would be the source of his major contributions to the building.

In the summer of 1954, while I was living in Paris, I received a "plan" from my father. It was a sketch of a proposed Seagram building that I found horrifying. Thus were the dancers set in motion. Over the next months, this unlikely cast of characters was brought together with their untested relationships, their affinities, and their antagonisms: architects who had danced, advancing and retreating in each other's orbit; father and daughter who moved, without touching, in non-contiguous circles. If not for these unlikely convergences how could Philip Johnson ever have dreamed of being the partner of Mies van der Rohe? Why would my father have placed me, a person without managerial or professional experience, in the position of selecting the architect for the Seagram building? And why would he have agreed to my appointment as director of planning for the building?

The story of *Building Seagram* offers insight into the arcana of commissioning buildings in New York City after World War II. In this volume I have also sought to explain in some detail Mies's approach to building—*Baukunst,* he called it, the building art. This encompasses the questions he posed about the time he lived in, the logical, the less than logical, and the spiritual, as well as instances of his auto-generative process. Rising prominently on Park Avenue, New York's broadest and most majestic street, Seagram was immediately perceived as the great exemplar of the prototypical American building type. What industry and lesser architects learned from it was not its exemplary form and proportions, not its refined details, not its astute siting (which changed the concept of public space in New York City), but the idea of the glass and metal curtain wall, which was roughly copied and deployed in countless buildings that are insensitive to site, context, or proportion and, one must say, far removed from the philosophical and cultural foundations of the art of architecture in which Mies was immersed. Like all, or almost all, of the buildings Mies forged, the Seagram tower was bound to an open platform forming a podium establishing a vista and an oasis in the grid of the busy city. Mies had explored this spatial interrelationship of building and landscape from his first built work in the first decade of the twentieth century. The glass towers he drew in the early 1920s as revolutionary manifestos remained theoretical for forty years, until the circumstance materialized in which they could be built. However, neither his low-rise structures nor his towers were entities in themselves. Rather, each was resolved as a union of house and garden or building and plaza, as elements bound together to become clearings in the "forest" of the city. In looking back at the birth and life of the Seagram building, it is not enough to recount what happened, as complex and compelling as that might be. It is also necessary to reexamine the unfolding of Mies's course in architecture, the evolution of his ideas over a half century, from his first independent building of 1909 to the completion of Seagram and its plaza in 1958. Similarly, it is necessary to revisit Philip Johnson's Glass House to understand his contribution to the building. It is equally vital to consider the impact of the Seagram building in the public realm of the city over the next fifty years, from 1959 through the first decade of the twenty-first century, when the Seagram company ceased to exist.

The scene and the endgame are set to permit me, in retrospect, to understand both the *what* and the *how* of Seagram: I begin with the endgame, the *what*, the design of Seagram as I experienced it, and then probe the *how*, a reflected account of Mies's as well as Philip Johnson's evolutive process. For in 1958, just after he completed Seagram, Mies noted the importance of time in the resolution of concepts and, in parallel, the pragmatic: "Viollet-le-Duc . . . has shown that the three hundred years it took to develop the Gothic cathedral were above all due to a working through and improving of the same construction type. We limit ourselves to the construction that is possible at the moment and attempt to clarify it in all details. In this way we want to lay a basis for future development."[34]

This is a story that depends on my own enormous bank of memories, systematically accessed and reflected in the light of the archive—my files and papers and other documents including photographs, in the Canadian Centre for Architecture (CCA) archives; documents in Seagram's corporate archives at the Hagley Museum and Library in Wilmington, Delaware; the various repositories of Mies's papers; critical assessments of the building; documents relating to city and state legislation in which the Seagram building was implicated; interviews with the architects who worked in Mies's office; Mies van der Rohe and other architects' archives; oral histories and interviews; and the writings and commentary of Mies and Philip themselves. This dynamic process, recollecting and researching, has led to a number of insights that have in turn opened up fresh lines of investigation that might never have been undertaken otherwise.

The ability to reassess Mies's work critically was first made possible with the donation of his papers and library to various institutions. This began in the late 1960s, with Mies's gift of hundreds of drawings from his office to the Museum of Modern Art in New York City.[35] His personal library was given to the University of Illinois at Chicago in 1969–70, and his correspondence and texts to the Library of Congress in 1971 and 1973. Over the past twenty years, these archives have become fertile ground for research into the thought of this major figure of the twentieth century. Studies by other scholars and architects as well as materials in numerous archives have allowed me to continue to investigate fundamental aspects of Mies's oeuvre that were central to the design of the Seagram building.[36]

Reviewing Philip Johnson's involvement, I first had to abandon my long-held assumptions that denied him a significant role in the building's design. What emerged in the process was a little-discussed aspect of his practice, his involvement with lighting, which had a great effect on his role in the realization of Seagram. In addition, one finds the surprising coincidence between the design sensibility of Lapidus and that of Philip Johnson with respect to their mutual preoccupation with lighting for dramatic effect. This was Philip's particular domain, which he developed in collaboration with Richard Kelly, one of the pioneers of modern lighting design. This lighting of spaces distinguished buildings from his own estate in Connecticut to the Seagram building glowing at night, the elegant design and dramatic lighting of the Four Seasons dining rooms at the plaza level, and the interplay of radiance and human presence on Mies van der Rohe's Seagram plaza.

The question of the building's reception from different perspectives occasioned major new research aimed at bringing to light the double-edged sword of Seagram's impact on New York, with zoning and tax legislation both encouraging and discouraging a high quality of architecture in the city. On the positive side, the Seagram building and plaza prompted a revision of the city's zoning ordinance that ushered in incentive zoning to encourage the development of open public space at street level; on the negative side, the city levied special taxes on the property because the building did not occupy the maximum extent of its site, and at the same time questioned the company's motivation for erecting a structure so much more costly than any ordinary commercial office building. Seen in light of protests against the demolition of Penn Station and the Brokaw Mansion in 1963 and 1965, respectively, the cause célèbre of the Seagram building marked a turning point in public awareness of architecture in New York.

In the same way, my reflection on the subject of Seagram's cultural leadership, its pattern of collecting, and its public art programs for the plaza and the Seagram Gallery became the starting point for a close rereading of the documentation surrounding the collections that were formed and built under my direction for over four decades. From 1957, when the building enclosure was completed and we began to consider artworks for the plaza's public spaces and the Four Seasons Restaurant, the semiprivate corporate reception areas, and the more private executive and staff offices, my intent was to realize, as far as possible, the corporation's great potential to assume the role of urban citizen in the public realm. From the beginning, I was determined that Seagram should become an example of what a new building in the city could be: inside and out and on all levels, for those who work there, for those who visit and pass by, for the neighborhood, and for the city itself.

I have long planned to write an account of building Seagram, for it would be almost impossible to connect the threads, the individual ambitions, and interpersonal relationships without having been a deeply engaged protagonist. Yet after 1959, studying and working as an architect, founding and directing a research center and museum devoted to building public awareness of the role of architecture in society, together with promoting scholarly research and stimulating innovation in design practice, it took many years before I could do so. Following a close study of the Seagram building for the book and exhibition *Mies in America,* which opened at the Whitney Museum of American Art in summer 2001, I was able to begin writing from the singular perspective of having experienced the total venture and influenced its outcome.

Lecture invitations from universities and museums gave me the opportunity to construct each chapter of the book sequentially and to receive valuable feedback. Much had changed about buildings in the area as well as in the rest of the city, especially ownership. The ownership of Seagram itself changed twenty years after it was built but ten years before it was eligible to be landmarked. At the same time, the demolition of notable structures, and even whole neighborhoods in American and Canadian cities, from the 1960s on sensitized me to the problems of maintaining the built domain. In 2001 even the Farnsworth house—the exemplar of Mies's other seminal building type, the pavilion—was threatened when a change of ownership without protection raised the possibility that it would be moved to another site. In a lecture not directly on subject but on my "advisory" role in the selection of architects for corporate and institutional projects,[37] I began reassessing the problem of stewardship in relation to the fate of modern architecture. While a commitment to stewardship was inherent in the project for Seagram from the beginning, modalities concerning maintenance and preservation had to be put in place in order to ensure the building's future for the moment when—as indeed happened too early—Seagram would not live there anymore.

Regulation of the modern metropolis—zoning and taxation—and the impact of the economy in the urban culture of New York and, beyond that, in the culture of global capital, weighed heavily on ambitious architecture. At Seagram, sustaining architectural culture was a concern from the beginning. Threats existed at the time Seagram was being designed and built, and again when it was for sale in 1979, at which time I worked to put in place the means to protect the building. Seagram agreed to do so even if it meant lower revenue from the sale, and thus protection was achieved through "Article 26: Tenant's Exclusive Rights" of Seagram's lease agreement with the new owner, Teachers Insurance and Annuity Association (TIAA),[38] attached to the deed of sale. Article 26 protected not only the exterior enclosure but the first sixteen feet of the interior and all public surfaces and spaces, by imposing strict maintenance specifications and regulating public events and sculpture installations on the plaza. In 1972, a threat had already arisen when the company considered moving to Connecticut at a time when "everyone was doing it." Seagram's unused air rights continued to pose the threat of another high-rise being constructed on the block despite studies I undertook with the city regarding the transfer of the air rights. Landmarking of the building and plaza was enthusiastically granted on schedule in 1989, in stark contrast to the high drama that ensued when the Four Seasons Restaurant was presented to the New York Landmarks Preservation Commission, but ultimately it, too, was landmarked.

Over the years, as the urban context changed, Seagram continued its public program of art on the plaza and exhibitions in the Seagram Gallery with the provisions included in Article 26 of the original lease agreement still in force. When the building was sold again in 2000, these provisions could have remained in force, adding to the safeguards afforded by landmark designation, but they were abrogated with the meltdown of the Seagram Company in 2001. Even so, the oasis of building and plaza remains coupled to the Seagram name. In a capitalist democracy, corporations have immense power, and sometimes command respect. Much more than what they produce and sell, their worth is judged by their corporate behavior. Since it has ceased to have a corporate identity, the Seagram Company can no longer affect the public through its programs, but the building and plaza that will carry its name forever continue to enhance the life of the city like small European public squares that are wonderful places to be.

Throughout this book, I have largely used contemporary photographs, including documentation of events on the plaza. However, while the Seagram tower has been captured on film at many different times and under a variety of circumstances, the plaza has not. To overcome this lacuna, at my request, in 2000 and again in 2010 Richard Pare made sensitive studies of the different aspects of the plaza—the generosity of space Mies gave to the building's approach, the sidewalks, and the different areas of the plaza itself, the continuity of space through the block, the shade and texture of the trees and ground cover, the water, the pools, the fountains, the steps, and the benches and other places where people sit and meet.

1

A SITE AND AN ARCHITECT FOR SEAGRAM

Although Samuel Bronfman decided to erect a building for his company in New York City in 1950, Seagram's initial solution to acquiring more office space than the Chrysler building afforded was to continue to rent (fig. 5). In October 1951, the company signed a long-term lease for six floors in a nine-hundred-thousand-square-foot, twenty-five-story office building that was to be constructed at 380 Madison Avenue between Forty-Sixth and Forty-Seventh Streets by the Uris Brothers (see fig. 16), a rapidly rising firm of developers producing office space by the yard.[1] In retrospect, I am surprised that SB would have agreed to such a lackluster location.[2] Accustomed to the lofty premises at the well-built and architecturally accomplished Chrysler building, he had a strong negative reaction to the cut-rate character of Uris's commercial structures. The idea of erecting a building for the company in New York was also undoubtedly fired by two other factors: the approaching seventy-fifth anniversary of Joseph E. Seagram & Sons, Ltd., and the company's ascendance. Already in September 1948, a major article in *Fortune* had asserted, "If there is a whiskey king in America, it is Samuel Bronfman of Montreal, chief of the House of Seagram."[3] The first documented reference to Seagram's search for a building site dates from March 1950. Real estate agent Anton L. Trunk, apprised of Seagram's interest in acquiring either the Metropolitan Club at 1 East Sixtieth Street at Fifth Avenue (fig. 6) or a block front on Park Avenue, wrote to Seagram treasurer James E. Friel comparing the cost of obtaining the Metropolitan Club—which was "to be left substantially as is except for some modernization" and the addition of several floors—with the cost of the site of the Montana apartment house between Fifty-Second and Fifty-Third Streets on the east side of Park Avenue (fig. 7), which was "to be improved with an eleven-story office building."[4]

5 Samuel Bronfman at home, Montreal. Photograph: Arthur Schatz, January 1, 1966.

The Montana site had previously been occupied by the venerable Steinway factory built in 1853, which fronted onto the open railroad tracks of the New York Central. The tracks were covered when trains were electrified, and Park Avenue was created, with an elegant sinuously landscaped median, earning its new name; on that strip of green, residents of a new crop of prestigious apartment buildings could sit or stroll (fig. 8). The Montana, designed by Rouse and Goldstone architects, was completed in 1913 (the year Grand Terminal was finished);[5] the Steinway family kept an apartment in the building.[6] This section of Park Avenue was solidly covered by residential buildings, after New York's 1916 Zoning Resolution divided Park Avenue at Fiftieth Street, allowing residential use to the north and commercial to the south.

A decade and a half later, as Christopher Gray of the *New York Times* recounted, "a full-fledged movement led by the New York Central Railroad and the Goelet family—the

6 Stanford White of McKim, Mead & White, architects, Metropolitan Club, entrance to courtyard, 1 East Sixtieth Street, New York, 1891–94. Photographer unknown.

7 Rouse & Goldstone, architects, rendering for the Montana Apartments, 375 Park Avenue, New York, 1913. Draftsman unknown.

8 Park Avenue, median landscape, over the New York Central railway tracks, rendering, c. 1913. Draftsman unknown.

9 Diagram of Midtown Manhattan buildings erected, under construction, or proposed by George A. Fuller Company, April 1957.

major property owners on the avenue—had begun to rezone the residential section in the [blocks from Fiftieth to Fifty-Seventh Streets] to permit commercial construction. When the question of rezoning came to a vote at the Board of Estimate a month after the stock market crash of October 1929, there was little protest."[7] The amendment passed, but the new zoning for these blocks was acted on only after the war.

While there were plans to build in 1930, the Great Depression and World War II postponed major changes to Park Avenue until after 1945. Wartime rent restrictions imposed in 1943 limited the financial return that Park Avenue landlords could earn; commercial buildings offered a better return, so residential proprietors were eager to sell. This precipitated a postwar office-building boom on Park Avenue, which became a notable district of 1950s architecture. As one historian comments, "It had been widely expected that many business firms would relocate to the suburbs after the war, and in later years many did; in the

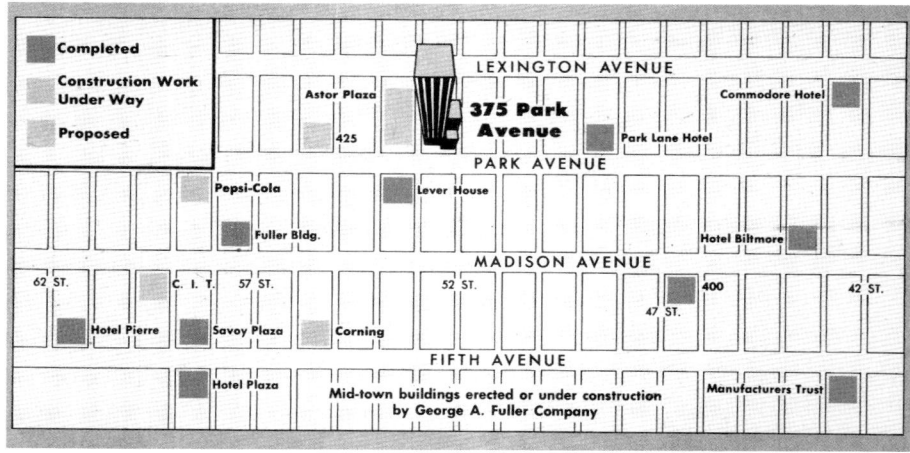

10 McKim, Mead & White, architects, Racquet and Tennis Club, 370 Park Avenue, New York, 1916–18. Photograph: Jack E. Boucher, 1965.

immediate postwar era, however, most chose Manhattan for their corporate headquarters, and the first choice was Park Avenue."[8] Building activity in the area was so intense that by 1957 eleven new structures in some forty blocks (Lexington to Madison Avenues, Fortieth to Fifty-Seventh Streets) by one contractor alone had been or were in construction (fig. 9).

Seagram had its eye not only on the Metropolitan Club but also on the Racquet and Tennis Club on the west side of Park Avenue between Fifty-Second and Fifty-Third Streets (fig. 10), directly opposite the Montana, as possible spaces to move into.[9] Both clubs were designed by the eminent architectural firm of McKim, Mead & White and are two of the most notable historic buildings of this time in New York. Stanford White's stately Metropolitan Club of 1894 presents itself as a palazzo on Fifth Avenue. It has a grand Mannerist entrance sequence on Sixtieth Street, where a columnated portico screens a large courtyard and the entry to the building. At right angles to the portico, the entry leads into an immense two-story hall faced with Greek, Italian, and American marbles. The Racquet and Tennis Club, completed in 1918 and considered the best of the firm's late work, drew on fifteenth-century Florentine palaces with its heavily rusticated base, quoins, and pointed arches.[10] Nonetheless, it is infused with American pragmatism: brick is the main material of revetment over a steel structure, and the blind arches on the fourth floor indicate the presence of the tennis courts.[11] The building was commissioned by Robert W. Goelet, who leased it to the club on completion. Like so many ironies in this story, the club purchased the lease in 1942, just before the wave of office buildings changed the avenue below Fifty-Seventh Street.

Lacking other evidence, I can assume only that a certain euphoria of the time and its own success led Seagram executives to seek out the finest buildings for their company headquarters, spurred by SB's obsession with quality and legitimacy. On two consecutive days at the end of May 1950, the real estate firms Douglas Gibbons and Anton Trunk each recommended to Seagram the purchase of the Montana site.[12] Trunk continued to urge its purchase in a series of memos and letters offering enticements: on July 19 he noted that a new Hotel Astor was to be constructed on an entire block owned by the William Waldorf Astor Estate immediately north of the Montana; on September 25 he mentioned that an offer of $4.4 million from former ambassador Joseph Kennedy for the Montana site had been refused two months earlier;[13] on November 9, that William Zeckendorf had purchased 300 Park Avenue in the vicinity[14] and a new Ritz Hotel (no longer the Astor) was to be built on the entire block to the north.[15] Ultimately, office buildings were constructed to the north and south of the old Montana site after Seagram was completed, but Trunk was correct in his understanding that "from what Mr. Bronfman has said . . . if 'Seagram's' [sic] was to have its own building in New York, he wanted it on Park Avenue."[16] Although numerous realtors proposed sites on Sixth Avenue that were also being offered for development, I recall SB's disdain for a Sixth Avenue site, for on no level could Sixth Avenue compare with the urban character and social cachet of Park Avenue.

After some six months—during which Seagram reviewed financial implications and such potential constraints as federal and state regulations regarding rights of tenants and the postwar availability of steel and other building materials—on January 19, 1951, Trunk wrote an authorized offer of four million dollars to the 373 Park Avenue Corporation to purchase 375 Park Avenue, the Montana and its site, as well as 114–20 East Fifty-Third Street and 121 East Fifty-Second Street.[17] The offer specifically stated that the purchase was to be made in order to demolish the Montana building. The consequences of this limitation became a critical design issue, as will be seen. After further discussions concerning the means of purchase and the tax consequences, at a special meeting on April 26, 1951, Seagram's board of directors adopted the resolution to purchase the property in order to erect an office building "as soon as practicable."[18] The transaction was closed on May 12, 1951.[19]

Three and a half years would intervene between the purchase of the site and the signing of a contract with the architect who would design the new building for the Park Avenue property. Seagram was discernibly at a loss faced with the new problem of how to proceed, and indeed if to proceed to build. An internal unsigned memo dated July 16, 1951, outlined a program for development that included a six-month period to explore whether the building should proceed and to assess whether a building occupied solely by the Seagram companies would be practical and give the proper impression to shareholders, the trade, and the public. Would it have advertising value? Would a building with maximal rental space lower the cost for the company's own space? Should the building be modern or traditional? What type of building would compete best with Skidmore, Owings & Merrill's Lever House (fig. 11), whose presence permeates this and any account of the area, or the Ambassador Hotel at Park Avenue from Fifty-First to Fifty-Second Streets (1921, later destroyed), or other buildings to be erected on neighboring sites?[20] Seagram lawyers studied tax issues related to demolition; company executives pushed for hiring consultants to assess what should be built; financial institutions sent lists of buildings under construction and the names of architects were put forward.[21] On March 24, 1952, Lou R. Crandall presented a study entitled "Project 'Skytop,'" consisting of various schemes based on the allowable building size and their relative breakdown of cost and income.[22] This study answered many of the questions posed. Crandall was president of the George A. Fuller Company, the preeminent construction firm in North America at the time. Mies used to say that the Fuller sign was like Walgreens drugstores in Chicago: there was one on every corner. Bronfman knew and respected Crandall, and he was already very much in the picture: just four days

11 Skidmore, Owings & Merrill, architects, Lever House, 390 Park Avenue, New York, 1951–52. Photograph: G. E. Kidder Smith, 1952.

after he presented the Skytop study, on March 28, 1952, Crandall signed an agreement with Joseph E. Seagram & Sons, Inc., for the demolition of the Montana at 375 Park Avenue.[23]

The Skytop study had been prepared by the Fuller Company in collaboration with architects Kahn and Jacobs and the real estate firm of Cushman & Wakefield.[24] The schemes ranged from a multitenant structure with a rentable area of 1,079,450 square feet, to a building of 331,400 square feet that would be occupied exclusively by the owner. Every scheme reserved 200,000 square feet and two basements for the owner, unless otherwise noted. Scheme 1 used the entire site and the maximum area allowed by the building code, calculated on the height of forty-three stories; Scheme 1C was fifty stories, with five setbacks to the tower and two or three basements. Scheme 2 (fig. 12), similar to the first

12 Project Skytop, Scheme 2: Study developed by George A. Fuller Company, Kahn and Jacobs, Cushman & Wakefield, perspective view, March 24, 1952.

scheme (and calculated for both forty-three- and fifty-story structures), used the whole site, except for the apartment house on Fifty-Third Street, in addition to the square footage of unused air rights from the apartment building, which was smaller than the zoning laws permitted.[25] Scheme 3A covered the entire site with a seven-story building without towers or embellishments, and two basements, to be used exclusively by the owner; Scheme 3B (fig. 13), described as a "'distinctive' type building," was twenty-three stories, to be used exclusively by the owner. Comprising 331,400 square feet of rentable area, it took Lever House as a model, and was estimated to cost almost seventeen million dollars—21 percent more than the seven-story structure estimated to cost fourteen million dollars. Scheme 4A (fig. 14), which used the entire site for a forty-three-story building with two basements,

13 Project Skytop, Scheme 3B: Study developed by George A. Fuller Company, Kahn and Jacobs, Cushman & Wakefield, perspective view, March 24, 1952.

14 Project Skytop, Scheme 4A: Study developed by George A. Fuller Company, Kahn and Jacobs, Cushman & Wakefield, perspective view, March 24, 1952.

introduced a new concept: a setback of one hundred feet from, and parallel to, Park Avenue, for the owner to use "for distinctive landscaping or building." Interestingly, containing 558,900 square feet of rentable space and setting back from Park Avenue (one hundred feet rather than ninety feet), it would be very close to Mies's solution. Furthermore, the cost, estimated at twenty-two million dollars, also closely matched the figure used by the City of New York as the value of the completed Seagram building during taxation discussions in 1960.[26] Since none of these calculations was kept confidential, Mies must have become familiar with the Skytop study by Kahn and Jacobs, who would become his associate architects. Scheme 4B is similar, but turns the building ninety degrees to Park Avenue with a "Tower dominating Park Avenue [and] 'Advertising' space or landscaping on front one hundred feet." Scheme 4C was similar to 4B, but with a fifty-story tower.

Lou Crandall sent the study to three leading New York real estate companies: Cushman & Wakefield, Cross & Brown, and Charles F. Noyes. He also specified the new technologies for first-class office structures: the building was to be air-conditioned and of "superior construction," including soundproof ceilings, recessed fluorescent lighting, and other "modern facilities"—defined as acoustical ceilings, electronically controlled elevators, window-washing mechanisms, and parking facilities. Furthermore, Crandall asked each real estate company to answer three questions about a hypothetical building forty stories high, with twenty-eight tower floors of more than ten thousand square feet each and three basements:

1. If such a building were constructed and completed between January 1st, 1955 and September 1955, will it be rented successfully?
2. What would be your estimated schedule of rentals at current, prevailing market rates for a building having all the advantages of "Skytop," and the estimated schedule of operating expenses at the present cost of labor, services, materials, supplies and other charges?

3. Would your schedules of rental and operating expenses still prevail for "Skytop" if constructed and completed in 1955?[27]

Crandall then had the responses tabulated and a financial analysis was undertaken by General Realty & Utilities Corporation, an affiliate of the Fuller Company presided over by Edmund Wagner. Its report concluded that the average of annual rentals for tenants would be $5.63 per square foot, while the owner's annual square foot cost would be $2.29.[28] This extremely favorable rent structure for the owner, far less than the average cost of $4.26 per square foot then paid by Seagram in the Chrysler building, was encouraging for the company.[29] In an attached memorandum, Wagner commented on the three surveys and concluded that he was highly enthusiastic about the site, feeling that for many years to come, choice clients would move from downtown or other less desirable locations to fill up a building of Skytop's character. Wagner admitted that "there may be some feeling among certain types of people about renting in a building built for a liquor company but that there will be plenty of tenants available."[30]

This "feeling" was a nightmare for SB. The Kefauver Committee, the Senate Special Committee to Investigate Crime in Interstate Commerce, which convened between 1950 and 1951, concerned itself also with the Prohibition era, thereby newly tarnishing the whisky trade.[31] The possible stigma might well have been on SB's mind much later, when the building under construction failed to rent as fast as he had hoped.

A year after purchase of the property at 375 Park Avenue, Seagram executives were still questioning what to do with the site: Should we build a new building? Should we invest our own money? Should we arrange investment through an insurance company? Should a building be built in Westchester or elsewhere outside of metropolitan New York? Is this a peak period for building costs? The need to manage the new property required these questions to be answered by the company's newly formed Advisory Committee, whose members—top officers of the holding and operating companies—were to meet bimonthly to make decisions on issues regarding company operations such as pensions, taxes, and packaging, as well as the building.[32] In the first meeting, a "Decision as to Park Avenue building" was the first item discussed; its conclusion, "We are to build a building."[33]

But this decision was not firm. For seven months, in meeting after meeting of the Advisory Committee, no action was reported regarding the New York property until, at the beginning of 1953, a real estate proposition for a Seagram building was offered in Chicago and fuzzy proposals were being made for the New York site—one for a hotel-office building and another for including a "center of interest" (a museum for drinking vessels).[34] Still more months passed until August 1953, when SB met with David Tishman, who made a suggestion that he called a "drastic departure" from his firm's usual building transaction: to construct the building for Seagram and then to rent the balance of the space from Seagram.[35] There was no follow-up. In November, with Chicago real estate still in play, supersalesman Victor A. Fischel, president of Seagram-Distillers Corporation, was appointed as a committee of one to review this matter with "management"—undoubtedly SB.[36] Owing to Fischel's keen interest in this project, shared by other members of the Advisory Committee, things moved ahead, and within five weeks the Advisory Committee was notified that Seagram had purchased a property in Chicago, at the northeast corner of North Michigan Avenue and Pearson Street.[37] (By coincidence, Mies van der Rohe lived on Pearson, and later he would be involved with that property.)

SB was undoubtedly at the root of the languorous pace at which things proceeded with the Park Avenue site. His slowness in making decisions, he claimed, was a lesson learned from the executives of DCL of Scotland, who rather than deciding too quickly, like Americans and Canadians, took their time and made fewer mistakes; however, he added, "'It sometimes takes them what seems to be an interminably long time to get things done.'"[38] When I eventually embarked on a six-week search to identify the architect for the New York building, my father told me not to speak to him about it in the meantime, undoubtedly because he knew the oscillations attendant on decision-making. Beyond that, in general he resisted making decisions, especially when it came to issues that were not critical to his core business. By mid-1953, SB's attention was focused on diversifying his company into oil. In June, the Advisory Committee agreed to put in a bid by which the Royalite Oil Company of Alberta and Frankfort Distillers would each take one-third interest in the offering of state-owned land by the Louisiana State Mineral Board.[39] Subsequently in the oil business for many years, Seagram Company eventually found that its destiny turned on the consequences of the diversity of focus.

But Fischel was focused on the matter of building on Park Avenue. In December 1953, Seagram's Advisory Committee expressed the hope that the purchase of the property in Chicago would precipitate "action" in New York,[40] and at a meeting on April 15, 1954, it was reported that "the letter to tenants had been sent" notifying them they would have to vacate apartment houses on the Seagram site, and twelve architecture firms were reviewed by the subcommittee on building that had been created by this date.[41] The next meeting of the Advisory Committee was only eleven days later, but the subcommittee on building had moved with greater speed than before. Fischel was anxious to move ahead with the building program as rapidly as possible: two candidates to coordinate the building program had been identified and would be interviewed by the full Advisory Committee and the Management Committee, and one of them would be hired without delay; Fischel explained that his "Summer Sales meeting program bears a direct relationship to the new building."[42] Thus, Fischel precipitated action that led eventually to the engagement of Mies van der Rohe as architect of the Seagram building in New York, though this was not what he had in mind.

Today's intense competition among corporations and developers to hire "signature" architects was not yet in play. Emulation has always been a factor in choosing an architect, but only later in the 1950s did prestigious banks set a pattern that other banks and corporations would follow.

The architects and buildings named in the correspondence between Seagram's Advisory Committee and various real estate agencies reveal the nature of building practices in New York City during the decade following World War II. Real estate agencies and the Fuller Company were "promoters" who provided lists of architects, whose buildings were taken to be "indicators." The new buildings were mostly tall and bulky masses composed of a series of floors progressively set back from a ten-story high base covering the whole site. They were known as ziggurats, referring to the ancient stepped pyramid, or, more familiarly, as "wedding cakes." Before the Zoning Resolution of 1961, their form followed the setback provisions of the zoning ordinance: the building could rise ten stories at the street line, but above that height, it was required to set back behind a series of inclined "sky exposure" planes, rising as a tower when the volume of the building reached 25 percent of the site area. Large floors had recently become possible because of technological improvements in lighting and the advent of air-conditioning, but this meant that workers could be far from windows, in a completely artificial environment.

On February 8, 1952, an officer of the Bankers Trust Company forwarded to Friel an announcement for the "Building Identification Prize Contest," an advertising campaign sponsored by Cushman & Wakefield in October 1951, with three dozen images of

FAIRCHILD AERIAL SURVEYS, INC.

How well do you know your New York?

CUSHMAN & WAKEFIELD, INC.
BUILDING IDENTIFICATION PRIZE CONTEST

How many buildings can you identify?

Win one of 23 Prizes

To be awarded, subject to the rules of this contest, to those who identify by correct name or address the largest number of the 36 new office and commercial buildings in Manhattan, erected since 1947, or now underway,* and who submit an essay of not more than 100 words, entitled:

WHY MANHATTAN IS THE IDEAL LOCATION FOR AN OFFICE

*During the same period since 1947 there has been little or no construction of similar buildings in many large cities in this country. New York is the World's Center of Business — and still growing!

15 Announcement for the Cushman & Wakefield Building Identification Prize Contest, February 8, 1952. Photographs: Fairchild Aerial Surveys, Inc., Adolph Studly, Dirk Duryea, Inc., Apdix, Willis Photo Art, and Ezra Stoller.

How many buildings can you identify?
SUPPLY ANSWERS ON OFFICIAL ENTRY BLANK

The illustrations on this page are miniature reproductions of 36 larger pictures on display during the contest, in a show window at the main offices of CUSHMAN & WAKEFIELD, INC. For easier identification, view the original pictures at 281 Madison Avenue, New York, where official entry blanks are also available.

CREDITS { Photographers — Adolph Studly, Dirk Duryea, Inc., Apdix, Willis Photo Art, Ezra Stoller.
Architects — Sylvan Bien, Emory Roth & Sons, Carson & Lundin, Skidmore, Owens & Merrill, Kahn & Jacobs.

Important

All but two prints of the buildings pictured above are reproduced from actual photographs or architects' perspectives of 36 new office and commercial buildings in Manhattan, erected since 1947, or, now underway. The two exceptions are architects' perspectives of buildings in the site clearance or excavation stage at locations of former well known landmarks. Four buildings pictured show only newly constructed extensions or additions to buildings erected prior to 1947. This contest is not intended to represent that CUSHMAN & WAKEFIELD, INC. is agent for any of these buildings, except where such is the fact.

16 Emery Roth & Sons, architects, 380 Madison Avenue, New York, 1953. Photograph: Felix Gilbert, Uris Buildings Corporation.

important New York buildings either under construction or recently completed; the Bankers Trust officer "picked fourteen as having characteristics of possible interest to you" that included architects "qualified by experience and ability to advise you and prepare preliminary drawings covering their idea as to the best utilization of your Park Avenue plot" (fig. 15).[43] Among the fourteen buildings and nine architects singled out for consideration by the officer of Bankers Trust were Reinhard, Hofmeister & Walquist, cited for Chrysler East and Dun & Bradstreet. The elegant Esso building (1947), at the northern end of Rockefeller Plaza, was designed by Carson and Lundin, who as staff architects for Rockefeller Center were obliged to make it fit in with the rest of the complex. The firm's Sinclair Oil building (1952), also on the list, employed a similar vocabulary of alternating limestone piers and windows of the same width, the windows and spandrels set inches back. Shreve, Lamb & Harmon, who had designed the Bankers Trust Company addition at 16 Wall Street in the early 1930s, were mentioned for their Mutual Life building. Kahn and Jacobs were included with three of their buildings. The Universal Pictures building (1946–47) had been the first to break the residential vocation of Park Avenue.[44] Located at the southeast corner of Park and Fifty-Seventh Street, it was also the first structure in the city to take its inspiration from the European experiments of the 1920s, notably those of Eric Mendelsohn's dynamic horizontalism, in which solid floor bands seemed to float above the continuous glass window strips. Regarding 100 Park Avenue (1948–49), Friel advised his colleagues that "it was more-or-less discussed around town that . . . from an engineering, architectural, standpoint, [it] is one of one of the best buildings that has been put up in recent years."[45] The firm's forty-two-story 1407 Broadway (1950) was also listed. The Look building (1949–50), designed by Emery Roth & Sons and developed with Percy and Harold Uris, had gained a certain notoriety in defining the aesthetics and economics of market-rate office building

17 Wallace K. Harrison, director of planning, United Nations Secretariat building, United Nations plaza, New York, 1947–53, United Nations Board of Design. Photograph: J. Alex Langley, c. 1950.

design,⁴⁶ and thus was also on the list. Emery Roth's 380 Madison (1953; fig. 16), the Uris building in which Seagram had taken space that it would later relinquish, was included.⁴⁷ Walker & Poor's 575 Madison Avenue was also recommended, as was 260 Madison (1952) by Sylvan Bien, one of Roth's competitors.⁴⁸ The latter was so typically corporate, Robert Stern tells us, that it was chosen to represent New York office life by *Life* magazine.⁴⁹

Two major International Style high-rise structures were on the "list of fourteen." The firm of Harrison & Abramovitz is recorded as the architect of the United Nations Secretariat building (1947–53; fig. 17).⁵⁰ Lever House (1951–52) was the other (see fig. 11). Nothing distinguishes these slab buildings—so different in form, intent, and international engagement—from the other commercial buildings singled out. Only the names of architects and their buildings were given in the Bankers Trust list: with the exception of a note or two, there is no mention of formal issues, nor are there any indications of architectural judgment. It is not surprising, then, that a major voice in architecture went unheard: Frank

Lloyd Wright, whose fame was again on the rise. But Wright was, in a manner of speaking, considered as architect for the Seagram building.

Wright had been the first American architect to propose glass towers, both in his National Life Insurance Company building for Chicago, drawn in 1924, as well as in his unrealized high-rise residential towers for St. Mark's-in-the-Bouwerie (1927–31), which reflected Mies van der Rohe's Berlin projects of 1921–22. A period of decline then set in for Wright, but in 1952 his exhibition *Sixty Years of Living Architecture* traveled from Florence to Zurich, Paris, Munich, and Amsterdam. Through his son-in-law Kenneth Baxter, a Seagram executive, Wright was in contact with SB's brother Allan Bronfman.[51] In a letter of April 1952 to Allan, Wright expressed his keen interest in building in New York: "I have always felt that the New York skyscraper was only half-baked—pushing ordinary guillotine windows way up into the sky—a dangerous and silly extravagance. They are all too heavy also—not scientifically built to be *tall*. Now I believe I could show you something else," something, he wrote further on, "that would enable you to astonish and delight the world."[52] And so he made his pitch: "Great ideas are involved—so having them up in my sleeve, as the final grand act of an architectural career by no means insignificant, I am anxious to shake them out so they can be seen and appreciated. You could give me this chance, I believe."[53] Wright correctly surmised that Allan's brother Sam was a stumbling block, but he was confident "that would change after the revelation which I propose and believe could convert him."[54] Namely, Wright suggested to Baxter that the "Bronfman Brothers could knock off a million dollars worth of advertising . . . by putting up a sign on their vacant lot on Park Avenue. 'Tallest building in the world will be built on this site for Seagrams [*sic*] (or whatever) by Frank Lloyd Wright.' This is to be followed up by presentable sketches of the project—price only one hundred thousand dollars, payable ten thousand per month after delivery of sketches."[55] SB was skeptical of Wright's proposal for a one-hundred-story building: "I don't want to meet my maker so soon."[56]

Despite Wright's correct assertion that "the work I would present to you would have a great international advertising value if you cared to present it that way,"[57] disregard for Wright and an endemic disrespect for architecture among Seagram executives (with the exception of Allan Bronfman) was apparent in the comments of Ellis D. Slater, who would eventually head up the Building Committee. Of a potential Wright building, Slater wrote: "Wright will undoubtedly design the most unique building in New York and it will surely be good architecture. . . . But, he can not get beyond the sketch stage. . . . The roof will probably leak; the heating system and the lights probably won't work; he will make it extremely difficult to house your employees because he will place them where he wants them, not where they are practically located. When you get through (if you ever finish it) it will cost twice as much as any other building."[58]

Wright's name never appeared on a Seagram list of prospective architects, although he designed two projects constructed in New York at the end of his life. The first was the Hoffman automobile showroom, with a curving, ramped turntable, at 430 Park Avenue, which opened in 1954.[59] Then, as design of the Seagram building was commencing, he was building the Solomon R. Guggenheim Museum, commissioned in 1943, which was finally located at Fifth Avenue between Eighty-Eighth and Eighty-Ninth Streets, across from Central Park. It was constructed in tandem with Seagram, opening in October 1959, when the Seagram building received its final certificate of occupancy.

In mid-April 1954 members of Seagram's Advisory Committee (Allan Bronfman, but not Sam, was copied on the memo) had reviewed a list of architects that was similar to the list drawn up two years earlier, but this time they were rated A, B, or C.[60] New to the list

18 Pereira & Luckman, architects, model made for Seagram annual national sales meeting and Seagram official Victor A. Fischel. Photograph from the *New York Herald Tribune,* July 13, 1954. Photographer unknown.

were Voorhees, Walker, Foley & Smith, Eggers & Higgins, William Lescaze, and Pereira & Luckman, all rated A. They were probably proposed, and were certainly approved, by Lou Crandall, whose firm had served as contractor for structures by each one. The first two were large New York firms Crandall insisted I visit when I undertook the search for the architect. Eggers & Higgins were known for having built John Russell Pope's Jefferson Memorial and the National Gallery in Washington by 1941, and three buildings at the Gateway Center in Pittsburgh in 1952. Voorhees had built more than any other firm on Fuller's List of Current Work, which included seventy-five buildings constructed by the Fuller Company across the United States.[61] Lou Crandall later told me how impressed he was by the successful partnership between the European modernist Lescaze and the American Beaux-Arts–trained George Howe in creating the earliest European Modernist high-rise building in America, the Philadelphia Saving Fund Society building (completed in 1932). The firm of Pereira & Luckman was also put on the list, but in this case, undoubtedly by Victor Fischel.

As president of the Lever Company, Charles Luckman had consolidated the firm's offices, acquired the Park Avenue site, and, with daring, commissioned Skidmore, Owings & Merrill to design the first International Style building in the center of New York, following the completion of the United Nations complex at the edge of the island, along the East River. However, in 1950, before Lever House was completed, Luckman returned to his original training as an architect, and four years later, on joining William Pereira to establish the Los Angeles architectural and planning firm Pereira & Luckman, he was asked by Seagram to develop some ideas for a new building to be presented at its annual national sales meeting, which was to take place in three weeks.[62] As Seagram's most powerful salesman, Victor Fischel recognized another master salesman in Luckman, and under the pressure of time due to the imminent summer sales meeting he had organized around the idea of a new building, he plainly had convinced SB to meet with Luckman. Years later Luckman recalled the encounter:

A SITE AND AN ARCHITECT FOR SEAGRAM

> I was surprised when one day I received a telephone call from Samuel Bronfman, president and largest stockholder of Seagram Distillers Corporation, a man I had never met. He invited me to his office in New York to discuss a headquarters building for Seagram. Bronfman, a rugged, forceful executive, knew just what he wanted. . . . Over a few drinks, Bronfman told me that he planned to construct a 35-story building of about 500,000 square feet on Park Avenue, across the street from Lever House. That did it. I was hooked. I wanted to do that building more than anything else. As he elaborated on the building of his dreams, I could visualize the unique challenge and opportunity of building a sister edifice to the glass-sheathed Lever House.[63]

On July 13, 1954, the *New York Times* ran the story "Park Ave. to Get New Skyscraper; Seagrams [*sic*] Plans a Gleaming 34-Story Headquarters—Voisin to Lose Home," announcing a fifteen-million-dollar project.[64] On the basis of a Seagram press release, the *Times* story reported: "The preliminary proposals for the new building call for a four-story facing of marble and bronze, forming a massive pedestal from which would rise a thirty-story tower with striking verticle [*sic*] lines of metal and glass." It then reported that the facilities proposed for the new structure included individual entrances for the three major corporate divisions (these were, according to business practice of the time, competing companies: Seagram, Calvert, and Frankfort distilleries), three large sales and advertising rooms, and a large auditorium. It is important to note that the company's press release referred to Pereira & Luckman as "Seagram's consultant for the new project," but it was instantly assumed that the firm was the architect designate. The press release also stated that Victor Fischel presented a powerful and unusual sales incentive program, providing an opportunity for each distributor to earn recognition. Every distributor who met his sales quota would contribute a symbolic "brick" to Seagram House, which would be memorialized by a plaque, and distributors who met higher sales quotas would have their portraits placed in the "Distributor's Hall" of the new building.[65] Fischel posed with a six-foot-high model Luckman had produced for the meeting (fig. 18). Luckman stated in the *New Yorker* that he held the firm conviction that "architecture is a business, and not an art." Luckman's visualization of "the unique challenge and opportunity of building a sister edifice to the glass-sheathed Lever House" was clearly sales driven.[66]

On July 26, 1954, *Newsweek* reported that the building was also being considered as a new home for the Metropolitan Opera.[67] The concept, preposterous considering the relatively small site, was proposed by the architects Fordyce and Hamby, who wrote to SB that Seagram needed more than a design for a building: "we think you need an idea."[68] The opera story, printed by a responsible magazine, indicates the general view of the time that anything was possible. The *New York Times* quoted General Frank R. Schwengel, president of Joseph E. Seagram & Sons, Inc., as saying that the move to build "is a pledge of faith in the growing prosperity of the American economy. . . . Major depressions are a thing of the past." The *Times* went on to cite several factors that General Schwengel said were making the economy less volatile: "Measures to prevent bank failures; sounder regulation of bank credit; the revolution in home financing through wider extension of mortgage amortization."[69]

Working as an artist in Paris, I was aware only of the image that my father had sent to me ahead of time. Over a period of a few days, I wrote him a long letter dated June 28, 1954.[70] My letter strongly advocated the abandonment of the Luckman plan: "This letter starts with one word repeated very emphatically NO NO NO NO NO. . . . I find nothing whatsoever commendable in this preliminary-as-it-may-be plan." In the note he wrote when he sent me the "plan," he had used the term "Renaissance Modernized" in reference to the future Seagram building. I had taken him to see the Palazzo Farnese in Rome earlier that year, so I explained:

> I did not make clear to you what I meant. I have used the Renaissance as an example and it happens to be the one period in architecture that I know a little about, and also about the most fascinating period of general culture and creativeness from every point of view and what has interested me most is that a building or a painting or a statue is never an isolated "work of art" but part of a whole society, of a way of life, of a philosophy. . . . You can't modernize the Renaissance—you can only *learn* from it—understand what it meant and why their buildings were beautiful. By analyzing what is beautiful in the past one can analyze what is beautiful in the present, but the present has different conceptions and a different vocabulary.

In continuing the letter, it was necessary to comment on the image I had been sent. In order not to be too heavy-handed or "academic," I chose to use the language of country "bumpkins" to formally criticize the Pereira & Luckman scheme:

> Knock them between the eyes, boys, that's the way. Show 'em you can do sumpthing new, sumpthing terrific. Yup a nice big high skyscraper popping up to the sky without letting it stop. Accentuate the verticals so that she goes streaking up like a comet . . . nothin' to stop her . . . good and futuristic . . . a Flash Gordon job . . . that's it, flashy . . . real rich materials . . . make the man in the street realize what you've got there . . . bowl him over . . . impress him with your power, your wealth . . . keep him out of it . . . make him scared to go in . . . all that lower part . . . just a mass of polished marble . . . no one can penetrate that except those that know that they go in there and belong . . . what's them funny sort of tower things going up the side?—dunno sorta looks like silos but ain't this the Seagram's building?—make whisky, guess that's where they store their grain . . . [and after learning that they were for executives] why them towers just cut off all the light from the rest of the building, but I guess it don't make much difference where the ordinary people work, they gotta work some place.

I learned what I thought as I wrote:

> The more I think of it, the more I am convinced that there are two very exciting new buildings in New York . . . the UN building and Lever Brothers. I might have scoffed at them, and it is easy to scoff at something that quite changes what we are used to and what we have considered quite comfortable. New conceptions are put into the flesh and sometimes quite violently change our way of looking at things and we take a while to even be able to look at these "new" things.

I wasn't sure what I thought of a glass high-rise building:

> At first, my reaction was that maybe it was wrong to make a building which weighs tons look as if it floats and to make the walls not quite definite because they are always changing. But why have a building crushing down on us? In the best architecture the aim has always been for lightness for elegance. . . . And is there anything wrong in having the interest in a surface due largely to changing reflections? . . . decoration through

your pattern of glass and your reflection. . . . How wonderfully simple, how elegant, how lovely.

My overwhelming concern was for the ethics of building:

> In putting up a building in New York, you have two choices—first you are erecting a building which is just a place to work in, with no specific appeal to men's imagination or intelligence or agreement, and in this case as long as your building is sound, and functional, and fairly agreeable, it does not much matter what it looks like because it will just be another vaguely modernized skyscraper office building like so many others and you won't be affecting anyone much one way or the other. This is not what you plan to do, but if you do not plan to do this you have *one alternative and one alternative only:* you must put up a building which expresses the best of the society in which you live, and at the same time your hopes for the betterment of this society. You have a great responsibility and your building is not only for the people of your companies, it is much more for all people, in New York and the rest of the world.

My father's response to my letter was to telephone and ask me to come back from Paris to choose the marble for the ground floor. I was stunned. I received the needed support from my mother, who suggested that he invite me to come to New York to see what I could do. According to the story as it is told in my family, my father wanted to lure me back from Paris,[71] but despite my lack of training in architecture or business, it was the fire and conviction with which I wrote of the importance of the role of architecture in society and my belief that my father really wanted a great building that must ultimately have engaged his attention at a moment when the business-as-usual procedures that Seagram executives and building professionals were applying to the project could hardly have galvanized him.

In New York, I first talked with architectural critic Lewis Mumford, whom I met through the stage designer Lee Simonson. Mumford was keen on Marcel Breuer and Naum Gabo's recent solution for De Bijenkorf in Rotterdam (in which a large sculpture by Gabo was installed instead of a projecting section of the building as mandated by the city in order to provide accents along the street front). He also recommended Louis Kahn, who had recently completed an extension to the Yale Art Gallery in New Haven. Subsequently, I found both wanting: Breuer's Student Arts Center of 1950–52 at Sarah Lawrence College in Bronxville, New York, like all his work I had seen in publications, was essentially suburban; about Kahn's extension to the Yale Art Gallery, I wrote to Mumford, "there was also something terribly self-consciously moralizing about the interior—the exposed air-conditioning ducts for example."[72] I found the expression of the ducts at the entrance to be unrelated to the building's heavy concrete ceiling structure. Furthermore, this tetrahedral structure was not read in the curtain wall. In my view, neither this building nor Kahn's Radbill building for the Philadelphia Psychiatric Hospital (1948–54), nor his very beautiful Bath House for the Jewish Community Center (completed 1955) on the outskirts of Trenton, New Jersey, both of which I visited later, had a sense of scale or articulation appropriate to New York City.

Through Marie Alexander, a Vassar friend, I met with the founding director of MoMA, Alfred Barr, who advised me to talk to Philip Johnson, but warned that Johnson was resigning his post as curator of architecture at MoMA to develop his own practice. My father arranged for me to meet with Lou Crandall, which made me somewhat uneasy, wondering how I would get along with a hardheaded businessman, but I was so convinced that we could create a distinguished building at a time when the greatest contemporary architects, who were equal with those of the Renaissance, were still alive, and I already knew so much about current work that Crandall essentially got me my job. On his advice Seagram hired Fred Kramer as coordinator for the new building. Kramer was an old-fashioned architect whose love of Oriental rugs I perceived as retrograde, and he was extremely proud of having worked in Washington, DC, for the French Neoclassical architect Paul-Philippe Cret, who was in my view even more retrograde. Nonetheless, my father assumed that Kramer would be the person to search for the architect.[73] An incident burnt into my memory indicates how little my father understood about the difference between business and the arts: driving to New York City from Tarrytown, where I was living temporarily with my parents, he told me that I could sit at Kramer's feet and learn, as his sons did in the business with him. My answer was something he had rarely heard: "No." Crandall, however, told my father that I should be the one to search for the architect. By the middle of August, I wrote to Eve Borsook, another Vassar friend, that my "real work began":

> Now I really have a job. I shall be travelling all over. . . . Crandall wants ME to do the research, talking to the architects, etc. He told my father that I could do a job that no one else could have done, going to these people and talking to them. Certainly no one employed by Seagram could (by virtue of being employed), and a daughter who is interested in seeing that her father puts up a fine building seems to have everyone's sympathy. And now I must say my prayers every day to be able to do the job as it should be done. What a unique chance I have![74]

I continued the letter, giving an account of my search: "Through [Philip Johnson] and Mr. Crandall I was to meet and talk to the leading architects, the heads of the architectural schools, the architectural historians and critics (among them, Aline Bernstein Saarinen, Vassar 1935), the editors and writers of art and architecture magazines and the members of museum staffs."[75]

In the early days of my search, I met Eero Saarinen at Philip Johnson's Glass House in Connecticut. An inveterate list-maker, he was most helpful in proposing that we draw up a list of architects according to three categories: those who could but shouldn't, those who should but couldn't, and those who could and should. Those who could but shouldn't were on the Bankers Trust Company list of February 1952, including the unimaginative Harrison & Abramovitz and the work of Skidmore, Owings & Merrill, which Johnson and Saarinen considered to be an uninspired reprise of the Bauhaus. Those who should but couldn't were the younger architects, none of whom had worked on large buildings: Marcel Breuer, who had taught at the Bauhaus and then immigrated to the United States to teach with Gropius at Harvard, and, as already noted, had recently completed Sarah Lawrence College Art Center in Bronxville; Paul Rudolph, who had received the AIA Award of Merit in 1950 for his Healy Beach Cottage in Sarasota, Florida; Minoru Yamasaki, whose first major public building, the thin-shell vaulted-roof passenger terminal at Lambert–Saint Louis International Airport, was completed in 1956; and I. M. Pei, who had worked with Breuer and Gropius at Harvard and became developer William Zeckendorf's captive architect. Pei's intricate, plaid-patterned curtain wall for Denver's first skyscraper at Mile High Center was then under construction.

The list of those who could and should was short: Le Corbusier and Mies were the only real contenders. Wright was there-but-not-there: he belonged to another world. By reputation, founder and architect of the Bauhaus Walter Gropius should have been on this list,

19 Mies van der Rohe, architect, Apartment towers at 860–880 Lake Shore Drive, view from Lake Michigan, Chicago, 1948–51, detail. Photograph: William S. Engdahl, Hedrich-Blessing Studio, after 1957.

but in design, he always relied on others, and his recent Harvard Graduate Center was less than convincing. Unnamed at that meeting were Saarinen and Johnson themselves, who essentially belonged to the "could but shouldn't" category.

I projected six weeks as the period of research, during which I visited the architects in their offices. Buildings that would be under construction over the next years were in the drafting rooms, and through other visits and the architectural magazines, I became acquainted with some of the new work in the United States, as well as Le Corbusier's Unité d'Habitation in Marseille and various buildings under way in other parts of the world. It was most important to see the recent buildings. In New York were the United Nations building and Lever House. Elsewhere were a fair number of buildings. Eero Saarinen's thin-shell auditorium and round chapel at MIT were under construction. Near Boston, Gropius's firm, The Architects' Collaborative (TAC), showed me houses and schools using the lift-slab technique of which they were inordinately proud. In Connecticut, I visited houses and a small Miesian office building for Schlumberger by Philip Johnson. Philip took me to Philadelphia to show me the Philadelphia Saving Fund Society building by George Howe and William Lescaze, built during the Depression, which he considered still to be the exemplary modernist office building and an object lesson in high-quality interior detailing. Also in Philadelphia was the psychiatric wing of the Jewish Hospital by Lou Kahn, and in Elkins Park, Pennsylvania, Frank Lloyd Wright had completed the Beth Sholom Synagogue in 1954. One could see Harrison & Abramowitz's 1953 Alcoa building in Pittsburgh, with its aluminum spandrel panels creased to avoid tin-canning, and the firm's auditorium for Oberlin University. In Detroit, I visited Eero Saarinen's Miesian General Motors complex; in Chicago, the wealthiest American city architecturally, I saw Mies van der Rohe's 1951 towers at 860–880 Lake Shore Drive (fig. 19) and his growing campus at IIT; and in Racine, Wisconsin, I viewed Frank Lloyd Wright's 1939 Johnson Wax building (fig. 20).[76]

Toward the end of the search, after dinner at the Saarinen home in Bloomfield Hills, Michigan, Aline Bernstein Saarinen, who was writing an article on the avant-garde for the *New York Times Magazine*,[77] posed the question: "In the 1920s, would you choose Behrens or the younger Mies? And in the 1950s, would you choose a younger man or Mies?" Philip Johnson was also present that evening, having traveled to Michigan to visit Saarinen's General Motors Plant with me. I do not remember the conclusion; maybe there was none, for Eero and Philip were the "younger men," both contenders for the building (Eero later came to New York to see me to make a special pitch).[78] In the 1920s, it would have been clear that the architect should be the young, visionary Mies. In 1954, he still had not been surpassed, but for me, for some time the choice lay between Mies and Le Corbusier. A letter written on October 30, 1954, makes clear my conclusion about the selection of an architect:

> It has been said that Frank Lloyd Wright was the greatest architect of the 19th century. . . . To me the Johnson Wax [building] is a complete statement of "Manifest Destiny," the embodiment of all the philosophy of that period in America. It has a force and vitality that is almost cyclonic. It's crazy as hell and as wonderful as it is crazy. The greatest errors of taste—not errors, just plain bad taste—turn out to be magnificent. . . . His is not the statement that is needed now. America has grown up a bit, and Frank Lloyd Wright has expressed what it was when its energies were unharnessed.
>
> Le Corbusier has not built a building in this country. (The UN was unfortunately only an emasculation of his plan.) Would he be a great and good influence here? I am afraid not. . . . One is fascinated by his spaces, his sculptural forms, but are not people

likely to be blinded by these and skip over the surface only? Mies forces you in. You have to go deeper. You might think this austere strength, this ugly beauty, is terribly severe. It is, and yet all the more beauty in it.

The younger men, the second generation, are talking in terms of Mies or denying him. They talk of new forms—articulating the skin or facades to get a play of light and shadow. But Mies has said, "Form is not the aim of our work, but only the result." In his Farnsworth house in 1951 and the Twin Towers at 860 Lake Shore Drive in Chicago in 1952, he has articulated the skin, at the same time creating a play of depth and shadow by the use of the basic structural steel member, the I beam. This ingenious and deceptively simple solution is comparable to the use of the Greek orders and the Flying Buttress. It is not a capricious solution; it is the essence of the problem of modern architecture that Mies had stated in 1922: "We should develop the new forms from the very nature of the new problems."[79]

It is in the nature of making decisions, at least meaningful ones, to wish to go back on them, to undo, and I agonized that Le Corbusier would have been best after all, but I knew this did not make sense. Lou Crandall agreed that working with Mies was "do-able," and when Mies met my father at his apartment in New York (the conversation was facilitated by the presence of my mother and Philip Johnson, who both spoke German), they took each other's measure with genuine respect.[80]

On October 4, 1954, Charles Luckman sent SB new plans to show me, "not . . . in any last minute hope that she will change her mind about the man she has chosen to design your building," but expressing the hope that his firm might continue in the capacity of consultant.[81] SB returned the photostats, declining Luckman's offer to be retained as consultant on call.[82]

Like an éminence grise or a deft puppeteer, Lou Crandall, it is now clear to me, was highly influential in the formation of the Seagram building design and construction team. He suggested to me the association of Philip Johnson with Mies, reasoning that it would ensure continuity should anything happen to Mies at his age (it is worthy of note that Mies was only sixty-eight at the time).[83] I welcomed the suggestion because of Philip's social skills, adapted as they were to a world little known to Mies and completely unknown to me. Mies, grateful to Philip, who had championed him for a quarter of a century, offered Philip a partnership: "Shall we make it 'Van der Rohe and Johnson'?" he asked. On October 28, 1954, Mies van der Rohe and Philip Johnson signed a Memorandum of Agreement "for the sole purpose of doing architectural work and design of a building to be constructed at No. 375 Park Avenue."[84] By December 1, 1954, I was named Director of Planning.[85] Crandall also recommended as associate architects Kahn and Jacobs, with whom he had collaborated on the production of the Skytop study and whom he considered to be one of the most competent firms in New York. He also effectively selected the consultants Severud-Elstad-Krueger Associates and Jaros, Baum & Bolles as structural and mechanical engineers, respectively, both of whom had previously worked with Kahn and Jacobs as well as the Fuller Company. Jaros, Baum & Bolles had collaborated with Kahn and Jacobs and Fred N. Severud on the Universal Pictures building (1946–47), and later with the Fuller Company on Lever House (1952). Jaros, Baum & Bolles, Kahn and Jacobs, and Severud-Elstad-Krueger all worked together on the construction of 100 Park Avenue (1948–49). At Crandall's recommendation, Fred Kramer had already been appointed clerk of the works, in charge of monitoring schedules, accounting, and site coordination.

20 Frank Lloyd Wright, architect, Helios Laboratory, Johnson Wax Company Complex, Racine, Wisconsin, 1936–39. Photographer unknown.

It must be said that SB placed complete trust and confidence in his architect and in Crandall, who was not only in charge of construction but was also to help determine and watch costs. SB in fact asked Crandall to treat the building as if it were his own. Crandall and I became, virtually, the clients. The stage was set, and the actors proceeded to play their roles: "And so began four fascinating years of work."[86]

2

MIES VAN DER ROHE'S UR-BUILDING

Clients almost invariably present their architects with endless ideas they have dreamt of and reams of efficiency charts and studies prepared by a hierarchy of committees. Samuel Bronfman stated his requirements very simply: he told his architects and contractor that the building was to be the crowning glory of everyone's work—his own, Crandall's, and Mies's. He did, from time to time, emit design preferences: he did not want a building on "stilts" like Lever House, and he liked "bronze," he said, in response to Mies's questions about materials. He also let it be understood that Seagram's head office was to have two hundred thousand square feet and the rest of the roughly half-million-square-foot building would be rental space.

By the end of November 1954, Philip Johnson had set up the design offices at 219 East Forty-Fourth Street in a recent, nondescript building by William Lescaze (1896–1969), located within an easy walk of Seagram's executive offices in the Chrysler building, where they had been for twenty years. Beyond an enclosed conference room at one end near the entrance and an enclosed model shop at the other end, the office was essentially one large room. A few small, boxlike semiprivate offices were aligned along the outer wall of the building, one cubicle each for Mies and Philip, and one for me, as I had chosen to set up my office with the architects. Lying hard against another structure, the windows of the outer wall were protected by iron grating. Philip masked them with translucent fiberglass sheets covered with fishnet. On the advice of lighting consultant Richard Kelly, lights installed between the fiberglass and the window wall gave off a pleasant glow. Apart from the oak partitions six or seven feet high forming our cubicles, this wall was the only element of luxury in the lofty open space that measured about fifty feet in length by twenty-four feet in width, with ten-foot-high ceilings. During the preliminary design stage, this space was used for making and studying models and also accommodated six drafting tables for two or three members each from Mies's and Philip's offices. They were replaced by secretarial desks as well as full-scale study models by mid-February 1955, when work on production drawings got under way, and a special drafting room was created on the floor above to house the architectural teams assigned to the project from the offices of Mies, Johnson, and the associate architects Kahn and Jacobs.

At the insistence of Lou Crandall, Mies came from Chicago to New York. He would sit in his small space silently puffing on a cigar and drinking coffee—which he told me moistened the tongue to counteract dryness induced by smoking (fig. 21). At times he tilted his head back in order to blow the smoke upward. If he made sketches, I know of only two, both of which focus on the plaza at the foot of the building (figs. 22, 23). In his cubicle, Mies was mostly thinking.[1] This was his general disposition, as I observed then as well as later, during the decade I spent in Chicago between 1960 and 1970. Philip, or one of the architects who had moved to New York from Mies's Chicago office, would enter his space to discuss a design problem. Gene Summers recently wrote that, for architects working with Mies, "The only way you knew how you stood with Mies was if he called you into his office."[2] I rarely entered his cubicle, but I would see and talk with him in the conference room for meetings, mostly with salesmen or technicians from the various building trades,[3] or for weekly project meetings.

Under more captivating circumstances, I joined Mies in the larger space when he studied the successive models set up there. These were, successively, a cardboard model of the urban context around the building site; a full-scale model of a section of the bronze curtain

21 Mies van der Rohe in his apartment, Chicago. Photograph: Phyllis Lambert, 1964.

22 Mies van der Rohe, architect, bird's-eye-view sketch, Seagram plaza, [1955]. Graphite on notepaper, 11¾ × 9 in.

23 Mies van der Rohe, architect, perspective sketch, Seagram plaza, [1955]. Graphite on tracing paper, 6¾ × 8½ in.

24 Full-scale wood model for Seagram bronze skin, with mirror extension studied by Phyllis Lambert, Mies van der Rohe, and Gene Summers, 1955. Photographer unknown.

wall that was extended by the use of mirrors (fig. 24); and full-scale steps built in wood (as was the model of the curtain wall) to test the proportions of riser to tread so that everyone in the office could judge the easiest flow up the three steps from the sidewalk to the plaza along Park Avenue. In a letter of August 1955, I made a sketch of the riser-to-tread proportions that were being discussed: Frank Lloyd Wright's outside stairs were four inches high to sixteen inches deep; ordinary exterior stairs, six to twelve inches; and Mies's at Farnsworth, five and three-quarters to fourteen inches.[4] For Seagram, the ideal was a riser five inches high and sixteen inches deep. (It was adjusted, in reality, to the slope of Park Avenue, as I discuss below.)

I recall one occasion when Mies spent most of the night sitting in his cubicle. He was there, he said, "to encourage" the architects who were finishing another model (to be presented the next day) of one of two great sixty-foot-square plaza-level spaces at both ends of the east wing. These grand spaces eventually formed the great rooms of the Four Seasons Restaurant. Initially, Seagram executives considered a bank or an automobile showroom for these spaces. The idea of an automobile showroom was inspired by Frank Lloyd Wright's Hoffman Auto Showroom on Park Avenue (1954, now Mercedes-Benz Manhattan). I decided to stay that night to watch the model being finished. Having been trained as a sculptor (not yet as an architect), I hoped to help. My offer was rejected, and later I came to realize that someone outside of the loop would have slowed the process. Those great rooms gave rise to Philip Johnson's later critique of Mies. Like others who worked closely with Mies, Johnson claimed that his logic was "a very flexible kind of logic": "In the dining room[s] of the Four Seasons, the central column is just taken out. All right, you say, 'Take it out,' but what happens to the beam? The beam should get twice as deep! But we couldn't make the beam twice as deep because of the ceiling. On the outside, the size of the spandrel had to be kept. Oh boy, so you see, I lost all respect for honesty, the logic of buildings."[5] Johnson, never a structuralist, then gave an example of his own early sin, committed years before Seagram: "Look at the Glass House. Look at that chimney. That chimney goes right through the beam!"[6]

The office was not the only point of contact. Philip, Mies, and I met elsewhere, often during luncheon at a nearby Italian restaurant, where both architects began the meal with two martinis, or when visitors came to the office (I recall in particular Richard Neutra, whom I first met in California, and the iconic Sigfried Giedion, whose *Space, Time, and Architecture* every modernist knew by heart), or at various evening parties with Nelly van Doesburg, Mary Callery, and Friedrich Kiesler. For me these were people from another world, people whose work I had read or read about and, with the exception of Callery, people who had been part of Mies's life decades earlier in Berlin, before he left for the United States. Feeling most comfortable with Philip or with old acquaintances, Mies would talk. He loved to recount the drama of removing, at the last moment, the dusty footprints of workmen on the black carpet of the Barcelona Pavilion just before it opened or finding the great block of onyx that set the pavilion's height. He told stories about the Bauhaus, about Paul Klee and Wassily Kandinsky.[7] He told most of these stories many times over, always with relish, and more expansively the more he had to drink. "One more martini and I will be doing Louis Quinze," he would to say with his hand overhead drawing large arabesques in the air, invoking the way he had worked in the stucco factory of a man named Max Fischer in his hometown of Aachen, where he learned to draw, "swinging [his] whole arm," full-size decorative ceilings.[8] Mies also would come to my apartment on the first floor of a three-story brick house on Seventy-Ninth Street between Lexington and Third Avenues. These evenings were spent with friends with whom I took courses at the Institute of Fine Arts at New York University and others, talking and listening to jazz. Martinis or Scotch flowed until Mies would greet the dawn, the *blaue Stunde,* as he would say.

The preliminary design for Seagram was undertaken by Mies and Philip with five members of their two offices. Philip Johnson's right-hand man at that time, Richard Foster, ran the project office, functioning as the project manager during design as well as construction. He was not involved in design: his responsibility throughout was to get the job done and to coordinate with the contractors and manufacturers. John Manley, a low-key person and very good draftsman and problem-solver, had also come from Philip's office.[9] Three people initially came from Mies's office in Chicago: David Haid, Henry Kanazawa, and Edward Duckett, a skilled draftsman and Mies's model maker.[10] All three worked with Mies developing the initial building concept. Mies drew my attention to Duckett's extraordinary draftsmanship for the building elevation, where the closely spaced lines denoting the mullions never wavered. I asked Duckett to teach me mechanical drawing, and sat in my office by the hour drawing variations on the hyperbolic paraboloid. I took my drawing board and T-square with me when I traveled, even to Paris.

At the end of April, Gene Summers arrived in New York after twenty-one months of military service in Korea. Summers had previously worked in Mies's Chicago office, where as he proved his skills and competency, he was given increasing responsibility.[11] On his release from service on April 22, 1954, when he visited Mies to tell him he was going back to Texas, before he could say so, Mies asked if he wanted to work on the Museum of Fine Arts, Houston, or the Seagram building—the two major new projects in the office.[12] Summers chose New York.[13] Shortly after he joined the Seagram project, Duckett and Haid returned to the Chicago office, where Haid took charge of the Houston project. Summers assumed the lead role in detailing the Seagram building. This, then, was the composition of the talented young team involved in the design of one of the major high-rise buildings of the twentieth century. Summers did not then have a license. Mies did not yet have a license to practice in New York. Philip had just obtained his. Summers laughingly remarked: "Nobody had a license. Not really."[14]

Some years later, Richard Foster wrote about working with Mies and the preliminary design team:

> Until I got accustomed to [Mies's] ways, his working habits were quite disconcerting. His usual hour of arrival was at 11:00 a.m., with meeting days the rare exception. At twelve-thirty it was lunch time and the heavy decisions were made very late in the afternoon. He would give direction as to which way the design would proceed, and the drafting force would make a number of sketches relative to the plan or details requiring an answer. The results of the previous day's work, and the drawings accomplished that morning were mounted on a wall in the drafting room during the lunch hour. That method was quite time consuming, and became progressively cumbersome as the work progressed. It was specially so in light of the fact that the building foundations began long before we knew what the exterior treatment would be, and before most of the interior work was designed, much less detailed.
>
> To complicate matters, Mies began bringing in, one at a time, his staff from Chicago. They began to establish their own office within an office, until the situation became impossible to control. I spoke to Mies several times about the division of authority, and received his marvelous *non sequitur* when he wanted to avoid a decision, Deeek, we'll think about it!
>
> Finally, I brought it to a head by telling him I was leaving the project effective immediately and that his staff from Chicago could run the project. I came to that conclusion after a number of unhappy days and nights, worrying about the design, progress of our information to the contractor relative to his construction schedule and the personalities involved.
>
> I chose a country inn site as the pleasantest place to tell him. Mies loved to stay weekends at the Fox Hill Inn in Ridgefield, with a commanding view of the surrounding countryside. It was a gracious hotel built in what was once a mansion. I would drive him up Friday nights in his car, and he would be driven back Monday mornings by a friend. I drove him up one Friday afternoon and called him on Saturday morning to ask if I could come over and have lunch with him, and discuss the job. He agreed.
>
> Mies suspected the reason for the call I'm sure, because he didn't seem at all surprised when I told him. After a long pause, he completely disarmed me by asking if my wife and I could join him for dinner that evening. I agreed, and we had a pleasant relaxed dinner. He was charming and gracious, and since I was no longer connected with the project, I probably told him more about how I felt than I would have otherwise. He at least knew I was sincerely interested in the building, and would quit rather than risk my commitment to its excellence.
>
> Sunday, I received a call from a Bob Wylie, who was both Mies's and Philip's business advisor, telling me that Mies had reached him, that he had spoken to Phyllis Lambert, and that I should reconsider since Mies had decided to send the Chicagoans home. Under those conditions I returned, and Monday morning they were all gone. From that point on we got along very well.[15]

Project meetings in which design, rental, and construction were coordinated took place every Wednesday in the conference room at Forty-Fourth Street. Richard Foster and sometimes Philip, Mies, and Ely Jacques Kahn, and later Gene Summers, all attended, as did the structural and mechanical engineers, L'Huillier Sheaff, a consultant and leasing representative from Cushman & Wakefield,[16] and two field coordinators from the Fuller Company, the experienced Matt Grogan and the younger Tom Hood. Fred Kramer and I attended on behalf of the Building Committee. These meetings were run by Foster, who commented, "The meetings were informative, and short—no more than one hour in length. Detailed problems between individuals were worked out later and their determination reported at the following meeting."[17] Foster also noted how attentive Mies was and how finely he read people. Mies clearly must have had this attribute, though I never heard him judge others. Foster recalled that "Mies listened carefully to whatever was said and made very few comments. He did, however, remember in detail all that transpired, and would go over it with me after the meeting to make certain there were no loose ends. He made carefully succinct personality observations of each new member present, and could wisely read the motives behind the posturing, questions and information given by those present."[18]

Commenting on my role, Philip said: "Just her presence meant that there was no hanky-panky, nobody cut corners. It wasn't that she knew anything about buildings, but it was like having the crown prince present."[19] In fact, my job was to be the link between Seagram executives and the designers, builders, and leasing representative. Most important to me was my self-assigned mandate to make sure Mies would build the building as he saw it.

The Building Committee, which had formally assumed its name by January 10, 1955, was also part of the process.[20] Its members were officers of the company: Ellis D. Slater, president of Frankfort Distillers Company, who chaired the committee; Joseph G. Friel, Seagram's treasurer; and Frederick J. Lind, Seagram's vice president and general counsel. John A. Handy, Jr., had joined the company as assistant to the president and became secretary of the committee.[21] From early on, Handy mentored me in working with a business organization and, most important, encouraged me to state my position and stand against the resistance he knew I would meet. I practiced with him how to tell the chair of the committee that I should be made a member, and with his help, I screwed my courage "to the sticking place" to do so. By the time the committee was named, I was a member.

This group performed a crucial role in the preliminary stage, obtaining building licenses, evicting tenants, and preparing, approving, and signing contracts, but when these objectives were no longer at issue, the only competence left to the members was the ability to go on record for cutting costs. Given such arbitrariness, I considered the process a sham, one that explained, at least in part, the mediocrity of corporate construction. My determination to build the building Mies envisioned meant skirmishing with the Building Committee on various matters, such as the question of the brick bond Mies wanted: English bond, in which cross members (headers) bond every row, rather than the common American bond, in which the headers bond only every seventh row. This principle of good construction was applied to the brick end wall of the east wing, which is located in an alley. Members of the committee argued that no one would ever see it. I used Mies's rejoinder that "God would see it." The English bond was voted down, but I arranged with Crandall to reinstate it; the difference of cost would be made up somewhere else. A few years later, after the building was completed, I wrote about the range of my activities:

> A good building depends on the clarification and ordering of information by the artistic volition, and on the freedom of the framework in which the architect can work. My

job was to make sure of this freedom and to avoid the rankling lack of understanding and short-sighted compromise that have atrophied or killed too many buildings.

This "keeping of the concept" involved a thousand decisions every day. I followed every step of the development of the building in the architect's office and we consulted with Crandall to make sure that the costs were in line before presenting them to the building committee. For example, we wanted nine-foot ceilings instead of the present standard eight-foot or less and fought bitterly for ten feet until we graciously accepted nine. Then I would explain why it was important that the stair wells be of good brick rather than the initially cheaper but in the long run just as expensive cinder block construction. I would insist that a graphic designer develop a lettering standard for use throughout the building. The mural decorations are an integral part of the space and I bought and commissioned prints, posters, tapestries, paintings, and sculpture for the offices of the Seagram Company, the public areas, and the restaurant. These procedures involved every part of the building, from desk handles and bathroom tiles, to the bronze extrusions, the glass, the plaza.[22]

Although I had planned to go back to Paris, I remained in New York, convinced that if the one person who really cared about the building was not there, Mies would not build Seagram. This insight proved to be accurate. Returning to New York from a summer vacation in 1955, after excavation had begun and numerous telegrams that spelled trouble had reached me, I found the project in crisis.

Fred Kramer [clerk of the works for the building recommended by Crandall was] trying to play the hero, per usual, and Mies even called his lawyer this time to see how he could get out of his contract.... Fred Kramer just has no idea of what anything means, he thinks that he is an architect and that Mies knows nothing and I wasn't there to dampen his spirits.... So Kramer decided to "architect" the core with Kahn & Jacobs, told [Ellis D.] Slater (the chairman of the building committee) some long song and dance, and Slater really doesn't know where he is at, and the whole thing got to be a mess. Mies felt that Seagram's [sic] had no confidence in him as an architect and the way things were handled and Slater & Kramer acted it certainly looked that way.[23]

By adding a bay to each side of the three-by-one-bay spine, Kahn and Jacobs's plan transformed the elegant proportions of Mies's three-by-five-bay tower into a clumsy, almost square four-by-five proportion. Enraged, I went downtown to Kahn and Jacobs's office to tell Mr. Kahn, in no uncertain terms, that as associate architect, and not the design architect, he did not have the authority to change Mies's concept. Incredibly, Kahn insisted that he had changed nothing, that after all it was still a five-bay building. Kahn's lack of discernment is corroborated by the story Philip tells about Kahn's first meeting with Mies at Forty-Fourth Street: "Kahn said, 'I tell you how we do it, Mies. We start with a ground plan and then we work the elevator core out. And in this building it would be about this many elevators to do the job quickly. And then we start decorating the door like this, you see.' Mies was a very, very quiet man, but right in the middle of this long speech—he must have been talking for ten or fifteen minutes—Mies stood up and hit the table, an enormous thing, with his hand, and said one word, 'No.'"[24] The details might be apocryphal, but the gesture is totally believable; I knew that, in substance, Mies did in fact dismiss Kahn from his office. And Kahn, who considered himself a master builder of numerous high-rise buildings, thought of Mies, with his "simple" Chicago apartment buildings, as a child in the

25 Meeting of the Building Planning Service Council of the National Association of Building Owners and Managers, Hotel Commodore, New York, May 2–3, 1955. Seagram's representatives, seated on the far side of the table from right to left: L'Huillier Sheaff, Ellis D. Slater (Seagram Building Committee chair), unknown, Phyllis Lambert, Gene Summers (behind Lambert), Philip Johnson, Dick Foster, Mies van der Rohe, Ely Jacques Kahn, Fred Kramer, and John Handy (seated at the head of the table). Photograph: Tommy Weber, May 3, 1955.

sophisticated business of designing office structures in New York City. Slater had the same attitude. He must have (quite correctly, although I did not think so at the time) brought the conflict to L'Huillier Sheaff, so that a two-day meeting of the Building Planning Service Council of the National Association of Building Owners and Managers Association was convened to resolve the quarrel that the associate architects Kahn and Jacobs raised with Mies's plan—the placement of the elevator cores and the shape of the building—as well as to give advice and point to any aspect they considered to be uneconomical (fig. 25). I was very nervous—I am sure that we were all nervous—but Mies was vindicated. George R. Bailey, chair of the Building Planning Service, read into the record the committee's approval of the design and the proportions and the materials of the building: "We think this is a magnificent conception."[25]

Mies was at pains not to think of the Seagram building as "different from any other building that I might build." He approached its design, he said, as he had approached all his buildings, by ascertaining the "facts": "Since [Seagram] was the first major office building which I was to build, I asked for the two types of advice for the development of the plans. One, the best real estate advice . . . as to the types of desirable rental space and, two, professional advice regarding the New York City Building Code."[26] At the same time, a philosophical and spiritual sense was communicated by his aura of quietude, assuredness, and strength. Large, silent, Mies referred to himself as "solid as an oak tree." He worked intensely, rooted in practical considerations, first gathering facts like minimal office size according to real estate agencies, zoning regulations, and vertical transportation, progressing to preliminary notions of building form, siting, structure, enclosure, and the plaza—all of which he then refined through painstaking studies, but rapidly, "hitting the nail on the head," as he would put it. The speed and flow of the work was transmitted in a letter I wrote on December 1, 1954, recounting the issues broached in preliminary design of the building:

> Three weeks ago, the contracts were signed and Mies came up—he and Philip found offices. Then the architects' offices (where I will work) had to be installed, and then they got to work. Mies wanted the facts and the problems began.
>
> The first facts were the zoning laws—and the first problem, the air rights. According to the zoning laws, a tower can cover only 25 percent of the plot. Seagram intended to demolish only 375 Park Avenue, now the Montana apartment house, but with the area of 375 alone, we would have an unworkable tower, only 8,000 square feet gross [per floor]. It is much too small for everything. However, Seagram also owns some land behind 375—116 East 53rd Street and two smaller buildings on 52nd Street. We could enlarge our tower if we could borrow the air rights to these buildings, but we find we can't unless they are included as a part of the new building, i.e., converted to offices. So in a meeting in Crandall's office, we looked again at 116 and the small houses on 52nd (someone long ago had said, "Oh, let's not pull them down," and the question stayed there) and we discovered that it was ridiculous to leave them as they do not make financial sense anyway. . . . Later, we bought a 100 by 100 foot plot on 52nd Street rounding out the site to 200 by 300 feet. This allowed for a still larger tower.[27]

Mies responded calmly to what had been a potentially disastrous situation—the lack of enough land for a viable tower. To increase the floor area of the building, once the additional land had been acquired and more volume allowed, Mies added a one-by-three-bay spine to the east side (one could say backside) of the three-by-five-bay tower. Then he replaced the small apartment houses east of the tower by a long, narrow, three-by-nine-bay east wing, three stories above the ground floor to connect the east wing with the tower, and to further increase the volume, Mies added on top of the east wing a six-story square volume we called the "bustle" (fig. 26). It was deceptively simple. Philip thought that for Mies, this would be an unthinkable compromise, denying the pure prism. He was convinced that it was a temporary phase. As was frequently the case, Mies's design solutions did not follow "Miesian" lore, and his inventive solutions surprised his followers.[28] The spine and the added volumes remained, providing the Seagram Company with larger floor areas and the building the promise of richly articulated spaces at the plaza level.

Mies's calm in the face of the potentially disastrous problem was in stark contrast to Philip's excitable nature when faced with similar difficulties. This contrast between the two men was evident throughout the process of design. I described the problem and Philip's reaction in my letter of December 1, 1954:

> Last week when Mies was not here X. [Philip Johnson] was doing some preliminary work for him, getting the facts—and the biggest fact in getting this skyscraper equals the elevators. They determine your bay system (in a columnar building a bay is the area between columns), the height of your building and heaven only knows what else. On the first try X. called me up—disaster—no building just elevators. Now all is getting in order—the Otis people are constantly consulted and asked to do their most brilliant best—but no matter what you do the elevators take up 3 bays![29]

26 Model for the Seagram building, Mies van der Rohe, architect, Edward Duckett, model maker, February 1955. Milled brass, composition stone, plastic marbling, and blond hardwood, 26 3/8 × 34 1/4 × 26 1/2 in. Photographer unknown.

The letter continued, describing Mies's interaction with the site model:

> Mies has [had] a cardboard model made of Park Avenue between 46th and 57th streets with all the buildings on the Avenue and some going in the blocks and then he has a number of towers for different solutions that he places in the empty place of the old 375 and this model is up on a high table so that when sitting in a chair his eye is just level with the table top which equals the street—and for hours on end he peers down his Park Avenue trying out the different towers. . . .
>
> Now to the building—what can we do without a wedding cake (buildings that set back from the street in layers until they get to the tower)? There are three solutions. First, a square tower—which is out.[30] Second, a 7:3 rectangular building set at a right angle to Park Avenue, the solution of Lever House. The third solution, set a 5:3 rectangular building back 90 feet from Park Avenue, creating a PIAZZA. . . .
>
> Guess what solution will be picked? Mies hasn't said which yet, but he is only thinking in terms of the last one. There will also have to be STEPS leading to the Piazza as there is a big drop (eight feet) from Park to Lexington and you can't have a building with columns of different heights marching down the hill, and so it has been placed on a podium.[31] This solution for the building has promise for terrific things—set back you hardly see it from the street coming up or down the Avenue *but* now what an impression—when you arrive there—almost Baroque, you don't know what is there and then you come upon IT—with a magnificent plaza and the building not zooming up in front of your nose so that you can't see it, only to be oppressed by it and have to cross the street to really look at it, *but* a *magnificent* entrance to a *magnificent* building all in front of you.[32]

Mies had taken a small apartment at the Barclay Hotel on Forty-Eighth Street, a few steps east of Park Avenue, and each morning he walked the five blocks to Fifty-Third and Park, studying the site. He was certainly mindful of the two major buildings nearby across Park Avenue: the imposing masonry presence of McKim, Mead & White's neo-Florentine Racquet & Tennis Club to the west (see fig. 10), facing the Seagram site, and Skidmore, Owings & Merrill's sleek, glass-enclosed Lever House on pilotis immediately to the northwest (see fig. 11). Mies usually worked through several solutions, especially when approaching problems such as the structural clear span at the Farnsworth house, or formal aspects of the urban oasis at 860–880 Lake Shore Drive, and later at the Federal Center in Chicago, Westmount Square in Montreal, and the Toronto-Dominion Centre in Toronto. He studied the limited number of innovative solutions presupposed by the New York site, working quickly and volumetrically using rough models. The Racquet & Tennis Club exerted a magnetic pull, even though we lack models and drawings to prove this. It was certainly a factor—if unacknowledged by Mies—in his decision to set the building back from the Park Avenue property line.

In closing my letter of December 1, 1954, I reiterated how rapidly decisions were made: "Mies just came back here on Monday and all these actual building things have happened since then."[33] On December 8, 1954, Ellis Slater reported to the other members of the Seagram Advisory Committee. He covered the activities I had described in my letter and conjectured that "Mr. van der Rohe should have his concept of the new building completed within the next two or three weeks."[34] The Advisory Committee began to work on space layouts. The Seagram companies were to occupy just over a hundred thousand square feet net, that is, without counting corridors and other ancillary spaces. If these had been included, they would have added some 30 percent, which amounted to considerably less than the two hundred thousand square feet the company had planned for, and which almost doubled Seagram's existing space.[35] As Slater had predicted at the end of December 1954, the key design concept was in place.

In December 1954, Duckett had made a cardboard model of the buildings surrounding the Park Avenue site, and in the first days of 1955, he began work on a small presentation model of Mies's building milled out of brass (see fig. 26). It was completed by the middle of February.[36] The model was small, only twenty-six inches high. Although Mies used very large drawings[37]—and had made a six-foot brass model, intended as a sales tool, for 860–880 Lake Shore Drive in 1950—he had clearly decided on a jewellike presentation for his first office building and his first building in New York. The model was made of "three-eighths-inch bronze plates put together in a box form with a T behind it. The . . . mullions were all milled out [of the plate by] . . . an old-timer down on 42nd Street. . . . For the spandrels, we let the bronze show through, and for the glass, we put on . . . Zipatone [sic] . . . it's waxed on the backside and you can put it on and peel it off."[38]

When Duckett had assembled the pieces and placed the tower on the wood base that represented the plaza and the sidewalks around the site, wire trees were placed at the sides to conceal the "stilts." With a high level of expectancy Mies, Philip, and I showed the model to SB at our Forty-Fourth Street offices in early March. We thought it to be so very fine—a proud bronze tower, set back on its plaza, a revolutionary concept—that he would immediately be convinced. I think Lou Crandall and L'Huillier Sheaff were with SB, and I do remember that nothing was said. Philip, Mies, and I, desolate, went to Laura and James Johnson Sweeney's for an intended celebration. In their beautifully bare apartment, its one large room furnished with a Mies couch, a large mat of woven grass, and perhaps an African sculpture, we talked about leaving. I would go back to Paris, Mies to Chicago, and Philip, I don't recall. I wonder now how we could have expected a go-ahead based on such an elementary presentation without a briefing on cost and scheduling. Within a short time it was worked through, so that on March 18, 1955, I wrote to friends that "the whole project is accepted."[39]

The building represented by the presentation model is within the same syntax as 860–880 Lake Shore Drive, with subtle but key differences—Mies always strove to develop a common language rather than particular solutions.[40] "I'm not working on architecture. . . . I'm working on . . . architecture as a language. And I think you have to have a grammar in order to have a language. . . . And then you can . . . speak in prose. And . . . if you are good at that, you speak a wonderful prose. And if you are really good, you can be a poet."[41] In developing a language, Mies's search—letting one solution grow out of another—demonstrated an extraordinary will to consequential thinking. The single building for Seagram rises monumentally on a plaza, its skin inferring its structure—"skin and bones."[42] The two buildings at 860–880 have a more informal relationship to their site. The skin is graphically drawn: I-beam mullions are composed directly upon the primary division of the structural frame, inducing a gridlike materiality that is quite different from the reflectivity of glass that had generated the forms of Mies's skyscraper projects of the 1920s, which I discuss in the next chapter. Seagram brings both together. The underlying difference between the glass skyscraper and 860–880 Lake Shore Drive was the separation of skin from structure. This had been the modality of Mies's skyscraper projects of the 1920s through the unbuilt projects he drew in 1939 and 1940 for the Armour Institute of Technology (AIT, later renamed Illinois Institute of Technology, IIT) in Chicago. In these proposals the curtain

27 Mies van der Rohe, architect, George Danforth, draftsman, Armour Institute of Technology (AIT) campus, view southwest from beneath the Chemistry building, Chicago, [1939/40]. Graphite on tracing paper, 24½ × 37¼ in.

walls of the buildings were cantilevered, projecting beyond the columns so that the skin was inherently separate from the structural frame (fig. 27).[43] This disjuncture of elements was consonant with Mies's great leap in designing the Barcelona Pavilion in 1929, where walls became spatial rather than supporting elements (see figs. 66, 67). This was the moment of his realization of the architectural implications of separating structure and enclosure, an idea he had absorbed from Karl Friedrich Schinkel's separation between the expression of a columnar gridded structure and infill. Mies knew the work of Schinkel (1781–1841) from his four years working in the Berlin office of Peter Behrens (1908–12). Later, in 1959, just after Seagram was completed, Mies would acknowledge this separation of structure and enclosure: "Das Alte [sic] Museum in Berlin . . . you could learn everything in architecture from it—and I tried to do that. . . . In the Alte [sic] Museum [Schinkel] has separated the windows very clearly, he separated the elements, the columns and the walls and the ceiling, and I think that is still visible in my later buildings."[44]

A decade later, in 1939, Mies arrived in Chicago, the heartland of American industry, where by the end of World War II, more than half the world's steel was being produced. Therefore, in his search for an "architecture of our time," he was able to investigate this medium as no architect had done before. Having begun to study the architectural potential of the raw structural shape of I- or H-sections while still in Germany, Mies pursued their possibilities in the American context as both structure and enclosure in buildings he designed for an entirely new campus for AIT.[45] Step by step he moved from the brick and glass skin placed in front of the column and mullion to brick and glass grasped in the flanges of the I-shaped mullion. With Mies's first steel-frame building for the campus, the Minerals and Metals Research Building, completed in 1943, the mullions of the curtain wall are unsuccessfully embedded in the brick spandrel, resulting in cracked bricks. With the Navy building (later Alumni Hall), in 1945, brick and glass are brought into alignment with the mullion, creating a curtain wall in which the exposed steel flanges of the mullions represent the structure below.[46] Mies further had begun to investigate a glass and steel curtain wall with projecting mullions in studies for high-rise skeleton structure buildings he first assigned as a student project in 1943, just after the Minerals and Metals Research Building was completed. Joseph Fujikawa, then a student but later a key architect in Mies's office, described how in one of these studies, "he even had his columns, structural columns,

28 Mies van der Rohe and Edward Duckett, model makers, cardboard model for the concrete Promontory Apartment building, [1946], Mies van der Rohe, architect. Photograph: Hedrich-Blessing Studio, August 31, 1946.

29 Mies van der Rohe, architect, perspective sketch for a steel version of the Promontory Apartment building, [1947]. Graphite on laid paper, 5 × 8 in.

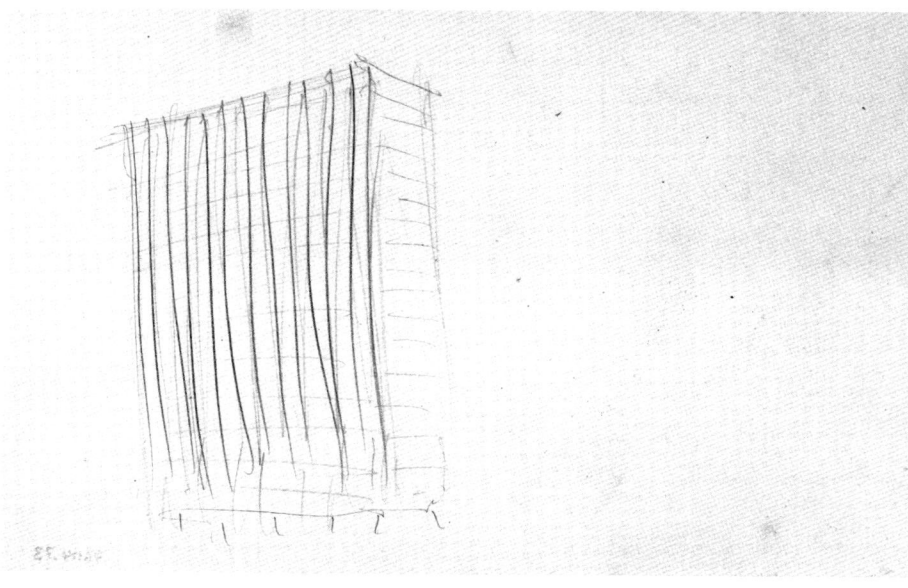

expressed like a mullion, only bigger."[47] Mies of course knew of the use of structural elements on the outside of Behrens's AEG Turbine Hall in Berlin (1910). In Chicago he also would also have seen the deep perforated braces projecting from the back of Louis Sullivan's Wirt Dexter building on South Wabash Avenue (1887), near the Blackstone Hotel, where Mies lived when he arrived in Chicago.[48]

The projects Mies assigned to students in 1943 were not for specific buildings; rather, they were visual studies resulting from an intuitive sense based on years of thinking about the constructive potential of steel and concrete as expressions of the building art. Clearly, this was more than a theoretical proposition. Mies continued to ponder the skeletal high-rise, and after the completion of the steel-skeleton drawings, he posed the question: "We have one example in steel. What do you think it could be like in concrete?" He then asked his students to draw the building in concrete. To express concrete as a more plastic material, Mies suggested: "In concrete maybe you could step the columns back."[49] For Mies, the nature of concrete resided in plasticity, the ability to mold the column. The solution of stepped-back columns was used in his first built high-rise, the concrete Promontory apartment building in Chicago's Near South Side (1946–49; fig. 28). An exposed concrete frame with brick infill was not unusual and had already been used in the 1920s in Chicago for high-rise apartment houses and industrial loft buildings.[50] Promontory was a speculative project whose design was determined largely by economic factors. Dissatisfied with Promontory as it was being built, Mies took a momentous step in asking his student Myron Goldsmith to draw the building with projecting steel mullions. Mies made a quick sketch himself to indicate the idea (fig. 29). As Goldsmith explained: "[He] was thinking already with mullions."[51] At the end of 1947, while Promontory was under construction, the opportunity to build a steel-skeleton high-rise building finally presented itself.

The steel skeleton towers of 860–880 Lake Shore Drive (1948–51), under construction (fig. 30), were a graphic illustration of the intention Mies announced in 1922: "Only skyscrapers under construction reveal their bold constructive thoughts, and then the impression made by their soaring skeletal frames is overwhelming. . . . On the other hand, when the structure is later covered with masonry this impression is destroyed and the constructive character denied. . . . We must not try to solve new problems with traditional forms: it is far better to derive new forms from the essence, the very nature of the new problems."[52]

The genius of 860–880 is this: deriving new form from the essence, the very nature of the new problem. The steel-clad structure was directly expressed by the raw material itself—the standard rolled H and I shapes, engineered for strength, which compose all steel skeleton structures, became components of the skin—the I-beam mullion, projecting beyond the steel-and-glass wall plane, only the back flange remaining in alignment, connecting to the enclosure. Thus the enclosure was a three-dimensional representation of the skeleton frame beneath. This remarkable invention has always seemed to me comparable to the evolution of the highly restrained, refined, and sculptural marble members of Greek temples, which represent the wood columns and architraves of earlier structures.

Innovative and architecturally satisfying as it was, the skin of 860–880 Lake Shore Drive was not Mies's ultimate solution for the high-rise building. A photograph taken from Lake Michigan showing the two steel and glass towers and, adjacent to them, Mies's aluminum and glass towers at 900 Esplanade (1953–57),[53] shortly after the latter were built, reveals a decisive change in Mies's handling of the skin (fig. 31). The surface planes of 860–880, clinging to the structure, are cool, clearly reticulated, black against a light field. The darkly veiled mass of 900 Esplanade (which was in the late stages of design when Seagram was begun)—cantilevered beyond the structure—is shrouded in mystery. Three decades

30 Mies van der Rohe, architect, apartment towers at 860–880 Lake Shore Drive, 1948–51, Chicago, under construction. Photograph: Hedrich-Blessing Studio, c. 1950.

after proposing something he did not yet know how to build, at 900 Esplanade Mies now wrapped the skin outside the high-rise skeleton, for the first time using a cantilevered skin for a skyscraper. Although somewhat clumsy at 900 Esplanade, this solution was significantly refined for Seagram. One might ask whether the differences between 860–880 Lake Shore Drive and 900 Esplanade—buildings of similar size, function, and conformation—are attributable to the considerable technological changes taking place in the building industry at the end of the 1940s and into the mid-1950s or to Mies's own volition? At 860–880, the steel mullions are, so to speak, "glued" to the structure, and heating elements

31 Mies van der Rohe, architect, apartment towers at 860–880 Lake Shore Drive, 1948–51, and 900 Esplanade, 1953–57, view from Lake Michigan, Chicago. Photograph: William S. Engdahl, Hedrich-Blessing Studio, after 1957.

buried in the floor and ceiling are supplemented by small electric units integrated with the base of the windows. Beyond opening the low window hoppers, the client had decided that there was to be no ventilation system except for aeration ducts needed in the kitchens and bathrooms. When 900 Esplanade was in design, however, air-conditioning had become essential in new high-rise buildings.[54] Water and air circulating at the perimeter of the buildings was required to feed the heating and cooling units. Mies took the opportunity of cantilevering the floor plane to accommodate the ducts and pipes, and this led to moving the enclosure to the outer edge of the cantilever, beyond the structure.

Aluminum was a handmaiden in this shift toward separating skin and structure. Joe Fujikawa talked of the role of aluminum manufacturers in encouraging Mies's office to design an entirely aluminum skin: "In the mid-'50s, when you found these huge aluminum plants with no place to sell their products, they became interested in buildings and doing parts for buildings. Alcoa had a big extrusion plant in Lafayette, Indiana, and they were the ones who first encouraged us to think in terms of aluminum on Commonwealth and 900, to do a whole building in aluminum. They had the capacity to extrude something with a twenty-one-inch diameter, they told us, and so they were really pushing."[55] Mies spoke of the difficulties involved in learning to work with aluminum: "When we changed from steel to aluminum they worked for about a year to develop this skin. . . . You have to change so many things. The expansion in aluminum is so much greater than in steel, and you know tall buildings wave—you have to allow more tolerances, and so we really had to change quite a lot."[56]

Another significant change was the use of tinted glass. At 900 Esplanade, a newly developed heat-absorbing gray-tinted glass was used floor to ceiling, while at 860–880, the glass was clear, untinted.[57] Tinted glass significantly differentiated 900 Esplanade from the clear glass at 860–880 Lake Shore Drive. Although the glass industry initiated the use of heat-absorbing gray glass at 900 Esplanade as a technical solution intended to reduce the impact of solar gain, for Mies, this was "just a problem in physics. It could be solved. Why don't they solve it?"[58] He had used tinted glass to emphasize the separation of planes in the Barcelona Pavilion and to attain varying levels of reflectivity, but at 860–880, which was built before a color of tinted glass acceptable to Mies was commercially available, a unified effect was achieved by installing silver-colored curtains throughout the building that would also inhibit the sun's penetration into the interior (a second curtain track permitted occupants to install curtains of their own choosing). Most important to Mies was the fact that from the outside, tinted glass obviated the patchwork of colors and patterns of the disparate window treatments installed by occupants. Joe Fujikawa remarked that, for Mies, "anything to help pull the wall together as a monolithic unit he was all for, which did include tinted glass."[59]

The advance in building materials abetted the decisive role aesthetics played for Mies in articulating the tall building. The use of a regular building module and an enclosure coplanar with the structure meant that the columns, which were wider than the mullions, impinged on the width of the glass, resulting in two glass sizes. A standard-sized window throughout the building was thus not feasible. With the skin separated from the structure at 900 Esplanade, the glass and metal of the windows was one size, continuously repeatable. In Mies's view, this was a modern solution. Although he had rejected the "rationalization" and "typification" that became slogans for modern housing in the late 1920s, he came to understand the powerful role that standardization would play in the economy of building in the United States in the twentieth century. The continuous enclosure composed of a regular rhythm of window divisions together with the use of tinted glass allowed the building to be treated as a volumetric whole. Tinted glass and dark metal create dark buildings while the contrast of light metal and dark tinted glass abrogates monolithic authority.[60] Mies frequently expressed his preference for the dark building in the city, a condition he would create at Seagram and later in his major urban projects in Chicago and Toronto. The language for Seagram was to become the symbolic embodiment of the Miesian tall building.

Retracing the development from the concept represented in the bronze model for Seagram, through the many exigencies that arose in designing and completing the building, it is useful to follow the order of work, from the first essential task of establishing the exact dimensions of the tower to defining the structure, designing the enclosure or skin of the building, integrating the heating, ventilating, and cooling systems, and finally designing the plaza. These were the issues of greatest importance to Mies in his effort to create a language. My account of how the Seagram building came together reveals, like Akira Kurosawa's *Rashomon,* a number of versions of the story, each told from a different point of view.

From the original concept of a sheer bronze and glass tower allied to an open plaza as expressed in the model, the first move, establishing the tower's dimensions, was like unpacking a puzzle. The module, the basic unit of measure determining the smallest practicable operating unit, had first to be defined. For an office building, the module is directly related to the width of an individual office. In common parlance, offices were defined by window units: a two-window office, a three-window office, and so on. Nonoperable windows, which are in effect panes of glass, are separated by mullions: so many mullions define a bay, and the number of bays establishes the floor area of the tower, which, according to code, could not be greater than 25 percent of the area of the site. The leasing representative, L'Huillier Sheaff, set the ideal office width at nine feet. A module of nine feet would limit offices to a multiple of nine. However, half that width, a module of four feet, six inches, would be more flexible, allowing two-mullion offices nine feet wide, three-mullion offices thirteen feet, six inches wide, and so on. Given a tower of five by three bays, to meet the 25 percent test for the tower measured to the exterior of the mullions, the module actually became four feet, seven and one half inches, and the bay size (initially set at roughly thirty feet square) therefore measured twenty-seven feet, nine inches square. In the 1950s the bay size of commercial skyscrapers was twenty to twenty-five feet, and a thirty-foot bay was considered unusual.[61] Gene Summers remarked that the four-foot-seven-and-one-half-inch module "seemed like a very mysterious number. Not four foot six or not five feet, but four seven and a half. And, people would always go back to Mies and say, 'Oh, how did you design this proportion? It's so beautiful.'"[62] The nonstandard dimensions created complicated conditions in the use of standard manufactured materials, but Mies accepted this, even as it contradicted his sense of the rational way to build, for the real estate people firmly emphasized that every half inch made a difference to the rent that could be charged. Six mullions per bay allowed Seagram to appear all glass head on and to possess an almost corporeal solidity when viewed obliquely, and thus a sculptural change of surface occurs with the viewer's movement. Twelve mullions per bay would result in an almost solid appearance with the verticals emphasized, as they were in Minoru Yamasaki's twin towers for the World Trade Center completed in 1973.

The differences between Seagram, Mies's first office building, and his two built metal and glass residential projects are noteworthy. Although there are similarities in structure and enclosure, office towers demand larger bays than residential buildings, so that fewer columns act as obstructions, allowing greater flexibility in the use of space. The basic structure of the Seagram building is a clear and straightforward Miesian skeleton frame, similar to his residential towers. However Mies initially considered something else, about which we know tantalizingly nothing. At the end of December 1954, he wrote to his former student Myron Goldsmith, who had also trained as an engineer and had worked in Mies's office. He asked him to come back from Italy to work on the Seagram building: "Is there any possibility that your work on your Fulbright is far enough along so that you could return sooner to work with us? Even if you cannot return sooner we would like to have you in the office upon your return, since the Seagram job gives us the possibility not only of paying more money than before but of working on new developments structurally."[63] Goldsmith replied to Mies that his letter had made "a very big impression" on him: "The idea of working on the tall building is something difficult to resist. At the same time I'm hoping that something good will come out of my studies with Nervi, and therefore, unless reasons for not doing so are overwhelming, I would like to finish my Fulbright grant. This should last into August."[64]

Goldsmith's engineering background might have been invaluable at this point in the design. Seagram's relatively slim tower, almost twice as high as Mies's residential buildings and half again as deep, raised the question not of structural safety but of possible cracks in the interior walls that would occur were it not rigid enough. In fact, I later lived at the top floor of 860 Lake Shore Drive, and I saw such cracks in one of the walls. The steel frame at 860 was stiffened by a K-joint between columns and girders, which allowed a certain flexibility. Mies wished to implement the same method at Seagram, while Severud-Elstad-Krueger Associates, the structural engineers, insisted on greater rigidity, stressing that neither the smallest cracks nor movement was acceptable in New York office buildings. This was in opposition to the relatively flexible frame that Mies believed to be an inherent attribute of the steel structure, evidenced in the design by Mies's Chicago engineer Frank J. Kornacker for 860–880 Lake Shore Drive. At Seagram, Severud used the one-by-three-bay spine and the elevator cores to stiffen the building as well as poured concrete floors to add weight.[65] Vertical trusses composed of diagonal steel braces were placed from the foundations to the twenty-ninth floor at the ends of the elevator cores and the sides of the spine, where they were embedded in twelve inches of concrete up to the seventeenth floor,

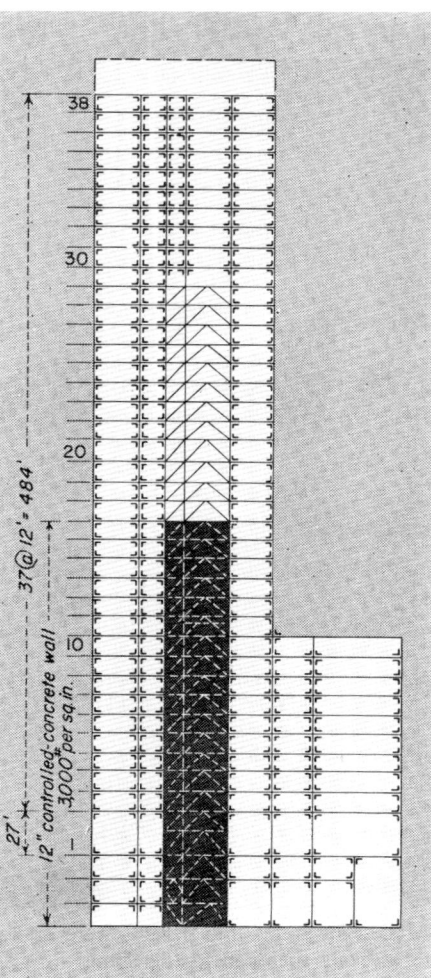

32 Severud, Elstad & Krueger Associates, structural engineers, schematic drawing of the steel frame for the Seagram building braced by vertical trusses embedded in elevator walls, from *Engineering News Record*, June 1957.

as sheer walls (fig. 32). The engineers also insisted on inserting an extra column at the Park Avenue end of the elevator cores, which Mies agreed to, having satisfied himself that it was possible to do so, but would require extra and costly steel bracing; consequently, the core does not end in a column as initially planned but projects beyond the column line.[66]

The solutions proposed by Severud to stiffen the building had other architectural consequences. The use of marble in place of glass on the north and south walls of the spine elicited controversy from members of Mies's office and other critics. Mies carried the skin across the sheer-wall face of the spine, replacing the glass with an opaque material, a dark green–veined Virginia serpentine marble whose finish was honed rather than lustrous. The marble panels (an inch and three-quarters thick) are held by the same bronze frame that carries the one-quarter-inch-thick glass and the three-sixteenth-inch-thick metal spandrel panels in the rest of the building. I recall the objections of a young architect in Mies's office to the use of serpentine because it required changing the profile of the interior stop holding the panel in place to accommodate the thicker material; using a thicker material was illogical, he argued, suggesting that a thinner material be used, either bronze like the spandrel panels or, preferably, obscure glass. Mies laughed, and said, "Ya, you have something to learn."[67] In an interview, Mies stated that to cover the concrete wall of the spine with glass or with bronze, "We would have made the structure of our building unclear."[68] During an interview with Philip Johnson, a critic called the surfacing of the spine end wall a "fake façade," saying, "Mies simulated the grid design on that solid marble wall, and that's fake."

Philip's response to him had to do with the idea of a glass building and the rhythm of the mullions: "It seemed most logical to Mies and me that the building all look the same. And you don't really notice it. That solid wall even goes around the corner of one window bay. That happened just before the construction started because the air-conditioning people said we didn't have enough vertical risers."[69]

Severud had still another reason for stiffening the Seagram tower. Having unleashed the atomic bomb that ended World War II, a decade later Americans were constructing bomb shelters throughout the country, still haunted by the possibility of retribution. Fred Severud, whose *The Bomb, Survival, and You* was published in 1954, wanted a structure with "unusually great resistance from any lateral forces, even those that might be created by a nearby bomb explosion."[70] He also designed baffles that could complete the enclosure of the Seagram elevator lobbies to transform them into temporary areas of refuge, and the bomb shelters in Seagram's basement and subbasement were designed to admit a certain amount of blast pressure, rather than futile resistance to total force. World history might have been different if Severud had been involved in erecting the World Trade Center.[71]

The bay size and air-conditioning design had other consequences for the design and articulation of the Seagram building enclosure. The larger bay required a deeper edge beam, and therefore a deeper spandrel, which confers a certain visual weight and gravitas to the horizontal expression of the skin compared with that of 860–880 Lake Shore Drive and 900 Esplanade. More decisively, however, the three-foot-deep spandrel at Seagram was required to accommodate ducts carrying the air below the floor slab at the perimeter of the building. Air-conditioning—meaning humidity control, air cleaning, and heating, as well as ventilation—was not in general use until the 1950s.[72] By that time, it had become sine qua non that no windows would open in order to ventilate tall office buildings. In fact, opening a window would disequilibrate the system.[73] Fresh air was drawn from outdoors and heated or cooled, and humidity added or subtracted depending on the season. The treated air was distributed through vertical risers and horizontal ducts, and a certain proportion of fresh air was mixed with the ambient air inside. The proportion of ambient to fresh air and the ability to control the temperature in different parts of building, as well as in individual spaces, defined the sophistication of the system in the mid-1950s. Kahn and Jacobs's Universal Pictures building of 1947, supposedly New York's first fully air-conditioned building, was still quite primitive: a central spine duct had its own fan room on each floor, and horizontal ducts carried in the corridor blew air directly into the offices through the corridor wall.

At Seagram, this young art was already very refined: on sunny, cold winter days, the air in one part of the tower could be cooling while it was heating in another. Air rises in vertical ducts within interior shafts in the elevator cores. High-velocity, high-pressure double-duct (hot and cold) air risers serve special air-mixing units to establish zoned temperature control on each floor extending to interior rooms, permitting individual temperature control. At the periphery, the air is distributed through low-profile air induction units, eleven inches high by twelve inches deep, along the base of the nine-foot-high glass window wall, but separated from it by a few inches. Mies had designed the first building in New York to carry the glass the full height from ceiling to floor, and the induction unit running between the columns gave tenants a feeling of security by forming a barrier between them and the glass. For the leasing agents, this was a serious consideration at a time when many potential tenants were extremely uncomfortable looking outside and steeply downward. In the United Nations Secretariat building and Lever House, the window wall stopped at desk-high window air-handling units backed by a masonry spandrel, in compliance with New

York's antiquated code governing fire safety: in both cases, the required masonry spandrel was covered with glass, making the exterior appear to be an all-glass curtain wall (fig. 33).

Bringing conditioned air into the Seagram building occasioned another demonstration of Mies's remarkable ability to transform necessity into art. Outside air is brought in and treated at the top and bottom of the tower. At plaza level on both sides, air enters through an invisible horizontal grill at the top of a boxlike travertine clad plenum projecting beyond the lobby enclosure. Lower than the travertine cores to which they are attached, together they form an elementarist cubic sculptural edge, interpenetrating with the glass enclosure of the lobby (see PF 6). At the tower's summit, the assembly of mullions and louvers that form a continuous screen around the air-intake and mechanical equipment for washing, heating, and cooling the air brings the building to a strong architectural conclusion. This screen was closely studied. The louvers replace glass and spandrels between two-story-high mullions aligned with those below. The louvers had to be open enough to admit the desired quantity of air and the V-shaped blades designed to make the view from any angle impenetrable. Summers said that the height was set "pretty close" to the requirements for the cooling tower. "It was really not an aesthetic decision."[74] The tendency to explain Mies's proportions as a consequence of necessity was consonant with Mies's office colleagues; had the proportions of the screen not satisfied Mies, he certainly would have made the necessary adjustments.[75] Seagram's strong expression of top, middle, and bottom was allied by Philip Johnson with a tendency by Mies toward the classical order of architecture.[76]

Air-conditioning was beginning to be understood as an environmental issue, as Reyner Banham made clear in his prescient book of 1969, *The Architecture of the Well-Tempered Environment*. Banham's brilliant history of artificial control of the environment indicates a shift away from structure as the generator of architectural form and toward systemic environmental control. (This had been a subject of great interest in Europe in the late 1920s, a period lacking the technology to advance implementation.)[77] In the 1950s,

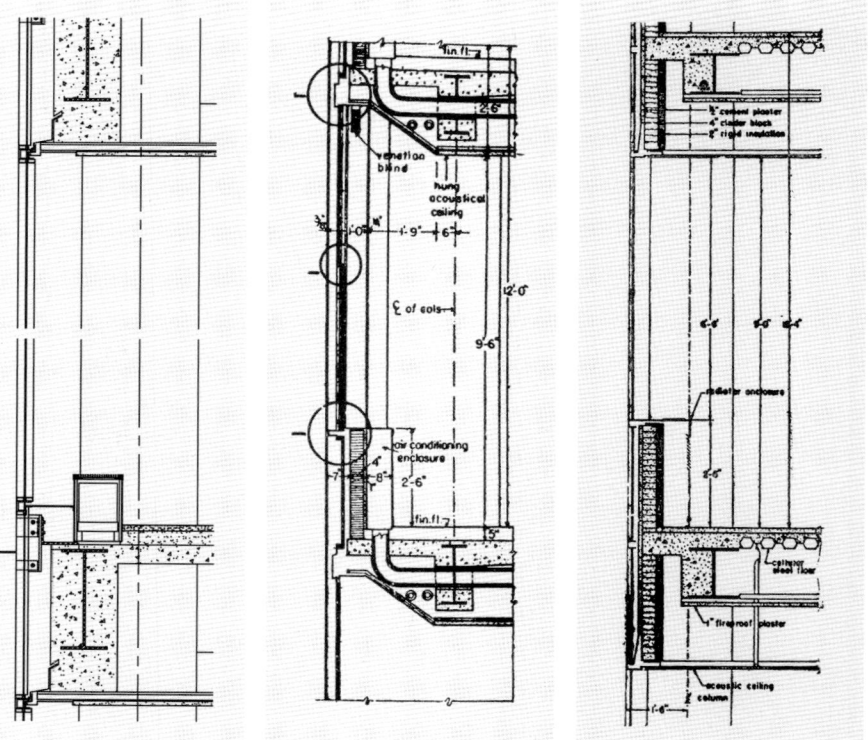

33 Comparison of vertical sections of the Seagram building, the United Nations Secretariat building, and Lever House, showing spandrel and window relationships. For Seagram, digital drawing, Alvin Ho, 2000; for the UN building and Lever House, from Reyner Banham, *The Architecture of the Well-Tempered Environment*, 1969.

office buildings required not only central and/or peripheral air-conditioning but hung ceilings, covering the air-handling ducts, incorporating air diffusers, fluorescent lighting, and sound-absorbing material. The cost was only about 8 percent more than a building without air-conditioning and illuminated by ordinary incandescent lighting.[78] Furthermore, the numerous functions contained within the suspended ceilings necessitated the cooperation of structural, mechanical, electrical, and acoustical engineers and designers all working together. The hung ceiling, like the curtain wall, was in essence a multipurpose membrane.

The luminous ceiling hung at the periphery of the Seagram building was a special case with respect to the ceiling membrane. Mies wished for Seagram to be illuminated at night. In 1928 he had already proposed using opaque glass to illuminate the (unbuilt) Adam Department Store in Berlin for advertising purposes: "Walls of opaque glass give the rooms a wonderfully mild but bright and even illumination. In the evening it represents a powerful body of light and you have no difficulty affixing advertising. . . . Such a brightly lit advertising on an evenly illuminated background will have a fairy-tale effect."[79] Mies had also used luminous surfaces in the *Wohnraum in Spiegelglas* (Glass Room) he designed with Lilly Reich for the technical section of the Werkbund exhibition *Die Wohnung* in Stuttgart in 1927, and the freestanding wall composed of two panels of etched glass lit from within—the only light source in his Barcelona Pavilion of 1929.

In 1950 Mies worked with lighting consultant Richard Kelly to create luminous cores on the ground floors of 860–880 Lake Shore Drive, which were deliberately intended to announce the building at night. Since the glass walls of an office building were necessarily transparent, Mies thought illuminating the Seagram building could be achieved using sealed-beam PAR lamps in pots shining onto and reflecting off the ceiling at the periphery of the building. Philip, working with Richard Kelly, proposed that the ceilings themselves be illuminated.[80] Together they developed the concept with engineers from Lightolier, the company that also manufactured and installed them throughout the full perimeter of Seagram's thirty-eight-story tower: a grid of fifty-five-and-a-half-inch enclosed-steel plenum box cells housing fluorescent tubes. The sealed cells both increased light output and stopped sound from transferring between offices (fig. 34). Translucent vinyl film was stretched over each cell to diffuse the light in an even pattern. I recall the test frames, which were made on the principle of embroidery hoops, over which the material was stretched. These were hinged for relamping. Four warm-white fluorescent tubes provided hundred-foot candles of light, and two others on a separate circuit were switched on as the sun set,

34 Spreader channels assembly for the luminous ceiling in the Seagram building. Photograph: Alfred Auerbach Associates, Inc., c. 1957.

so that the building glowed at night. The original night lighting was deactivated during the 1970s energy crisis and has never been revived.[81] Seagram's luminous ceilings, inspiring the building to be called "A Tower of Light" at night,[82] expressed the building's reticulated structure. They found a critic in Rem Koolhaas. He pointed out that instead of the expression of the massive floor slabs one would expect, the light boxes fragment the building as a glass monolith and represent "an almost exhibitionist display of the false ceiling, and the theoretical Mies—'Beauty is the Radiance of Truth'—is incompatible with any kind of falsehood" (fig. 35).[83]

At the beginning of August 1955, Mies was hard at work on the Seagram building curtain wall. In that first summer, working drawings got under way, and the articulation of the elements of the enclosure were continuously refined. The mullions of bronze and the color of the glass presented new problems in themselves. But why *bronze*? Samuel Bronfman's answer to Mies's query about what materials he liked ignited another leap of artistic insight in Mies. His experience with 900 Esplanade had prepared him. Mies was disturbed by the reflective properties of aluminum, which took on different shades and sheen in light and in shadow. On the other hand, bronze was a noble, time-tested material; it is resistant to corrosion; its surface becomes richer with time; it is ductile, and therefore, like aluminum, it can be extruded. If 900 Esplanade and Commonwealth Promenade had been the first buildings designed in Mies's office (and probably anywhere) to have a skin entirely made of aluminum, the bronze skin of Seagram was unprecedented, and I believe it remains so.[84] The success of the Seagram tower lay in the discipline of structure and enclosure, the proportions, the quality of the materials, and the refinements of the curtain wall. Developed only months before the design of Seagram began, the pioneering extruded-aluminum curtain wall of 900 Esplanade proved to be a constructive mock-up for the bronze skin of Seagram. Whereas Mies had not paid particular attention to detailing 900 Esplanade, he worked on Seagram more closely than he had any other building.[85] Piping for air-conditioning units carried behind the mullion at 900 Esplanade was exchanged in New York for deeper spandrels to carry the more complicated systems required for an office building; thus the clumsy depth of the 900 Esplanade skin beyond the column and the crude spandrel covers became the elegant framed low-relief spandrel panels at the Seagram building (fig. 36). Gene Summers recalled the experience of working with bronze:

> Bronze [was] a new material for me to deal with. And I worked probably more closely with Mies at that time than I ever did before or after. . . . He had a little cubicle, little office, next to Phyllis's office. . . . And I'd be able to go in there and sit down and talk to him about it. We discussed and tried different kind of mullions. We had been doing the wide-flange mullions on all the steel buildings for good reason. That's a standard shape. And because this was extruded, this mullion on the Seagram Building, we had more freedom. We could change the shape. So we tried shapes that were curved, shapes that were rectangular. And we tried in the drawing, and then we tried in sketches, and then we would build it full size, a full-size model of it. But in the final analysis, the simple H-shape, like the steel wide-flange, was still the better aesthetic shape.[86]

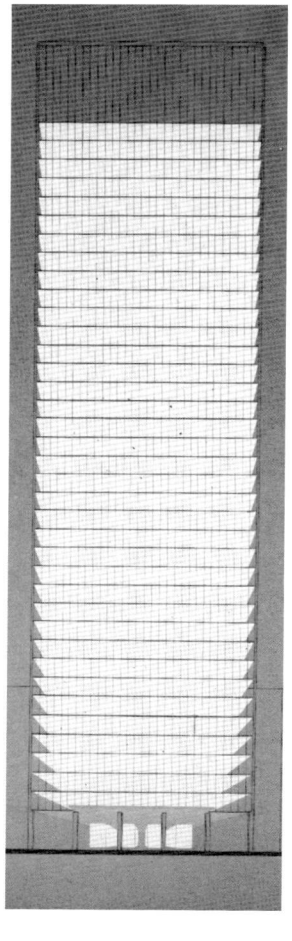

35 Richard Kelly, lighting consultant, graphic concept for the Seagram building as a "tower of light," c. 1957, from *Architectural Forum*, February 1957.

I asked Mies why he would use in bronze a shape that had been developed as the basic structural profile for steel beams and columns.[87] Mies explained that he had tried other profiles, but none allowed the same play of shade and shadow (he used the words "umbra and penumbra") as the I-beam. Even in full revolution against Miesian architecture, Philip Johnson spoke of the "exquisite shadows" caused by the I-beam mullions of

36 Seagram building, study of facade proportions, articulation, and relationship of skin to structure, detail. Photograph: Werner Blaser, 1963.

the Seagram building (which he referred to variably as H-beams or H-columns): "That H-column, which makes that shadow, was an absolute revolution, because it gave you your third dimension . . . the application of a common, ordinary H-beam was a turning point . . . in façade design."[88]

Compared to working with aluminum, bronze had certain disadvantages. Summers, who had worked with both, commented that larger diameter dies could be used in the aluminum extruding process: "We were limited in the bronze to, as I recall . . . 6-½-inch diameter die. [Actually it was initially a six-inch diameter die. Aluminum had the capacity to extrude a section twenty-one inches in diameter.] And so we wanted to make that mullion a little larger for visual reasons. But we were limited. So that's a little bit smaller mullion than, say, 860 [Lake Shore Drive]."[89] However, in collaboration with the General Bronze Corporation, specialists in architectural metal work and curtain walls, an extrusion technique was developed that increased the allowable diameter of their extrusion dies (fig. 37). Still, the six-inch-deep bronze mullions of Seagram are three-quarters the depth of those at 860 Lake Shore Drive.[90] At the same time, there were definite advantages to working with extrusions over rolled-steel sections, as Summers explained:

> You have the flexibility of incorporating . . . such things as the alignment pin between one mullion and another mullion. To make [them] line up, we put a pin from one

37 Seagram building window and spandrel unit being lowered into place, billet-to-mullion extrusion sequence, and mullion assembly, from the *Copper and Brass Bulletin*, February 1957.

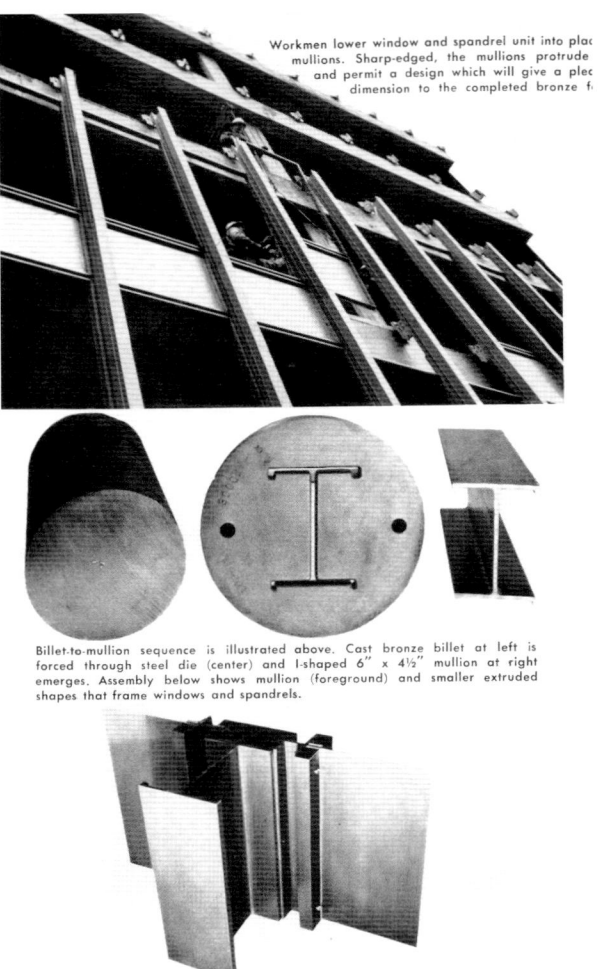

flange to the other flange. . . . And that was able to be done by changing the shape at the end of that flange. . . . The back of that mullion could also be altered, because it was an extrusion, to accept the window frame. And I detailed a window frame that had teeth in it. And then there was a set of teeth on the back of the mullion so that they interlocked. . . . You could get more refinement in the detail. More from a technical point of view than certainly an aesthetic point of view.[91]

But this development was not totally smooth. I recall considerable concern over the thickness of the section, a concern Philip Johnson must have felt since he spoke of it. He called the mullions "bronze trim," saying that the thickness of the flange had to be changed from seven-eighths to three-quarters of an inch, "because of the method of fabrication."[92] However, the rationale for this change was not the method but rather the cost. I recall that the price of copper, which kept fluctuating, was a problem. The cost was considerably reduced by removing material where it was not needed. Mies, however, thickened the end of the flange not only to incorporate the alignment pins but for visual reasons, to give the edge some substance. Summers recounted the collaborative work in refining the mullions:

After I worked on the skin and the development of the details, and got them to where Mies was happy with them, I was working then with a member of Kahn & Jacobs's team [who] was going to do the working drawings of the skin. And he was an Indian from

India. A wonderful guy. I liked him very much, and we worked together well. He had had more experience than I had. So we actually made some technical changes, due to his suggestion. And then, of course, that's drawn up in working drawings. And at the same time we were dealing with General Bronze, with the company that we felt sure was going to get the job, and we would work with them, ask them questions, as well.[93]

Similarly, the extrusions forming column covers, the stops holding the glass and the spandrel panels, and the profiles making up the grill at the top of the building were studied to resolve their proportions and connections. Richard Foster spoke about researching the color of bronze:

The Seagram's [sic] Building is notable for a number of reasons, beyond wide acclaim it received for its design. From the beginning, a bronze exterior was considered as one of the options. It was my job to contact the brass company and research how best to achieve the intended result. It was imperative that we get samples to assess the results of years of weathering, so there would be no future surprises as to its appearance. We found that it turned a dark color much the same as the building looks today. I also found a somewhat skeptical attitude on the part of the brass company. They had trouble conceiving of a building with a bronze "skin," using the quantity of materials far beyond any that they had ever furnished on a single job before. They were accustomed to building with store fronts and an occasional bronze door or grille.[94]

Summers's account differs:

I worked with one specific man [at General Bronze]. I had him give me a series of panels and sheets of the same alloy that we were using on the panels in the building, as well as extrusions, to see what patinas were, in fact, possible. But it was Mies that wanted this sort of old penny look. In fact I specifically remember Mies seeing the—I was walking with him on the sidewalks around the Seagram Building when the skin was going up, and he said, "It's wonderful," he said. "It's like an old penny."[95]

Generally, it was thought that the bronze would turn green. The color of the patina depends on the proportions of copper and zinc smelted to make the alloy that is bronze. It might also contain additives. Bronze statuary has a small amount of zinc, between 2 and 20 percent, compared to the Seagram building, where the extruded sections are composed of 56 percent copper, 41.5 percent zinc, and 2.5 percent lead, whereas the sheet-metal spandrels consist of 61 percent copper and 39 percent zinc.[96] The patina coating that would prevent corrosion and give a certain coloring was applied to Seagram's bronze skin essentially by hand, so that the surface was at first quite blotchy (fig. 38). When it was exposed to weather, the color rapidly evened out, eventually becoming a deep rich brown, almost black, as Philip Johnson and Richard Foster thought it would be.

Preventing water infiltration was a serious concern in the early days of curtain wall fabrication. General Bronze announced the "Skyscraper of Bronze, Another 'First' for General Bronze." The other "firsts" the corporation claimed were the United Nations Secretariat, the first skyscraper with complete aluminum window walls (see fig. 17), and Lever House, the first skyscraper with a stainless steel grid curtain wall (see fig. 11).[97] At their plant in Garden City, New York, General Bronze induced a "hurricane" to test the skin's ability to withstand winds and rains of force "equivalent to those that flatten buildings."[98] A two-story section

38 Alan Dunn, "Never mind. On thinking it over we decided to let it age," cartoon from *Architectural Record*, March 1957.

of the building's curtain wall was set up in the Garden City test tower at the beginning of July 1956 to measure the effects of natural onslaughts.

Mies was strongly set against the green-tinted glass used for Lever House, which was the only commercially available heat-absorbing glass at that time. The reason, I am sure, is that the color would contrast with any metal used to frame the glass, thus precluding a unified appearance. Furthermore, Mies was very sensitive to the architectural implications of the material, having used differently colored glass compositionally in the 1920s. For Seagram, Mies wanted to find a warmer gray than the glass he had used for 900 Esplanade, one that would relate to bronze. During the winter of 1956, the office of Van der Rohe and Johnson searched for a company to produce glass in the desired color, but the large manufacturers claimed they were unable to do so. I could not believe this, thinking that Libbey-Owens-Ford, which made bottles for Seagram, would surely make a special effort. A visit to the company's plant in Toledo, Ohio, revealed why it was not possible. The glass was made using a continuous tank process. From a huge tank furnace, the hot, molten material was poured onto a metal surface a mile long. In order to make a special run, it would take one day to clean the current material out of the tank, one day to produce the glass needed for the building, and one day to clear the tank again. This was economically indefensible. At a time when President Dwight D. Eisenhower's secretary of defense declared, "What's good for General Motors is good for the country," the bulk of Libbey-Owens-Ford's production was devoted to automobile windows. Hence, in the absence of a commercially available warm gray glass that would complement the bronze, it was finally produced for Seagram in Butler, Pennsylvania, by the Franklin Glass Corporation, using small batches by the ancient pot method, rather than the new industrialized method of the continuous pour.

Although an intention in building Seagram was to reform and encourage new manufacturing processes, certain specialty processes employed of necessity (to get the right color glass, for example) were soon industrialized as building escalated across the country. It is paradoxical that, given Mies's rhetoric on industrialization and technology, many elements of the Seagram building—the tinted glass, illuminated ceilings, granite surfaces, and bronze curtain wall—were in effect artisanal but ultimately set new industrial standards.[99]

Design of the Seagram plaza was a litmus test of everyone's position about what this open space in the city could be. In Luckman's scheme, the ground floor of the building was to be a sales tool, with pavement bricks bearing the most successful salesmen's names.

Discussions in this mercantile vein persisted while Mies's building was in design. In a letter written in late summer 1955, my perception of the overriding character of the building was "its calm on Park Avenue—its noble elegance and beautiful proportions," and I wondered, in the pell-mell of the avenue with its racing flow of cars, "should the plaza carry this calm—an exciting calm with the splash of fountains—or should it have some feeling of the Trevi Fountain?"[100]

Mies's two perspective sketches of 1955 show his intent for the design of the plaza (see figs. 22, 23). The elevated point of view of these drawings was unusual for Mies, who almost always considered the view of the pedestrian, both as he drew or when photographs were to be taken. From a vantage point above Park Avenue, which includes a partial view of the tower, looking down on the plaza, these two studies show Mies thinking about the elements that would modulate the space—steps, low walls, a tree, paired sculptures. Variations may be seen in the point of view and the location of the sculpture. The sketch drawn from the higher vantage point positions the paired sculptures unconvincingly close to the building, and receding lines emphasize the depth of the plaza. The sketch drawn from a perspective closer to the ground plane shows the sculptures placed toward the front, at either side of the wide stairs. In this position, they are conceived as repoussoirs, much like the role they later assumed in the large study model made in Mies's Chicago office in 1956.[101] Mies had returned to Chicago at the end of 1955 owing to bureaucratic difficulties with licensing in New York State. The local chapter of the AIA turned down his application for a license, finding that his secondary education was not equivalent to a New York high school diploma. The AIA even suggested that Mies take a high school graduation examination.[102] On leaving New York, Mies asked Philip to work on the plaza. Philip conceived of the plaza as a body of water with the building rising out of it. He gave the problem of the plaza design to students at the University of Pennsylvania. I was invited to jury that studio, and recall that most of the students proposed a highly active plaza surface. Philip's concept, allowing only a central path of access from sidewalk to the entrance, precluded something that was always fundamental for Mies: freedom. Freedom not only of space but of movement, for movement was basic to the perception and experience of Miesian form and space. Later, I wrote:

> I can only speculate on why Mies would have rejected the water-plaza solution—his practical sense (maintenance leakage). He would have had a sense that the plaza was to be a pedestrian sector, and the ability to approach the building from various directions, and reject a directed path—this would be part of the philosophical intent of the 1920s when the avant-garde rejected formal processional space. His ground plans for IIT, for his court houses, show a complex spatial organization created by overlapping solids (buildings). I also think Mies had an inherent affinity for classical order.[103]

Commenting on his own design, Philip recalled: "I did design fountains, which Mies hated. I changed them to suit Mies. . . . They were elaborate waterworks. I had them mocked up in a place in Massachusetts. The water would go bub-bub-bub-bup-bup-bup. You know, playing waters. And much, much more. They weren't small the way fountains are now. They went all around the building."[104] Philip had commissioned Professor Arthur T. Ippen, director of the Hydrodynamics Laboratory at MIT, to make a hydraulic model of an "innovative" fountain for the Seagram plaza—one that was to involve water motion that would be horizontally rather than vertically dynamic, as is the case in conventional fountains.[105] Gene Summers elaborated on Johnson's design: "Philip had a scheme that the pools actually were sort of dog-leg shaped or L-shaped. And those pools on either side of the building went under some of the columns so that the columns are actually standing in the water. Then the pool went out to the very edge of the building where it became a razor-sharp edge, and the water came right to the edge of that plaza wall so that you couldn't walk there at all."[106]

Working drawings for the plaza of August 27, 1956 (later superseded), include a diagram of Philip's configuration, as well as details of the mosaic lining and pool edges. Summers recalled Mies's reaction to Philip's design: "Philip was describing [to Mies] the building 'rises out of the water,' and how wonderful this was. And Mies says, '*Ja*. That's exactly what doesn't happen, the building rises out of the water.'"[107]

Mies then took the design back to his office in Chicago. In a large model he studied all the components, including sculpture. The model was to be included in the exhibition *Buildings for Business and Government* at the Museum of Modern Art in early 1957.[108] Summers commented, "Without really saying anything [about it] to Philip . . . [Mies] had me start finishing up this big model that I made. It was a quarter-inch-scale model—so it was a big model—that took the tower up only five stories. . . . And we ended up with the solution that is there today, with a much smaller pool. The pool did not extend back in the back where we put the trees. . . . And then these wonderful benches which were Mies's idea. . . . Big hunks of the green marble from France."[109] On this model, Mies placed trees at each edge of the tower's open ground floor and a pair of sculptures at the front of both pools. The sculpture for each pool was composed of three large leaflike forms made of aluminum foil—a leadlike sheet, a black sheet, and a bronze sheet, which emphasized the symmetry of building and plaza. However, Mies was not willing to attempt a de novo work himself, and at the opening of the MoMA exhibition *Buildings for Business and Government* in early 1957, he invited Jacques Lipchitz to make sculpture for the plaza. Lipchitz declined. Apart from a proposal by Picasso that never materialized, the subject wasn't taken up again until 1964, when sculpture by Henry Moore was considered.[110]

Philip later reflected that "Mies did much better, of course, adding the trees. Mine was all water. I think the trees are very important. So he was right."[111] The trees were romantically twisted weeping beeches: "Mies chose the weeping beeches because he liked their structure even when bare."[112] They did not thrive in the atmosphere of New York and were replaced in 1959 by ginkgos.[113] While Mies was working on the plaza in his office in Chicago, SB came to see the big model. Discussion quickly turned to the freestanding columns at the base of the building. My father called the columns "pilasters," as Summers remembers: "I think the first thing he said was, 'Mies, I thought you were going to get rid of those pilasters.' And Mies answered him only by saying, 'Come over here. Come over here, Mr. Bronfman. Come over here.' He called him 'Mr. Bronfman.' 'Look down through here. Look through those columns, through the lobby. Isn't that wonderful?' And that was that. And I think Bronfman probably said, 'I'm not going to change his mind.' So he dropped the whole subject."[114]

The Seagram tower rises visually from the plaza, which is the top plane of the podium that establishes the datum of the two-hundred-by-three-hundred-foot site. Integrally, the entire surface is faced with slabs of Swenson pink granite quarried in Maine.[115] Four feet, seven and a half inches square, the three-and-one-half-inch-thick slabs are five inches deep at all edges. The granite carries down the vertical walls of the podium, which drop some eight feet on the side streets, following the slope from Park Avenue to Lexington Avenue. Along the steps at Park, the podium negotiates the slope of the street and sidewalk, where there is a three-foot, three-inch change in height from south to north. This change was carefully managed by Mies, who took up the difference in the joints between the eighty-three-foot-long steps cut into the plaza podium, so that while one *reads* a five-inch step, the actual height varies from five and one eighth inches at the southern (Fifty-Second Street) end to seven and seven-eighths inches at the northern (Fifty-Third Street) end, and the depth of the treads varies from sixteen inches to fifteen and a quarter inches (see PF 8). The podium itself is set back seven feet, four inches from the property line along Park Avenue, so that the largesse of the wide sidewalk prepares everyone walking there for the broad, open space of the plaza. The podium is also set back some two feet on the side streets (see PF 9).[116] Today the sidewalk is paved in granite, but Mies did not indulge in this expense; perhaps he wished to separate the two realms—the place of movement flow and the place in which to be immersed in another world. He did, however, insist on replacing the city's standard, mean-spirited, sheet metal edge binding the concrete walkway with a six-inch-wide granite curb. When he was asked why—since "no one would notice"—I recall Mies's response: "Exactly, they would not notice the granite, but they would notice the steel curb."

Raised three steps above the sidewalk along Park, the plaza becomes a place of calm, distancing us from the commotion and turbulence of the street. It gives us back shades of our primal selves, which can be sensed near the building, under the sheltering trees, where at their base the granite slabs give way to mounds of English ivy.[117] Here one might sit on the massive marble benches to think or to read. This treescape at the edges of the tower and the area beneath the soffit become part of a secreted world, haptically architectural in the para-niche where the travertine walls encounter the glass enclosure of the lobby and its myriad reflections (see PF 1–PF 7).

The richly veined, deep green *verde* antique marble benches that guard the edges where the podium drops to the pavement are examples, once again, of Mies's leap in creating art from prosaic necessity, not to mention (as the son of a marble cutter) his love of fine materials (see PF 10). Summers explained how the benches came about:

> When I first came to the office, there was a wall in the little model . . . there was a wall on the edge of it to keep people from falling off the edge. But as I started working on the details of the plaza, Mies said, "Let's try a bench." And I said, "Well, we really have the problem that a bench is only 18 inches, at the most, high—16 would be better." And he said, "Well, let's make it wider." I went to the city and got permission from them to be able to count that 36 inches—it was 36 inches for a railing then (it's 42 now). But you'd go up, and you'd go across. Their logic was that you can't fall over that. I'm not sure if that's great logic either. But it was wonderful that they let it happen, and as far as I know there's never been an accident.[118]

The benches take root at the western edge of the eight-foot-high stairways at both side streets leading to and from the plaza and tower. One hundred and eighty feet long, they stretch beyond the sheltering trees all the way to the edge of the plaza at Park Avenue. For most of this length they are hugged by the pools, and despite the narrow space between pool and bench, they are part of another plaza atmosphere, the more public area in which to sit or lie, to watch and be watched. According to Philip Johnson: "We designed those blocks in front of the Seagram Building so people could not sit on them, but, you see, people want to so badly that they sit there anyhow. They like that place so much that they crawl, inch along that little narrow edge of the wall . . . . Mies told me afterward, 'I never dreamt that people would want to sit there.'"[119] The pools, forty-six feet wide by sixty-nine feet long, approach the proportions of the golden rectangle, the "divine proportions" of the Euclidian mathematical ratio, which Mies would use.

The two pools symmetrically placed on either side of the eighty-foot-wide central stairs along Park Avenue are visually continuous with the rest of the plaza. The fifteen-inch depth is safely modulated by three shallow steps. Mies had anticipated the possibility that the pools would not always be filled with water and therefore thought plants could be placed on the steps on such occasions. As Summers remarked, "[That] worked out very well because they [later] put Christmas trees in there once a year, which they still do. They just fill that whole thing up with Christmas trees."[120] The installation of some 130 to 150 spruce trees ranging from three to twenty feet in height, decorated with some twelve thousand small white lights became a New York tradition.[121] A columnist for the *New Yorker* wrote in December 1959, the first Christmas after the building was fully opened:

> One pleasantly nippy afternoon last week, we passed a couple of hours strolling about in Midtown, dodging shoppers and admiring the decorations in, on, and round about some of the biggest of our citadels of supposedly heartless commerce. In our opinion, the prettiest of these decorations are to be found at the Seagram Building, whose designer, Mies van der Rohe, is famous for saying "Less is more," and whose three little words were evidently borne in mind on this occasion. The display consists of a hundred and fifty not very tall but very green and very sweet-smelling balsam firs, tucked into the shallow basins of the fountains in the plaza in front of the building. The jets of the fountains having been turned off, the delicate trees, bearing among their branches many thousands of tiny white lights, stand reflecting themselves in the still water—bewitching to gaze on and, at close range, to sniff, as far-away-from-New-York-seeming as the Canadian woods from which they came.[122]

Beyond Philip's original proposal for a building rising out of water, for which he had invoked phenomena such as tidal waves at MIT's hydraulic research laboratories, he designed the fountain display for Mies's pools—twice. I accompanied Philip, Mies, and Gene to one of the labs at MIT, where we studied possible spray effects.[123] The first set of fountain heads was distributed symmetrically over the length of the pools. Realizing that this arrangement lacked force, Philip gathered them toward the front of the pools, where, finally, like Mies's proposed sculpture, they function as repoussoirs.[124] The cluster of water sprays at the front of the plaza pools create a locus of interest for those sitting on the benches, steps, or ledges at the perimeter of the podium—and for pedestrians passing by. A few times a year the large, central area of the plaza is an open-air gallery in which sculpture creates another focus, stimulating diverse perceptions.[125]

But the plaza almost didn't happen. In the summer of 1957, a serious threat arose in the form of a Seagram initiative that jeopardized the half-acre plaza and imperiled Mies's fundamental concept for the building. Gene Summers described the crisis:

> All the steel was there. The concrete slabs were there, but the granite had not started being brought in. And one day . . . Bronfman comes in and says let's put a bank there. Mies about died. . . . [He] said, "This is a real dilemma." . . . Crandall was against it, although he knew he had to listen to Bronfman. Crandall actually brought in Bunshaft. Crandall told Bunshaft about it, and Bunshaft is, of course—was, of course—a person of very strong personality, and didn't mind telling anybody what he felt about something. So he went to Bronfman with Crandall, and said, "You can't do this." He said, "Your building is not finished, but this is already a national monument. This is a major national monument, and you cannot destroy it." And it was Bunshaft that convinced

Bronfman. It's not something that Mies could or really [do]—it wasn't the best position for him to, in fact, do that. But Bunshaft could do it. I mean here is somebody totally independent, didn't have anything to do with his design. And Phyllis was against it.[126]

Philip Johnson recounted his version:

Once Crandall went to Sam directly with some drawings.... [Sam] called me into his office—the only time he ever did—and said, "I [don't] want you to tell Phyllis about this. I want your opinion as one of the architects." You see he really accepted me.... He didn't usually interfere in the building, but he said, "This I've got to do. Mr. Crandall has brought me these drawings."... "I want your frank opinion. What would this do to the building? I want to know the relative importance of the harm we'd do to the building." I said, "It's very simple. This would totally ruin the building and nobody would build it." He said, "That's what I wanted to know," and threw the drawings away.[127]

My account begins earlier and ends later. Early in 1957 L'Huillier Sheaff mentioned to me that there was some interest in placing a bank on the plaza. I could not believe that this was serious, dismissed it out of hand, and would not hear of it when it was again put forward. Sometime later, Philip did tell me that he had been approached to study the relation between cost and income were a bank pavilion to be built, and I recall that he said it proved to be a wash—the rent would only cover the cost of construction. Because of my opposition from the beginning, Philip had been told not to speak to me about the project. That Crandall went to my father with the proposal makes sense, for he was the only one in a position to approach him on such a problem. But I never knew that Crandall had done so, and I never knew that Bunshaft had been called in. I only remember being asked, together with Mies, to drive an hour from New York to visit my father at his house in Tarrytown. I must have been anxious, but I was determined. To give up the plaza would have been to give up the building's birthright. I remember just the three of us sitting in cast-iron chairs on the lawn outside the wisteria-covered pergola, and my father saying, "Well, Mies, what should I do?" Mies responded, "If I were you Mr. Bronfman, I would not do that." With Mies's words, the subject was closed.

From the beginning, Mies had said that the building would take eighteen months to design and eighteen months to build. Which it did. Design began in December 1954, and Seagram moved its executive offices into the building in December 1957. The project was put on a fast track, so that construction followed close behind design: When excavation began on the Seagram site in January 1956, design was ongoing and interior tenant changes continued to be made well into 1959. Excavation itself took more than three months, because with bedrock close to the surface, blasting was necessary in order to create the three subterranean levels that would accommodate a garage, a vast mechanical room, and various Seagram facilities. I recall vividly an incident concerning the construction fence surrounding the building while this was going on. Completed at the end of March 1956, it was painted in early summer while I was on vacation. It was not painted gray, not white, not with an abstract pattern, but with tulips against a sky blue background. Seagram's public relations department apparently considered this to be appropriate.

Construction photographs, beginning January 12, 1956, were taken to document the progress of building month by month. This was, and is, a common practice at major construction sites, primarily for legal reasons. Historically, the images provide evidence of progress of construction and building techniques (figs. 39–50).

OPPOSITE TOP

39 Seagram building site being cleared, view looking northwest from Fifty-Second Street, January 25, 1956. Photograph: The House of Patria.

OPPOSITE BOTTOM

40 Seagram building site, excavation within newly poured perimeter concrete walls; view looking southwest, May 28, 1956. Photograph: The House of Patria.

41 Seagram building steel framing rising above ground level; aerial view looking southwest, June 27, 1956. Photograph: The House of Patria.

42 Seagram building ground-floor steel framing of east wing in progress; view at Fifty-Second Street looking west, June 27, 1956. Photograph: The House of Patria.

43 Seagram building steel framing of east wing complete and steel of tower rising behind; view at Fifty-Second Street looking west, July 26, 1956. Photograph: The House of Patria.

44 Seagram building formwork for concrete fireproofing being installed at east wing and steel framing of tower up to tenth floor; view looking west, August 27, 1956. Photograph: The House of Patria.

OPPOSITE

45 Seagram building tower steel frame eighteen floors high; concrete fireproofing ten floors high; east-wing fireproofing completed; and ground-floor bronze mullions attached at east wing; view at Fifty-Second Street looking west, September 27, 1956. Photograph: The House of Patria.

OPPOSITE TOP LEFT

46 Seagram building tower steel frame rising above twenty-sixth floor; concrete work up to twenty-first floor; bronze mullions attached at first floor; view looking southeast, October 26, 1956. Photograph: The House of Patria.

OPPOSITE TOP RIGHT

47 Seagram building tower steel thirty-six floors high; concrete fireproofing being formed from twentieth to twenty-sixth floors; concrete fireproofing completed up to twenty-third floor; mullion connectors reach twelfth floor; bronze mullions attached up to eighth floor; glass inserted on first two floors; view looking southeast, November 26, 1956. Photograph: The House of Patria.

OPPOSITE BOTTOM LEFT

48 Seagram building tower steel frame up to thirty-eighth floor and mechanical penthouse being framed; concrete up to thirty-fifth floor; bronze mullions attached up to fourteenth floor; glass being inserted at seventh floor; view looking southeast, December 26, 1956. Photograph: The House of Patria.

OPPOSITE BOTTOM RIGHT

49 Seagram building steel tower steel framing, including mechanical penthouse, complete; bronze mullions attached up to thirty-seventh floor; glass inserted up to twenty-ninth floor; canopy framing completed at ground floor; view looking southeast, February 27, 1957. Photograph: The House of Patria.

50 Seagram building tower exterior complete; cladding of canopy and ground-floor columns being completed; granite on plaza being installed; view looking southeast, September 26, 1957. Photograph: The House of Patria.

51 "Topping Out" ceremony marking the placement of the highest steel beam on the Seagram building, with Tom Hood, construction supervisor, holding flag at left, December 17, 1956. Photographer unknown.

52 Samuel Bronfman with Seagram building construction workers, April 1956. Photographer unknown.

OPPOSITE

53 Mies van der Rohe and members of the Seagram Building Committee visiting the construction site. Photograph: Frank Scherschel, July 1956.

In contrast to 860–880 Lake Shore Drive, the entire skeleton frame was never seen at Seagram. The different phases of construction followed hard upon one another. Before the steel frame reached the tenth story, concrete was being formed around the steel spandrel beams and outside columns as fireproofing; by the time the steel was twenty-five stories high, concrete flooring was being poured and the mullions were being attached to the spandrel beams. In the construction photographs of November 26, 1956 (see fig. 47), all the phases of the whole operation could be read: the steel skeleton of the top six stories stood out against the sky above the thirty-fourth story; concrete was being formed and poured around the columns and edge beams seven or eight floors below, making eminently visible Mies's clear structural system; concrete floors were being poured below these layers, and connectors for the mullions dotted the outer spandrel beams. Farther down, the mullions were already attached to them, and on the floors below, the window frames, which had been raised on dollies on the outside, had been put in place from the inside and connected to the mullions; the lowest two stories were the most advanced: tinted glass had been inserted into the window frames, obscuring the structure that had become almost invisible behind that dark glass. On December 17, 1956, the "topping out," as is the tradition of high steel workers, took place above the thirty-eighth floor (fig. 51). Not until nine months later, in September 1957, was the building completely closed in (see fig. 50). Earlier on the owner greeted construction workers (fig. 52), and the architect visited the site

54 Mies van der Rohe studying the Seagram building in construction. Photograph: Frank Scherschel, July 1956.

55 Samuel Bronfman commending Phyllis Lambert on the first day he occupied his office in the Seagram building; Mies van der Rohe and Saidye Rosner Bronfman (to the right with back to camera), December 23, 1957, detail. Photograph: Tommy Weber.

with members of the building committee (fig. 53). Mies was also caught by the camera on a side street, studying his building (fig. 54). Then on December 23, 1957, three months after the building was completely closed in, when the first nine floors of the building and the basement facilities were finished,[128] and the interiors were advanced enough, my father welcomed Mies, Philip, myself, and family members to his new office for a champagne toast (fig. 55). He spent the rest of the afternoon shaking hands with the members of the Seagram staff who were moving into the building. Seagram personnel would, over the next months, occupy six floors, amounting to 25 percent of the building's useable space. Some 115 other tenants moved in over the course of 1958 and 1959.[129]

Ultimately, building was only fully completed when the Four Seasons Restaurant opened in July 1959 (the restaurant is discussed in detail in chapter 4). Because the restaurateurs were nervous about its reception (needlessly, since it received a chorus of praise), the Four Seasons opened quietly to the public on July 29, 1959. In their book *The Four Seasons: A History of America's Premier Restaurant,* John Mariani and Alex von Bidder chronicled the event: Just before noon that day, Bronfman came down from his fifth-floor office in the Seagram building, "entered the restaurant, turned to [Jerome] Brody and the assembled RA [Restaurant Associates] personnel, nodded, said 'Thank you very much,' and went back upstairs to work."[130] In contrast to the quiet opening of the restaurant, the official dedication of the Seagram building exactly two months later, on September 29, 1959, was staged as a remarkable public gesture: a luncheon for fifteen hundred invited guests followed by a symposium on the theme of *The Future of Man*. This gesture was completely consonant with the wide reach and search for legitimacy that characterized the visionary man who loved to quote Robert Browning, "Ah, but a man's reach should exceed his grasp, or what's a heaven for?" The symposium was similar in scope and intent to SB's projects of the company's early days in its baronial Montreal office, when a building in New York was merely being contemplated: the 1941 publication *Canada: The Foundations of Its Future* and the international travelling exhibition *Cities of Canada* a decade later.[131] *The Future of Man* symposium was his last great public gesture. Aside from the building and the ongoing programs of art on the plaza and the fourth-floor exhibitions, they remained so. Beyond charitable contributions, such imaginative, public-minded gestures were never again initiated by the company.

Because of the large number of people who were invited to attend, the event dedicating the new building and its plaza was held in the grand ballroom of the Waldorf-Astoria rather than in the Four Seasons Restaurant. Dr. Milton S. Eisenhower, president of Johns Hopkins University, chaired the symposium; speakers included the poet Robert Frost, evolutionary biologist Julian Huxley, visionary businessman and philanthropist Devereux C. Josephs, anthropologist Ashley Montagu, geneticist Hermann J. Muller, and the absent philosopher Bertrand Russell, who was represented in a five-minute broadcast and then participated "live" via two-way radio communication. An "interviewing" panel composed of major media personalities included Douglas Edwards, William L. Laurence, and Inez Robb—the only woman on the podium. The theme of the symposium was posed as a question that seems poignantly paradoxical today: "If, as is now expected, man, in the next century, gains control over his physical environment, what will happen to him as an individual? When science gives him greater leisure than ever before, will he use it to develop his great reservoir of potentials? Will he use this new time to bring about a renaissance in the arts, sciences and the humanities? Or, is there a danger that he will fall into a state of decadence?"[132]

The uses to which the atom would be put, one-world government, and overpopulation weighed heavily as each speaker made a statement, followed by general discussion among

56 Mies van der Rohe at the Seagram building. Photograph: Maurey Garber, 1958, copy print by Elijah Cobb, 1993.

them. In his introductory remarks, SB talked about how the occasion that had prompted this gathering, the formal dedication of the Seagram building in New York City, was in "closest harmony" with the theme of the symposium: "For every dedication is looking to the future. As such, it is an act of faith; it is a gesture which proclaims belief in the advent of a good tomorrow."[133]

I believed in the advent of a good tomorrow, too, but these issues were not ones I was thinking about that day. The symposium was anticlimactic for me. There was still much to do to complete the Seagram building and to experience its meaning and role in the city. There had been the mind-boggling experience of working with Mies and Philip and all the others on the building's design; learning how to direct planning and being involved in construction while remaining oblivious to the high stakes involved; anticipating the outcomes of the bidding process with the excitement of a horse race; and assuming the role of a watchdog to keep cohorts at bay. As the structure was rising, I reveled in the privilege of driving onto Seagram plaza, which was the staging area during construction, and riding in rigged-up construction elevators to visit the various stages of work on different floors. I still recall the very beautiful space of the open floors—the gray expanse of concrete rhythmically bound at the edge by the mullions. The brightness at the edge, and the ceiling low in the open field, caused the central groups of columns to fade into the penumbra. I wanted the building to stay this way. The physical pleasure, the apprehension by the senses of the essence of architectural space, this is what was on my mind that September day as the dedication ceremony carried on, and that is what I most vividly remember today—that, and Mies's affectionate smile, caught by a photographer as the architect of Seagram turned to look at his building (fig. 56).

Mies said the Seagram building would have been as good a building in steel as the Barcelona Pavilion in brick, but he commented wryly that he was sure Barcelona would not have been as successful had the walls been brick rather than marble. Writing to students about the Seagram building in 1960, Mies insisted on the generality of principles. He emphasized "clear structure and construction" and the universality of architectural issues, and eschewed the notion of individuality. However, the issues that underlie and sustain the mediating aspects of design—purpose, function, place—and modulate the qualities of space and material were not acknowledged by Mies in his letter to the students. Yet he had long recognized that historically, buildings reflected the "needs of inhabitants" and the "rhythm and character of the landscape in which they are embedded at the same time that they connected to the specific spiritual atmospheres that we perceive as characteristic cultures."[134]

The mature Mies held the concepts of the young Mies. The systems of the Seagram building—air, light, working space—reflect the summum of the physical needs of mid-twentieth-century office building inhabitants. The "specific spiritual atmospheres" Mies would bring are embedded in order, the finest proportions, materiality, and detailing—the way elements meet, the prospect, and the rhythm and character of the landscape the building creates. When the building was being completed, *Architectural Record* summed up in one page the architectural facts (fig. 57). It shows the clarity and generosity of plans at all levels, starting with the plaza and sidewalks, the pools, benches, trees, the sweeping passage between the glass-enclosed west and east lobbies, through the four elevator cores to steps on each side leading down to the side streets, and in the center, a short rise to the Four Seasons Restaurant. The order and regularity of the structural bay permit exceptional planning throughout the tower, and with the east wing only three stories high at both ends, Mies eliminated two columns at the center, allowing him to create at the high ground floor something he dearly loved—two clear-span great rooms. Mies created these large spaces because the possibility was there—only three stories above to carry—and he had a great affinity for the clear span, for the large room.[135]

Architectural details show the proportions and lightness of the bronze and glass skin: mullion, glass, or spandrel frame, and the elegant connection of partitions to enclosure. A vertical section shows (as does the corner plan detail) the basic I-beam steel structure encased in fireproofing concrete, the skin projecting beyond the structure, the floor-to-ceiling glass, and the conditioned air distributer, low, near the window (also shown in plan). The most difficult problem in architecture has always been the corner.[136] It is represented here in plan details. The very beautiful exterior corner turns symmetrically, allowing the same conditions in all directions. One finds such corners on the bases of ancient Greek pedestals and in the work of Schinkel, especially his Altes Museum. The interior, or re-entrant corners of courtyards, on the other hand, was a nightmare for Renaissance architects.[137] I witnessed Mies working on this problem in the New York office—an architect from the Kahn office made a complicated drawing using various color inks for the different strata where plates and angles, framing and glazing bars met. Mies asked him to make three different solutions in black ink so that he could clearly see the differences.

Seagram's material qualities are integral to its urban presence—the dark bronze, bronze tinted glass tower and its *souriant* plaza. The tooled surface of the granite paving of the podium extends throughout the site, from Park Avenue across the wide sweep of the

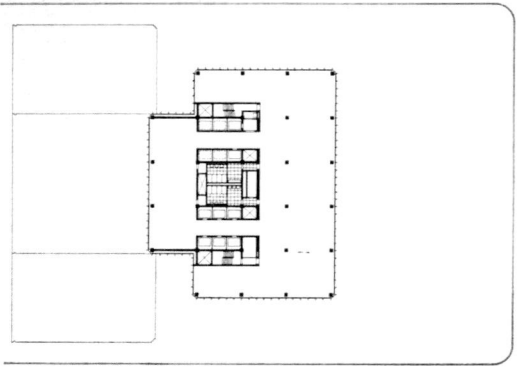

Plan at tower level

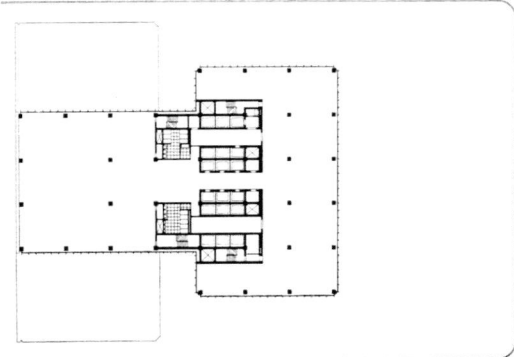

Plan at intermediate level

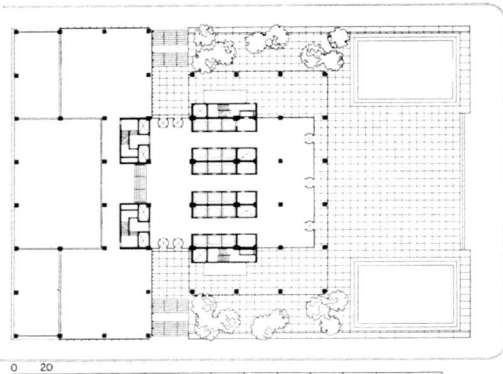

Plan at plaza level

Typical intersection at mullion and glass

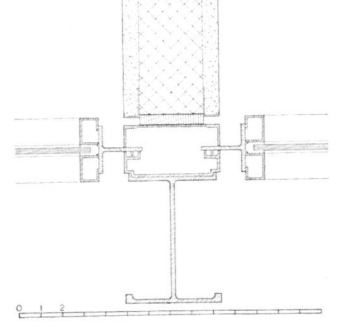

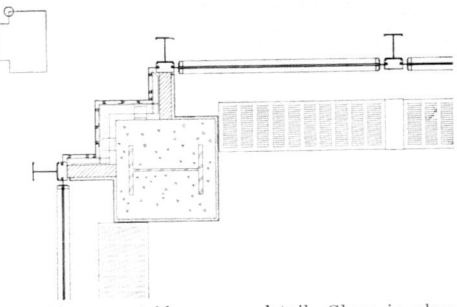

Above: outside corner detail. Glass is glare reducing pink which appears without color from inside. Bronze mullions were extruded from 7½ in. diameter tubes which are 2½ in. larger than the former maximum diameter available. Bronze covering columns was fabricated in long narrow extrusions fitted together. Extrusions were used because they wave less than plates.

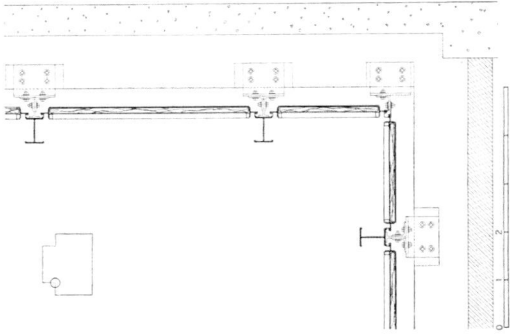

Above: Inside corner detail showing serpentine marble facing. Solid concrete wall is part of wind bracing system. Below: elevation and section of window and spandrel. The section shows the special low profile, high pressure, high velocity air-induction units used on the periphery of the building. They are recessed in the floor construction to achieve an even lower profile.

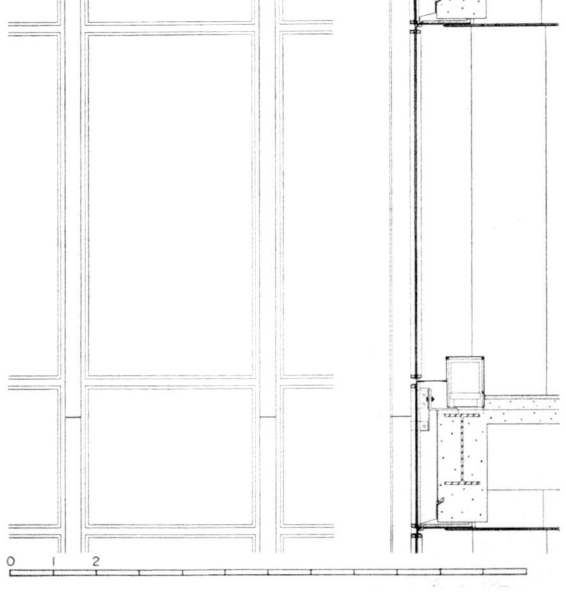

ARCHITECTURAL RECORD *July 1958* 141

57 Seagram building details: floor plans at plaza; tower floors five to ten and eleven to thirty-eight; skin plan details of exterior and reentrant corners, vertical section detail, elevation detail, and detail of mullion at interior partition, from *Architectural Record,* July 1958.

plaza through the west lobby and elevator cores to the east lobby, where one may either enter the Four Seasons Restaurant or descend the stairs to Fifty-Second and Fifty-Third Streets. Material sensuality is heightened as the pedestrian crosses the plaza: the sound and the movement of the fountain jets, the water of the pools mirroring the warm colors of the bronze-and-glass skin, the power of the massive slab benches, the trees at the edges of the building, the liquidity of the water in the pools, the semireflective surface of the striated, bronze-covered columns, the reflections of the revolving doors in the glass enclosure of the lobby, the shadows of its framing projected onto the granite, the subtlety of colors and textures—pink granite, pale butter-yellow travertine, bronze-tinted glass, the different green marbles of the spine and of the benches—and at night, the luminous ceilings emphasizing the building's reticulated structure.

Unlike the cavelike entrances to elevators in conventional high-rise buildings, Seagram's travertine elevator cores function as spatial elements creating fluid passages as the pedestrian moves through the building. Philip Johnson talked of the clarity of procession arising from Mies's insistence on walking directly from the street to the elevator: "Philip, we will not turn the elevator banks no matter what that does to the practicality of the rooms above. You must walk from the street to your elevator."[138] An itinerary from Park Avenue leads to Picasso's *Le Tricorne*, the great stage curtain painted in 1919 for Sergei Diaghilev's Ballets Russes, which hangs in the lobby entrance to the Four Seasons Restaurant. Under certain lighting conditions, McKim, Mead & White's Racquet and Tennis Club is reflected in the glass at the entry, so that it can be seen together with *Le Tricorne*. At such moments, interior and exterior space is inextricably entwined (see PF 14).

Materiality is the aspect that would be emphasized by the New York Landmarks Preservation Commission when the Seagram building was designated in 1990 without any reference to the radicality of its urban form. The innovative gesture of the building set back on a plaza was acknowledged by the New York City Zoning Resolution of 1961, which permitted additional building bulk in exchange for the amenity of open space at the ground level. Yet critics have not brought into focus the power Mies discovered in the low building on the plaza. The great rooms at each end of the east wing take on the nature of pavilions, bringing to the vocabulary of the urban oasis—composed of tower, podium, benches, trees, pool, and sculpture—the presence of a constant human reference counterweighing the short duration of visitors and occupants drawn up into the tower like water into the stem of a plant. The Seagram building, the solitary tower set on its podium in the quietude of a recess carved out of the urban jungle, is unsurpassed in its immanence, yet the building and its plaza established the terms of reference for Mies's future high-rise complexes: the oasis of the dark building in the city wedded at ground level, inside and out, to human presence and activity (figs. 58, 59).

58 Seagram building, Mies van der Rohe and Philip Johnson, architects; Kahn and Jacobs, associate architects; Phyllis Lambert, director of planning, view from northwest in the afternoon, 375 Park Avenue, New York, 1954–58. Gelatin silver print, 17⅞ × 14⅛ in. Photograph: Ezra Stoller, 1958.

59 Seagram building, Mies van der Rohe and Philip Johnson, architects; Kahn and Jacobs, associate architects; Phyllis Lambert, director of planning, view from northwest at dusk, 375 Park Avenue, New York, 1954–58. Gelatin silver print, 17⅞ × 14⅛ in. Photograph: Ezra Stoller, 1958.

PORTFOLIO

RICHARD PARE: PLAZA STUDIES, 2000 AND 2010

PF 1 Ivy beds, gingkoes, and tower, view looking south from above, April 15, 2010. Chromogenic laser print, 28 × 18 in.

[Concrete, steel, and glass] are genuine building elements . . . of a new building art. They permit a measure of freedom . . . that we will not relinquish any more. Only now can we articulate space freely, open it up and connect it to the landscape.
—*Mies van der Rohe, 1933*

PF 2 Ivy, gingko, colonnade, and lobby, view looking south, June 8, 2010. Chromogenic laser print, 18½ × 24 in.

PF 3 Ivy, gingko, pool, and fountain, view looking west, June 8, 2010. Chromogenic laser print, 18¾ × 24 in.

PF 4 Plaza panorama, looking south from the first setback of 399 Park Avenue, April 15, 2010. Chromogenic laser print, 24 × 22¾ in.

PF 5 Beneath the trees near the travertine core and lobby enclosure, view looking southwest, June 8, 2010. Chromogenic laser print, 24 × 18⅞ in.

PF 6 Interplay of travertine cores and lobby enclosure, view looking east, April 2000. Chromogenic laser print, 24 × 19⅛ in.

By employing glass, it is not an effect of light and shadow one wants to achieve, but a rich interplay of light reflections.
—*Mies van der Rohe, 1922*

PF 7 Columns, trees, and glass reflections, view looking northeast, June 8, 2010. Chromogenic laser print, 18 × 29 in.

PF 8 Granite sidewalk, steps, podium, plaza, and bronze building view from Park Avenue, looking east, August 31, 2010. Chromogenic laser print, 19⅛ × 24 in.

PF 9 Podium set back from property line marker set in sidewalk lower left, at Park Avenue and Fifty-Third Street, August 31, 2010. Chromogenic laser print, 19⅛ × 24 in.

OPPOSITE
PF 10 *Verde* antique, granite, and water, May 2000. Chromogenic laser print, 18⅞ × 24 in.

PF 11 Outside, inside, "a rich interplay of light reflections" at the Fifty-Second Street entrance, June 8, 2010. Chromogenic laser print, 18 × 27⅝ in.

PF 12 Canopy and reentrant tower corner showing serpentine marble of spine, Fifty-Third Street entrance, June 8, 2010. Chromogenic laser print, 24 × 19⅛ in.

OPPOSITE

PF 13 Inside, outside, Four Seasons Pool Room, viewing plaza, fountains, and trees, September 15, 2010. Chromogenic laser print, 24 × 19⅛ in.

99

PF 14 From lobby through elevator cores to view of Picasso's *Le Tricorne* and reflection of Racquet and Tennis Club in Four Seasons lobby entry enclosure, April 2000. Chromogenic laser print, 18 × 26¾ in.

PF 15 Reflection of Racquet and Tennis Club in lobby enclosure, April 2000. Chromogenic laser print, 18¾ × 24 in.

3

UNION OF BUILDING AND PLAZA IN THE URBAN LANDSCAPE

What led Mies to create the union of skyscraper and plaza on Park Avenue, a binding together so profoundly important in his oeuvre? In the 1950s, it would have been difficult to answer, let alone to ask. Would or could Mies have retraced his own trajectory? A few iconic buildings were known. The mullioned high-rise towers of the 1950s did not seem to derive from the sheer glass skyscrapers of the early 1920s. A genealogy of the plaza could not have been constructed: the "podium" at 860–880 Lake Shore Drive was not recognized as such. And Mies's Zeitgeist? Philip Johnson proclaimed that he was tired of hearing Mies quote Augustine's "Beauty is the radiance of truth."

Who noted the contents of the library in Mies's Chicago living room? Or paid attention when he retold the story of how he had to select three hundred books from his collection of three thousand when he left Germany for Chicago? Mies said that he could have retained just thirty, but before that, he would have had to read the three thousand.[1] The only publication on Mies before 1950 was Philip Johnson's exhibition catalogue *Mies van der Rohe,* published by the Museum of Modern Art in 1947.[2]

When I directed the 1977 exhibition *The Seagram Plaza: Its Design and Use* in collaboration with Ludwig Glaeser, then curator of the Mies van der Rohe archive at MoMA,[3] research was not yet far enough advanced. At the time, Glaeser wrote, "There is no direct precedent for the configuration of the Seagram plaza in the work of Mies van der Rohe. As an urban space it is more closely related to the more intimate enclosed space of Mies's courthouses than to the urban spaces which Mies had either proposed or built."[4] In my text, I likened the Seagram plaza to the parvis before a cathedral.[5] While this may be so, it really doesn't get to the essence of the matter of Mies's deep interest in the interrelationship of building and landscape, which historians and critics have largely overlooked. To a great degree, Mies himself is responsible for this gap in the reception of his work. During his American years, he declared more than once that his first job was to design a good building, and only then could he take into consideration the surroundings. But the facts contradict this assertion. Strong principles underlay his architectural design, what he called the "building art," yet Mies's buildings and building complexes were mostly informed by the particularities of the surrounding context and the special circumstances of their sites. In America, only in talking about the Farnsworth house did Mies express his sensitivity to site: "Nature should also live its own life. . . . We should attempt to bring nature, houses, and human beings together in a higher unity. If you view nature through the glass walls of the Farnsworth house, it gains a more profound significance than if viewed from outside. This way more is asked from nature, because it is becomes a part of a larger whole."[6] This, a long-held concern, must have been almost innate in him, a given, like everyday things to be attended to.

Barry Bergdoll has definitively connected Mies with the German *Wohnreform* movement of the late nineteenth and early twentieth centuries.[7] In his discussion of the twenty-one-year-old Mies's first independently built work, a house commissioned by the philosopher Alois Riehl and his wife, Sofie, in 1906 and completed in 1907, Bergdoll wrote that Mies "bound house and garden together to form a podium."[8] Reading this was for me an epiphany. I could see, almost in a flash, the unity of building and landscape developing throughout Mies's building art, ultimately morphing into the podium that binds the Seagram tower to the urban landscape—plaza, platform, an oasis amid the chaos of New York. This led me to reevaluate the importance of surrounding context, whether garden or urban fabric, in Mies's architecture throughout his career and to understand in a new light some of his statements, drawings, and photomontages. The reexamination begins with his early houses.

Wohnreform was a late nineteenth- and early twentieth-century formal and ideological reform of the everyday environment, advocating new spaces at the green edges of the city that would support healthful living and an ethical renewal of German culture.[9] Hermann Muthesius, an influential architect and a leader of the movement, spoke of house and garden as a unity whose "characteristics should be infused with the same spirit," and advocated the extension of the interior spaces of the house into the garden.[10] In the 1910 edition of his *Landhaus und Garten,* he published Mies's Riehl house, in the Babelsberg district of Potsdam, on the outskirts of Berlin, as a model of these principles (fig. 60).

Street views show a modest middle-class house, half hidden by a continuous wall. The peaked roof, eyebrow dormers, and unadorned stucco walls evoked the local vernacular, recalling the unostentatious bourgeois Neoclassicism of the early nineteenth century.[11] Beyond the wall lies a geometric parterre of flower beds contained by a retaining wall, and beyond that, a distant view of the valley comes into focus when the visitor turns toward the house, takes one step up, and enters the *Halle,* or central communal space. To the right one is attracted by the open veranda, a loggia where four pierlike columns frame the landscape beyond; closer at hand, in a sheer drop, the lower garden comes into view, its sloping lawn separated from the surrounding dense forest by a path culminating in another contemplative viewing place. The outer wall of the veranda, as it supports the piers, is a continuation of the retaining wall, and the veranda floor continues the upper garden, so that together they form a podium as an outlook to the distant view. The lower garden elevation of the house belongs to a different world from the modest street front. From there, the parapet is revealed as a long, massive retaining wall traversing the site, ingeniously created by Mies to solve a difficult, steeply sloping site. The wall contains the house and upper garden, and

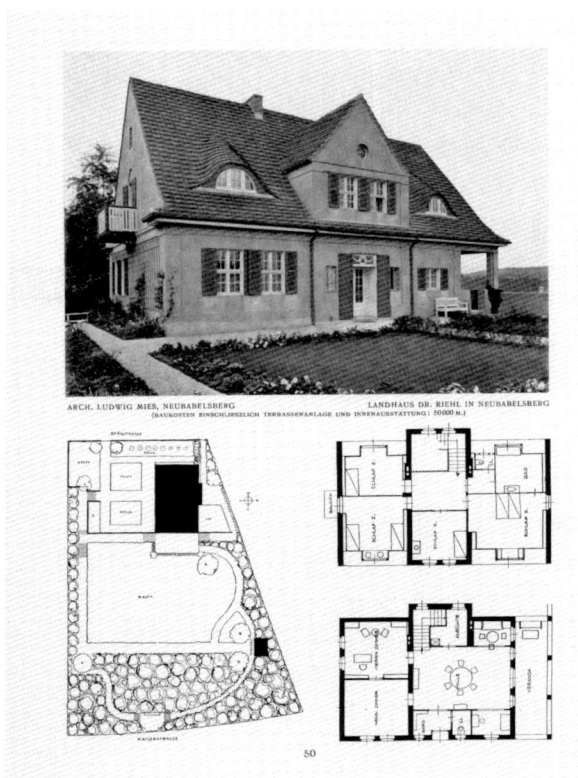

60 Mies van der Rohe, Riehl House, Neubabelsberg, Germany, 1906–7. Clockwise from top left: view from upper garden, view from street, view from lower garden, site plan, and plans of ground floor and upper story, from Hermann Muthesius, *Landhaus und Garten: Beispiele neuzeitlicher Landhäuser nebst Grundrissen, Innenräumen und Gärten*, 1910. Photographer unknown.

one section acts as the stylobate for the four piers supporting the gable roof as pediment, so that this east face of the Riehl house invokes a temple front. Its imposing presence bears an ancestral kinship with the Seagram building and plaza Mies would situate on Park Avenue fifty years later.

The dialogue between house and garden was at the heart of Muthesius's argument: "If the house belongs to architecture, the garden must also.... What is appropriate to human formal invention in every medium is rhythmics, submission to principles.... the same fundamental principles that prevail in the house, the same organic relationship of the individual parts one to another, the same unification of the parts into a harmonic whole must also prevail in the garden."[12]

To Muthesius's precepts, the architect Peter Behrens added the concept of space in his essay "Der moderne Garten," published in 1911, while Mies was working in his studio. Behrens's essay seems obliquely to honor the Riehl house.[13] For Behrens, the opposing forms of house and garden, harmoniously unified, provided an opportunity for giving form to space; as he explained, "giving form to space is obviously the highest principle of architecture," emphasizing that "this interlocking of forms, this aesthetic evaluation of the opposing form, is one of the most important moments in the fine arts in general."[14]

The double face of the house embodies Riehl's maxim governing all action, the conflict of ancient faith with a priori order and the new laws modern society made for itself: "The ancient Good—hold fast to it! The new Good is but a transformation of the old."[15] Much later Mies would similarly say: "It must be possible to fuse into a harmonious whole the old and the new energies of our civilization."[16] However, the *retardataire* language of the house, without considering its other strengths, no doubt caused Mies to excise the work from his oeuvre when he refused Philip Johnson permission to include it in the first major exhibition of his work at MoMA.[17] Nevertheless, the Riehl house and garden prefigured

61 Mies van der Rohe, competition project for a monument to Bismarck, longitudinal elevation, Elisenhöhe, Bingen, Germany, 1910. Pencil and colored pastel on tracing paper, 39¾ × 85½ in.

62 Karl Friedrich Schinkel, the Royal Palace at Orianda, Crimea, Ukraine, 1838. Chromolithograph on beige paper, 24⅞ × 14 in.

what was to come in Mies's work. The relation of house and garden and the sense of calm they imparted attracted the attention of numerous critics, which was unusual for such a young and unknown architect. One critic writing in 1910, in the journal *Moderne Bauformen*, praised the generous impression made by the siting of the Riehl house on the terrain and wrote approvingly of its classical simplicity and clarity of design.[18] Both characteristics would forever exemplify Mies, but the deep attention to site and landscape so highly praised at the time—the interweaving of building and site to form a podium and the strong retaining wall that classically defines a sacred precinct—were ignored as "old history" until the houses Mies designed in and around Berlin during the 1910s and 1920s were identified and analyzed while the exhibition *Mies in Berlin* (MoMA, 2001) was being planned.

Mies's next independent project, his competition entry for the Bismarck Monument of 1910 on a site that rises four hundred feet above the Rhine River, envisioned a powerful masonry podium on which he set two long, parallel colonnades joined by a semicircular exedra, which was to house a portrait statue of Otto von Bismarck (fig. 61). The debt to Karl Friedrich Schinkel's utopian proposal for the royal palace at Orianda in Crimea of 1838 is clear (fig. 62); a volume illustrating the design was a fixture on his drawing table.[19]

UNION OF BUILDING AND PLAZA IN THE URBAN LANDSCAPE

63 Karl Friedrich Schinkel, view of Schloss Charlottenhof from terrace framed by exedral bench and *velum*, Park Sanssouci, Potsdam, Germany, 1826–29. Lithograph, 14¾ × 19 in., detail.

In the office of Behrens, young architects were encouraged to study Schinkel's buildings and gardens in and around Berlin.[20] Schinkel's design for Schloss Charlottenhof, a small estate for the crown prince of Prussia in Park Sanssouci in Potsdam, held many lessons for Mies. In transforming the "rather small and unattractive" villa,[21] as Schinkel referred to it, and flat grounds formerly belonging to a businessman, Schinkel constructed a great terrace garden to the height of the upper level of the house become villa by constructing massive retaining walls at both short ends. At one end he added to the house a coplanar portico opening onto the terrace; at the other, a large semicircular exedral bench behind which a trellis rises: it is a place for viewing the villa, the upper fountain, and the environs, with the Neue Palais in the distance (fig. 63). A pergola closes one long side of the terrace, which on the fourth side slopes down to terminate in a basin with small fountains. Similarly Mies's Riehl house encompasses vistas from the geometric garden that interweaves and is coplanar with the reception floor of the house and the far vista, while a massive retaining wall containing house and upper garden drops the height of one story to the lower garden, a lawn differentiated from the surrounding forest by a path terminating in a contemplative, semicircular space (see fig. 60, site plan). Bergdoll points to Schinkel's use of the viewing platform, "introduced to provide ruptures and discontinuities in the landscape that might cause one to reflect on distant, almost pictorialized views."[22] The trace of viewing terrace, pergolas, the semicircular exedral bench, and trellis would become part of Mies's language as he pursued the unity of house and garden in the spirit of Schinkel over the next years.[23] At the same time, on either side of the built-up terrace and villa, which are connected at the portico, Schinkel pragmatically cut openings in the two lower courtyards in order not to "take away light from the lower story" containing essential rooms.[24] For the same reason, with the Riehl house, Mies punched openings in the massive retaining wall.[25]

What was nascent in the Riehl house would evolve in different ways in Mies's avant-garde Tugendhat house and Barcelona Pavilion, two breakthroughs of 1929. In the Tugendhat house, the podium is contained within the volume of the house, and the broad flight of steps leading to the garden hugs the massive wall, behind which lie service functions (fig. 64). Even though an elusive distant view is glimpsed from a carefully controlled opening at the entrance court at street level, the panorama is viewed fully only on the floor below, from the principal room of the house, which is itself the podium. When in a technological feat the enormous floor-to-ceiling glass wall sinks behind the massive podium wall, this family living space becomes a viewing platform completely open to the outdoors (fig. 65).

64 Mies van der Rohe, Tugendhat house, view from the garden, showing punched opening in basement wall, Brno, Czech Republic, 1928–30. Photograph: Rudolf de Sandalo, c. 1930–31.

65 Mies van der Rohe, Tugendhat house, main floor with floor-to-ceiling glass wall lowered, Brno, Czech Republic, 1928–30. Photographer unknown.

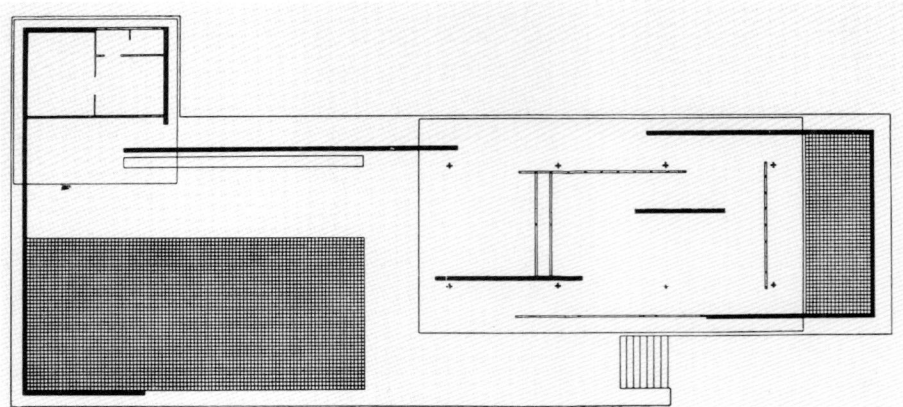

66 Mies van der Rohe, view of German Pavilion, International Exposition, Barcelona, 1928–29 (demolished). Gelatin silver print, 8 × 10 in. Photograph: Berliner Bild-Bericht, 1929.

67 Mies van der Rohe, plan of the German Pavilion, International Exposition, Barcelona, 1928–29 (demolished). Photograph of plan: Berliner Bild-Bericht, c. 1929.

The presence of the large, sloping garden from above and the garden itself are places for the contemplation of and communion with nature. Like Riehl, the viewing platform at Tugendhat is part of an *occupied* podium. The podium at Seagram also encloses occupied spaces (see figs. 58, 59, and PF 8), but at the same time, and significantly, it relates most prominently to the platform at the Barcelona Pavilion (figs. 66, 67), and indeed, to the upper garden and viewing platform of the Riehl house, where the interior and exterior spaces are coplanar and interpenetrate in a unity of building and garden—the garden-become-platform—and, eventually, plaza.

Mies's first ideas about the skyscraper may be linked to Schinkel's assertion that "architecture is the continuation of nature in her constructive activity" and "the whole essence of the construction of a building must remain visible,"[26] bringing to bear the organic themes in European architectural thought that resonated for Mies. These are summed up in a two-page spread for the 1924 "Nasci" issue of *Merz,* published by El Lissitzky and Kurt Schwitters, in which Mies's 1922 Glass Skyscraper was juxtaposed with a human femur redrawn by Lissitzky after an illustration by Raoul H. Francé.[27] The Latin *nasci,* "becoming" (*Gestaltung* in German), refers both to form and to the process of formation, implying "a self-generating process of form-creation through which inner purposes or designs become visible in outer shapes."[28] Later, talking about his work, Mies quoted an aphorism by Goethe: "'It is neither core nor shell—it is all one.' The interior and exterior of my buildings are one—you can't divorce them. The outside takes care of the inside."[29] And Mies's sense of the organic evolved: In his inaugural address at the Armour Institute of Technology he would "emphasize the organic principle of order that makes the parts meaningful and measurable while determining their relationship to the whole."[30] At one of the Thursday evening dinners at his apartment in Chicago, Mies characterized to me his sense of the organic as distinct from Frank Lloyd Wright's: Whereas Wright's buildings grew from the soil like trees, Mies metaphorically demonstrated that for him it was the relation of the part to the whole, as a segment of the finger is related to the finger, the finger to the hand, the hand to the arm, and so forth.

The immediate inspiration for the glass skin was, above all, the play of light on the large glass apron suspended over the tracks at the Friedrichstrasse station, which was under construction in 1920. It must have been as exciting to Mies as it was for the architect August Endell, who declared it to be particularly beautiful at dusk, when "the many small panels begin to reflect the sunset and the entire plane assumes a colorful, shimmering life."[31] With his project for the Friedrichstrasse Turmhaus, Mies was equally inspired by the structural skeleton seen in buildings under construction. In a well-known statement, he observed: "Only skyscrapers under construction reveal the bold constructive thoughts, and then the impression of the high-reaching steel skeletons is overpowering.... The novel constructive principle of these buildings comes clearly into view if one employs glass for the no longer load-bearing exterior walls."[32]

Glass was the quintessential material of the future. The architect Bruno Taut wrote ecstatically in his journal *Frühlicht*: "Long live our realm of non-violence! Long live the transparent, the clear! [Long live purity!] Long live the crystal. And long and ever longer live the fluid, graceful, angular, brilliant, sparkling, light—eternal building, long may it live!"[33] The glass curtain wall was integral to Mies's concept of a new order, one tied to the landscape. In 1933 he unreservedly proclaimed: "The glass skin, the glass walls alone permit the skeleton structure its unambiguous constructive appearance and secure its architectonic possibilities.... They are genuine building elements from which a new, richer building art can arise. They permit a measure of freedom in spatial composition that we will not relinquish any more. Only now can we articulate space, open it up and connect it to the landscape, thereby filling the spatial needs of modern man."[34] Mies had first proposed the curtain wall with projects of 1921 and 1922 for glass skyscrapers in Berlin that electrified the world of architecture. His startling entry drawing for the 1921 competition for the Friedrichstrasse Turmhaus, or skyscraper—an entire prismatic building sheathed in glass—made him a leading figure of the European avant-garde (fig. 68).[35]

The play of transparency and reflectivity in glass was immeasurably intriguing. Although the prismatic form of Mies's Friedrichstrasse Turmhaus—which grew out of

 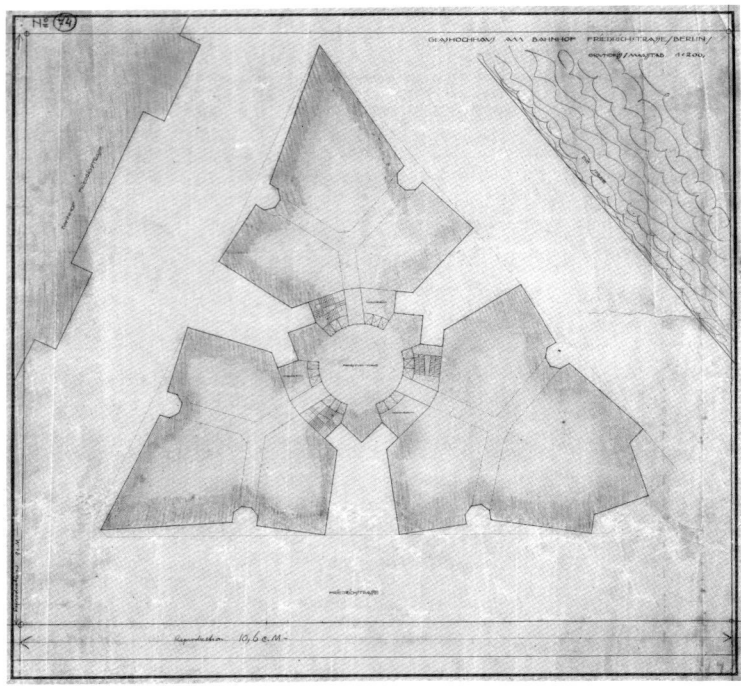

68 Mies van der Rohe, architect, competition project for a skyscraper, Friedrichstrasse, perspective view from north, Berlin-Mitte, 1921. Charcoal and graphite on brown paper, mounted on board, 68¼ × 48 in.

69 Mies van der Rohe, architect, competition project for a skyscraper, Friedrichstrasse, plan, Berlin-Mitte, 1921. Vandyke print with pencil, 23½ × 25¼ in.

the triangular site (fig. 69)—calls to mind Bruno Taut's enraptured paean to glass, Mies explained it with matter-of-fact sobriety: "A prismatic form corresponding to the triangle appeared to offer the right solution for this building, and I angled the respective façade fronts slightly toward each other to avoid the danger of an effect of lifelessness that often occurs if one employs large glass panels."[36]

A caricature by coworker Sergius Ruegenberg comments on Mies's methodology in seeking to overcome the "lifelessness" of large glass panels by crouching to be at eye level as he studied different configurations of glass in bright sunlight on his balcony.[37] Even in the 1950s and 1960s, lifting his right hand high, Mies would reenact how he wedged long strips of glass into Plasticine, at different angles, and out of doors, learning through the use of the model. Mies continued: "My experiments with a glass model helped me along the way and I soon recognized that by employing glass, it is not an effect of light and shadow one wants to achieve but a rich interplay of light reflections."[38] With this text Mies published the experimental glass model of 1922 in which the expressionistic, faceted lobes of the Friedrichstrasse Turmhaus gave way to an organic, deeply sinuous, irregularly lobed ground plan (figs. 70, 71).

The tall building, of consuming interest to architects in Germany after World War I, was stimulated by numerous competitions for the design of the *Grossstadt,* or big city, aimed at fulfilling the needs of a growing population and offering a new way of postwar life. Peter Behrens had drawn a vertical city landscape for the journal *Das Plakat* in 1920, in which masonry predominated as in the other contemporary projects; he found "the germ of a new architecture" to be inherent in the commercial buildings of New York.[39] Fascination with the tall building, fueled by the American example, was intensified in avant-garde circles.[40] The rash of proposals for prominent sites in Berlin in 1920 set Mies's Turmhaus competition project across the street from the Friedrichstrasse railway station in high relief.

For German artists and architects, the devastation of World War I had shaken faith in technology and industrial progress as rational forms of organization for the modern world,

70 Mies van der Rohe, architect, project for a glass skyscraper, second project, plan, 1922. Ink on illustration board, 30 × 40 in.

71 Mies van der Rohe, architect, project for a glass skyscraper, second project, photograph of model, 1922.

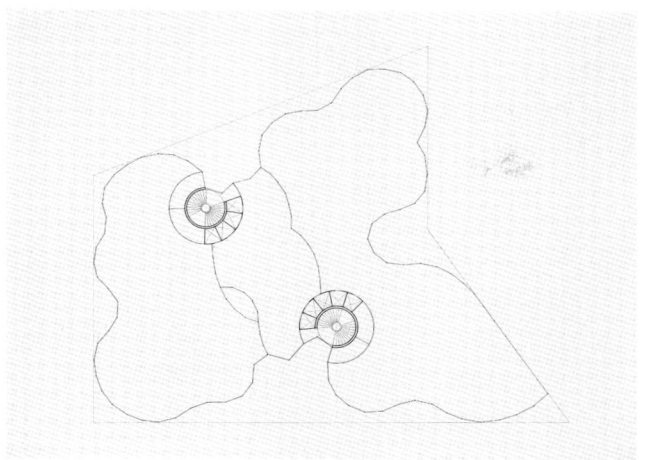

and as Fritz Neumeyer has put it, "The debris of values and vacuum of meaning that the war had left in its wake made utopian visions almost a matter of mental survival."[41] Bruno Taut envisioned himself becoming a "master builder of the universe," whose mission was to realize "an ideal become building, bringing happiness," giving people the sense "that they are part of one great architecture," and to overcome the density of matter in order to infuse it with spiritual life.[42] The impulsion to glass architecture had been inspired by the author of "fantasticated" novels, Paul Scheerbart, with his unillustrated and almost prescriptive 1914 publication *Glasarchitektur*.[43] Scheerbart's ideas were given visual substance in Bruno Taut's *Alpine Architektur* of 1919,[44] which presented a dream world of glazed arcades, crystalline needles, and bridges of glass and rock, above the vegetation line, hewn into crystalline form, with mountains surmounted by filigree structures in concrete and colored glass illuminated at night (fig. 72).[45] Taut dedicated his book to Scheerbart, whom he had asked to provide mottoes for his House of Glass pavilion for the Deutsche Werkbund exhibition of 1914 at Cologne. Most of the mottoes applied to the interior drum had the general

72 Bruno Taut, architect, *Der Kristallberg* (The crystal mountain), showing alpine peaks decorated with crystalline formations, 1918. Lithograph, 11½ × 9⅜ in.

sense of the first one: "*Glück ohne Glas—Wie dum ist das!*—Happiness without glass, How dumb is that!"[46] The last motto declared, "Glass opens up a new age / Brick building only does harm."[47] Taut used glass throughout his Cologne pavilion, which comprised a dome of faceted panes set on a drum made of glass bricks—even the stairs inside were glass. A photograph of the model showed how the glass was colored.

Scheerbart inspired artists and architects of the Bauhaus: Lyonel Feininger's medievalizing crystalline woodcut was used on the cover of the first Bauhaus program; Moholy Nagy's "crystalline architecture" paintings and Kasimir Malevich's crystalline Suprematist paintings were displayed together at Gropius's Bauhaus; and Gropius himself admired Scheerbart's writings.[48] Scheerbart became the spiritual father of the Dadaists, who published his writings in their journal *Der Sturm*. One is somewhat amazed at Mies's connection to this ecstatic atmosphere. In his closer circle, Hannah Höch had an extensive Scheerbart library, Mies collaborated with Taut on the publication of *Frühlicht*, and his valued colleague Ludwig Hilberseimer, writing on Scheerbart's work, gave a rationalist interpretation of his utopia.[49] There is sufficient evidence to affirm that Mies was ready to absorb many aspects of Scheerbart's fervor for glass. With "both feet firmly on the ground," wanting to reach with his head "to the clouds,"[50] knowing that "no one can shape the past or the future, only the present,"[51] and understanding the necessity to "create form out of the nature of the task with the means of our time,"[52] Mies would have agreed with numerous ideas in the 111 short chapters of Scheerbart's *Glasarchitektur*. He would have agreed that glass is unthinkable without the Gothic and that the iron skeleton was indispensable to glass architecture (although he would have reversed the order).[53] Mies would also agree with Scheerbart's deductive reasoning, that "we live for the most part in closed rooms. These form the environment from which our culture grows. Our culture is to a certain extent the product of our architecture. If we want our culture to rise to a higher level, we are obliged . . . to change our architecture. . . . We can only do that by introducing glass architecture."[54]

Mies clearly was taken with Scheerbart's vision. Aspects of the Barcelona Pavilion certainly bear out the implications of some of Scheerbart's commonsense proposals: "double glass walls . . . ornamentally colored . . . with the light between them,"[55] is found as such in the Barcelona Pavilion, where the double-panel, luminous wall was of etched glass and others were of transparent gray and bottle green glass.[56] They all heightened reflectivity, as did the polished marble walls. According to Scheerbart, while "the iron skeleton . . . is of course indispensable for glass architecture," protecting iron against rust "can only be done by nickelling or coating with paint."[57] This practical solution was taken up by Mies in the nickel-plated sheets covering the steel columns at Barcelona; they almost melt in reflectivity, so that the whole—columns, glass, and marble walls—could seem more chatoyant than substantial, "an interplay of light reflections" that he had observed in playing with the model of the Friedrichstrasse tower.[58] Of Scheerbart's pronouncements about the need to temper the glare of light with colored glass, and of America as the country where glass architecture would be fulfilled and the "patina of bronze would also be suitable" for exterior metal panels,[59] critic Reyner Banham commented that, in 1914, Scheerbart stood closer to the Seagram building than did Mies.[60]

It was only in the United States, after his immigration in 1938, that Mies would build glass skyscrapers, but his concern moved from expressivity and reflectivity to what he called "a structural architecture": "My idea, or better, 'direction,' in which I go is toward a clear structure and construction—this applies not to any one problem but to all architectural

73 Richard Pare, Seagram tower, view of northwest corner, April 2010. Chromogenic laser print, 19⅛ × 24 in.

problems which I approach,"[61] and he bound the placement of his buildings to the landscape of the city. At the Illinois Institute of Technology Mies set for himself a rigorous learning process in creating a structural architecture, working on a representational expression of structure in which the enclosure was made with the same structural steel members as the building's basic constructive steel skeleton (but at a different scale).[62] From this process Mies took a creative leap, crafting his first glass-steel-mullioned tower at 860–880 Lake Shore Drive. The mullions, however, were attached to the structure, so the skin of Mies's first steel and glass tower was not free from the load-bearing structure as he had proposed in his visionary skyscrapers of the 1920s. They denied the fact of a wrapped skin or sheath, whereas at Seagram, the structure-free cantilevered enclosure allowed the building an uninterrupted, nuanced surface (see fig. 58). The skin separated from the structure allowed the building to be treated as a volumetric whole, a monolithic unit, and moreover, the tinted glass—so loved by Scheerbart—helped to secure this effect. At Seagram, the issue was no longer one of light reflections, for the surface is now gridded by three-dimensional elements: the glass can be transparent or reflect the surrounding buildings, interacting with the play of light and shadow on the mullions and flickering more subtly on the bas-relief frames surrounding spandrels and windows during the day (fig. 73). At night the glass is absent, transmitting the luminosity of the rooms and, like an X-ray or film negative, showing us the bones, revealing the structure of the building (compare figs. 58, 59).

In articulating the interplay of vertical and horizontal elements defining the structure—the mullions and the spandrels—at Seagram the curtain wall took on new dimensions. Architectural historian Kurt Forster has observed that the spandrel panels of the Seagram building resonate with the articulation of the leaf motif of the Carolingian bronze doors of the Chapel of St. Hubert at Aix-la-Chapelle, and that the proportions of spandrel and glass evoke the relation of solid and void in Schinkel's New Guardhouse on Unter den Linden in Berlin—both buildings intimately known to Mies in his early years. Forster sees in the five centuries connecting the classic leaf motif of the chapel door to its twentieth-century incarnation as a facade grid "the Miesian synthesis of Gothic height and classic balance."[63] Applying similar reasoning about the fusion of Gothic and Classical elements "in a supremely elegant whole," *New York Times* art critic Herbert Muschamp declared the Seagram building to be his choice "as the millennium's most important building." Muschamp concluded that "the business of civilization is to hold opposites together. That goal, often reached through conflict, has been rendered here by Mies with a serenity unsurpassed in modern times."[64]

Mies continued to bind building to site. He translated the union of house and garden into the union of building and greensward, building and podium, and plaza in the city, where the platforms became oases amid the rush of traffic in the city streets. To critic Michael Hays, this was Mies's great achievement: Like a clearing in the forest, the platform had the potential "to open up a clearing of implacable silence in the chaos of the nervous metropolis."[65] Some years later Mies would explain the need for a relief from the city's density: "There are no cities, in fact, any more . . . it goes on like a forest . . . that is the reason why we cannot have the old cities any more . . . that is gone forever . . . planned city and so on. . . . We should think about the means . . . that we have to live in a jungle . . . and maybe we do well by that."[66]

Mies's photomontage depicting his project for the 1942 IIT campus in Chicago superimposes a series of academic buildings, interwoven with the open spaces of a greensward, onto a bird's-eye view of the endless dense blocks of small buildings of Chicago's Near South Side (fig. 74). He had conceptualized the campus as clearing in the "jungle," set apart on a virtual podium realized as a greensward—literally, a grass plane. With antecedents in his built work of the late 1920s, this "clearing in the chaos" would ground Mies's future projects as the paradigm for his high-rise urban complexes of the 1950s and 1960s.

With a triangular site for 860–880 Lake Shore Drive, the building no longer took the form of espousing the trace of the site of the 1920s skyscrapers. The two rectangular Chicago towers set at slightly overlapping right angles to each other accommodate their

74 Mies van der Rohe office, photomontage of Illinois Institute of Technology campus model and aerial view of Chicago near south side, 1947. Photograph: Hedrich-Blessing Studio, September 6, 1963.

UNION OF BUILDING AND PLAZA IN THE URBAN LANDSCAPE

75 Mies van der Rohe, architect, apartment towers at 860–880 Lake Shore Drive, site plan, Chicago, 1948–51. Delineator: Richard Bachand, 2000.

OPPOSITE

76 Mies van der Rohe, architect, canopy and plaza between apartment towers at 860–880 Lake Shore Drive. Photograph: Hubert Henry, Hedrich-Blessing Studio, between 1950 and 1969.

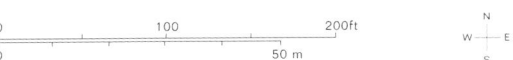

triangular site as well as the view-corridor easement required for the apartment house behind. Organized on a defined travertine plane—a virtual podium one step up from the grass—the complex of buildings becomes a clearing in the city (figs. 75, 76, and PF 4). It was also the first construction in which Mies lifted his buildings off the ground, as he had proposed in his early campus drawings, in order to establish the podium plane. The steep change of street levels between Park and Lexington Avenues, the change of grade along Park Avenue between Fifty-Second and Fifty-Third Streets, and the presence of McKim, Mead & White's neo-Florentine Racquet and Tennis Club directly across Park Avenue, as well as city zoning regulations, set up certain conditions in the design of the Seagram building (see PF 9). On the Seagram podium we find other elements of Charlottenhof in the trees and benches, first delineated in Mies's 1955 sketches for Seagram. In bringing order, nature, and revolutionary spatiality, Mies's urban clearings give rise to a new sense of the urban condition. His architectural language of freestanding towers, and pavilions carefully arranged on podia, offers a method for creating discreetly intervening urban patterns in cities across the system of real-estate development and building production in North America, "optimizing the space for life to unfold and spirit to play wherever the opportunity presented itself."[67]

In the evolution of Mies's architecture from the Riehl house to Seagram, podium and building are united as elements of a sacred precinct for everyday life. The mullioned skyscraper is enriched in its modulation from transparency to solidity with the union of the plaza and the building. The movement of the pedestrian and the shadows of surrounding structures as the sun moves from hour to hour frame a view that evokes the dialectics of the two faces of the Riehl house. Here the plaza is like the lower garden of the Riehl house;

77 Seagram building lobby looking west toward the Racquet and Tennis Club. Gelatin silver print, 7⅝ × 9⅝ in. Photograph: Ezra Stoller, 1958.

Mies has translated the space of quietude and contemplation into the city (see figs. 36, PF 1, and PF 8). As Ludwig Hilberseimer commented, "Like the individual building, the entire city can be open and spacious . . . leaving behind the traditional narrow, closed space of the streets and city, the urban space emerges free and open on all sides. Just as the house unites with the landscape, the room with the garden, and the exterior and interior become one, so the city with the landscape, and the landscape now also exists in the city" (fig. 77).[68]

The use of Seagram plaza by New Yorkers has made evident its qualities as a public space. The ebb and flow of people across the plaza intensifies the awareness of how crucial movement is to Mies's oeuvre. In testing the design of a building in relation to its site and context, Mies investigated two kinds of movement.[69] From his earliest built work, he considered the visitor's flow of movement, as he first did in the Riehl house, through individual elements such as walls, columns, stairs, and furniture, which were composed as part of an unfolding progression through space (see PF 8, PF 9, PF 11, PF 12, PF 14, and PF 15). But Mies also explored the visual effect of parallax—that is, the perception of change in the appearance of an object or building, relative to other objects, owing to a change in the observer's position.

Beginning in 1910 he experimented with montage as a means of testing his projects in their surroundings. This practice evolved into a cinematographic methodology involving the comprehension of parallax in relating a building to its site and to neighboring buildings. In the United States, where his practice flourished, Mies applied this principle in composing the low-rise buildings of the IIT campus from the point of view of a pedestrian walking through it and ultimately brought parallax to bear on the design of the curtain wall of the tall building, so that it would be perceived to be open or closed, transparent or solid, depending on the position of the observer.

Of course, the podium occasioned movement. Mies's interest in movement, in addition to the itinerary he carefully plotted through the Riehl house and its landscape, was manifested early on in his photomontage studies for building projects in relation to their site. These studies eventually made use of parallax to consider building projects as they might be seen by an imaginary subject from a range of viewpoints. Ultimately it is inherent in

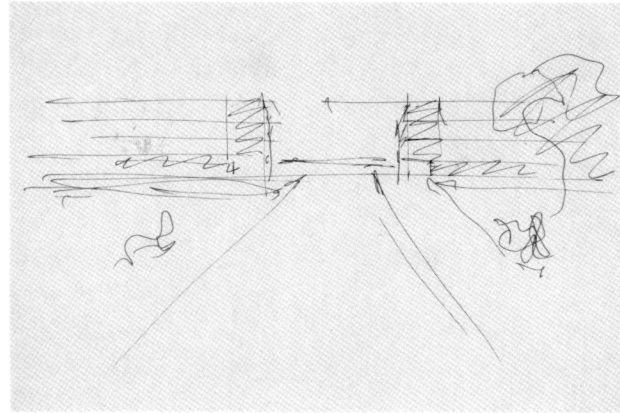

78 Mies van der Rohe, sketch for Armour Institute of Technology (AIT) campus, perspective view north toward the Student Union building with the Chemistry building auditorium at right, Chicago, [1939/40]. Pen and black ink on Apex notepaper, 6 × 8¼ in.

79 Mies van der Rohe, sketch for Armour Institute of Technology (AIT) campus, perspective view west along Thirty-Third Street toward the Mechanical and Civil Engineering buildings and Rock Island Railroad tracks, Chicago, [1939/40]. Pen and black ink on Apex notepaper, 6 × 8¼ in.

80 Mies van der Rohe, sketch for Armour Institute of Technology (AIT) campus, perspective view looking southwest, including the Civil and Mechanical Engineering buildings and Library building with Chemistry building auditorium to the left, Chicago, [1939/40]. Pen and black ink on Apex notepaper, 6 × 8¼ in.

Mies's articulation of the mullioned skyscrapers. For the Bismarck Monument competition of 1910, Mies combined photograph views of the terrain from below looking downriver, which had been made available to all contestants to use as they please, with his model for the monument. He then tried another view, looking upriver. Eleven years later, in 1921, even though the technique of photomontage was apparently not allowed in submissions for the Friedrichstrasse competition,[70] Mies merged photographs of his drawings and of the site to produce montages looking both up and down the street. This early practice of exploring subjective positional shifts takes on another dimension in Mies's photomontage studies for the Stuttgart Bank competition of 1928. All contestants were required to use the same image,[71] but Mies also studied his proposed building by moving the point of view to the right, and in another montage he moved in closer, so that the series allowed him to visualize the effects of the changing relationship of buildings, one to the other.

Most striking is the fact that Mies's habit of using montage to study projects elicited a new sketching modality—cinematographic conceptual sketches for the IIT campus.[72] It is possible to plot the movement and sequence of viewpoints he adopted. Three images from the sequence of Mies's perspective sketches illustrate the mode: The first sketch looks north toward the Student Union building, with the Chemistry building auditorium at the right (fig. 78); the second looks west on Thirty-Third Street toward the Mechanical and Civil Engineering buildings, which frame the opening leading to the Rock Island Railroad beyond (fig. 79); and the third, which looks southwest, includes the Civil and Mechanical Engineering buildings, the Library building, and the Chemistry building auditorium, which is now to the left (fig. 80).[73] In this series of rapid pen-and-ink sketches, Mies

81 Walker Evans, *[Man, Seagram Plaza, New York]*, May 17, 1963. Gelatin silver print, 9⅛ × 13½ in.

studied the spatiality of the campus from the changing points of view of a pedestrian moving through it—the varying relationship of one building to another, overlapping and shifting in scale, appearing small in the distance, looming larger as the imagined pedestrian moves closer, some parts revealed, other hidden.

Mies eventually brought the phenomenon of parallax into the articulation of tall buildings in the city, into his urban oases. Beginning with his high-rise apartment building at 860–880 Lake Shore Drive, the raw elements of construction—the steel I-beam, the mullion—not only played in the light with the earth's movement, but the series of mullions changed the building's surface with the movement of the observer. The repetitive rhythms play against one another, elaborating the effect of parallax. The projecting mullions at 860 and Seagram, as in all of Mies's later high-rise buildings, reveal varying degrees of opacity and transparency. The change from permeable to solid induced by the shift of an observer's viewing position was convincingly compared by art historian Rosalind Krauss to the perception of changing qualities of texture in the grid paintings of Agnes Martin. Krauss proposed that three different vantage points allow for distinctly diverse visual experiences: the engagement with the materiality of the individual line and the tactile surface of the canvas viewed at close range; dematerialization—a "haze" of lines—perceived as the viewer backs away from the canvas; and the opaqueness and impermeability of the grid—"immovable as stone"—when looked at from a greater distance.[74]

Mies's engagement with the continuity of architecture and landscape is best known from the famous 1939 montages for his first American project, the Resor house, viewed against the dramatic landscape of the Grand Tetons in Wyoming,[75] and the 1943 project "Museum for a Small City," in which Picasso's *Guernica* and two Maillol sculptures are seen against a landscape of foliage and a body of water.[76] For the museum project, Mies wrote, "The barrier between the art work and the living community is erased by a garden approach for the display of sculpture. Interior sculptures enjoy an equal spatial freedom, because the open plan permits them to be seen against the surrounding hills." This passage may be transliterated to mean the high-rise tower and the plaza seen against and within the landscape of the city; as Mies concluded, "The architectural space, thus achieved, becomes a defining rather than confining space."[77] Above all, it was the *idea* that counted. The idea of the house unified with the garden, the tall building and the city both separated and united by the podium, calm and contemplative, distanced and made sacred, precincts set apart from the cacophony of the streets, inducing observation of the play of light and transparency, the shifting reflectivity and openness and opacity of the glass wall with the movement of the visitor.

In a *New Yorker* review of September 1958 entitled "Lesson of the Master," architecture and urban critic Lewis Mumford captured the essential spirit of the building:

> It is at ground level, in the public spaces, that van der Rohe's sense of architectural order remains unqualified and supreme. . . . The fact that 375 is set back from Park Avenue some ninety feet not merely makes it visible but makes it approachable, and the open plaza in front, plus the arbored green rectangles at the sides, gives the same satisfaction that the building itself does. This plaza is open without being formidable; the absence of any kind of ornament, except the tall bronze flagpole, seventy-five feet high, slightly to the right of the main entrance, and the fountains and rectangular, step-rimmed pools of water on either side, only emphasizes the quality of the space itself.[78]

Russell Lynes, inimitable commentator on American taste and manners, said that the Seagram building "is an architectural ornament to the city [and] has also provided the city with a small pleasant square of open space which every lunch hour in good weather is crowded with New Yorkers hungry for a bit of open space in which to sun themselves" (fig. 81).[79]

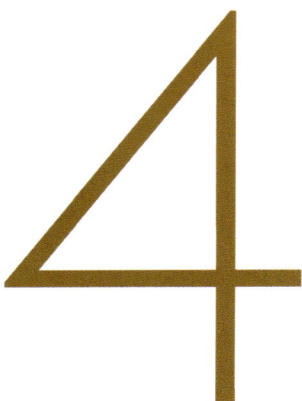

4

LIGHT: PHILIP JOHNSON'S *STIMMUNG*

By his own account, Philip Johnson's eyes filled with tears when Mies van der Rohe offered him a partnership as co-architect of the Seagram Building: "Shall we make it 'Van der Rohe and Johnson'?"[1] Although he had been an acolyte of Mies, and his own Glass House had been so strongly inspired by Mies's models, Johnson was just beginning to break away, to develop his own approach to architecture (fig. 82). From the outset, he was interested in the Seagram building as a *Gesamtkunstwerk,* a synthesis of elements that results in a work of "total design." Alfred H. Barr, director of the Museum of Modern Art in New York, had oriented him in this direction in 1932 when he suggested that Johnson put together an industrial design exhibition. The same year, when Johnson became the first director of the Department of Architecture, Barr predicted that his program "would be of equal importance to anything we do in painting or sculpture,"[2] and indeed, with the exhibition *Machine Art* of 1934, MoMA gained a reputation for establishing standards in design. Twenty years later, before I selected Mies as architect for the Seagram building, Philip took me to Philadelphia to visit Howe and Lescaze's Philadelphia Saving Fund Society building (1929–32), where he commented on the attention paid to the interior in relation to the exterior of the building. While his appreciation of the interior was greater than his interest in the exterior, I recall that Philip considered this Depression-era work to be the epitome of "total design." And *Stimmung* completes the physical with the mood or atmosphere it creates. Like the tuning of an instrument, it depends on the conjunction of different forces or on a certain harmony between different variables.

Knowing that Mies's primary concern was the articulation of structure, form, and material, Philip quickly grasped that Seagram presented an unusual opportunity to improve on many of the standard industrial design elements used in office buildings: doors, elevator

82 Philip Johnson with his Brick Guest House and Glass House, New Canaan, Connecticut. Photograph: Arnold Newman, July 1, 1949.

cabs, hardware, lighting, plumbing fixtures, and room partitions, as well as lettering and signage. Johnson reserved this role for himself, but his contribution to Seagram would prove to be even more far-reaching than he could have foreseen, eventually expanding to include the design of entire office floors, lighting strategies for the whole building, the display of artwork, the fountains on the plaza, and the design of the great rooms that merged with the public space at the plaza level. Philip used powerful theatrical effects to interiorize the dramatic exterior substance of Mies's building.

As Seagram began to be more fully occupied by the summer of 1958, the July issue of *Architectural Forum* carried a first glimpse of the completed building in an article titled "Seagram's Custom Look: 13 New Ideas for Better Skyscraper Design." The article proposes Seagram as a locus of applied research, "a half-million-square-foot laboratory in which new and special office designs are being tested in actual use," crediting the architects with refusing "to accept a standard material or standard method if they could see ways of improving it."[3] The numerous pragmatically captioned illustrations stressed those elements destined to become part of commercial product lines, "a whole catalogue of innovations that may soon affect office building design throughout the U.S.," not only captured Philip's intentions but inadvertently pointed up the state of the building art in the late 1950s.

Two of the thirteen "new ideas" featured in this article were rooted in Mies's fundamental architectural conception and language: the bronze and glass curtain wall (fig. 83) and Seagram's air-conditioning system, which "made floor-to-ceiling glass walls practical for the first time." However, one could easily imagine that Philip was the *Forum* critic's amanuensis, because the other eleven "new ideas" were his, albeit in Mies's vocabulary: his

83 "Seagram's Custom Look," title page from *Architectural Forum*, July 1958. Photograph: George Cserna.

controlled Venetian blinds, "specially designed to stop in only three positions," producing "façade patterns that always look neat" that cartoonist Alan Dunn parodied (fig. 84); the "floor-to-ceiling doors" that "added nothing to the cost" and were made to "look like integral parts of [the] paneling," giving the "interiors greater unity"; movable floor-to-ceiling partitions, stock items redesigned and "greatly simplified in detail" for Seagram; and floor-to-ceiling elevator doors revealing the custom-designed panels of an interwoven stainless steel and bronze mesh lining the elevator cabs (fig. 85).

On the same page, the floor-to-ceiling travertine slabs installed in an executive washroom allowed the *Forum* critic to discuss the ceiling grid and custom-designed fixtures. There was no mention that the marble slabs of the executive washroom were clearly not a stock item and instead derived from a sumptuous Johnsonian concept for a travertine room. In fact, this introduced a new Philip Johnson, one who had begun to lavish rich and

84 Alan Dunn, "Oh, Mr. Mies! Tenant on the 34th floor brought his own window shades!" cartoon from *Architectural Record*, September 1958.

85 "Seagram's Custom Look," controlled venetian blinds, partitions, elevator doors, travertine slabs, and floor-to-ceiling doors, from *Architectural Forum*, July 1958. Photographs: Ezra Stoller and George Cserna.

2. *Controlled Venetian blinds* were specially designed to stop in only three positions: all the way up, all the way down, and at half mast. The angle of the slats is fixed at 45 degrees to let pedestrians get full impact of lit-up building at night. These controls produce façade patterns that always look neat.

3. *Floor-to-ceiling doors* (far left) added nothing to the cost of each opening, made doors look like integral part of paneling, hence gave interiors greater unity. This corridor is part of Seagram's executive suite.

4. *Floor-to-ceiling partitions* (near left) are stock units reworked for Seagram by the architects. Greatly simplified in detail, partitions have reveals at panel joints, recessed wiring chases behind baseboards, specially designed doorknobs and hinges, and continuous tubular rubber stops around door frames. Panels were finished with many different materials, all washable. The system is now standard with its manufacturer.

5. *Floor-to-ceiling travertine slabs* (far left) divide washroom on Seagram's special executive floor. Orderly appearance was achieved in part by use of ceiling grid as module for partitions. All fixtures in all washrooms were specially designed, including pipe-connections at lavatories and toilets.

6. *Floor-to-ceiling elevator doors* reveal interior of cab lined with panels of stainless steel and bronze mesh designed for Seagram in a cartridge-belt pattern. These metal panels are removable, easily maintained (because they do not show scratches), reflect light from luminous ceiling above. Elevators are of the electronic brain type, which adjusts to changing loads at different times of day, eliminates need for elevator operators.

sensuous materials on bathrooms. Already in the late 1940s he had used leather "tiles" to line the walls of the circular bathroom in his own Glass House, forming a warm, tactile skin that exuded a musky scent. Ten years later, another critic described the men's and women's washrooms Philip designed for the Four Seasons Restaurant as "palaces," "the former in Bardiglio Fiorito marble and Macassar ebony, the latter in Rose Portas, rosewood, and gold Fortuny [cloth], with theatrical vanities surrounded by [low-watt] bulbs . . . [and] . . . marble shelves containing ashtrays adjoining each stool."[4]

The next page shows signage in a serif Egyptian Bold font designed by Elaine Lustig for use throughout the building, custom faucets and other washroom fittings, and door handles and signal hardware fabricated in brushed aluminum and stainless steel at a "very, very, minimal" cost over top-quality hardware, according to the manufacturer (fig. 86). The left-hand side of the last page of the *Forum* article is devoted to three "New Ideas" in lighting. A grouping of small images points to certain specific lighting effects employed in the

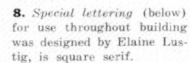

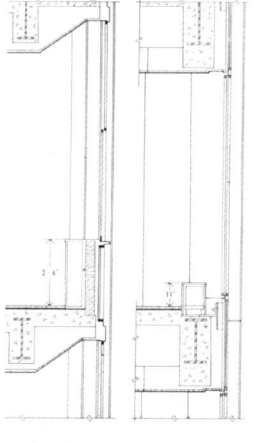

86 "Seagram's Custom Look," floor-to-ceiling glass, special lettering, faucets, and hardware, and new air-conditioning system, from *Architectural Forum*, July 1958. Photographs: Ezra Stoller and George Cserna.

Seagram Company offices as well as other spaces in the building: display lights that disappear into the ceiling when not being used, and "invisible" or "concealed light sources" that "spill a wash of light over conference-room walls, and make a pool of light on [a] conference table" (fig. 87). The text also commented on the role of lighting designers—members of a profession, I may add, that was underdeveloped as an art form at the time:[5] "Lighting Consultant Richard Kelly, in collaboration with Lighting Consultant Edison Price, used concealed light sources to illuminate [the] marble-faced elevator stack in [the] lobby, and to light paintings and tapestries in [the] Seagram offices. Result: one of the best-illuminated buildings ever constructed." The right-hand side of the last of "13 New Ideas for Better Skyscraper Design" is devoted to what at the time must have been an astounding image of the Seagram Building glowing at night, which the *Forum* critic evocatively described: "Each night, the luminous ceiling band is lit up on every floor, [and] provides a dramatic spectacle on Manhattan's sky line."

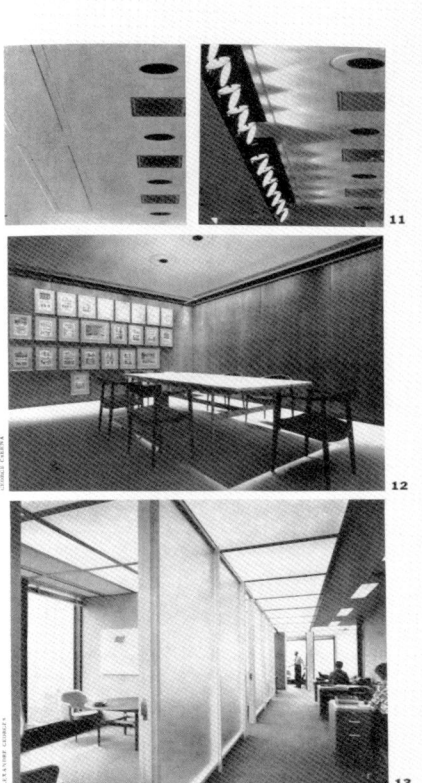

87 "Seagram's Custom Look," display lights, invisible light sources, and luminous ceiling, from *Architectural Forum*, July 1958. Photographs: Ezra Stoller, George Cserna, and Alexandre Georges.

LIGHT: PHILIP JOHNSON'S *STIMMUNG*

Philip's involvement with all aspects of the lighting for Seagram, though unacknowledged by the *Forum* critic, is a pivotal part of my story. Lewis Mumford's "The Lesson of the Master" appeared in his regular column in the *New Yorker* on September 13, 1958, summing up his critical assessment of the effect of the Seagram building shaft, the plaza, and the lighting: "It needs no ornamental fixtures other than those it has in order to increase this human quality [serenity]; all it needs—and it already has these, both by day and by night—is people capable of enjoying the primal aesthetic pleasures: ordered space, air, the spray of fountains on one's face, and sunlight or the regal mixture of black and gold that greets one from the lighted building at night."[6] Alluding to the different "hands" involved in the design, Mumford wrote: "In accounting for the qualities that distinguish this edifice, one is safe in assuming that they derive, directly or indirectly, from the Master himself. To acknowledge this is not to diminish the contribution made by his associate, Philip Johnson, an avowed if by now an independent disciple."[7] Within ten days of the publication of Mumford's piece, I wrote to him: "You might be interested in knowing who did what.... Philip played a very minor role until Mies suggested that the building would be nice lit up at night. Then came the ridiculous business about Mies's license and Mies went back to Chicago. At that point Philip's office took over."[8]

From the end of December 1955 until early February 1957, Philip Johnson was legally the principal architect of the Seagram Building owing to the denial of Mies's license in the state of New York.[9] For Philip, who had only recently left MoMA to open his own office, Mies's physical absence gave him a newfound authority that enhanced his growing sense of assuredness as an architect. Although he sought Mies's approval on all major design decisions, Philip was now in charge of the office, and he remained so even after Mies's application was accepted in July 1956. From then on, Mies "visited" the office rather than heading it. So, left in charge early in 1956, Philip began to work on the lighting and on two autonomous interior spaces in the Seagram building: the Seagram Company's executive offices and the restaurant Mies asked him to design—or, as Philip put it, "give up" to him.[10] The Four Seasons Restaurant was installed in the ground floor of the low east wing, in the great free-span volumes Mies had created at each end. With the exception of the lighting, the "good design" elements Philip contributed to Seagram (those lauded by the *Architectural Forum* critic) constitute a body of two-dimensional elements applied to the surface planes of the building. They affect perception of the building rather than its essence. However, the restaurant Johnson designed, still unseen in 1958, would come to have an importance that exceeded what anyone could have imagined.

With the Four Seasons, Philip achieved the ultimate *Gesamtkunstwerk,* in which theatrical interior effects are locked into reciprocity with Mies's structural language. Furthermore, the executive offices for the Seagram Company and the lighting design for the building, although treated matter-of-factly in the pages of *Architectural Forum* and also by myself in the abovementioned letter to Mumford, were highly distinctive. Paradoxically, Philip made his most significant contributions to the Seagram Building as he was moving away from Mies and beginning to find his own voice.

Philip's first built move away from Mies had occurred during the remodeling of a bedroom in his Brick Guest House, conceived as a foil to his Glass House at New Canaan, Connecticut (see fig. 82). In 1953, four years after it was finished, Philip remodeled two of the three rooms of the Brick Guest House to form one long, narrow space, in which he hung a series of canopied plaster vaults from the ceiling, carrying them to the ground on thin "pilasters" (fig. 88). In 1966, Henry-Russell Hitchcock remarked on this shift,[11] and thirty years later, Philip himself confirmed it, calling the insertion of a vaulted ceiling in the brick

88 Philip Johnson, architect, Brick Guest House, view of remodeled interior, New Canaan, Connecticut. Photograph: Ezra Stoller, 1953.

building "my first break from the International Style."¹² He continued, "The insertion of the vaults came out of discussions with Dick Kelly, my lighting man. Lighting from around a concealed roof [sic] gives a wonderful light in the room. Having got that idea straight, then I thought at once of John Soane's breakfast room at his house in London. . . . This is the first time I used that vault. . . . It's a copy of Sir John Soane. It's the first time I used anything as definitely historical as that."¹³

Philip later commented that the solution had more to do with Robert Adam's remodeling of the long, narrow space of the Library at Syon House.¹⁴

Much has been made of Johnson's use of historical sources, beginning with his now famous *Architectural Review* article of 1950, in which he cited the sources for the design, composition, and siting of his houses at New Canaan.¹⁵ In addition to claiming Mies as his generative model, Johnson referred to Mies's contemporaries Theo van Doesburg, Le Corbusier, and Kasimir Malevich on the relationship of forms and to Mies's "mentor," Karl Friedrich Schinkel, for the "pure neo-classical Romantic—more specifically Schinkelesque" way of siting buildings.¹⁶ He attributed to Claude-Nicolas Ledoux the idea of separating the functions of the Glass House and the Brick Guest House into two absolutely cubic forms, pointing to the influence of nineteenth-century historian Auguste Choisy's analysis of movement on the Acropolis at Athens, and quixotically—always wanting to surprise— Philip linked his own interest in bucolic settings and eighteenth-century British models to the obscure estate of Carl Friedrich von Pückler, count of Silesia.

Johnson initially learned about architecture by following a curriculum laid out for him by Alfred H. Barr at the end of the 1920s, when he undertook a firsthand study of both historical and contemporary architecture in Europe. However, on his own, in 1930, Johnson focused on Mies, and then in 1930 and 1931, with his recent acquaintance Henry-Russell Hitchcock, he visited and studied buildings by Schinkel. Hitchcock was influential in orienting Philip toward the aesthetic and perceptual aspects of architecture, and even encouraged him to pursue a doctorate (a short-lived project) on Schinkel's most brilliant and eclectic follower, Ludwig Persius. The work of both Schinkel and Persius surely legitimized Johnson's departure from Miesian modernism. But referring to models did not necessarily constitute a "break" with Mies, since Mies himself valued historical examples: the structure of medieval barns, Gothic cathedrals, and Schinkel's Altes Museum in Berlin (from which he said "you could learn everything in architecture").[17] Recalling his reaction to the "careful construction, absolutely honest" in the work of Hendrik Petrus Berlage, Mies said: "After I returned from Holland [1910] I fought with myself to get away from the Schinkel-classicism."[18] It was a difference of intention that would constitute the break between Johnson, whose models were sensually evocative, and Mies, whose models were tectonic.

The drama of the décor at New Canaan struck me on first visiting Johnson's domain in the summer of 1954. The brick and glass houses and their setting had palpable presence. An ecstatic aura pervaded the guest room. One was not aware of entering a tall, narrow, windowless, tomblike space but rather was captivated by the glow of light washing the sandlike expanse of pink, silver, and gold Fortuny cloth covering the enclosing walls. Turning the knob of a substantial dimmer box at the head of the bed (an early use of this new technology), one had the sense of nightfall in the desert, under the vaulted canopy—a sheltering firmament—as the light gradually faded.[19] I realize now that another model was lodged deep in Philip's psyche.

Even though Philip seems never to have referred to any but British sources for this room, he had to have known another room with the same sense of enclosure, curtained walls, and magical lighting: the bedchamber Schinkel designed between 1809 and 1810 for Queen Luise at Schloss Charlottenburg in Berlin, which was open to the public from 1918 through at least 1937 (fig. 89).[20] Barry Bergdoll's description of this remarkable room intensifies the comparison with the bedroom of Johnson's Brick Guest House: "By the simple means of white muslin stretched over rose-papered walls, light was reflected and filtered through the material to create the glowing effect of [the] sunrise, breaking down the boundaries between nature and architecture, and testing in concrete terms . . . the capacity of visual art to evoke specific moods, emotions, and states of mind."[21]

The same light magic experienced inside the Brick Guest House was conjured up in the glass pavilion every evening, as the induced light would slowly rise and fade among the

89 Karl Friedrich Schinkel, architect, Queen Luise's bedroom, remodeled in 1930, Schloss Charlottenburg, Berlin, 1809–10. Photographer unknown, c. 1930–43.

90 Philip Johnson, architect, Glass House, exterior view at night, New Canaan, Connecticut. Photograph: Alexandre Georges, c. 1960.

surrounding trees (fig. 90). Philip called this landscape his continually changing wallpaper. Added to this luminous experience were effects manifested within the glass walls. Against the dark brick floor and the large brick cylinder connecting floor and ceiling, uplights reflecting off the ceiling cast a glow over an early copy of Nicolas Poussin's *Burial of Phocion* resting on its easel. And by 1954, a Johnson-Kelly–designed floor lamp (placed next to the Mies-designed daybed and table) emanated a soft pool of light (fig. 91).[22] The glow of the fireplace added atmosphere in cold weather. The striking image of the steel-framed structure poised on a plateau at the edge of a precipice, the view framed by the structure of the Glass House, and the trees and valley beyond are reminiscent of Karl Friedrich Schinkel's evocative early paintings such as *Landscape with Gothic Arcades* of 1812, which Philip, who found Schinkel to be "almost as good a painter as Caspar David Friedrich," must have known (fig. 92).[23] Likewise, Poussin's *Burial of Phocion,* installed at the spiritual center of the house, resonates with the peopled landscape and architectural elements of Schinkel's *Antique City on a Mountain* of 1805: both works situate a story and embed a particular view in the earth's topography.[24] Poussin's landscape, invoking Schinkel's view, can be seen as the ideal for the site of the Glass House, which Philip strove over the years to distance from the actual topography of the Connecticut woods. All of this reveals the extent to which Schinkel was on Philip's mind.

Clearly, Philip's break from Mies was fed by their very different understandings of the Schinkel connection they shared. This move to independence was instrumentalized through lighting design, not only because Mies's architectonic approach was out of reach for Johnson but also because it lay outside his concerns, which were only beginning to surface. These concerns were nurtured by his haunting memory of the Hofgärtnerei in Potsdam in 1930, where, Philip wrote, Schinkel succeeded in "the creation of emotional space, by such casual and eclectic means."[25] Through the control of artificial illumination, using techniques acquired during his highly rewarding collaboration with Richard Kelly, Philip could bring together the pictorialism and atmospheric romanticism he found in Schinkel within the tectonics Mies so admired in Schinkel, the "wonderful constructions, excellent proportions and good detailing."[26] Schinkel was for Mies "the greatest building master of classicism [representing] the end of an old and the beginning of a new time."[27] For Philip, the Altes Museum "is Schinkel's most restrained and classical building. The Hofgärtnerei in Potsdam is romantic. Schinkel the classicist—Schinkel the romantic—both appeal to us."[28]

Beyond historical models and influences, more pragmatically, the introduction in North America after World War II of buildings enclosed by glass walls created new lighting problems for architects and lighting designers. Solid enclosing walls that acted as reflecting surfaces were replaced by large sheets of glass that appeared black at night. This troubled Philip Johnson when he first moved into his Glass House: "There was no light—other than the sun. You can imagine the problem of reflections [at night]. If you had one bulb you saw six."[29] Richard Kelly developed the solution. Philip said Kelly "founded the art of residential lighting the day he designed lighting for the Glass House."[30] He might have said that Kelly developed a new art of lighting that articulated a new architectural language. Kelly's technique for lighting the Glass House, which would be taken for granted today, must have seemed revolutionary in the mid-1940s. In the first sentence of one of his earli-

91 Philip Johnson, architect, Glass House, interior view with Mies sitting group, *Burial of Phocion*, and landscape beyond, New Canaan, Connecticut. Photograph: Alexandre Georges, c. 1960.

92 Karl Friedrich Schinkel, *Landscape with Gothic Arcades*, c. 1812. Oil on canvas, 24¾ × 39⅜ in. Photograph: Jörg P. Anders.

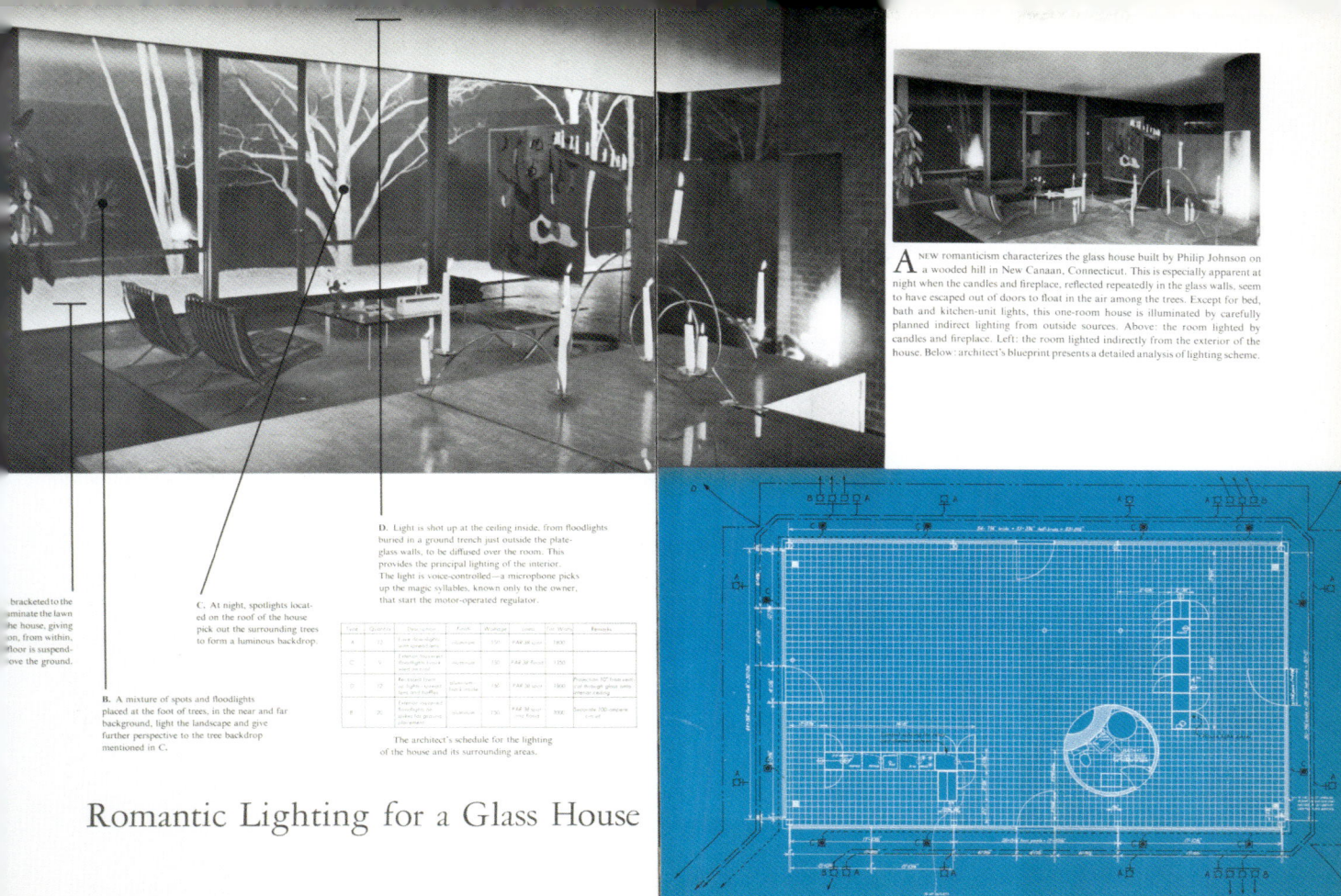

93 "Romantic Lighting for a Glass House," layout from *Flair*, February 1950. Photograph: Louis Faurer.

est articles, Kelly asserted that "good lighting is a vital part of good living," and proposed to eliminate glare that tires the eye "by diffusing bright sources, by shielding the sources of light, [and] by arranging for a proper relation between bright objects and their surroundings." He demonstrated how these effects could create drama, even in a living room—albeit fashion designer Lilly Daché's living room: "Noticeably free of glare and sharp contrasts, the general lighting is indirect—from sources subtly concealed," certain objects like plants "are sharply silhouetted by baby spotlights, sculptures are made to reflect light, . . . [and] lighting can create drama."[31]

By 1950, in the obscure periodical *Flair,* Kelly was more polemical, claiming (under the headline "Focus on Light") lighting design to be an art: "It is not nature, but the artificial control of selected natural elements. Light and seeing are inseparable conceptions. We in fact make what we see by making things visible, and we make them appear and disappear to suit nuances of our desires."[32] Among the effects illustrated in the article were Kelly's use of a combination of indirect light and glittering highlight to enhance fine fabrics worn by the clients of the Stork Club in New York; color lighting to achieve distance; and dimmers to control the intensity of light and thus the sense of scale. The essence of the article, however, is a two-page spread on Johnson's Glass House titled "Romantic Lighting for a Glass House" (fig. 93). It consists of a large and a small version of the same panoramic view photographed from the inside looking out at dusk. These are also probably the earliest photographs of the house: candelabra with movable tapers provide incidental lighting in the sitting area, and a Miró (whose installation there preceded the Poussin) rests on an easel. The larger of the two images carries captions that use such theatrical terms as "bracketed," "spots," "floodlights," and "backdrop" to describe the lighting effects:

LIGHT: PHILIP JOHNSON'S *STIMMUNG*

Lights bracketed to the eaves illuminate the lawn around the house, giving the illusion, from within, that the floor is suspended above the ground. A mixture of spots and floodlights placed at the foot of trees, in the near and far background, light the landscape and give further perspective to the tree backdrop. . . . At night, spotlights located on the roof of the house pick out the surrounding trees to form a luminous backdrop. Light is shot up at the ceiling inside, from floodlights buried in a ground trench just outside the plate-glass walls, to be diffused over the room. This provides the principal lighting of the interior.[33]

The smaller image captures the same view at night, but without exterior illumination. The glass wall is black, so that "the candles and fireplace, reflected repeatedly in the glass walls, seem to have escaped out of doors to float in the air among the trees."[34]

The key design invention is buried in the body of the article. After a general discussion of new technical developments in local lighting designed to meet exacting requirements for comfort in seeing under changing conditions, Kelly writes that "to give such concentrated lighting a reasonable relation with our natural backgrounds, we require some general lighting. This need is exaggerated in the Johnson glass house by lighting the immediate surrounding landscape, in contrast to firelight and moveable tapers indoors."[35] In other words, lighting the landscape counterbalances the illumination of the interior. The continuity and flow between interior and exterior implied by this concept was a basic premise of the new architecture theorized in the 1920s. The lighting scheme Kelly and Johnson created for the Glass House evoked Schinkel's aesthetic vision of a stage "essentially atmospheric in nature, employing lighting and painterly *Stimmung* as the main devices for the creation of theatrical effects."[36] The Glass House at night must have seemed somewhat garish, initially: Mies laughed and said that it made the house look like a hot-dog stand. Mies had proposed neon lighting to dramatize a drive-in restaurant for a commercial strip in Indianapolis and was still hoping to build it in 1950 when he most likely first saw Johnson's Glass House. But Kelly and Johnson soon discovered how to make evident the reciprocity between exterior and interior through the use of lighting. And this was something neither Johnson nor Kelly could have achieved without the other—a picturesque, Schinkelesque effect that could only have been achieved within the sublime frame of Miesian architecture. Kelly and Johnson would go on to refine lighting at the Glass House as they collaborated on numerous projects before Johnson took charge of Seagram in 1956 and Kelly was contracted to consult on the architectural lighting for the building.[37]

The sense of drama Johnson found in Schinkel's work must have drawn him to Kelly, who had studied theatrical design at Yale University. They met at least by November 1946, when both served on the "Affordable Lighting" jury organized by Eliot Noyes, then director of the Department of Industrial Design at MoMA, to stimulate better design of objects for everyday use.[38] Kelly had already experimented with lighting as a high school student, and after completing courses and joining the theater department at Columbia University in 1932, he experienced the new architecture as a lighting designer and consultant. This led him to enroll in architecture school at Yale in 1942, where his most telling experience was surely at the Department of Drama, which, like architecture, belonged to the School of Fine Arts. There, Kelly was exposed to the work of the peerless lighting designer Stanley McCandless, one of the earliest instructors in stage lighting and author of the highly successful treatise *A Method of Lighting the Stage,* first published in 1932.[39] McCandless's close attention to the instruments of lighting—fixtures and their technical characteristics—converged with the interests of Kelly, who had become a consultant to the founder of Gotham

Lighting in the late 1930s. After obtaining his degree in architecture from Yale in the mid-1940s, Kelly served as director for the newly formed lamp department of Knoll Associates (the US manufacturer of furniture designed by leading contemporary architects, established in 1938), following McCandless's basic concepts of lighting as a design method: stage lighting, which "in its brightness and darkness, its color and pattern . . . creates an atmosphere that is inherently dramatic." McCandless also embraced the notion that the conquest and control of the medium of light "in a sense provides a new horizon for artistic expression."[40] Lighting, McCandless would remind his readers (and doubtless also his students), "is not really visible until it strikes some surface so that it can be reflected to the eye."[41] Kelly emphasized this point when he quoted Le Corbusier, who wrote, "L'architecture est le jeu savant, correct et magnifique des volumes assemblés sous la lumière" (Architecture is the masterful, correct, and magnificent play of volumes brought together in light).[42] Taking from McCandless the notion of "motivating light" (light that sets temporality and mood),[43] Kelly was concerned with how lighting affects the occupants of space and therefore emphasized the psychological effects of his work: "To plan visual beauty by controlling light, it is important to know the psychological effect various light phenomena have on us."[44]

Kelly was a polemicist, and as early as 1946 he aimed to educate and convert through his writings in popular magazines. In 1952, first in *House and Garden* and then more formally and self-consciously in the *College Art Journal,* he formalized his principles as a "vocabulary" that expressed his theoretical position on lighting. In a piece for the *College Art Journal,* he introduced these principles through the metaphor of watercolor painting:

> A feeling for light and lighting starts with visual imagination, just as a painter's talent does. Think of the creation of a watercolor rendering—first, major highlights are imagined—then, graded washes of different luminosity are added and—then, the detail of minor lightplay makes the idea clear and entertains the eye. In front of the mind's eye are three elements in the perceptions of visual design—three elemental kinds of light effect which can be related to the art of painting for easier visualization: 1) Focal glow or highlight. 2) Ambient luminescence or graded washes. 3) Play of brilliants or sharp detail.[45]

With these three elements—"focal glow," "ambient luminescence," and "play of brilliants"—Kelly established the terminology and the principles that would form the foundation of his work. It is useful to consider how he applied the three elements of his thesis in practical terms in the *House and Garden* article:[46]

> 1) Floor lamp and hanging lamp provide pools of light for armchair and sofa reading. This is called focal glow.
> 2) Ceiling spotlights spread soft, general light over fireplace wall and rug, which in turn reflect light toward ceiling. This is ambient luminescence.
> 3) Candlelight adds facets of light and play of brilliants.

As an architectural lighting designer, Kelly was, in essence, applying the techniques belonging to stage design. His three principles of lighting became a point of reference in his own field. They were absorbed into Philip Johnson's design language, even as Johnson made the terminology more graphic, replacing the tongue-twister "ambient luminescence" with "washing the walls with light."[47] In 1954, Philip was captivated by these new tools, always saying "PAR 38, PAR 38," which referred to a parabolic aluminized reflector, or PAR lamp, now widely used in residential as well as in commercial and transportation illumination.[48] Enamored of this new type of controllable ambient light and "focal glow," Philip used it not only in his New Canaan Brick Guest House but also in the modest apartment he designed for me in a New York brownstone.[49] By 1958, his application of Kelly's lighting ideas was demonstrated at Seagram: the luminous ceilings that gave an even, shadowless light, the indirect display lighting, and the strongly light-washed travertine core walls of the building lobby were all "new ideas" highlighted in the July 1958 *Forum* article, which concluded that Seagram was "one of the best-illuminated buildings ever constructed."[50]

The genius of Kelly and Johnson's collaboration on lighting at Seagram lay in creating, as they had at the Glass House, continuity and reciprocity between interior and exterior spaces. These effects were epitomized in the Four Seasons Restaurant, which opened in 1959. Kelly's thesis about lighting required a particular architectural aesthetic in order to soar, perhaps even to develop. Philip's strong Miesian discipline and language combined with his own romantic and intellectual sensibilities. He supplied such an aesthetic along a six-year trajectory that led from the tentative moves he made with the Glass House in 1949 to the sophisticated levels achieved at Seagram. Behind the bronze and topaz glass skin of the east wing, set back behind the building shaft and visible from the street, the shimmer of light and people in the great rooms of the Four Seasons Restaurant imbue the place with the intriguing promise of something about to happen (see PF 11). The form is Mies's, but the drama belongs to Johnson.

The story of creating and designing the Four Seasons Restaurant began with an unlikely event. In the fall of 1956, Seagram decided to look for someone to operate a restaurant in the building, and I was invited by the manager of the restaurant at Newark Airport, the Newarker, to test the kitchen. All I remember is a consommé with small profiteroles floating around in it. What could one possibly say about the place—a cafeteria with faux-elegant food? The Newarker restaurant had opened only a few years earlier, in 1953, under the direction of Jerome Brody—young, inexperienced, but business-school trained. Brody had taken over the small, failing chain of Riker's cafeterias and lunch counters his father-in-law had come to own. Brody achieved success by running other concessions. He renamed the company Restaurant Associates (RA) in 1945 and then established the Newarker, which (my assessment notwithstanding) became known as a fine dining venue at a time when there were few. (One of these, Voisin, disappeared when the Montana apartment house, in which it was located, was demolished to make way for the Seagram building.) RA's achievements caused L'Huillier S. Sheaff of Cushman & Wakefield to recommend the company as restaurateur for Seagram.

The problem of what use would be made of the ground floor of the east wing of the building (at first just called the "back portion") was still undecided in June 1955, although working drawings for the base building were to be finished in November and a definitive program for Seagram spaces was being developed. The question of eating facilities for the building (whether for staff and executives, an executive luncheon club, or a public restaurant) was raised at a meeting of the Advisory Committee on June 1, 1955. After a long discussion, opinion inclined favorably toward providing a public restaurant "for the benefit of the Seagram employees, as well as other tenants in the building."[51] Function, not the art of dining, was at issue.

L'Huillier Sheaff, who was invited to the meeting, reported on having checked to see if Edward Levine, owner of the Brass Rail restaurant, had any interest in taking space at

Seagram. Given the committee's low level of ambition (calling to mind Eero Saarinen's definition of "committees" as groups that are assembled to design a horse but end up with a camel), Sheaff could not have been aiming very high: the Brass Rail at Seventh Avenue and Forty-Ninth Street was described as a Times Square establishment, "one of those places reminding the visitor somewhat of a cafeteria, without at all being one,"[52] "big, bustling," and catering "to a typical Broadway crowd; but the food is excellent and not expensive. Fine roast beef, noted Welsh rarebit. Convenient to Radio City and to many theatres."[53] A few days after the meeting, I explained: "The main problem for the moment is deciding what will go into the back portion or East Wing which consists, as you will remember, of an area roughly two hundred by ninety feet which divides itself pretty well into three parts—the central area which continues the core of the building and the North and South areas which are bound by glass walls." The large central area (which now contains the half-acre kitchen), it was proposed, "could be used for meetings, large and small, and such sporadic exhibitions as [the Seagram people] may wish to have, and the areas north and south as rentals . . . a restaurant and/or show rooms such as Herman Miller and Knoll Associates and/or a bank or just simply keep the area for Seagram's own space in which they could, as they please, have their own product display and library etc., which wouldn't be open to the public."[54] I was aghast at the parochial programming ideas, noting: "To work anything out there would be moral suicide and the important thing will be the plaza, which must be superb and [over] which I will try to keep some kind of control."[55] It is also clear that there was no concept of the immense scale of the entire area or of the difficulty of using it.

Twenty months after the Advisory Committee meeting in June 1955, the plan to create a restaurant in the Seagram building became a reality on February 1, 1957, with the signing of a lease agreement between Seagram and Brody's recently confected 375 Park Avenue Restaurant Corporation. I have no memory of how this came to be.[56] Six months after the Newarker luncheon, at which Brody talked endlessly about what a "terrific idea" it would be to have a restaurant in the building, and I reportedly "sat there, ate, but said nothing . . . listened and listened but just wasn't responding,"[57] it is recorded that Sheaff arranged a meeting between Edgar M. Bronfman and Brody, which led to a meeting with SB, which Brody described: "Sam looks me straight in the eye, flops down in his chair, and says, 'So I understand that you want to run a restaurant in my building.' That was all he said. . . . I was very nervous but well prepared, so I started to talk about how RA would build such unique restaurants that they'd do wonders for Seagram's corporate image, and how they would express everything that was wonderful about New York."[58] Brody encountered SB's habit of falling asleep during meetings, but as was generally agreed, he always heard what he needed to hear. Edgar Bronfman tapped on the desk, and Brody continued:

> Sam opens his eyes, and, without missing a beat, waves his hand and says to me, "All right, all right, I'll have my man contact you about working out a lease." I was flabbergasted. Then as I was leaving, I tried to break the tension by asking Sam, "Well Mr. Bronfman, since it's your building what kind of food do you think we should serve?" Mr. Sam waved his hand again and replied, "All I want is to be able to get a good piece of flanken, okay?"[59]

A twenty-year lease was drawn up between Seagram and 375 Park Avenue Restaurant Corporation for a 485-seat restaurant and a 150-seat coffee shop.[60] The rent was considered by RA to be "astoundingly low,"[61] and the rest of the terms were extraordinarily generous: the rider to the lease specified that the landlord, Seagram, would undertake the cost and expense of the necessary alterations to the plans (and structure) to furnish the necessary equipment, including finished floors, columns, stairways, door and partitions, all ceilings hung or otherwise, all fonts, marquees, vestibules, and exterior signs, all necessary air-conditioning, heating, and ventilating, including kitchen hood exhaust, and all other necessary mechanical systems. In effect, Seagram, in what might be called a "turnkey" operation, provided the restaurant operators with a complete architectural installation. Seagram would also furnish "works of art, including sculpture, painting, tapestries, murals, and stage curtains which the Landlord may require,"[62] since we—I—had concerns about the nature of the art that the restaurant owners might choose. Seagram also provided the initial cost of the necessary kitchen equipment, carpeting, and drapes; the excess over seventy-five dollars of the cost per chair (as approved by the Landlord) was to be reimbursed by the tenant according to an agreed-upon schedule.

Brody brought his top team from the Newarker to develop the new restaurant. Joseph Baum (1920–1998) was the ingenious spirit. With a strong background in hotels and accounting, he had joined Brody before the Newarker opened and was soon made director of all RA operations. Baum hired the classically trained Swiss chef Albert Stockli to develop the menu, then invested in fine china and furnishings. RA's food was initially flamboyant: It was noted that, at the Newarker, the "waiters brandish gigantic peppermills at the table, stick sparklers into the desserts, and flame everything in sight."[63] At RA's Forum of the Twelve Caesars, which opened in December 1957, there were "so many flaming dishes and so many chafing-dish specialties . . . that we built an extra ten percent capacity into the air-conditioning system."[64] One wondered how this team could create a restaurant in Mies's refined world. The answer lay in Baum's work-driven intelligence and his obsession with detail. For the Forum, Baum immersed himself in Roman culture, consulting Professor Frank E. Brown of the Department of Classics at Yale, asking Harry Levy, professor of Classics at Hunter College, to lecture to his staff, and having them read Suetonius. He researched food in the same way, studying a Roman manual on the culinary arts and traveling to experience restaurants in Europe.[65] Baum, who invented the seasonal theme, applied the same level of research and testing to create the Four Seasons menu, qualified as the "New American Cuisine" based on the freshest seasonal ingredients.[66] A nervous, energetic, meticulous, sharp-tongued perfectionist, Baum had a remarkable capacity to learn, and learned a great deal working with Philip Johnson.

I had assumed that Mies would design the restaurant, but he asked Philip to do so. Philip remarked on Mies's impatience with "anything that had to do with an elaborate program." This assessment was accurate, for Mies at seventy, and always, was a conceptualist, concerned with architecture's epochal role, the idea of structure, and the proper use of materials, not with intricate programming—especially with retrofitting of the kind Philip described: "No one could decide how to get into the restaurant. The more expert you are the less convinced you are that you have only one way of getting from a kitchen to a dining room. How do you get people in? There was no precedent for bringing people in from down below and walking them up. Americans don't do that."[67] On the other hand, Baum realized that Philip had no experience with restaurant layout and specialized equipment, so he suggested that Philip work with interior decorator William Pahlmann, who had designed Forum of the Twelve Caesars, which was under construction when Seagram and RA signed their agreement.[68] The ornate, eclectic décor of the Forum was so overbearing that it seemed as though a partnership between men of such disparate sensibilities would be difficult. At one point, the tension was so high that Philip (feeling unsupported by RA) resigned. On demanding that Philip be reinstated, I received a lesson in management from

L'Huillier Sheaff, who explained that to force an architect on a client meant the owner would be liable for all errors or difficulties or failures.[69] I cannot imagine what I would have done if, the day after Philip's resignation, Brody and Baum had not rehired him.

In their book chronicling the history of the Four Seasons, restaurant critic John Mariani and Alex von Bidder, general manager and co-owner of the restaurant, noted Philip's acknowledgment of Pahlmann's input on chair and table placement, as well as kitchen layout.[70] They also credited Pahlmann with the idea of installing a pool, to make the Pool Room (which Philip confirmed),[71] since the integrity of the very large space would have been violated by the installation of row after row of tables and chairs. To solve this problem, Mariani and von Bidder explained, "Pahlmann came up with a brilliant concept. Why not put a twenty-foot-square white Carrara marble pool in the middle of the dining room? Lighted softly from below and set at table level, a pool would have a softening effect on the geometry of the room, and the pleasant bubbling of the water would have a soothing effect on the diners."[72]

Mariani and von Bidder also characterized the enormous challenge of designing the Four Seasons in ways that I had never thought about: "Johnson had to contend with three different levels, the first being the entrance on 52nd Street, the next the two dwarfing spaces for dining connected by a hallway, and a third set back into the second." The authors quote Johnson as saying,

> I was faced with all the taboos about restaurant design. . . . They said that the toilets must all be on the same floor as the dining area. They said the entrance to the dining room must be as far as possible from the service station and kitchen door. They told me putting a stairway leading to the dining room was a no-no. I certainly had no idea about how to design a table. And right from the start, I knew that the space was much too big for a restaurant. So really, I was just trying to fill the space somehow, stay true to Mies's design for the building, and keep the commission. There's a lot of wasted space, you know. But there is in a great cathedral, too, isn't there?[73]

Philip made the one-story ascent from the entry on Fifty-Second Street to the restaurant above almost imperceptible with the grand Miesian (but differently articulated) stair he designed, rising from the low-ceilinged travertine room to the large, inviting stairwell opening above, where with each step one perceived more of the activity of the vast, dramatically lit Grill Room with its rich wood walls and Lippold sculpture (figs. 94, 95). Mies had provided the shell of the two grand rooms, sixty by ninety by twenty feet high. To create these impressive spaces, he had eliminated two center columns to make a sixty-foot clear span and raised the far end of the room by some four feet to accommodate car and truck entrances on the streets below, resulting in a terrace or mezzanine, so that the main impression is of sixty-foot-square volumes (fig. 96). Philip further defined these volumes with the mezzanine walls: in the Grill Room, a similar walnut mezzanine wall is pushed back, allowing the narrow end stairs to lead to a one-table-deep balcony space (two modules wide), whose long wall encloses two private dining rooms (three modules deep) (see fig. 101). In the Pool Room, the doors of a French walnut screen at the edge of the mezzanine can be open or closed, and a broad central stair gives access to the space behind (fig. 97). Between the two great rooms and at the same ceiling height, Philip created a travertine passage ninety feet long and three modules deep, behind which lies the kitchen, out of sight.

The twenty-foot-high ceilings, according to Mariani and von Bidder, had an inhuman scale that worked against any thought of intimacy in a restaurant, and lighting such spaces

94 Philip Johnson, architect, with William Pahlmann, interior designer, Four Seasons Restaurant, view of the Grill Room with Richard Lippold sculpture from staircase edge. Photograph: Ezra Stoller, 1959.

OPPOSITE TOP

95 Philip Johnson, architect, with William Pahlmann, interior designer, Four Seasons Restaurant, view of the Grill Room with Richard Lippold sculpture from mezzanine. Photograph: Louis Reens, 1959.

OPPOSITE BOTTOM

96 Philip Johnson, architect, with William Pahlmann, interior designer, Four Seasons Restaurant, floor plan, 1959.

PRIVATE DINING ROOM
DINING ROOM
KITCH. VEST.
SERVICE BAR
KITCHEN
WINE CELLAR
DINING ROOM VESTIBULE
LOBBY
BAR - GRILLE VESTIBULE
PRIVATE DINING
BAR & GRILLE MEZZANINE
BAR & GRILL
D'N
BAR
UP
PLAZA
EAST LOBBY
PLAZA
UP
UP
5

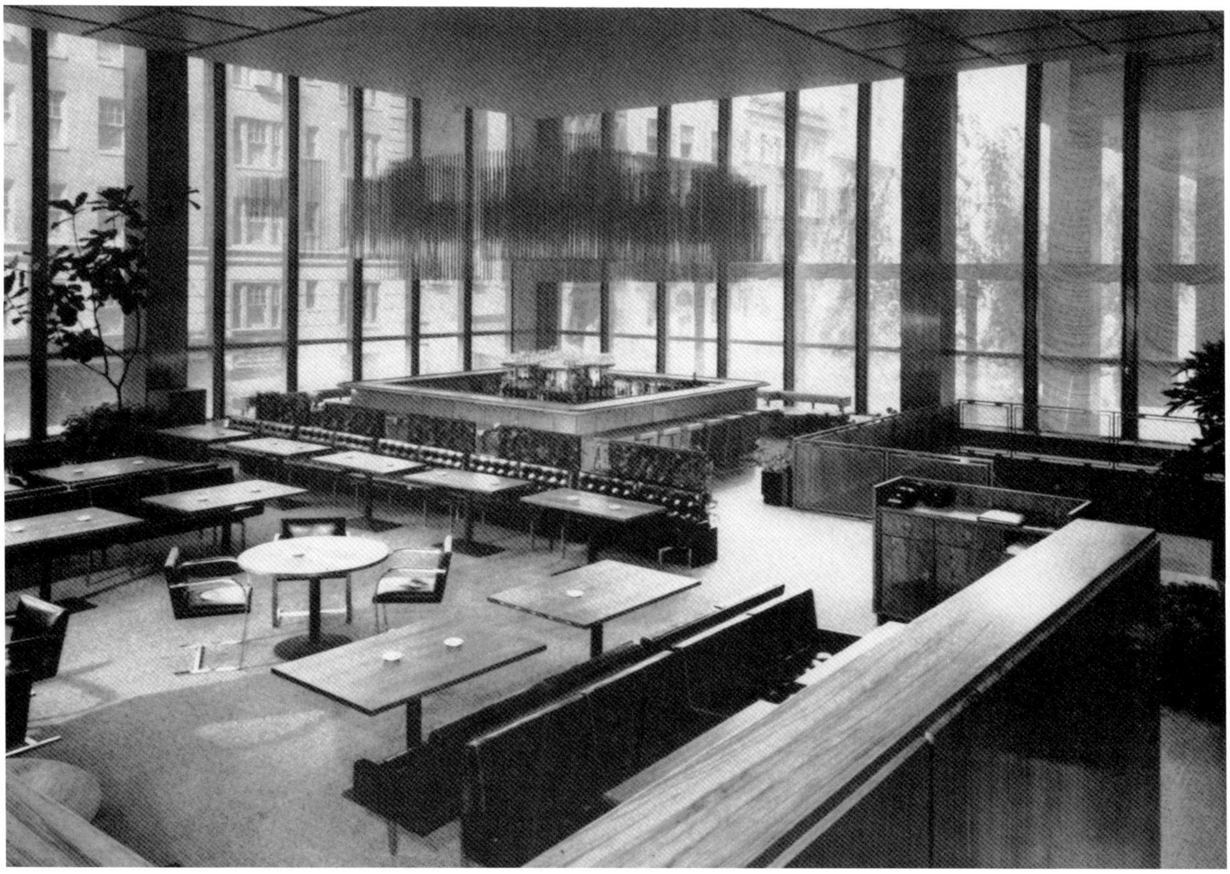

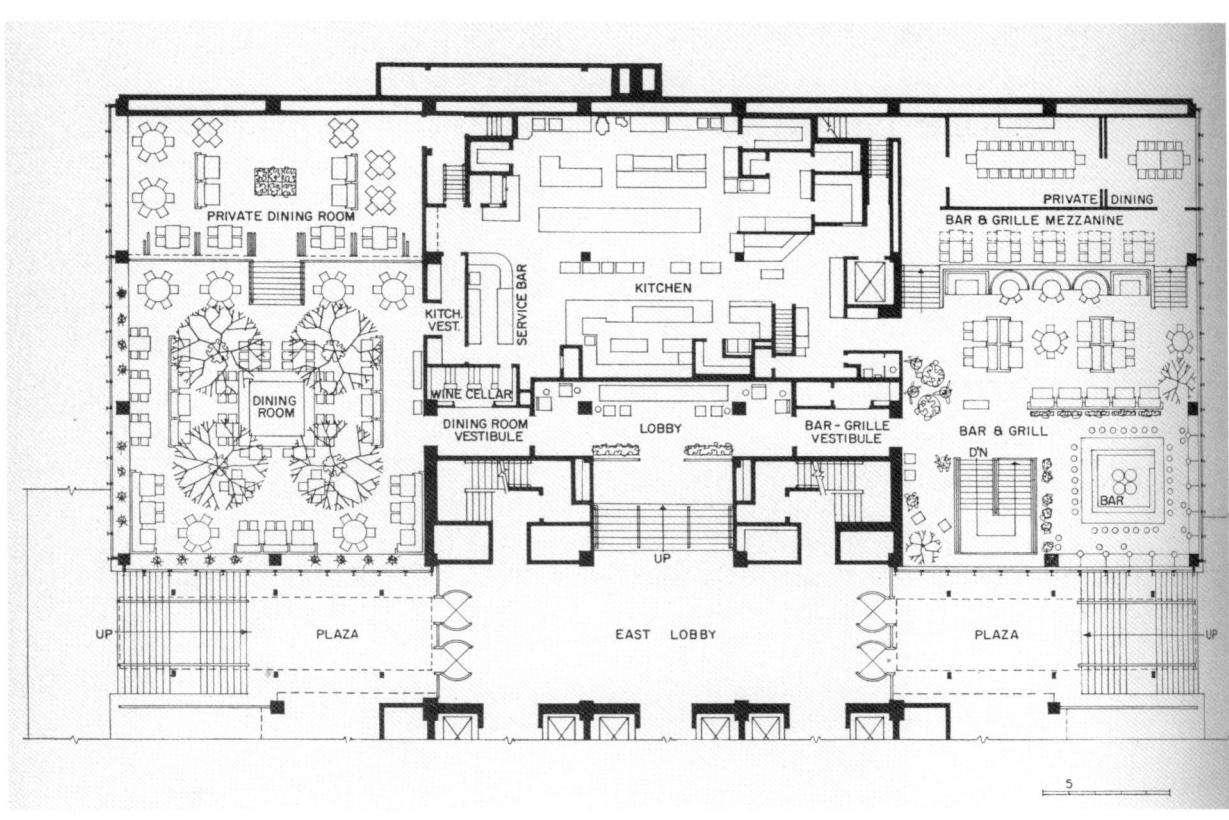

97 Philip Johnson, architect, with William Pahlmann, interior designer, Four Seasons Restaurant, view of the Pool Room looking toward the mezzanine screen wall with central panels open. Photograph: Louis Reens, 1959.

98 Philip Johnson, architect, Four Seasons Restaurant, multipurpose ceiling in construction, 1959, Richard Kelly, lighting consultant and Edison Price, manufacturer, photograph from *Progressive Architecture,* May 1960.

99 Philip Johnson, architect, Four Seasons Restaurant, sections through "darklight" and ceiling suspension system, Richard Kelly, lighting consultant and Edison Price, manufacturer, drawing from *Progressive Architecture,* May 1960.

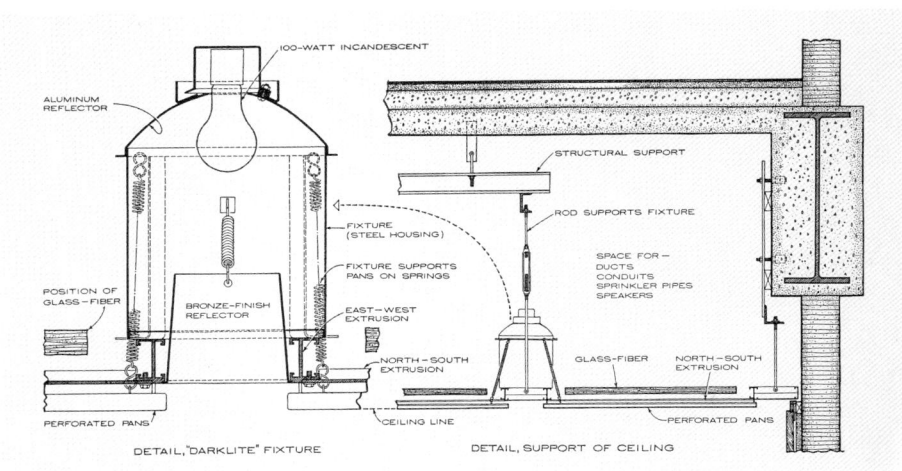

seemed impossible with existing technologies.[74] At that time, lighting fixtures that could achieve the kind of effects Johnson and RA desired didn't exist, so consultant Richard Kelly, together with manufacturer Edison Price, had to invent them.[75] The strongly articulated ceiling grids in the Pool and Grill Rooms continue the rhythm of the mullions of the glass walls that form the outer corners of the rooms, answered by the paneled walls forming the reentrant inner corners of the rooms. Over a network of ducts and wiring, the ceilings are permeable diaphragms from which flows most of the "well-tempered" environment: air, light, and sound. This membrane was developed by Philip and Richard Kelly together with Edison Price, who designed, produced, and installed the light fixtures and rib and panel system composing the ceiling surface, which is coordinated with the building module (fig. 98). Acoustic speakers are unseen behind the gridded dark gray aluminum ceiling canopy, and stage lights may be attached to the grid when necessary (fig. 99). In order to modulate the fine distinctions of mood that are key to successful restaurants, illumination throughout the restaurant spaces is variable according to the time of day, weather conditions, number of people, or type of meal or event. This theatrical ambience is achieved through a lighting console forming part of the maître d'hôtel's reception desk, which controls seventy dimmers and almost as many circuits, with presets that allow for fifty-four different changes.

In the Four Seasons, Kelly brought light-washed walls, his principle of "ambient luminescence," to a highly controlled level of expression. At the Fifty-Second Street entrance, the travertine walls and floors are similarly light washed by Price's "dark-lights" in the ceiling. This tomblike space is not Mies but Johnson (fig. 100). We are reminded of the bedroom at the Brick Guest House and its ethereal guest room—with its memory of Schinkel's fabric-draped walls for Queen Luise—in the pink and silver Fortuny cloth that lines the walls of the Ladies' Powder Room, which opens off the travertine entrance to the restaurant.

The swags of Queen Luise's bedchamber also resonate in an unexpectedly spectacular aspect of the two great Four Seasons dining rooms: the veil of the "Venetian" curtains made of fine-gauge aluminum chains falling in a catenary curve at the window walls (see figs. 94, 95, PF 12, and PF 13). I was impressed by the genius of the idea when Philip and I visited the studio of Marie Nichols, the textile designer who developed these curtains with Richard Kelly to give sparkle, after sculptor Richard Lippold suggested using metal chains that "would echo the shimmering light of his own sculptures."[76] Yet only when they were hung did we understand the extraordinary effect of the movement induced by the heated or cooled air rising from the convectors at the window wall, causing the lightweight yellow-gold, copper or reddish gold, and darkish silver anodized aluminum chains to move with slow, wavelike motion.[77] When first installed, they were considered a potential disaster:

100 Philip Johnson, architect, Four Seasons Restaurant, Fifty-Second Street Lobby staircase. Photograph: Louis Reens, 1959.

101 Richard Pare, view of Richard Lippold bronze sculpture installed over the mezzanine, Grill Room, Four Seasons Restaurant, 2011. Chromogenic laser print, 24 × 19 in.

Johnson thought that they might make diners feel ill. But when he saw Baum's enthusiastic reaction, Philip said later, "I got the feeling that when Baum saw those lighted chain curtains, he was going to let me do whatever I wanted in the restaurant."[78] As in Schinkel's bedroom for Queen Luise, "light [is] reflected and filtered through the material."[79] At times during the day the curtains are almost transparent, but in the evening they gain varying degrees of opacity and reflectivity as the maître d'hôtel manipulates the controls on the lighting console to change the mood in the room by orchestrating the intensity of "ambient light," the "focal glow" of pools of soft light on the tables, and a "play of brilliants" among sculpture and plants—thus manifesting Kelly's three principles for creating a seductive environment using light.

Richard Lippold's sculpture over the bar in the Four Seasons Grill Room was Philip's answer to Brody's request to create a more intimate space in the vast, high-ceilinged room. This tiered piece, measuring some twenty-two feet square, is constructed of fifteen hundred quarter-inch-square bronze rods, composed in square and rectangular bundles one to five feet long, suspended by nearly invisible wires. To balance this, Lippold added a pendent sculpture mounted high on the mezzanine wall of the Grill Room, explaining that "because the room is square and the general disposition of the elements it contains are asymmetrical

". . . a second sculpture in the opposite corner would be desirable to respect the room's symmetry" (fig. 101 and see fig. 111).[80]

The solution was brilliant. The principal piece over the bar is effectively a transparent, luminous volume. The sculptural construct seems to float like a cloud, creating a new plane virtually lowering the height of the ceiling over the bar area. It fosters an ambient intimacy (fig. 102) and creates the excitement inherent in a work whose aspect changes with the viewer's position. This piece, and its smaller complement installed diagonally across the room, which infer the building's architectural intention and the room's space, are at one with the form and materials of Mies's building.[81]

The myriad elements of the two sculptures, which "sparkle" when light is focused on them, allowed Kelly to introduce his third principle of lighting: the "play of brilliants." This "aesthetic ocular stimulus" is also unleashed in a private dining room just off the mezzanine. A "sparkling" ceiling composed of miniature incandescent lamps mounted in metal panels hovers over the room (fig. 103). Although made especially for Kelly by Edison Price, was this Kelly's idea or Philip's? In an April 1959 issue of the *New Yorker*, the author described a sparkling gossamer curtain Kelly designed as being "strung with countless electric bulbs so infinitesimal as to be practically invisible by daylight."[82] Nevertheless, the

102 Bar with Lippold sculpture above, Four Seasons Restaurant. Photograph: Louis Reens, 1959.

LIGHT: PHILIP JOHNSON'S *STIMMUNG*

103 Four Seasons Restaurant, private dining room with "play of brilliants" ceiling designed by Philip Johnson, architect, with Richard Kelly, lighting consultant, and Edison Price, manufacturer. Photograph: Superior Electric Company.

104 Karl Friedrich Schinkel, *Hall of the Stars in the Palace of the Queen of the Night,* set design for Mozart's *Magic Flute,* act 1, scene 6, 1815. Aquatint after Schinkel by C. F. Thiele, 1874, 17 × 24 in.

boldness of the starry field recalls the 1874 aquatint representing Schinkel's most famous stage set, the *Hall of the Stars in the Palace of the Queen of the Night,* which he designed for the first act of Mozart's *Magic Flute* (fig. 104). This image is one that anyone thinking of Schinkel's extraordinary range, especially Philip Johnson, would know.

In the travertine passage linking the Grill Room to the Pool Room, Picasso's *Le Tricorne* exerts a powerful presence (fig. 105). The nineteen-foot-square stage curtain, originally commissioned by the celebrated impresario of the Ballets Russes, Sergei Diaghilev, is the height of the travertine wall as if it were made for the space. It marks the summit of the plaza entry sequence: designed to be seen from afar, its magisterial presence is the focal point of the long vista of successive spaces leading from the building to the restaurant entrance, making it wholly and intimately connected to both the Seagram building and the restaurant. (The remarkable history and acquisition of *Le Tricorne* is detailed in the following chapter.) One of the numerous ironies of this integration into the space is that

105 Pablo Picasso, *Le Tricorne* stage curtain, 1919, viewed in "Picasso Alley" linking the Grill Room and Pool Room, Four Seasons Restaurant, Philip Johnson, architect. Photograph: Ezra Stoller, 1959.

Philip originally wanted to place the curtain elsewhere. He referred to "the big battle of where to put the Picasso,"[83] wanting to install *Le Tricorne* in the Pool Room. Where remains a mystery, for the mezzanine, at fifteen feet high, is not high enough, and the only twenty-foot-high free wall is bisected by the entrance and encumbered on one side by the captain's station. Joe Baum reportedly objected to placing it in the dining room: "Picasso depicted a bullfight . . . and I just didn't think that would go down well with customers dining on tournedos of beef."[84]

What came to be the Pool Room unfortunately lacks what would have completed the *Stimmung* of Philip's design of the space: a suite of paintings originally commissioned from Mark Rothko for the mezzanine space. Elevated almost five feet above the rest of the room, the mezzanine is in effect a stage framed by a proscenium-like screen wall, composed of five paired door panels in the fifteen-foot-high French walnut wall, which when closed create a separate room (see fig. 117). When these are opened like a drawn-back curtain revealing the room behind, a suite of Rothkos on the far wall would have spiritually and phenomenally dominated the larger room.

Philip was a longtime admirer of Rothko's work; for years during the design of the Seagram building we lived with one Rothko painting that Philip hung in the office.[85] I was intrigued and enthusiastic about the possibility of a group of paintings that would create a dialectic; I outline the specific details of the commission's tortuous history in the following chapter. The commission was a curatorial decision taken by Philip Johnson, architect of the interior of the room, who willed a *Gesamtkunstwerk,* and myself, a young woman who willed the creation of a building that expresses "the best of the society in which we live." Had Rothko provided us with the paintings as planned, the upper portion of what is now the room would have emanated a glowing, spiritual presence. I very much regretted Rothko's decision not to participate, but I came to understand: he was creating a series of sacred works. Eating and drinking with his paintings in the background would constitute the same inattention, the same lack of conviction and authenticity as chatting with friends while someone is playing a Bach cello concerto.

Although it was never intended to be so, the major feature of the room is now the central thirty-foot-square white marble pool. The tall trees at each corner emphasize the volume of the square within a square.[86] Seductive as the Pool Room is, however, it lacks the conceptual wholeness that the great suite of Rothkos would have brought to the space.

A single painting on the wall—even the large Lichtenstein that hung there for years, like all other paintings that have been placed on the east wall of the Pool Room, was only an addition, not an integral component of the room. It is impossible to conceive of the Bar and Grill Room without the Lippold sculptures or to think of the Seagram lobby and the Four Seasons without Picasso's *Le Tricorne.* There is no substitute for the essential dimension that art brings. Without critical art in the Pool Room, there is no object that possesses or exercises a comparable presence and ability to engage both attention and imagination. Although it is a wonderful space, the Pool Room is orphaned for lack of a link to the other two spaces.[87]

In the late 1990s, Philip proposed an architectonic sculpture for the mezzanine of the Pool Room in the lexicon of Da Monsta, the 1995 visitors' pavilion at his New Canaan estate. Three-dimensional wall surfaces composed of folded planes were to rise from the floor, engulfing the ceiling, the end wall, and the upper part of the screen wall, with planes forming an integral work of art that is inhabited by people, who in turn inhabit the space (fig. 106). The walls would have modulated light and engaged movement, changing as the viewer moved through the space. The plan's genius was to treat the room as a whole, just as Rothko had intended. This proposal, in a work of art of his own devising, would have completed Johnson's imprimatur on the art of the Four Seasons Restaurant. I championed it, but it did not go ahead.

Plants were to be an integral part of the interior design of the Four Seasons, as suggested by the restaurant's name. Landscape architect Karl Linn's concept was to have "permanent specimen planting, strong entities, and decorative 'exhibition' flower displays" during each

106 Philip Johnson, architect, model of project for the Pool Room mezzanine, Four Seasons Restaurant, 1996. Photograph: Robert Walker, 1996.

season.[88] In contrast to Johnson's Glass House, where the building structure frames the landscape, in the Four Seasons Restaurant, the play of the natural forms of leaves and branches heightens the effect of the disciplined architecture. Kelly placed uplights in the bronze housings at the base of each plant, which project patterns of light onto the ceiling (see fig. 97). This effect is especially dramatic in the Pool Room, where at the four corners of the square pool, large ornamental *Ficus decora,* or fig trees, were originally placed to dominate the space and at the same time create an intimate environment. Downlights in the ceiling cast subtle shadows onto the surface of the dining tables, while uplights in pots illuminated the underside of the leaves, transforming the trees into a sheltering canopy. It soon became clear that the light in the room was not sufficient to keep the ficus trees alive, and they had to be replaced, but trees and the pool became the counterpart of Lippold's sculptures in the Grill Room. Given the geometry of the half-cubic rooms and the clarity and purity of the decorative treatment of their two solid and two transparent glass walls, the Four Seasons is not an indoor garden, despite the strategic placement of plants. Rather, Johnson and Kelly established a fine balance between the architectural frame and the refined surfaces—the rippling chain curtains and parchment paneling in one room, the book-matched French walnut paneling in the other, all bathed in light—and the pointillist effect of the light-dappled plants.

These rooms were orchestrated with a theatrical sensibility, where lighting played a crucial role. The subtle effects used to light the trees and pool in the dining rooms of the Four Seasons connect the interior of the restaurant with the illuminated trees and fountains on the plaza and the glow of the Seagram building day and night (see PF 13). Philip Johnson did not have to struggle with tectonics: he had only to conjure up an interior environment within the space of Mies's structure. With the unleashing of his refined responsiveness to light and materials, as well as his sense of history, Johnson came into his own. He brought Schinkel's genius for evoking *Stimmung* to Mies's appreciation of Schinkel's "wonderful constructions, excellent proportions and good detailing."[89]

5

ARCHITECTURE AND ART ALLIED

Together, the Seagram building and plaza constituted a model of what could be done on all levels, inside and out, a total work, a *Gesamtkunstwerk*. Philip Johnson's keen interest in art as well as design and my own interest in the relationship among architecture, art, and the public realm motivated Seagram to support a contemporary art program for the new building. This extended to the purchase and commissioning of works for its offices and markedly for the public spaces of the Seagram building, as well as mounting public exhibitions.

Corporations had always collected art, but not at the time—to my knowledge—the work of contemporary artists. However, this began to take hold over the course of the 1950s.[1] Although a few collections formed immediately after World War II were oriented toward established European art, interest in American art was keenest and the fastest growing: of the twenty corporate collections with American art in the 1950s, half of those holdings were contemporary by the end of the decade.[2]

From the moment Seagram moved into its new building in December 1957, artifacts and eventually exhibitions began to animate the company's offices, the building, and the plaza, playing a significant role over five decades in the public life of the building.[3] My account of collecting and public art programs initiated by Seagram is intended to give a sense of the dynamic interplay between art and architecture, the private domain of the company, the public realm of the building, and the players: Philip, myself, and those concerned with the integration of art and architecture. Our approach was consonant with the architect John Soane's intent "to shew . . . the union and close connexion between Painting, Sculpture, and Architecture,—Music and Poetry" in his house and collections at Lincoln's Inn fields in early nineteenth-century London.[4]

My intention in forming collections for Seagram was to recover interconnections among the arts.[5] Seagram's collections were formed at three different scales: the public realm of the ground level, with the Four Seasons Restaurant and the plaza; the company's semiprivate reception areas; and the private domain of the company's offices. All three were being considered during the summer and fall of 1957 when the building enclosure was being completed and spaces for Seagram were successively finished from below grade to the ninth floor.[6] The responsibility for forming the collections was mine, and remained so over four decades. I had been trained in the study and practice of sculpture from an early age, but it was through the extraordinary education, opportunities, and connections afforded me at Vassar College that I developed my interest in the interconnections of the arts and in modern art. Especially resonant for me was the National Intercollegiate Arts Conference, at Vassar in February 1948, with the theme the Creative Arts in Contemporary Society, where I curated the exhibition *Modern Design: Art and Architecture*. This exhibition was immensely important for me, as much so as formal classes, in leading to my role in building Seagram. Hence it establishes the first image for this chapter (fig. 107).[7]

These interests and animated conversations with those in the arts continued in the 1950s, while working on the Seagram building. My environment from 1954 to 1959 was fueled by the quest for the highest values in artistic life. On weekends, Philip Johnson invited me, along with a coterie of friends, mostly architects and architecture students from Yale, to his Glass House in New Canaan, Connecticut, where aspects of architecture were always discussed: current projects, books, history. Looking at the drawings being produced in Mies's office raised many questions for me about modes of representation, notational conventions, and subject matter, some of which also encompassed the client and the builder across time and in disparate places. Thus, cultural inquiry became the basis for forming Seagram's collections in the 1950s—and ultimately led to my founding the Canadian Centre for Architecture (CCA) in Montreal in 1979 as a research center and museum.

Art for the public space of the building became of consuming interest as soon as Mies's project for Seagram was officially accepted in March 1955. The stories of research for

107 John Cage, Phyllis Lambert, and others during the National Intercollegiate Conference on the Creative Arts in Contemporary Society, Vassar College, Poughkeepsie, New York, February 27–29, 1948. Photograph: Haig W. Shekerjian.

ARCHITECTURE AND ART ALLIED

sculpture for the plaza, for theater curtains and tapestries and paintings for the restaurant, are legendary as they engaged Constantin Brancusi, Pablo Picasso, Richard Lippold, and Mark Rothko.

In the summer of 1955, I met Brancusi in his "whitewashed shack of a studio" at the Impasse Ronsin in the Fifteenth Arrondissement of Paris through an American friend who had a studio there. Brancusi, with a broken leg, his huge beard, and a nightcap covering his hair—all white—was propped up in bed. A gong the diameter of the bed hung above him, and he struck it whenever he needed help; the other inhabitants of the Impasse were quite at ease with him. I had brought him roses and asked for a vase, but he insisted that they lie a while, saying, "They must suffer to be beautiful." I recorded the visit: "We drank champagne with flies buzzing and a terrific heat, Brancusi telling me lovely stories. He is so very much like Mies—how right it seems to have their work together."[8] Brancusi proposed enlarging a piece titled *Le Coq*. I continued to correspond with him through the publisher H. P. Roché. For the Seagram "piazzetta," as he termed it, Roché thought *Bird in Space* would be ideal, and that Brancusi would certainly be pleased to collaborate with Mies on the plans for the fountains and reflecting pool of the plaza. Roché was emphatic about the choice of *Bird in Space,* preferring it, as did I then, to *Le Coq,* which was "too anecdotal"; he wrote: "It's the image of a *coq*'s crow."[9] *La Colonne sans fin* (The endless column), which I had thought to be a possibility for the plaza, Roché considered to be too much like Mies's tower; he added that it had already been realized in gigantic proportions, ninety-eight feet high, installed in a clearing in a public park in Târgu Jiu, Romania. In a letter written two weeks later, dated September 1, 1955, Roché wrote that Brancusi was doubtless waiting for a visit from me, Sweeney, and himself at the beginning of October.[10] Brancusi, he explained, was often in a state of "Nirvana," indifferent to money but not to glory, and we could succeed if we could interest him in the project, "like a great toy." In another ten weeks, Roché reported that Brancusi was pleased that I liked his exhibition at the Guggenheim in New York. He added, "We are quietly waiting for your visit."[11] (The Brancusi exhibition was installed by James Johnson Sweeney in rooms sheathed in white to cover the conventional interiors of the rather grand townhouse at 1071 Fifth Avenue that served as the Guggenheim's temporary quarters while Frank Lloyd Wright's conchoidal spiral was being constructed on the avenue further to the north.) This was the last Brancusi letter. No follow-up. I probably discussed with Philip Johnson my discomfort at the idea of enlarging a work of sculpture and did not further pursue the question of sculpture on the plaza.[12] I wonder if I would have thought differently had I seen one of the very fine photographs Brancusi made to study various arrangements of his work in his studio, like one dating from the early 1940s that includes two very large plaster versions of *Le Coq,* which he had been working on since 1923 (fig. 108).[13]

Attention turned to the great rooms of the Four Seasons as Philip Johnson was planning the restaurant. In 1957 Richard Lippold had already started working on the commission to create an intimate space over the bar area in the southwest quadrant of the Grill Room, which Johnson astutely proposed (see figs. 94, 95). This was well before the contract was signed in 1958.[14] What is remarkable is how Lippold conceived his work not only in relation to the interior space—what he called "one of the great rooms in the world for this century"—but to the architecture of the entire building:

> My first concern when I was asked by Philip Johnson and Phyllis Lambert to consider a work for this space, was to examine in great detail every aspect of the total building.

108 Constantin Brancusi, studio view with several versions of the *Grand Coq*, Paris. Gelatin silver print from original glass plate by Jacques Faujour, 9½ × 7 in. Photograph: Constantin Brancusi, c. 1940–45.

The first conclusion I arrived at is that . . . the two rooms which constitute the main dining areas of the Four Seasons Restaurant are squares, the most . . . beautiful kind of space that a human being can experience.

They are half as high as they are wide, so they actually constitute each, one half a cube. Not only that, but their significance in relation to the entire building is that they sit like space fundaments on which the towers of the building rise. . . .

I then considered the proportions of the rooms and was given the suggestion that all I should create is something that would not destroy the space of the rooms or diminish them, but to create a lowering of that part of the ceiling over the bar to create a more intimate effect.

This I felt I accomplished and I chose as material and form the suggestion of the great suspended mullions on the outside of the building. . . . The perfect section of these mullions in their verticality emphasizing the verticality of the building [surging]

ARCHITECTURE AND ART ALLIED

109 Richard Lippold, detail of bronze rods suspended on stainless steel wires above the bar, viewed from below, Grill Room, Four Seasons Restaurant. Photograph: Louis Reens, 1959.

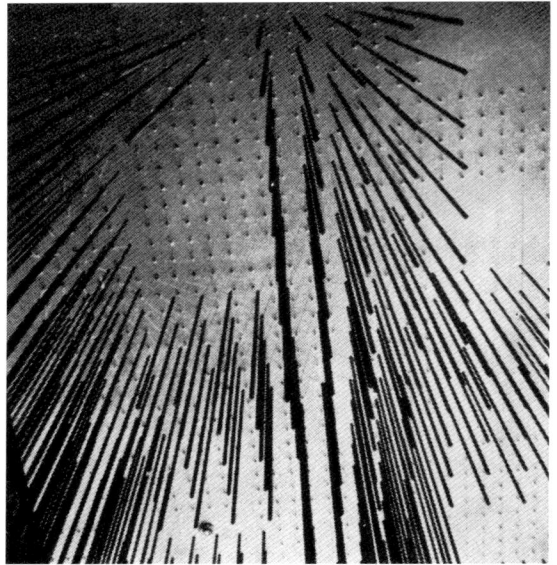

into the space . . . is what I reduced to human scale in the sculpture which now inhabits that space [figs. 109, 110].

The divisions, the spaces between each rod is in perfect proportion to the room itself, the large sculpture, occupies one fourth of the space and half of the height so it is actually in proportion one-eighth of the volume of that room.

The echo wing sculpture on the other side is half of that, so it is one sixteenth of it. So this creates a harmony of the large scale of the building to a detail at the interior which is the simple, you might say, of the nature of that structure [fig. 111, and see fig. 101].[15]

Lippold installed the sculptures himself with great care, suspending one tube at a time. An eyewitness described him working: "[He] would go up the ladder, put one [tube] up, adjust it, come back down the ladder, stare at it, then comb his hair. Then he'd go back up the ladder and put in another one."[16]

In the summer of 1957 another major work, Picasso's *Le Tricorne,* the magnificent stage curtain for Diaghilev's ballet of 1919, was acquired for the building.[17] It seemed a miracle to find a work whose size, muted tonality, and classical repose would fit Mies's building so perfectly (fig. 112). The subject of the canvas, ostensibly a bullfight, focuses on two groups of spectators in the foreground, *majas* wearing mantillas, a *mujer* sporting his red cloak, and, in the center, a boy selling oranges—none of whom pays attention to the scene represented in the background, where a pair of horses drag the vanquished bull (we see only his head) across an arcaded bullring. Ballet historian Nesta Macdonald intriguingly identified the figure on the left as Picasso himself; next to him, the ballerina Olga Khokhlova, whom he married in 1918; Stanislas Idzikowski, the diminutive, brilliant dandy of the ballet, is comically represented here as a ragamuffin; choreographer Léonide Massine is in the ring with a whip; and the Goyaesque *maja* in profile is as Diaghilev himself in drag.[18] Picasso had been drawing Ingres-like portraits of those around him for some time, and while in London he made drawings of many who were associated with the Ballets Russes, so it is readily conceivable that members of the ballet company could have served as models for the somewhat caricatured figures of the curtain.[19] For example, the *maja* to the left bears a resemblance to Picasso's portrait of *Olga Khokhlova à la mantilla* (June 1917).[20] However,

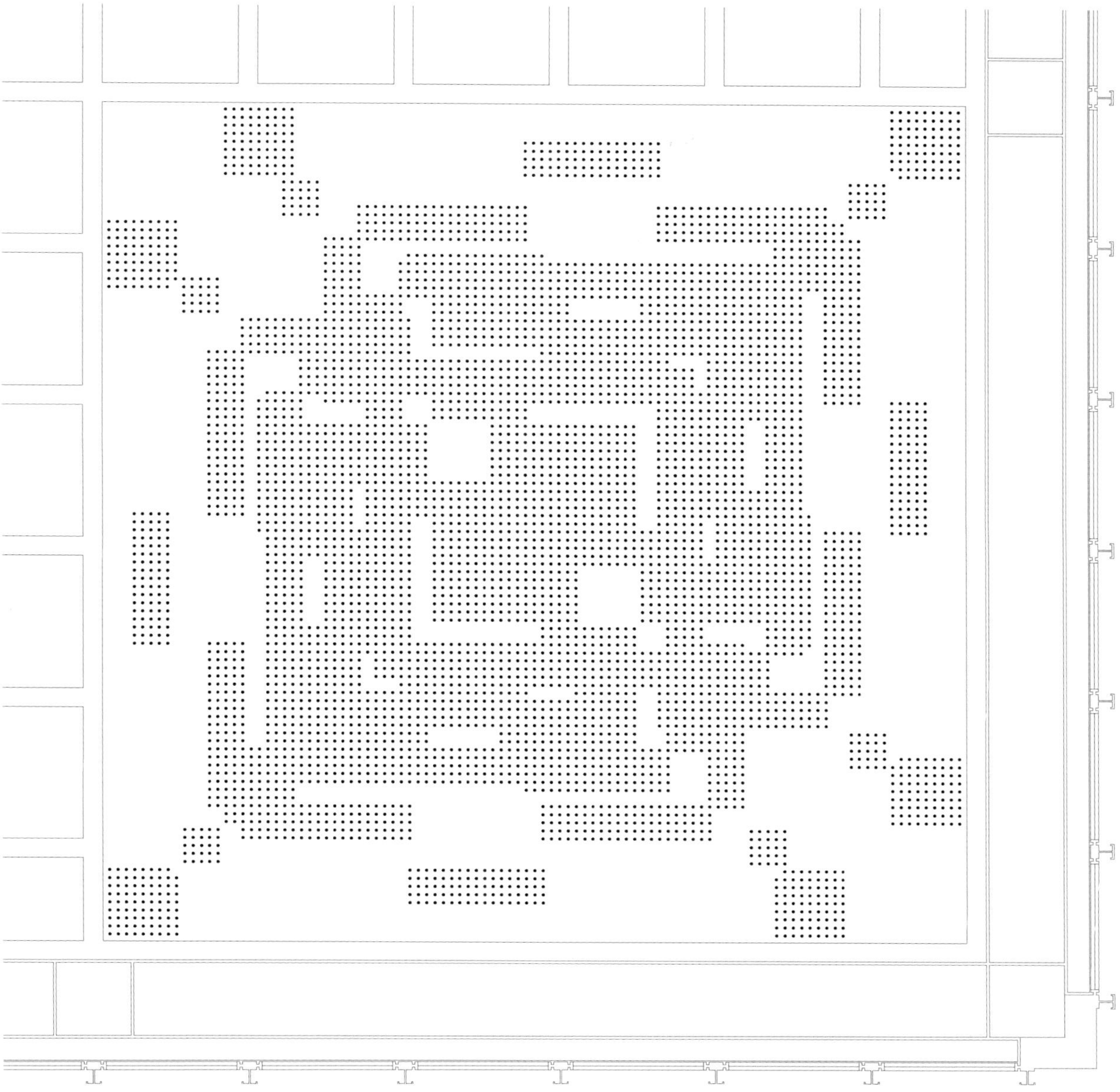

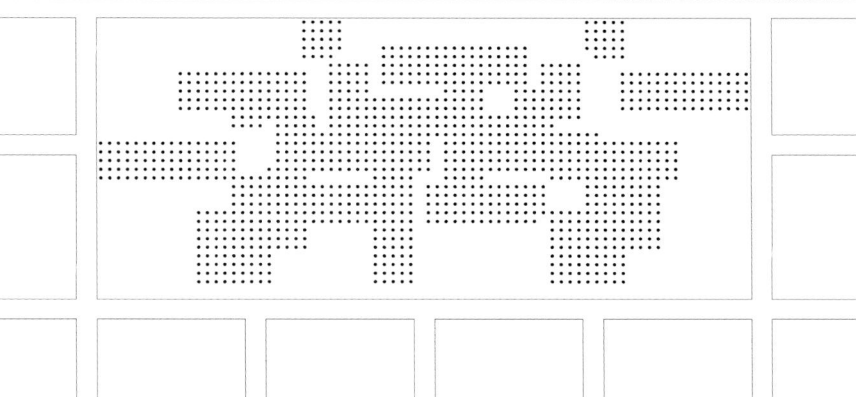

110 Richard Lippold, reflected ceiling plan for wire attachments suspending bronze rod sculpture above the bar, Grill Room, Four Seasons Restaurant, 1958. Redrawn by Catherine Bella, 2011.

111 Richard Lippold, reflected ceiling plan for wire attachments suspending bronze rod sculpture at the mezzanine, Grill Room, Four Seasons Restaurant, 1958. Redrawn by Catherine Bella, 2011.

112 Pablo Picasso, *Le Tricorne* stage curtain, 1919, in "Picasso Alley," Four Seasons Restaurant, Seagram building. Photograph: Richard Pare, 1979.

Picasso biographer and critic John Richardson considers the figures too generalized to support such attributions.[21]

Le Tricorne (The three-cornered hat) was an entirely new ballet. While in Barcelona in 1917, Diaghilev had commissioned Manuel de Falla to compose the music for a ballet based on Pedro de Alarcón's 1875 novel of Andalusian life, *El Sombrero de tres picos*. Léonide Massine choreographed the work. On May 25, 1919, Picasso, who was to be responsible for the sets and costumes, arrived with Olga Khokhlova in London, where Diaghilev would present a series of new dances. Diaghilev rented a large studio in Covent Garden, where the Russian scene painters Vladimir Polunin and his wife, Elizabeth Violet, produced the

113 Pablo Picasso, study for *Le Tricorne* stage curtain, 1919. Gouache and graphite on paper, 7¾ × 10½ in. Photograph: Hervé Lewandowski.

stage curtains. Polunin, who recalled that he and Violet executed most of the ballet's backdrop according to Picasso's studies and under his supervision, described the artist working directly on the canvas: "The drop curtain having been drawn and the general tones carefully roughed in, Picasso himself set to work on its central portion while my wife and I prepared the colors and helped him in everything. After working on the curtain for more than a fortnight, he asked me to stop him when, according to the demands of the stage (which he said I knew better than he did), he had achieved the most suitable result. This I did."[22]

The writer and critic Sacheverell Sitwell visited the studio (with Diaghilev and Massine in attendance) while Picasso was painting the *rideau de scène,* recalling that for broad effects, the artist used a brush attached to a broom handle, and for more detailed work, a toothbrush. Sitwell confirmed the assertion that Picasso painted the central section, the *corrida* scene: "Picasso in carpet slippers and with a bottle of wine standing near him, was at work. The canvas lay stretched upon the floor, and Picasso was moving around at great speed over its surface (he wore carpet slippers for this purpose) walking with something of a skating motion.... I recall ... thinking that this was the nearest that modern eyes would ever get to the spectacle of Tiepolo ... at work."[23]

Picasso's large curtain representing a Spanish bullring had been the central part of the much larger *rideau de scène,* the introductory curtain that is the pictorial equivalent of an overture, and indeed Picasso asked Falla to compose an overture to accompany this scene.[24] The ballet's plot—concerning a magistrate (the despot of the three-cornered hat) who is charmed by the miller's wife and attempts to seduce her, but fails, to the delight of the villagers—has nothing to do with bullfighting. Richardson tells us that Massine and Diaghilev decided that this front curtain must be ultra-Spanish, and hence *tauromachic*.[25] Picasso's first sketches show vertical tiers of balconies occupied by Goyaesque *majas,* framing the image of a picador charging a bull; he made numerous drawings depicting this violent scene.[26] In another sketch he set a Cubist still life with a guitar against a representational view of the bullring.[27] The final version of the complete *rideau de scène* is known only from a watercolor study at the Musée National Picasso in Paris (fig. 113). It indicates the central

ARCHITECTURE AND ART ALLIED

scene pretty much as we know it, but framed by curtains, with the addition of surrounding deep borders, the vertical areas consisting of a Cubist guitar within an elongated diamond shape. Interestingly, the overall *rideau de scène* evokes eighteenth-century tapestries based on cartoons by Francisco de Goya, in which an allegorical or historical scene at the center is surrounded by swags, arabesques, and ornate borders—a formal concept that, according to Sitwell, Picasso intended.[28] This schema seems not to have been carried out; the scholar Douglas Cooper noted: "As the music began the theatre curtains parted to reveal a grey drop-curtain in the centre of which was a rectangular painting."[29]

A number of writers, critics, and friends considered *Le Tricorne* to be outside Picasso's avant-garde pursuit. Roland Penrose wrote that "nothing of the revolutionary nature of *Parade* [Picasso's first work for Diaghilev] was involved, but the theme gave Picasso admirable scope to utilize and enjoy the atmosphere of his native country in the costumes and scenery."[30] Douglas Cooper characterized the project as "a sophisticated venture into the territory of folk and popular imagery [which] was an interlude for Picasso, though he made of it a great invention."[31] John Richardson, however, quite rightly I think, believes that for Picasso, *Le Tricorne* was "a useful vitrine for his emergent stylistic synthesis."[32] The costumes and the set, he posits, have come to be seen as Picasso's "supreme theatrical achievement."[33]

Surprisingly, beyond these major biographers, scholars have paid little attention to the curtain, which is formally, historically, and iconographically intriguing—both in the context of Picasso's oeuvre and in the culture of the Ballets Russes. In early 1957 not much of the curtain's history was known. It had traveled with the company, but in 1928, when Diaghilev needed money to finance new productions, he cut down the curtain himself and sold it to the Swiss collector G. F. Reber through the gallerist Paul Rosenberg.[34] The next known owner was a Frenchman, a Mr. Forest, who in 1948 offered the curtain to Alfred H. Barr, Jr., for the Museum of Modern Art.[35] At the end of 1956, the market for curtains designed for ballet performances was roiling, and by March 1957, Barr was at the center of another incident involving *Le Tricorne* when he wrote to Philip Johnson about three ballet curtains he knew were for sale. Léonide Massine, who then had a house and studio on Long Island, hoped Monroe Wheeler would be interested in purchasing Henri Matisse's 1938 curtain for *Rouge et noir* (*L'Étrange farandole*) and Salvador Dalí's 1941 curtain for *Labyrinth*.[36] In his letter to Johnson, Barr mentioned that he knew *Le Tricorne* was for sale, though he considered the price of fifty thousand dollars to be speculative: "So far as I know none of the curtains actually painted partly or entirely by Picasso has been sold but any work on that scale is a white elephant. I would not offer over $15,000 if you are interested and go up from there. The fact that the Matisse, if really holographic, is priced at $5,000–$10,000 certainly could be used as a bargaining point."[37]

Barr suggested that Philip and I carry on the discussion with art dealer Klaus G. Perls, who represented the owner. Two weeks later, Perls sent Philip "the best color transparency [he] was able to get."[38] A tedious hiatus in the negotiations ensued, during which a cat-and-mouse game I no longer recall had put me on edge. On July 12, 1957, I sent Perls (who was in Athens) a one-word cable: "SOLD."[39] In response to his reply dated July 13, 1957, I wrote him: "This fiddle faddling was unbearable and we still have not gotten a decision [presumably from Seagram]. There have also been other requests for it and so to simplify matters I am buying it myself."[40] The seller began pressing for payment immediately. In a subsequent letter to me dated July 20, 1957, Perls noted that the owner of the curtain had been bombarding Sickles (Perls's assistant) with requests for prompt payment and that he had replied: "I have told [Sickles] to tell her that no payment will be made before delivery."[41]

From this note it is clear that the last owner of the curtain was a woman, although her identity remains unknown.

On February 7, 1958, I received a letter from Perls and the "original" certificate for *Le Tricorne*, which consists of a statement written in red crayon in Picasso's hand on the back of a color photograph of the drop curtain: "This curtain for *Le Tricorne*, by my hand, was painted in London in 1919 Picasso/Cannes (A.M.) 20.2.1957."[42] Perls wrote: "Here are the photographs. I apologize for not having thought of this myself. And, at the same time I noticed that I was still in possession of the original Picasso certificate. . . . This is a valuable document."[43] I put little credence in such "certificates," which are part of a French dealer's practice with which artists sometimes collaborate. It was even less than convincing having been written decades after completion, when Perls was looking to sell the curtain. What mattered was that I had acquired, for the asking price, Picasso's curtain, which would be seen from Park Avenue on the long axis of the entrance to the building and the Four Seasons Restaurant. The curtain was delivered to me at Seagram on February 18, 1958,[44] Seagram purchased it from me the following year,[45] and thus *Le Tricorne* entered the public domain of New York City.

In a completely different venture, the summer of 1957 I visited Picasso with Marie Cuttoli (fig. 114). I loved Picasso's chunky plant studies and asked him to make four large ones for the Four Seasons Restaurant, which was then under construction, but alternatively he proposed *Les Baigneurs* for the plaza (fig. 115). However, I find in my files the draft of a letter I wrote in French to thank Picasso for my visit to his villa La Californie in Cannes, saying that it was almost too beautiful to be true that he had agreed to make the four sculptures for us. In the letter, "as promised," I provided technical details about the forms and materials of the building's skin, describing step by step the extrusion process used in making the mullions and keying these to enclosed photographs. I also noted the dimensions of the bronze sheets used for the spandrel panels and assured Picasso that we could send him the materials he would need so that he could fabricate the pieces in France, adding, "It seems to me difficult for you to make the sculpture without directing the work." Clearly, the sculptures were for the restaurant and not the plaza, for I wrote to him that "the building is splendid and waits for its Picasso sculptures—I will have three dimensional photographs made of your '*salle*' and of the building and will send them soon. . . . I will come to France instantly if you need me."[46] There was no follow-up. What remains is a faint memory of being told by Philip Johnson of the jealousy of Jacqueline Roque, whom Picasso would marry in 1961, who did not want Picasso to see me again. It might be the explanation of Philip's cryptic reference in the letter he wrote to Marie Cuttoli on January 3, 1958, saying, "Thank you for all that you have done for us with Picasso. Not only Mrs. Lambert, but all of us are extremely grateful for your tact and hard work."[47]

Another series of works, which were to my regret never installed in the restaurant, consisted of a sequence of canvases Mark Rothko was commissioned to paint for the mezzanine of what is now the Pool Room. As I write, I can visualize Rothko, Philip, and myself standing at the entrance to the room. According to Rothko, this was in the spring of 1958.[48] One could feel the rawness of the space. The floor, the ceiling, and the mezzanine were immense gray concrete fields. Their gloom was perpetuated in the two inner concrete block walls. The magnificence of the space was revealed as daylight suffused the room through the twenty-foot-high glass walls punctuated in the proportion of four-to-one by Mies's bronze mullions. Although I silently envisioned the paintings on the east wall, with the

114 Marie Cuttoli, Pablo Picasso, and Phyllis Lambert at Picasso's Villa La Californie, Cannes, viewing the *New York Times* advertising supplement on the Seagram building, summer 1957. Gelatin silver print, 9 ½ × 11 ¾ in. Photograph: André Villers.

115 Pablo Picasso, *Les Baigneurs*, 1956. Bronze after wood. Photographer unknown.

proscenium open, Rothko's handwritten notes about the commission (with certain words haltingly begun and then crossed out) indicate his somewhat conflicted understanding that the commission was:

> to fill a ~~pu~~[blic] space which was to be used as a ~~pub~~[lic] private room
>
> My one condition [was] that the place be an enclosed space. In so far as I have always maintained that if I should be given an ~~private~~ enclosed space which I could surround with my work it would be the realization of a dream that I have always held.
>
> The question of the dining room was always appealing to me for I immediately envisioned the refectory of the San Marco church with the wall painting by Fra Angelico. . . . What was obvious [was] that there was in me . . . a conception of a [place contained] and absolutely mine.[49]

On June 6, 1958, the preeminent dealer of the avant-garde, Sidney Janis, wrote to me on behalf of Rothko "to confirm conversations with Philip Johnson regarding the approximately 500 to 600 square feet of paintings the artist is to execute and install in quarters at 375 Park Avenue at the price agreed upon, namely, $35,000."[50] With seven thousand dollars issued at once by Seagram for Rothko's immediate expenses, at the end of June Rothko rented the gymnasium of a former YMCA at 222 The Bowery, where he erected a space approximating the dimensions of the Four Seasons' mezzanine. (According to Rothko's biographer James Breslin, the space was about nine feet shorter, two feet wider, and eight feet higher.)[51] Here, Rothko worked for the first time on a series, one painting in relation to another painting. Struggling, he made three separate series over two years: "The first pictures I made were in my old style. But soon I discovered that the old image would not serve the purpose. It became clear that to be a public man required a different attitude. Other pictures are made for nowhere. But once a specific place and permanence and the heterogeneousness of a public situation were involved a new image would have to be evolved."[52]

Rothko sold the panels separately as individual paintings. He said of the next series: "The second time I got the basic idea, but began to modify it as I went along—because, I guess, I was afraid of being too stark. When I realized my mistake, I started again, and this time I'm holding tight to the original conception."[53]

Of the first series of paintings, Michael Compton of the Tate observed that "they contain the merest suggestion of architectural elements."[54] With the second series, according to Rothko's assistant Dan Rice, he turned the paintings on their side. The result made the rectangular forms appear as vertical columns with openings between them, "suggesting windows, doors, portals."[55] The paintings were to be placed at least four feet, six inches from the ground to be above people's heads. Compton pointed out that, rather high, "they would . . . be seen from a variety of angles and would be scanned as a group by eyes moving predominantly in a horizontal plane, that is, they would be seen as architecture."[56] Rice believed that Rothko's decision to change the direction of the masses of his paintings, so that they read vertically rather than horizontally, represented a pivotal change in his work: "I think it was his absolute concern with architecture."[57] Like Lippold's, Rothko's art had a strong grounding in architecture, which is evident in his notes of 1960:

> There followed a series of steps in which every step was further and further reduced and at the last the extent of reduction was acceptable. In an age which has found no myths and symbols to express itself, the final image had to be free of interior connotations. The problem was to image an image which was whole and extraneous to

the several images themselves. In short to make a place rather than pictorial vestiges. When the project was achieved I realised that I had never forgotten M. A. [Michelangelo's] room which contained the stairway leading to the Lorenzo Library wherein the false bricked-in windows toward the top of the unrelieved brick walls made an interior world wholly pervasive and awesome [fig. 116].[58]

Rothko was always neurotically anxious about his work. Robert Motherwell wrote, "He liked one to treat him as a genius . . . [but] in his heart of hearts he also had a deep-rooted ambivalence, a persistent doubt, questioning his intimates as to whether he was a painter at all, that went far beyond an artist's usual doubts."[59] After eighteen months of strenuous work on the Seagram commission, Rothko was dissatisfied, disgruntled, and angry. Thus in the spring of 1959, he decided to take a vacation with his wife and daughter, sailing to Naples on the USS *Independence*. On the first night out, in the bar, he encountered John Hurt Fischer, to whom he vented his spleen. Fischer, inopportunely an editor at *Harper's Magazine,* transcribed the notes he took on their conversation. These formed the basis for his 1970 article published in *Harper's* as "Mark Rothko, Portrait of the Artist as an Angry Man," and thus became the source of the crude, often repeated reasons given for Rothko's disaffection.[60] Fischer asserted: "Rothko first remarked that he had been commissioned to paint a series of large canvases for the walls of the most exclusive room in a very expensive restaurant in the Seagram building—'a place where the richest bastards in New York will come to feed and show off.'" And further: "'I accepted this assignment as a challenge, with strictly malicious intentions. I hope to paint something that will ruin the appetite of every son of a bitch who ever eats in that room.'" Fischer also reported that Rothko was inspired by the [stone, not brick] vestibule of the Laurentian Library in Florence, in which Michelangelo "achieved just the kind of feeling I'm after—he makes the viewers feel that they are trapped in a room where all the doors and windows are bricked up, so that all they can do is butt their heads forever against the wall."[61]

Fischer recorded Rothko raging against art historians, experts, and critics, "the whole machinery for the popularization of art": "When a crowd of people looks at a painting, I think of blasphemy."[62] Yet to this Rothko added, "I believe that a painting can only communicate directly to a rare individual who happens to be in tune with it and the artist."[63] This last statement comes closer to Rothko's emotional and aesthetic responses. At Pompeii, he "had felt 'a deep affinity' between his own work and the murals in the House of the Mysteries," sensing "'the same feeling, the same broad expanses of somber color.'"[64] At Paestum, Rothko pronounced, "I have been painting Greek temples all my life."[65] Places like the refectory of the convent church of San Marco in Florence and Michelangelo's Laurentian Library, which for Rothko was an interior world wholly pervasive and awesome, particularly touched him. He also talked of his will to intimacy, "looking for a spiritual basis for communion":[66]

> I paint very large pictures, I realize that historically the function of painting large pictures is painting something very grandiose and pompous. The reason I paint them however—I think it applies to other painters I know—is precisely because I want to be intimate and human. To paint a small picture is to place yourself outside your experience, to look upon an experience as a stereopticon view or with a reducing glass. However you paint the larger picture, you are in it. It isn't something you command.[67]

It is one thing to rant and rave, as Rothko did, having escaped from the torture of the work

116 Michelangelo Buonarotti, vestibule of the Laurentian Library, Florence, begun 1524. Photograph: Alinari Fratelli, c. 1890.

in 1959. It is another to write thoughtfully and eloquently about the same experience, as he did in his notes of 1960 relating to his upcoming retrospective exhibition at MoMA, which not insignificantly he wrote after he had also resolved the problem of the Seagram paintings by withdrawing from the commission, returning the money he had received. These notes make clear that Rothko was leery of the Seagram commission from the beginning:

> My first instinct was the general distrust of all dealing promises of this sort. Therefore the first item of the contract was a provision that in the event of a desire on the part of my patrons to dispose of the pictures that they must be resold to me. Already was the hope that I would paint something which they could not endure. In this wish was embodied of the horror of the great maw which had developed which had a mouth and teeth anything that was offered. Nothing could any longer shock or repel. But on the basis of the aesthetic everything could be consumed.[68]

In an outline that precedes these notes, Rothko wrote: "The self deception that drives the project to conclusion in the hope of a miracle that the two can coincide."[69] At the end of the

ARCHITECTURE AND ART ALLIED

notes, he responded to that hope: "[Leaving for Europe] I locked the door and did not see the pictures for the next two months. When I saw them again their conviction persisted. By this time the place and the spirit for which they were made was functioning. Then I saw the completed destination. It was obvious that the two were not for each other."[70]

At the end of the 1960s, Rothko donated nine paintings from the third series to the Tate Modern in London, where they are now installed in a dedicated room. Based on these and others of the series[71] and Rothko's 1961 instruction on hanging them,[72] as well as his decision to raise the bottom edge of paintings four feet, six inches above the floor in order to clear the seated height of people, I have constructed a hypothetical montage showing how the Four Seasons murals might have been installed (fig. 117).

Rothko had told me he dreamed of placing his work in wayside chapel, places of special destination, where one could be alone with the work, where nothing else intervened.[73] As fate would have it, two such chapels with Rothko's work were built, both by Philip Johnson in association with St. Thomas University, Houston. I accompanied Philip to Houston in the mid-1960s when he was studying the height at which the university chapel paintings would be hung. In 1971, the nearby Rothko Chapel specifically dedicated to his work was initially designed by Philip but redesigned by Rothko. These commissions, particularly the second, fulfilled Rothko's dream, though his suicide precluded his ever seeing it realized.

In January 1958, when Philip was searching for tapestries for the Fifty-Second Street entrance to the Four Seasons, at my suggestion, he wrote to Marie Cuttoli, who had revived

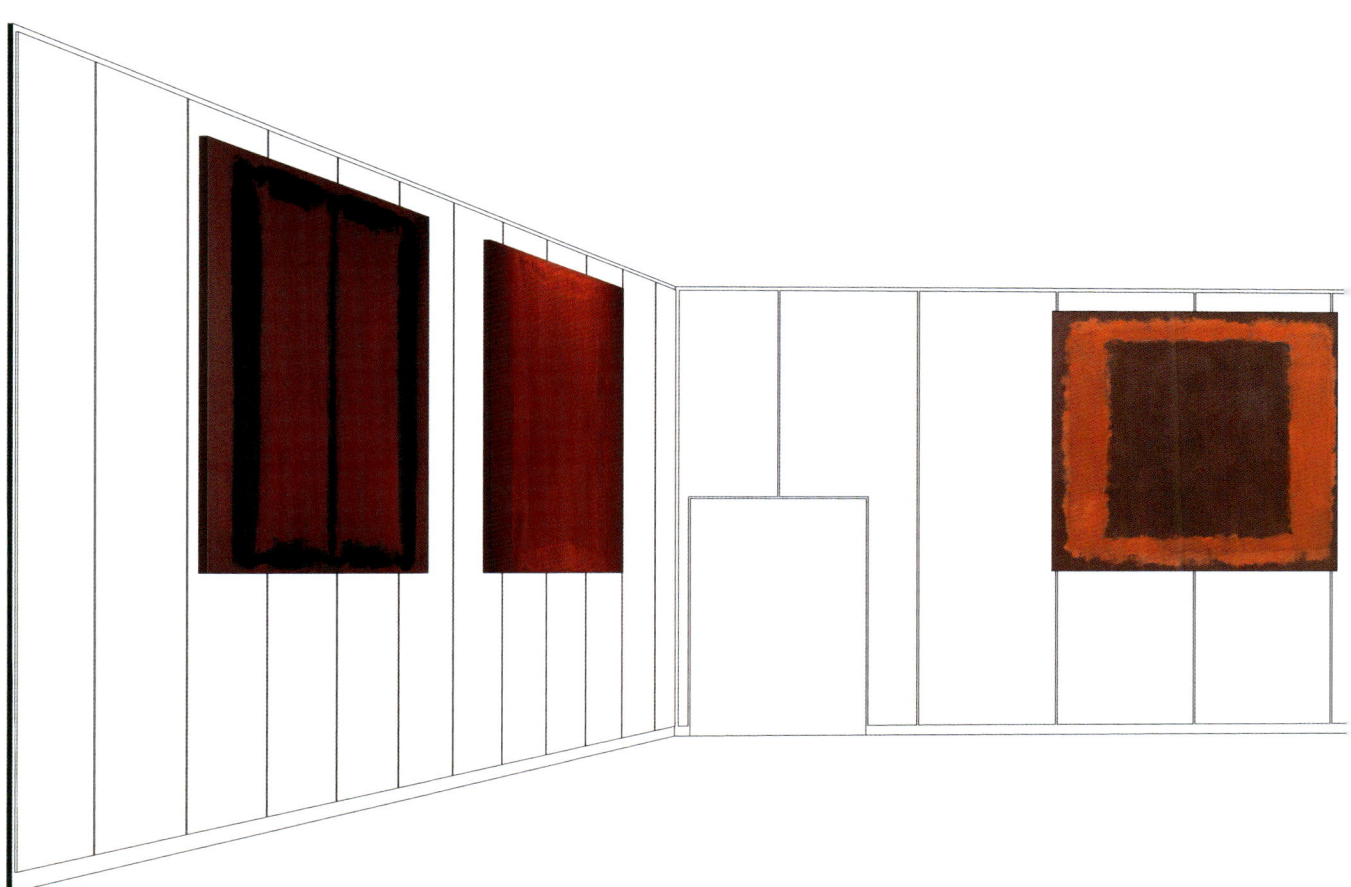

164   ARCHITECTURE AND ART ALLIED

117 Phyllis Lambert, hypothetical photomontage of Mark Rothko's Seagram murals as they might have been installed in the mezzanine of the Pool Room, Four Seasons Restaurant. Drawn by Catherine Bella, 2011.

fine tapestry weaving in France using designs by major contemporary artists.[74] He had hoped to procure six Aubusson or woven tapestries for the entrance hall of the Four Seasons, but he added that if she had none of the right size, "we should discuss the commissioning of new ones. . . . Concerning the artist that we like, Miró is to us the best designer for such pieces."[75] Through his dealer, Miró said he would paint seven full-scale oil paintings for a fee of $67,000; however, they would remain his property. Half the sum was to be paid on presentation of the paintings, and half on completion of the tapestries.[76] To this would be added the cost of making the tapestries. I found the price to be outrageous. It must be measured against the $10,000 Seagram would pay to Cuttoli in May 1958 for each of two Miró tapestries, *Escargot, femme, fleur, étoile,* and *Hirondelle d'amour;*[77] $40,000 for Richard Lippold's sculpture for the Bar and Grill Room of the Four Seasons Restaurant (commissioned in February 1958);[78] $35,000 for Mark Rothko to produce a series of paintings for the mezzanine of the Pool Room in the Four Seasons Restaurant (an agreement signed in June 1958);[79] and $50,000 for Picasso's 1919 *Le Tricorne* stage curtain (purchased in 1957). The Miró commission did not go ahead.

Apart from these major commissions and acquisitions to complete the architectural ambiance of the Four Seasons, the alliance of art and architecture required the offices and public spaces of the Seagram building to exhibit art that would enhance the experience of the building for all the members of the staff and the public at large. I also shuddered at the chaos that reigned in the personal spaces of Seagram's offices in the Chrysler building and

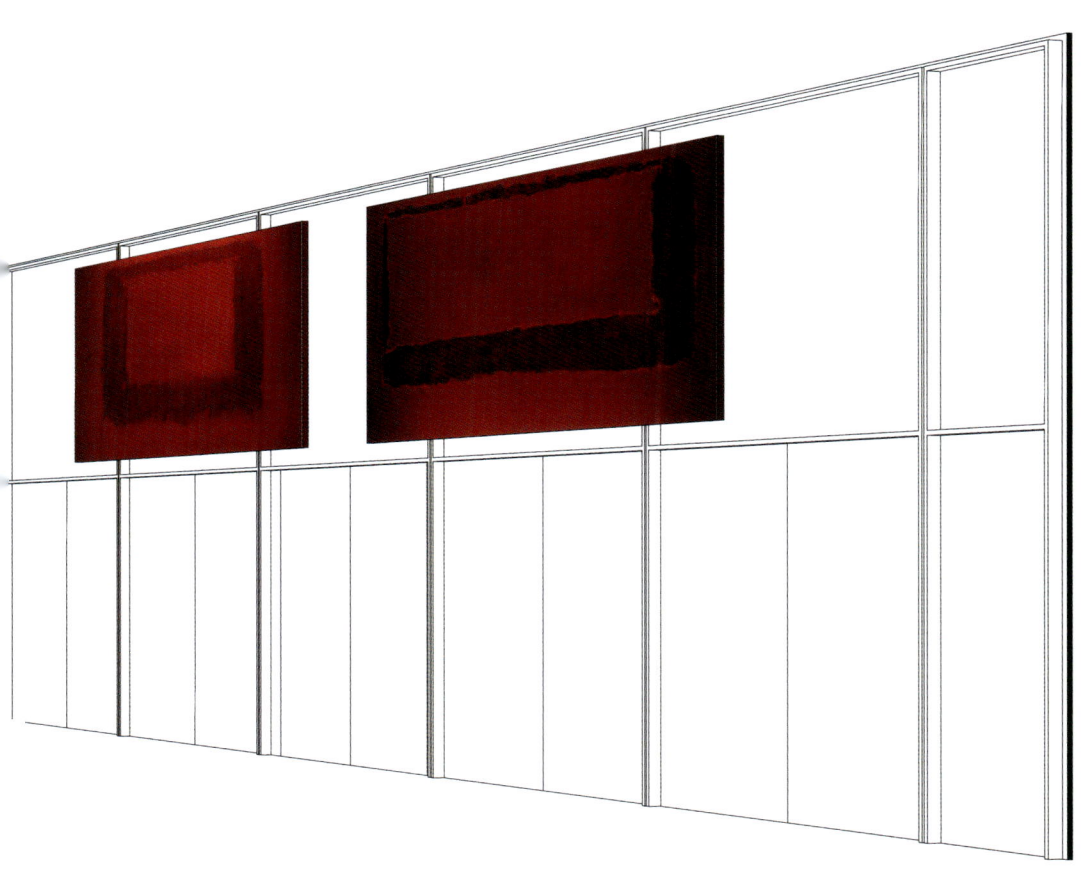

the banal images displayed in many of them, which, if transferred to the new building, would have resulted in discord rather than unity between architecture and art. The reality of the situation was made alarmingly clear by the Seagram Internal Planning Committee's decision, just before the move, to hang original artwork owned by the company, "documents, prints and pictures depicting the history of the distilling industry on the fifth floor [in the executive offices]. For other offices, prints of well-known paintings and pictures of the plants [Seagram's distilleries] will be used."[80] At the same time, I felt that it was essential for Seagram employees to be familiar with the history of wine and spirits and their related social traditions, so that everyday work in the present would be informed by the perspective of past traditions. Strategically, it seemed that the first acquisitions should engage the interest of executives who were conversant only with the visual culture of advertising, bottling, and labels but who would be paying the bills.[81]

In the months before Seagram executives and staff were to move into their new headquarters, I began assembling a collection of historical material related to spirits for the company's offices. In Paris I began *l'art de boire* collection, which included prints depicting the history of distilling from Denis Diderot's *Encyclopédie,* as well as other prints and artifacts.[82] To my surprise, I have discovered a letter of December 27, 1957, to William Lieberman, curator of prints at MoMA, referring to our recent discussion about commissioning artists to make prints related to the distilling and wine industries and my response to his request to provide him with some eighty photographs showing the various phases of the distilling processes, including the machinery used, and related material. I wrote that I had also asked for "any material we have on molecular changes that occur in the process of distilling, feeling that this might be of interest to some of the artists."[83] The intent was to create a series of prints that would be placed in the reception areas of the affiliated Seagram companies Calvert, Four Roses, and General Wine and Spirits, which (like divisions of IBM, Ford, General Motors, and other companies of the time) competed with one another. Only one of the artists named in the letter was commissioned, and the work had no relation to the company's business.[84] However, from this exchange emerged an interest in forming coherent collections and the goal of commissioning artists.

April through June 1958 was the most intense period of collecting for the Seagram offices. With the walls and furniture in place, it was possible to gauge more precisely matters of scale and placement of artworks for the company's semipublic and private areas. In mid-April, three large tapestries were ordered from Theo van Doesburg's widow, Nelly: we purchased Robert Delaunay's *Joie de vivre* and Fernand Léger's *Fleur du Mexique* and *L'Homme à la pastèque*, which were eventually hung in Seagram's main reception room on the fourth floor (fig. 118).[85] They replaced two paintings originally installed there, Franz Kline's *Composition* and Larry Rivers's *The Accident,* when it was acknowledged that textiles were better suited than oil paintings to heavily trafficked and semipublic areas.[86]

The fourth-floor reception area was one of six large spaces created when Mies added the three-by-three-bay "bustle" at the east of the building, which increased the typical 14,900-square-foot tower floor by some 8,000 square feet (fig. 119). This additional space accommodated large meeting rooms, one to three depending on the configuration of the movable dividing walls (fig. 120); they were entered through the oak double doors located in the display case wall of the reception area. The wall dividing this large room from the meeting rooms behind was spectacular, lined with the same elegant bronze-framed, illuminated glass-shelved cases Johnson created for the fifth floor. Here they held a sophisticated arrangement of vessels for wine, whiskey, cordials, and liqueurs made or distributed by Seagram companies, one brand to a shelf.

118 Philip Johnson, interior architect, Seagram fourth-floor reception room, Seagram building. Gelatin silver print, 8 × 10½ in. Photograph: Ezra Stoller, 1991.

In 1958 Mark Rothko's strong *Brown and Blacks in Reds* hung near the end of the long wall of the sparse, rectangular reception area anteroom. In this space between the travertine elevator core and the main reception room, a pair of Eames couches, separated by a low Knoll table, lined each of the long, parallel white-painted walls (fig. 121). Notwithstanding Rothko's painting (which was soon moved to the fifth floor), the area was a poor cousin to Johnson's richly appointed oak-paneled waiting room. I was dissatisfied with the arrangement, but the space remained unchanged until 1975, when I had the idea to commission Sol LeWitt, who proposed *Lines & Color*, a major series consisting of sixty-four monoprint silkscreens, thirty-two on each side, covering the parallel walls of the anteroom from floor to ceiling.[87] Everything tends to come at once. As fate would have it, when I commissioned LeWitt in mid-May, Seagram's Bicentennial photographic campaign on the county court house was well under way, and a series of exhibitions on photographs of court houses, discussed below, would soon be installed in the anteroom. This became the Seagram Gallery, where between 1975 and 2004 three public exhibitions were presented each year according to a publicized schedule (fig. 122).[88] By the fourth year, exhibitions were reviewed in the press.

In 1958, when Stoller first photographed Seagram's main reception area on the fourth floor and the executive offices on the floor above, works of art were still sparse, so Miró's *Escargot, femme, fleur, étoile*, *Personnages avec étoile*, and *Hirondelle d'amour* were moved

ARCHITECTURE AND ART ALLIED

119 Plan of Seagram fourth floor, printed in Joseph E. Seagram & Sons, Inc., brochure entitled "Our New Home," 1958.

120 Philip Johnson, interior architect, two of Seagram fourth-floor suites of conference rooms, Seagram building. Gelatin silver print, 7⅝ × 9⅝ in. Photograph: Ezra Stoller, 1958.

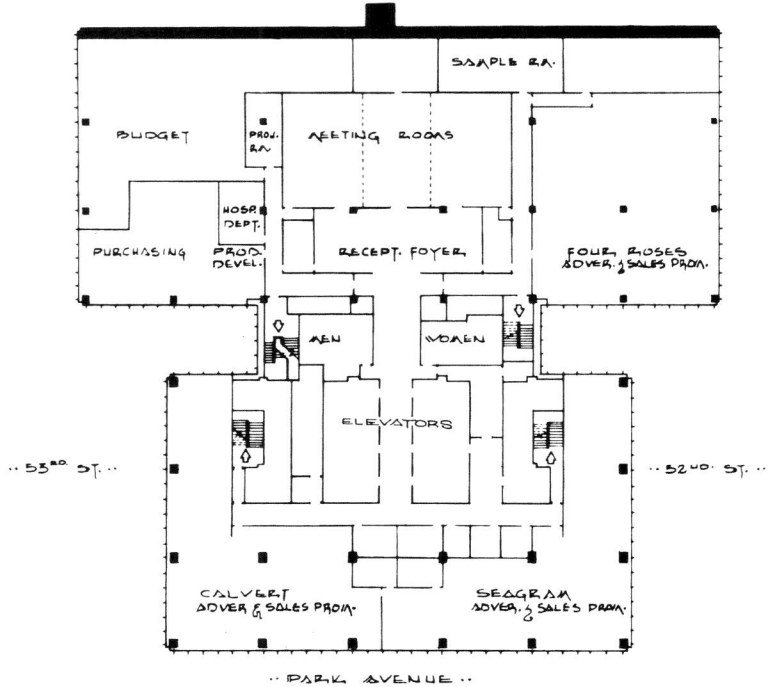

121 Philip Johnson, interior architect, view from elevator lobby anteroom and Seagram's fourth-floor reception room, Seagram building. Gelatin silver print, 7⅝ × 9⅝ in. Photograph: Ezra Stoller, 1958.

122 Seagram Gallery (former anteroom), fourth floor, as transformed by Phyllis Lambert, Seagram building. Gelatin silver print, 8 × 10½ in. Photograph: Ezra Stoller, 1991.

from place to place during photography—for example, from the fourth-floor meeting rooms, Miró's *Personnages avec étoile* was otherwise hung in the fifth-floor executive reception room (fig. 123). Here it could be seen framing Herbert Matter's mural diagramming the distilling process, which lay perpendicularly between the cases of the European and American drinking vessels (fig. 124).[89] When the Four Seasons Restaurant opened, the fine Miró tapestries migrated to the lobby of the Fifty-Second Street entrance (see fig. 100). For a while, two rugs—Stuart Davis's *Flying Carpet* and Miró's *Composition, or Le Rêve* were installed together with Lurçat's *Le Jardin* on the other side of the fifth-floor executive reception area, where Rothko's *Brown and Blacks in Reds* was eventually installed and remained for many years.

Through June 1958, dozens of lithographs and some etchings of the 1950s (the majority by Joan Miró, Pablo Picasso, Georges Braque, and André Masson), destined for the fifth-

ARCHITECTURE AND ART ALLIED

123 Philip Johnson, interior architect, Seagram fifth-floor executive reception room, with view to the Herbert Matter mural in reception hall, Seagram building. Gelatin silver print, 5⅞ × 8⅞ in. Photograph: Russell Hart, July 1979.

124 Herbert Matter, mural diagramming the distilling process, Seagram fifth-floor reception hall; display cases by Philip Johnson. Gelatin silver print, 5⅞ × 8⅞ in. Photograph: Russell Hart, July 1979.

floor executive offices and related spaces, were received on consignment.⁹⁰ By the end of October 1959, posters designed by artists in the 1950s for exhibitions in Parisian galleries and museums had been acquired for general offices throughout the company. Interest in that genre began to take hold in the United States, and Seagram's collection of prints and posters soon extended to include American artists.⁹¹

An inventory dated March 30, 1959, and titled "Art on Display at Seagram Building," lists the disposition of works on the fourth and fifth floors: thirteen lithographs by Picasso, Braque, and Masson were hung in secretarial spaces outside private offices, whereas others were hung together with paintings: Miró's colored lithograph *Gérmination nocturne* was installed with Gottlieb's *Black Silhouette* (1956), lent by the André Emmerich Gallery. Miró's *Moon and Stars* was installed in the fifth-floor executive suite, together with etchings on winemaking from Diderot and d'Alembert's *Encyclopédie*.⁹² Picasso's lithographs *David and Bathsheba* (1947) and *Scène antique* (1956) were installed with Conrad Marca-Relli's *St. Cyprian's Day*, lent by the Stable Gallery, in a large executive office with Seagram standard

125 Philip Johnson, interior architect, Seagram fifth-floor executive office with Jens Risom executive desk and Hans Wegner chairs, Seagram building. Gelatin silver print, cropped, 7⅝ × 9⅝ in. Photograph: Ezra Stoller, 1958.

126 Philip Johnson, interior architect, and Phyllis Lambert, Seagram fifth-floor executive office with Mies van der Rohe, Seagram building. Gelatin silver print, 7⅝ × 9⅝ in. Photograph: Ezra Stoller, 1958.

127 Philip Johnson, interior architect, fifth-floor office of Samuel Bronfman, Seagram building. Gelatin silver print, cropped, 7⅝ × 9⅝ in. Photograph: Ezra Stoller, 1958.

executive desks and chairs (fig. 125), and in the spare fifth-floor office I indulged a wish to pay homage to two great architects by hanging an Aubusson tapestry Marie Cuttoli commissioned from Le Corbusier opposite the north-facing window wall with Mies's furniture (fig. 126).[93] Rodin's *Balzac* was not yet on its pedestal in SB's office when photographed by Stoller. The room was furnished by my mother with a handsome English partner's desk and Chippendale chairs surrounding the marble table Philip Johnson designed (fig. 127).

The early collections for Seagram, composed of tapestries, prints, and posters from France on one hand and, on the other, paintings and prints by New York School artists, signaled a time of change: the medium of tapestry weaving was being revived in France and poster and print media, particularly lithography, began to take hold among the post–New York School in the 1950s.[94] These two poles of early acquisitions also resonate in the divergence of Philip's interests from mine at the time. From his connection to MoMA, Philip was a serious collector of contemporary American art. My background in art history and my interest in old master drawings and prints led me to historical material, and a major collection of European and American drinking vessels, in collecting objects related to

ARCHITECTURE AND ART ALLIED

128 Seagram collection of European drinking vessels displayed in cases designed by Philip Johnson, fifth-floor reception hall, Seagram building. Gelatin silver print, 10½ × 13⅝ in. Photograph: Richard Pare, 1979.

the company's businesses and with which Seagram employees could develop an eye and appreciation for art.

The collection of drinking vessels was the first of a series of commissioned projects for the Seagram offices. Olga Raggio, then assistant curator at the Metropolitan Museum of Art in New York and a friend, formed this collection at my request.[95] The objects were installed in the elegant, silk-backed, illuminated bronze and glass cases designed by Philip Johnson, lining opposite walls in the semipublic fifth-floor reception area. The European and American drinking vessels offered insight into the different social, technical, and cultural histories of the two continents (figs. 128, 129). The European artifacts, dating from the sixteenth to nineteenth centuries, are primarily related to the appreciation of wine. The earliest objects in the collection were fashioned of solid materials: shells, horn, and wood. The hard wood of tree bolls and knots was preferred in northern countries, where they were found to preserve the bouquet of the wine better than metal cups. In the sixteenth century, glass vessels were made in Florence and then Venice. European cups and flasks were crafted by artists and artisans, and varied not only in material but also in shape and ornament. Production of American drinking vessels took hold in the nineteenth century. Industrially fabricated, principally in glass, and dedicated to holding spirits, bottles and flasks rather than cups predominate, varying little in size and shape but gorgeously varied in color and impressed with American symbols and historical references.[96] The most distinctive aspect of American drinking vessels is the predominance of the American eagle in the pictorial and historical whisky flasks, made during the turbulent period of the "March of Democracy," from the end of the depression of 1817 to the end of the Civil War. The

129 Seagram collection of American drinking vessels displayed in cases designed by Philip Johnson, fifth-floor reception hall, Seagram building. Gelatin silver print, 10½ × 13⅝ in. Photograph: Richard Pare, 1979.

contrast between European and American drinking vessels is resonant of Henry James's depiction in many of his novels, particularly *The American* and *The Golden Bowl*, of the great inherited houses of Europe and the devastatingly polished comportment of their aristocratic occupants, in contrast to the energetic, straightforward American who made his fortune in commerce, manufacturing such lowly artifacts as washtubs.

A curatorial office was established at Seagram well after the inauguration of its public programs and special collections.[97] A combination of the high cost of space in the Seagram building and the company's growth led to the revision of corporate policy on the use of space in general and resulted in moving operational functions, including sales, to less expensive quarters at 800 Third Avenue. With new space requirements, the collections expanded through photography. For the new Third Avenue offices I first considered prints by American artists, but it seemed to me that contemporary minimalist artworks would not be accessible to Seagram's staff; rather, they could be an imposition. Instead, just as I sought to engage Seagram staff and management in art by building a collection related to the venerated traditions of their industry, I believed that the most accessible medium for the company to collect and exhibit would be photography, especially images with a New York or urban focus, which led to the formation of the collection we titled "Photographs of American Urban Life" in 1973.

The first third of these photographs, comprising between two hundred and three hundred photographs for the public spaces at Seagram's 800 Third Avenue offices and another three hundred or so for private offices,[98] was assembled by Pierre Apraxine,[99] advised by

ARCHITECTURE AND ART ALLIED

130 Paul Strand, *Wall Street, New York*, 1916. Photogravure, 5⅛ × 6⅜ in.

Denis Longwell and John Szarkowski, assistant curator and curator, respectively, of MoMA's Department of Photography. Images collected included works by Walker Evans, Hilla and Bernd Becher, Robert Frank, and Lee Friedlander; Garry Winogrand's *Animals* series and a 1974 William Eggleston portfolio called *14 Pictures*; and, from earlier in the century, works by Edward Steichen and photogravures by Alvin Langdon Coburn and Alfred Stieglitz. Later, after taking over the responsibility for the collection in 1977, Richard Pare outlined its scope, which he saw as encompassing "some of the major themes and ideas in photography during the period in which the collection was assembled. It describes this trajectory quite distinctly, including works of what might be called the Chicago School represented by Callahan, and Josephson, Sinsabaugh and Siskind; the uninflected realism of the photographers of the New Topographics, and the influence of minimalism can all be seen. The pleasure of the collection comes in part from the freedom of its parameters" (figs. 130–32).[100] In collecting photographs for Seagram, it seemed incumbent on us to go beyond the acquisition of existing prints and to take a direct approach in commissioning new work. Major historical events often generate a level of energy that exceeds their commemoration. The US Bicentennial in 1976 did so for me. My interests were allied rather with architecture's potential to shape society. Involved by the ongoing experience of documenting Montreal's evolution by photographing its gray stone buildings, and having discussed American public buildings with a much-respected friend who grew up in Ohio and convincingly evoked the presence and richness of county court houses along the river, my direction became clear.

We launched a project in November 1974 in order to investigate the image and character of county court houses across the United States. Our project was the first compre-

131 William Eggleston, *Untitled* (from *14 Pictures* portfolio), 1971. Dye transfer print, 12⅝ × 18⅝ in., signed "Wm Eggleston" in pencil on verso, black ink copyright stamp with plate and edition numbers inscribed in pencil on verso.

132 Danny Lyon, *Crossing the Ohio River from Kentucky,* 1966, printed 1978. Gelatin silver print, 8¾ × 13 in., dated, titled, and signed in pencil on verso.

hensive commission since the Farm Security Administration program, the monumental photographic undertaking created by Roy Stryker for the federal government during the Depression. As the most representative of American buildings, the county court house is the symbol and sentinel of needs, values, and aspirations with a multivalent presence in community life. As I wrote at the time, the county court house was:

> a public building with which everyone comes into contact in the course of a life span: those who own land which they register there, those who may be helped or punished there—every citizen visits it on ordinary and special occasions. Thus its architectural expression is apt to be more relaxed than that, say of the Statehouse. Those who built the county court house were not officials desiring to relate to a wider constituency, but citizens whose concerns were local. The standard was the next county seat, rather than a remote city, so that the buildings tend to reflect those local values rather than more

ARCHITECTURE AND ART ALLIED   175

formal architectural concerns, and they represent the institution for which citizens of the United States bear a profound respect—the law.[101]

County court houses had the advantage of providing a significant yet manageable sampling; not too many, not too few. Of the 3,034 American counties, more than one-third would be photographed, offering a generous cross section of time and place and the many symbolic architectural languages that builders considered worthy of their subject.

Black-and-white film was still the predominant working medium of the time together with large-format view cameras. Stephen Shore was the exception in that he made most of his pictures for the project using color negative film, and Lewis Baltz used a 35mm camera. Richard Pare, the project's editor, encouraged the photographers to be interpretive and to work within their own sphere of interest at the same time as they were producing the documentary photographs, because, as he wrote, "It is only from the interpretive images that the great richness of this collection is going to make itself evident" (figs. 133–35).[102] While photographing and editing was still in progress, John Szarkowski, who was initially skeptical about the venture, exhibited sixty-four of the court house prints at MoMA in 1977. On May 19, 1978, *Court House: A Photographic Document* was published just in time for a few copies to be available at the opening of the exhibition at the American Institute of Architects Foundation in Washington under the auspices of the National Association of Counties.[103] Subsequently, two identical court house exhibitions traveled concurrently throughout the United States in 1978 and 1979.[104]

The photography critic Gene Thornton wrote: "Nothing quite like this has been undertaken since the Farm Security Association of the 1930s."[105] Wolf von Eckardt, the architectural critic of the *Washington Post,* considered *Court House* to be as important a historic event in American architecture as the commissioning of Mies van der Rohe to design the Seagram building in New York, "perhaps more so. The Seagram Building acquainted the American public with the best the so called International Style of architecture could offer.

133 Nicholas Nixon, *Suffolk County Court House, Boston, Massachusetts, 1886–94,* with later additions, George A. Clough, architect. Gelatin silver print, 7¾ × 9⅝ in., 1975.

134 Jim Dow, *Cabarrus County Court House, Concord, North Carolina, 1875–76*, George S. H. Appleget, architect. Gelatin silver print, 9⅝ × 7⅝ in., c. 1974–77.

135 Ellen Land-Weber, *Janitor and Sheriff, Malheur County Court House, Vale, Oregon*. Gelatin silver print, 7⅜ × 9¼ in., c. 1978.

136 Richard Serra, study for *Flat Rock*, 1981. Paintstick, 35 × 50 in., from David Bellman, *Drawings by Sculptors: Two Decades of Non-Objective Art in the Seagram Collection*, 1984.

The courthouse project acquaints us with the richness and ingenuity of our own indigenous architecture. Even those of us who have long taken an interest in historic building will be astounded just how rich and indigenous it is."[106] A full set of 2,500 master prints and more than eleven thousand negatives, together with the documents collected, which compose the Seagram County Court House Archives, was presented by Joseph E. Seagram & Sons, Inc., to the Library of Congress as a gift to the nation in 1980.[107]

The last major collection formed for Seagram was *Drawings by Sculptors: Two Decades of Non-Objective Art,* assembled between 1978 and 1983. The idea to look at the phenomenon of drawings by contemporary sculptors was linked to my early practice as a sculptor and my interest in architects' drawings. *Drawings by Sculptors* would not, however, have become the basis for a collection without the arrival in Montreal of David Bellman from Vancouver to assume the position of curator at McGill University's McCord Museum. Bellman was passionately interested in contemporary nonobjective art, and we discussed the idea of assembling a collection of conceptual or working drawings for three-dimensional works by nonobjective sculptors. The catalogue of the collection, *Drawings by Sculptors: Two Decades of Non-Objective Art,* was published in 1984 to accompany an exhibition that traveled to museums across Canada. The artists ranged from Vito Acconci to Mel Bochner, Dan Flavin, Michael Heizer, Eva Hesse, Donald Judd, Sol LeWitt, Brenda Miller, Robert Morris, Bruce Nauman, Royden Rabinowitch, Fred Sandback, Richard Serra (fig. 136), Robert Smithson (fig. 137), and Michael Snow (fig. 138).[108]

A long-term public program of exhibitions in the Seagram building was initiated by the *Court House* project (see appendix 2). The Seagram Gallery was established in the company's principal reception area on the fourth floor in 1975 (see fig. 122) when the first photographs for *Court House* were printed. It struck me that, as they arrived, they should be displayed where the Seagram staff and visitors would see them, so that we could present an ongoing "report" on the project. Six exhibitions showed the progression across the country from the early Classical mansion-size court house in the East to those lost in the welter of

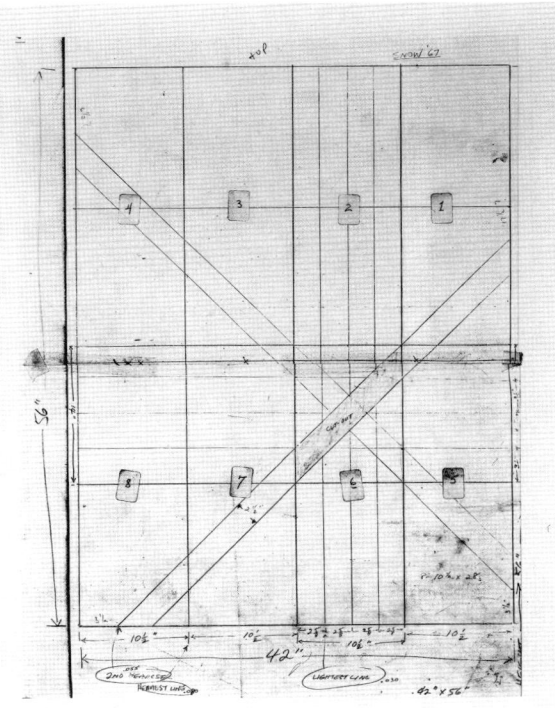

137 Robert Smithson, study for *Floating Island to Travel Around Manhattan Island*, 1970. Pencil, 18¾ × 24 in., from David Bellman, *Drawings by Sculptors: Two Decades of Non-Objective Art in the Seagram Collection*, 1984.

138 Michael Snow, study for *Sight*, 1967. Mixed media on paper, 16⅝ × 12¼ in., from David Bellman, *Drawings by Sculptors: Two Decades of Non-Objective Art in the Seagram Collection*, 1984.

growing cities; the Italianate or Baroque towered structures of midsized towns throughout the country; the flags, portraits, clocks, and the clerk's safe and other small details that reveal how people transformed the interior spaces; and the familiar symbols found on almost every court house square—memorials to war dead, artillery relics, plaques, fountains, trees, and lawns. By the fifth exhibition, the tone changed. Pare wrote with indignation: "Until now this space has been reserved to show only the finer aspects of the subject, [while] this is the first indication of the enormous amount of shoddy construction being undertaken in the name of 'improved working conditions' and being up-to-date."[109] The sixth exhibition was a plea for conservation: "The implications are that the buildings of the past should be treasured and can be replaced only at considerable risk to the whole community."[110]

Several of the ongoing series of exhibitions marked special events relating to the Seagram building itself, starting with the twentieth anniversary of its completion: *The Seagram Plaza: Its Design and Use* was presented from November 1977 to March 1978 (fig. 139). The exhibition was developed under my direction in collaboration with Ludwig Glaeser, curator of the Mies van der Rohe Archive at MoMA.[111] I wished to call attention to the role of the plaza, since that aspect of the building is difficult to represent and know unless one is actually in the space or walking by. Among the objects presented, MoMA loaned the small bronze model made in the project office of Van der Rohe and Johnson in 1955 (see fig. 26), refurbished for the exhibition, and William H. Whyte's time-lapse film, *A Day in the Life of the North Front Ledge at Seagram's*,[112] was displayed on a television screen. Photographs pertaining to the history of the site, as well as drawings for various installations of sculpture and art events that had taken place on the plaza, were presented. And the plaza itself offered an incomparable exhibition space—of both people and works of public art that made temporary homes there; its impact is taken up in the next chapter.

At the beginning of the 1990s the last of three exhibitions celebrating the designation of Seagram as a New York City landmark (discussed in chapter 7) was dedicated to the photographs Ezra Stoller made in 1958 after Seagram had moved into its newly completed headquarters and before the Four Seasons Restaurant was completed. Many of these are reproduced in this volume (see figs. 58, 59, 94, 105, 118, 120–22, 125–27, 175). Mies's directive to Stoller was to take "many pictures and we will choose a few."[113] A reviewer commented in the *New York Observer* that these images of "modernism reflecting modernism"

139 Exhibition installation, *The Seagram Plaza: Its Design and Use*, Seagram Gallery, Seagram building, November 22, 1977–March 1, 1978, Phyllis Lambert and Ludwig Glaeser, curators. Photographer unknown.

show that although the building had not changed in three decades, those images "looking out, [show that] the city around it had been transformed."[114]

Many more exhibitions, held in the Seagram building as well as traveling in variant forms outside New York, made the acquisition and exhibition program at the building a rich and diverse experience for all visitors. Small exhibitions have the ability to interpret an epoch and its dialectic, as the Seagram Gallery continued to do. It is evident from the earliest notices that Seagram Gallery exhibitions were a part of the New York scene.

The initial response from critics invoked a strong sense of place: In August 1979, a *New York Times* critic wrote that "during the warm spell, the fourth-floor art exhibition space of the Seagram Building . . . is a cool, restful and eye-filling haven."[115] In 1980, in a piece on Martha Beck's exhibition *Self Portraits,* John Russell found it to be "intermittently a distinguished and inventive capsule survey," but he also remarked that it was installed in "the season's most curious location."[116] In the *New York Times* "Going Out Guide" of August 30, 1982, under "Spaces," a critic noted that art galleries are often built into the most "unlikely premises," of which the Seagram's corporate reception room was one: "The gallery makes a brief stop during the midday hours, a good time to take in the scene in front of the Seagram Building itself."[117]

Just as much as the gallery, the plaza became a place for art for the public and a place for an open-air break from life of the office and the city: "At lunchtime the avenue front of the building is colorfully peopled with standees and step-sitters, and likely as not, there will be a jazz group performing for the passers-by. Very pleasant on a nice day."[118] This recalls nothing if not the *Lunch Poems* by Frank O'Hara, in particular, his "Personal Poem" of 1959:

> *I walk through the luminous humidity*
> *passing the House of Seagram with its wet*
> *and its loungers and the construction to*
> *the left that closed the sidewalk if*
> *I ever get to be a construction worker*
> *I'd like to have a silver hat please.*[119]

The value of an outdoor space where people could sit, talk, and maybe eat, like a European plaza, piazza, or *place,* had been my secret dream for the building. Sculpture became part of it. In August 1955, when construction had just begun, I wrote to a friend with this in mind:

> There shall be fountains—how where etc to be solved. . . . [With an architect friend] I was talking of having great prisms in the plaza in which or on which white lights (warm and cold) could play at night—prisms as in Dürer's etching *Melancholia* [1514]. I had conceived this as something calm and [my friend] . . . as an exciting welling-forth out of a pit of prisms and perhaps a huge chunk of travertine (if that is what the plaza material will be), with water playing. What sculpture—a huge Brancusi bird or cock? A trip to Egypt to wrest a beautiful sculpture from Egyptian government? Rodin, no. Brancusi or Egypt—I can't think of what would be more wonderful.[120]

As seen above, sculptures for the plaza by Brancusi or Picasso were not to be. The subject of installing permanent sculpture on the plaza was finally put to rest after 1964 when Edgar M. Bronfman, the newly appointed Seagram president, resurrected the idea. At his request for sculpture on the plaza, Mies proposed a reclining female figure by Henry Moore. A

140 Cover of *Progressive Architecture* showing Olmec Head, San Lorenzo, Tenochtitlan, Mexico, stone, 5th c., installed on Seagram plaza, spring 1965. Photograph: Maude Dorr, 1965.

photograph of Moore's *Reclining Figure* of 1955 was enlarged at two different scales and mounted on boards to make full-size mock-ups to be studied by Moore and Mies in situ.[121] Moore rejected the idea. In a letter to Edgar, I explained:

> [Henry Moore] felt that because the plaza is not a huge plaza that any sculpture placed there would not be part of the plaza or the building. Rather, it would become part of the environment to the north and south of the plaza. In this way Moore felt that the sculpture would be devalued and that it would detract from the quality of the plaza and the building. Mies thought about it further and came to about the same conclusion, that the plaza without sculpture is a quiet and serene space for people to be in or pass by in the business of New York. . . . Sculpture in public places has to do with scale, in relating the human being to space. . . . The wonderful living quality about the Seagram plaza is that it changes all the time, the people are the sculpture. It looks wonderful when it is empty, then it changes as people go in and out of the building or just wander on the plaza. When people sit on the benches and walls, it again has another character. Because of its intimate size the trees, the pools, the fountains and other people make a living environment and relate directly to the building, nothing is needed to make a transition. Static sculpture permanently on the plaza would not only be pompous, it would be too much and detract from the qualities it now has. . . . Fine sculpture on the plaza at times (and not often) has a different quality, it marks an occasion, and it is good to be able to do that if carefully controlled and selected. A permanent sculpture no matter how fine would create a formality and insistency inimical to a serene environment that changes itself.[122]

Seagram had already experimented with placing sculpture on the plaza. In May 1965, a sixteen-ton, nine-foot-high Olmec head (on its way to the Mexican Pavilion at the 1964–65 New York World's Fair in Flushing Meadows) was placed on the Seagram plaza (fig. 140).

141 Barnett Newman, *Broken Obelisk*, bronze, 1963–67, installed on Seagram plaza, fall 1967. Photograph: Fred W. McDarrah, September 27, 1967.

A previous proposal that the head be displayed at Rockefeller Plaza was, tellingly, declined for lack of "proper space."[123] The colossal head at Seagram "caused such a stir" that the two-week installation was extended for four more weeks.[124] Two years later, as part of the *Cultural Showcase Festival* sponsored by the New York City Administration of Recreation and Cultural Affairs, Barnett Newman's twenty-nine-foot *Broken Obelisk* was installed on the Seagram plaza by September 27, 1967 (fig. 141). During October and November 1968, an eight-foot-high Easter Island head was placed on a twelve-foot pedestal, initiating at Seagram a worldwide drive by the International Fund for Monuments to restore and preserve these remote islands relics.[125]

The occasional installation of sculpture on the plaza, rather than a permanent installation, became Seagram policy, requiring the approval of both Philip Johnson for MoMA and myself in my ongoing role as director of planning.[126] These events were of considerable interest to the public, who could observe the installation process, which was sometimes spectacular. In the case of Tony Smith's *Light Up* of 1998 (figs. 142–44), for instance, a series of photographs documents the enormous pieces being lowered into place by a crane. Like most photographs documenting sculpture on the plaza, they are seen against the

ARCHITECTURE AND ART ALLIED

142 Tony Smith, *Light Up*, painted steel, 1971, being installed on Seagram plaza, summer 1998. Photograph: Carla Caccamise Ash, June 1998.

143 Tony Smith, *Light Up*, painted steel, 1971, being installed on Seagram plaza, summer 1998. Photograph: Carla Caccamise Ash, June 1998.

144 Tony Smith, *Light Up*, painted steel, 1971, installed on Seagram plaza, summer 1998. Photograph: Marian Harders, 1998.

surrounding buildings, bearing out Henry Moore's concern. Richard Long's *Brownstone Circle* (figs. 145, 146), proposed by the Public Art Fund of New York City, was conceived as a site-specific piece in which the installation was a performance in itself, with Long positioning by hand each fragment of the familiar material used to build New York brownstone houses.[127] The public was able to evaluate and judge the works in their relation to the architectural context. Other images show the mystical aura of Willem de Kooning's *Seated Woman* or the poetics of an untitled Joel Shapiro sculpture in dialogue with the Seagram building (fig. 147).

145 Richard Long installing *Brownstone Circle* on Seagram plaza, spring 2000. Photograph: Carla Caccamise Ash, April 8, 2000.

146 Richard Long, *Brownstone Circle*, 2000, installed on Seagram plaza, spring 2000. Photograph: Carla Caccamise Ash, June 24, 2000.

147 Joel Shapiro, *Untitled*, bronze, 1974–75, installed on Seagram plaza, fall 1986. Photograph: James Dee, 1986.

148 Jean Dubuffet, *Milord la Chamarre*, painted stainless steel, 1973–74, installed on Seagram plaza, fall/winter 1974–75. Photograph: Richard Pare, 1975.

In the decade between 1971 and 1981, the changing sculpture program at the Seagram plaza was generated by private art galleries and museums in conjunction with their own exhibitions. A number of major works were installed for considerable periods of time. Jean Dubuffet's *Milord la Chamarre* was installed between November 1974 and January 1975 (fig. 148), during which time it withstood an early winter blizzard. Mark di Suvero's *Praise for Elohim Adonai* was installed for five months, from the end of 1975 through early 1976, in conjunction with his retrospective exhibition at the Whitney Museum of American Art (fig. 149). Engineering studies were made to spread the load of particularly heavy pieces, as were drawings showing the methods to be used for installation, such as those for Michael Heizer's forty-six-ton *Guenette* (figs. 150, 151). These studies, along with the many contracts and agreements between Seagram and various owners and contractors, made this

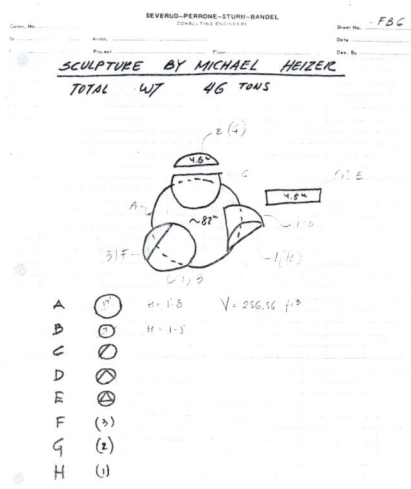

149 Mark di Suvero, *Praise for Elohim Adonai,* wood and steel, 1966, installed on Seagram plaza, fall/winter 1975–76. Photographer unknown.

150 Severud-Perrone-Sturm-Bandel, consulting engineers, diagram for the placement of Michael Heizer's *Guenette* on Seagram plaza, 1978.

151 Michael Heizer, *Guenette,* 1977–78, Laurentian Pink granite, installed on Seagram plaza, summer/fall 1979. Photograph: Michael Heizer, 1979.

152 Poster for Marilyn Wood and the Celebration Group performance, *Celebrations in City Places: The Seagram Building and Its Plaza,* September 29–30, 1972. Poster design and collage by M. Jackson Baum using photographs by Robert Wood.

153 Marilyn Wood and the Celebration Group performance, dancers silhouetted on the first three floors of the Seagram building, *Celebrations in City Places: The Seagram Building and Its Plaza*, September 29–30, 1972. Photograph: Phyllis Lambert.

practice complex and costly. The owner or consignee of the works bore the major expense; the curator of the Seagram Collections had only a small budget for this purpose.[128] At times, the sculptures were appropriated by the public. In some instances, artworks were overappreciated: In mid-November 1976, *Newsweek* reported that "Seagram was forced to remove a large foamed-plastic sculpture—*The Hill* by Horia Damian—after scores of children used it as a Jungle Gym."[129] A special event was staged in 1972 by performance artist Marilyn Wood and her Celebration Group. Traffic on one side of Park Avenue was blocked for the evening so that the audience could sit on chairs arranged on the street watching the performance, which drew on many dimensions of the building and plaza: flutists played all the while standing in the pools; the dancers' fluid movements were silhouetted against the glowing glass on the lower floors of the tower; a ribbon of red felt was unfurled, cascading down five hundred feet from the top of the building to the plaza; and gliding through the lobby, and round and around the revolving doors, the dancers moved onto the plaza, which at the finale was the stage on which both performers and audience danced madly (figs. 152, 153).

The Seagram plaza was unique in its role as a space for exhibiting art. The often experimental installations functioned as a barometer for understanding the public's interaction with art, architecture, and the urban environment—both through occasional special events and the ordinary, everyday life of the place. Walker Evans's 1963 photograph *Seagram Plaza*, in which a man is quite at home, lounging on the marble bench at Fifty-Second Street, epitomizes the plaza's spirit as an outdoor room (see fig. 81).[130] Sculpture became an amenity with the enactment of New York's new Zoning Resolution in 1961, which listed sculpture as an allowable "impediment" in the open space of privately owned plazas (legal language transforms a positive to a negative, an attractive feature to an obstruction, obstacle, barrier, hurdle, hindrance). The artworks installed outside the city's buildings were

ARCHITECTURE AND ART ALLIED

mostly permanent and rarely of distinction, since the selections were too often made by real estate developers themselves, without consulting institutions or individuals in whom such judgment resides.

My focus here is the social role of privately owned public spaces in the early 1970s, a decade after the new zoning resolution was enacted. The approach pioneered by Seagram in creating an open plaza led New York City officials to encourage builders to create open public spaces by offering a bonus: for one square foot of public space, builders could add ten square feet of commercial floor space over and above the amount normally permitted by zoning. This option was exercised almost without exception. William H. Whyte, a proponent of sustainable urban development and author of *The Organization Man* (1956), observed in 1980 that "every new office building provided a plaza or comparable space: by 1972, some twenty acres of the world's most expensive open space [had been so designated]."[131] Indeed, between 1963 and 1975, 121 plazas had been created for their host buildings.[132] But Whyte saw that most plazas lacked amenities, and consequently people did not frequent them.

> We discovered that some plazas, especially at lunch time, attracted a lot of people. One, the Seagram Building, was the place that helped give the city the idea for the plaza. . . . On a good day, there would be a hundred and fifty people sitting, sunbathing, and schmoozing—idly gossiping, talking nothing talk. But on most plazas we didn't see many people.
>
> It was obvious enough that the zoning requirements weren't working right. In exchange for the extra floor space builders were getting, they ought to have been required to come across with something better. The Planning Commission agreed and asked us if we could come up with some guidelines.[133]

Recognizing the need for objective analysis of what made a good public space, Whyte had established *The Street Life Project* research group in 1970 with funding from several founda-

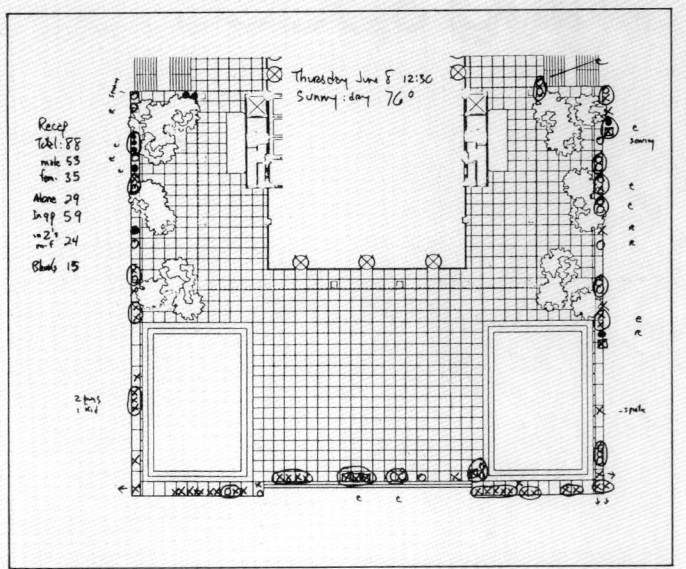

154 William H. Whyte, Seagram building and plaza, sighting map, "Thursday, June 8, 1972, 12:30, Sunny Day, 76 degrees," from *The Social Life of Small Urban Spaces*, 1980.

155 On the steps of Seagram plaza, from William H. Whyte, *The Social Life of Small Urban Spaces*, 1980. Photograph: William H. Whyte.

tions. Seagram was his primary model. "With such tools as time-lapse and telephoto photography, and especially our own eyes, we have been studying how people use the streets and open spaces of the city—where they gather, where they don't, what they do."[134] One of Whyte's time-lapse films tracked movement across the north corner of Seagram plaza. Sighting maps were compiled indicating with circles every sitter as either an individual "X" (male) or "O" (female), or various combinations of Xs and Os (fig. 154). Based on Whyte's studies, the Urban Design Group of the New York City Planning Commission developed guidelines that became known as the *Open Space Design Criteria*.[135] To make plazas inviting for the public, Whyte laid down detailed specifications concerning the quantity and nature of seating, the number and caliber of trees, the quality of paving, the lighting levels, and so on. With Seagram as his benchmark, Whyte summed up the lessons to be learned:

> *The Seagram Plaza is a Theater.* There is a superb relationship to the street—to the surrounding places. You can't tell where the social life of the street and the plaza leaves off. They are inextricable.
>
> *The Whole Periphery of Seagram is Eminently Sittable.* It is only slightly elevated, the steps practically invite you in, you don't have to make a decision. People are in the main traffic on the ledge. Those sitting further back and under the trees are not cut off; they are still part of the street.
>
> *The Seagram Plaza Offers a Choice.* That's very important for example on plazas where there are chairs, people will move them just an inch—at Seagrams [sic] the choice is very subtle—there is a cavey feel under the trees—People have said this in interviews. The trees give a sense of enclosure and protection—often people are back there reading. The benches are wide, and you see people lying down—They bring their lunch. [fig. 155].
>
> *There is a genial permissiveness.* The water at Seagrams [sic] looks unusually liquid. I know that if I put my hand in it or my foot in it, no thought that police will come along to stop me, as they do in many other places [fig. 156].

ARCHITECTURE AND ART ALLIED

156 Children placing their hands in the pools on Seagram plaza, from William H. Whyte, *The Social Life of Small Urban Spaces*, 1980. Photograph: William H. Whyte.

There is Always Something Going On. Sculpture sometimes, or maybe other events—the choreography of people moving across the plaza but there is activity around the plaza—vendors set up at the corner of 53rd Street—people put up their pictures along the granite walls—people just watching other people—there is always activity. This is a hallmark of a great urban space.[136]

In *The Social Life of Small Urban Spaces,* Whyte had also written, "If you want to seed a place with activity, put out food. One of the big contributions to Seagram plaza's success is Gus, the vendor who can be found day after day, year after year at the corner of Park Avenue and 52nd Street" (fig. 157).[137] And on the subject of "Undesirables," he posed the question, "If good places are so felicitous, why are there not more of them? The biggest single reason is the problem of 'undesirables.' They are not themselves much of a problem. It is the measures taken to combat them that is the problem."[138] He went on to say, "The best way to handle the problem of undesirables is to make a place attractive to everyone else. The record is overwhelmingly positive on this score. . . . The way people use a place mirrors expectations. Seagram's management is pleased people like its plaza and is quite relaxed about what they do. It . . . tolerates oddballs, even allowing them to sleep the night on the ledge" (fig. 158).[139]

Already in 1972 Whyte had summed up his appraisal of Seagram plaza in an article for the *New York Times*:

157 Gus, the food vendor at the corner of Park Avenue and Fifty-Second Street, from William H. Whyte, *The Social Life of Small Urban Spaces*, 1980. Photograph: William H. Whyte.

158 Itinerant woman on bench, Seagram plaza, from William H. Whyte, *The Social Life of Small Urban Spaces*, 1980. Photograph: William H. Whyte.

Many people actually like the city. . . . Complain as they will how horrible it all is, they enjoy the hustle and bustle. They like to watch the parade go by; they like being part of it; they like to schmooze, to girl-watch, and whenever any sort of decent open space is provided, they will quickly make it into a very sociable place. The Seagram Building is an example. On a pleasant day in spring or summer or fall this austerely elegant place throbs with life and color. You see people reading, talking, writing, picnicking, sunbathing, playing cards, necking. It is one of the great urban places of the world, in its way as significant as the Piazza San Marco of Venice.[140]

Yet despite Whyte's affirmation that the Seagram plaza was considered "one of the great urban places in the world," the story of *Building Seagram*, as it continues, is evidence of some of the harsher realities of architecture and municipal organizations.

IRONIES IN THE PUBLIC LIFE OF ARCHITECTURE: REGULATION AND THE MODERN METROPOLIS

A view through the lens backward, the historical perspective often results in the recognition of an entirely new optic. Humanist statesman Leonardo Bruni, inspired by Aelius Aristides' second-century panegyric on Athens, wrote his *Laudatio Florentinae Urbis* in praise of Florence at the beginning of the fifteenth century. Departing from a Greek model that never mentioned the physical form of the city, Bruni valorized the buildings and urban fabric of Florence, the physical appearance of the city and its amenities, and thus broke new ground. He conjoined the ethos of civic virtue and good government based on the Greek notion of the *polis* with enlightened understanding of architecture and public space rooted in the Roman sense of the *urbs,* inaugurating an early modern standard for public appreciation of the aesthetic dimension of the city. Five and a half centuries later, the Seagram building became the main stage on which ideas about new construction would be played out in New York City. My account of the reception of Seagram, exposing the deep ironies of its impact, both the highs and the lows, is presented through the lens of the various constituencies and bureaucracies that played conflicting roles in the public life of the building.

Before 1961, New York's high-rise buildings hugged the sidewalk property line for ten stories before setting back, according to code, creating relentlessly aligned building facades, or as Lewis Mumford put it, "greedy buildings, hogging every cubic foot of space the law allows."[1] Seagram was a liberating addition to Park Avenue. Even while it was still under construction, the effect of the opening that had been created in the massively walled avenue was startling. Architectural historian William Jordy described it in 1958 as "so deeply set in its plaza [that] it takes us by surprise."[2] Seagram effected a far-reaching innovation in the city's urban fabric. But for architects and critics of the 1980s who had grown up in a city by then almost riddled with small open spaces, no longer did the Seagram plaza "take us by surprise." Although the vaunted bronze skin of the building continued to be unique, the plaza, seeming so natural, was taken for granted.

The innovative nature of the plaza—its scale, quality and use of materials, the trees, water, benches, and often sculpture—is central to any discussion of the reception and influence of the Seagram building. Only in walking the streets of New York can one sense Seagram's qualities in relation to the space the building occupies: how it interacts with the buildings and streets surrounding it, the quality of the open space as one walks by, or on the plaza stops to talk, to sit, to recline, to watch, to read, to court, to think (see PF 4, PF 8, and fig. 155). However, just as the qualities of the Seagram building and its plaza caught the imagination of critics and passers-by in the years just following its creation, it drew very different responses from two New York City agencies.

Spurred by Seagram's example, in 1961 the New York City Planning Commission realized a new concept for zoning that focused on incentives rather than restrictions,[3] in order to encourage the development of privately owned public space. Proprietors were allowed to increase the floor space of their buildings in exchange for dedicating open plazas or arcades as public space. This legislation actually rewarded developers for emulating Seagram. However, at about the same time, the city tax department took what Seagram considered to be punitive measures in inflicting an "exorbitant" tax on its building—in effect, a luxury tax—because in building its own house, the Seagram company invested considerably more in the built fabric of the city than would a commercial developer whose business it was to make a profit from supplying office space. These issues placed Seagram at the center of New York's awakening to the importance of architecture in the public realm, making a case for small places of public enjoyment in contemporary North American cities, places that, in an advanced capitalist society, tend to be provided by private corporations.

To understand the impact of Seagram's plaza on New York City's urban form it is necessary to review zoning as it had structured built form since 1916, when New York enacted the nation's first comprehensive "zoning resolution." This legislation pioneered the establishment of height and setback limits to ensure light and air in the streets.[4] In order to control the speculative, upward growth of the new skyscrapers rising from the sidewalk, buildings were required to set back from the property line incrementally as they gained in height. While amendments were constantly made to the zoning resolution, not until 1961—half a century later—did the city revisit its zoning law in response to the massive societal change that promoted an entirely new regime of land-use ordinances after World War II. In a climate of high optimism, reformers led by New York's mayor, Robert Wagner, wished to "remake" the city through comprehensive municipal planning strategies.[5] By 1958 some twenty-eight million square feet of new office space had been built in the city. This activity was centered on two areas: Wall Street, which had long been dominated by office buildings, and the new Midtown business district on the East Side, where Seagram was located together with buildings erected between 1950 and 1956, within eight blocks of one another. The new zoning resolution was revolutionary when it took effect on December 15, 1961, reflecting a basic change in what was expected of zoning laws. It was no longer enough merely to prevent specific harms to the public. Proactive rather than reactive, the 1961 legislation was designed to secure particular benefits. Among these the concept of "incentive zoning" was introduced, offering a bonus of additional floor space in order to encourage developers to provide open public space at the ground level.

A proposal for the new zoning resolution prepared for the Planning Commission by the large architectural firm of Voorhees, Walker, Smith & Smith and submitted in August 1958, was illustrated with photographs of the newly completed Seagram building to exemplify open space at ground level, and Lever House, a tower occupying less than 40 percent of the lot area, both providing "a general feeling of openness at street level."[6] Another goal of the new regulations was to permit, in the highest-density commercial districts of Manhattan, "the maximum possible degree of design freedom in achieving economic, efficient, and attractive buildings."[7] Therefore, to encourage departure from "the widely prevalent 'wedding cake' building forms resulting from the rigid envelope imposed,"[8] the new zoning resolution introduced the floor area ratio (FAR), whereby the volume allowed is related to the lot area and district in which the structure is erected, replacing the setback rules. As both Seagram and Lever House were built under the 1916 Zoning Resolution, neither benefited from the new zoning legislation they inspired, but New York urban form, responding to architectural theories enunciated by the avant-garde in the 1920s, was irrevocably changed.

Taxation was another matter. From the beginning, the Tax Commission of the City of New York taxed Seagram as an exception. We do not know for sure the basis on which the building was finally assessed; we know only the conflicting facts and arguments used by lawyers to attack and defend the assessment and the differing, sometimes self-admittedly confused rationales of the many judges who supported the assessment. From fiscal year 1956–57 to fiscal year 1960–61, the city increased property taxes on Seagram's land by 31.5 percent, in contrast to a 17.5 percent increase on the land occupied by Lever House in the same period. Seagram established the building's estimated commercial value after the building had been fully occupied, that is, for 1959–60, 1960–61, and 1961–62, to be $15 million, $14.7 million, and $14.4 million, respectively, while the city's assessment for the same years was $20.5 million, $21 million, and $21 million.[9] Furthermore, the city based its assessment of the Seagram building on replacement cost—that is, on reproducing the building. This represented a major deviation from the well-established practice of determining the commercial worth of a building by capitalizing its rental income. Whether capitalization of potential income can be properly employed when the structure involved is not a completely adequate improvement and does not represent a full economic utilization of the land, the tax commission emphasized, went to the "very heart of the issue."[10]

Seagram responded to the city's assessment by making a long string of appeals challenging the tax increase. First, the company approached the tax commission with an "Application for Correction" that was heard on May 25, 1958. The commission refused to correct or reduce the assessments, and the application was denied. Seagram then brought the case into the New York State court system, beginning with a Petition for Review of Assessments on September 30, 1958, to the lowest court dealing with civil cases, the Supreme Court of New York County. The petition was argued first before the New York Supreme Court, Appellate Division, First Department, in the fall of 1962. In the argument about the method used to assess the land and the building, the city contended that Seagram was a "specially built" structure—that is, a building "designed to suit the purposes of a particular tenant, with emphasis on its individual prestige creating character, rather than on its commercial revenue."[11] The Tax Commission of the City of New York, the Respondent in the case, explained that capitalization of income would be used for a building of ordinary commercially profitable operation making full use of the land but that Seagram "covers only about one half of the plot on which it stands, and was specially built for Seagram's [sic] as something of a prestige asset."[12] The Respondent further explained that in keeping with this concept, the Seagram building "contains only half the amount of floor space which a normal office building would contain. It cannot be valued, therefore, as an ordinary commercial structure on the basis of capitalization of income, but must be treated as something in the nature of a specialty—a limited specialty might be the more appropriate term—and valued on the basis of depreciated replacement costs."[13]

After lengthy discussion of operating costs and amortization features, the Respondent stated that Seagram's actual net return of 5.3 percent had been shown to be more than ample to sustain the assessments "in view of a specially built type of structure involved," leading the lawyers of the Respondent to remark that the "Petitioner, under the circumstances, has little cause for complaint," thereby confirming the tax commission's assessment.[14] In its reply brief, Seagram, the Petitioner, caustically commented that underlying the term *fully adequate* lay the proposition that "the City is entitled to tax the petitioner not merely on the building that was built but on the building that should have been built."[15]

Judge Aaron Steuer held a Special Term of the Supreme Court, which concluded with five judges agreeing that "nowhere in the record is it explained just how . . . an experienced owner employing a reliable contractor and having the services of outstanding architects put $36 million into a structure that was only worth $17.8 million. Such a startling result requires more than speculation before it can be accepted as fact."[16] Judge Steuer's opinion reasoned that, for its owners, the building must have had another level of economic value, above that of conventional structures, and therefore should be treated differently.[17] In other words, a building of such great expense must bring to its owners value above and beyond rental income. This extra value was "prestige." Steuer wrote that "the prestige building has a rental value not based alone on commercially rented space, but on the building's value in promoting the economic interests of the owner," in effect contributing to its principal enterprise—in this case, increasing the sale of alcoholic beverages. In other words, prestige is taxable.

The court's attitude seems to have been pervaded by a strong puritanical streak. In expressing the court's dismay that the construction cost was materially in excess of utilitarian standards, Judge Steuer was equally irate that a corporation would sacrifice a substantial amount of the land that might be built upon with a consequent reduction of rentable space. For Steuer, it was a matter of ideological principle: such buildings "contribute to the owner's prestige" and "exemplify the economic theory 'Doctrine of Conspicuous Waste,' described by Thorsten Veblen as designed to impress observers with the owner's 'pecuniary strength.'"[18]

In the last possible appeal, Seagram put its case before the state's highest court, the New York State Court of Appeals, in 1964. Although the issue of the building's "prestige" was certainly discussed, particularly in the lower courts, the higher court did not conclude that "prestige" should be included in the valuation, or that the unbuilt air space of the plaza should be valued; nor did it adopt the concept of a "specialty building."[19] The court ruled seven to zero, with a majority of four and a minority of three, to uphold the City of New York's assessment.[20] The unifying thread between the majority and minority positions was on cost and the fact that Seagram's experts undervalued its income: it was shown that estimates even for Seagram space were about 14 percent below rental values of commercial tenants.[21] The Respondent averred that as long as no attempt was made to measure the value of the real estate by the profits of the commercial enterprise, there was no impropriety in taking quality into consideration, but the Seagram counsel failed to do so.[22] "Judged even by ordinary commercial standards his [Seagram's expert's] estimates were gross understatements of the real rental values."[23] The Respondent therefore found that the lower court was most convincingly justified in rejecting these rental values completely and, with them, Seagram's "'explanation' of the discrepancy between the construction cost and its expert's alleged capitalized values on which the explanation was predicated."[24] The court asserted that in the absence of a satisfactory explanation by Seagram as to why the tax was excessive, the cost of construction established the building's value for purposes of real estate taxation.[25] Furthermore, the court found that Seagram's explanation of the discrepancy between the actual construction cost of $36 million and its alleged capitalized building value $14.4 million was not satisfactory.[26] It has been noted that tax appeal cases are generally hard for the taxpayer to win because the presumption is that the assessed value is correct: the city does not have to prove its case unless the taxpayer is able to evidence a lower value taking all relevant factors into consideration. If there are holes in the taxpayer's argument, the taxpayer loses.[27]

An *amicus curiae* brief was brought before the Court of Appeals on March 16, 1964. The *Amici,* or friends of the court, consisted of a number of the most powerful associations involved in the built environment: the Regional Plan Association; the American Institute of Architects in New York; and the Fine Arts Federation of New York, which was composed of twelve other art, architectural, and landscape societies.[28] The *Amici*'s brief supported Seagram's contention "that the learned Justices . . . were in error when they ordered a novel method of assessment" based on "prestige" value, which departed from prevailing standards. They wrote:

> The Associations are here concerned with the broad implications of the issue; not merely with the confusions and inequities which will result from the application of the novel method of assessment but, of far greater importance, its prejudicial effect on freedom of architectural expression. Such freedom of expression, the ability to experiment with new forms and new ideas and to strive for perfection, is always aided by the architect's release from considerations of cost. We contend that when private wealth wishes, at its own expense and regardless of cost, to encourage the finest aesthetic expressions of the era, a form of support which characterized all periods of great artistic achievement, the courts should not be called upon unwittingly to frustrate such endeavors by the approval of novel and discriminatory methods of taxation which penalize and discourage such support.[29]

The *Amici* surmised that the only remaining value of such excess expense would be "an outstanding aesthetic quality, which can not be and in the public interest should not be subject to a real property tax."[30] The Court of Appeals disagreed, writing: "There is little of substance in the brief of the Associations. The arguments therein are obviously founded on misconceptions."[31] The court commented that the city's assessors "have leaned over backwards in their effort to extend every consideration possible in their assessment. . . . One of the best indications of this is their evaluation of the building here at the level of only $21 million, or little more than half its construction cost."[32] At Albany on June 10, 1964, the taxation levied on Seagram was unanimously upheld.[33]

Ultimately, it is not only a matter of considerable irony but also deeply disturbing that the courts could not agree on the terms and approaches to be applied. Real estate lawyer Timothy More commented that "unusual facts often result in muddled court decisions and the Seagram's case is proof in point."[34] However, one must assume a certain discrimination against Seagram: At least two notable prewar structures, the Chrysler building and Rockefeller Center, exhibited an extravagant use of materials and decoration, and Rockefeller Center had dedicated considerable open space to public use. The proceedings show evidence of a puritanical posture in the courts' deliberations that could have been allied to opprobrium levied against whisky makers going back to Prohibition and rekindled in 1950 and 1951 by the Kefauver Committee hearings on organized crime. The court of appeals departed from the concept of "prestige" that the appellate division had put forward, as well as the notion of "conspicuous waste." Instead, presiding Chief Justice Charles S. Desmond described the excess tax as a "realty tax," directly attributable to the space Seagram occupied in the building, coupled with the benefits of having its name attached to what the court acknowledged to be a "monumental and magnificent structure."[35]

Like so much else about the building that surpassed common standards, the assessment challenged established procedures and perceptions for valuing office buildings, and the courts' decisions and reasonings achieved notoriety on their own. The court of appeals effectively created a new category of taxable property, one that is "specially built to suit the tenant," and accepted the city tax commission's novel formula, whereby the cost of *reproducing* a building could be used as the basis for *assessment*.[36] That the influence of the Seagram building and plaza—beyond architecture, beyond urban form—extended to a formula for tax assessment, one attributable to new construction and "specialty properties," is yet another irony. The formula of reproducible costs persists today in New York as one of three approaches used in determining a property's market value.[37] Judge Steuer's misquotation of Veblen, referring to "conspicuous waste" rather than conspicuous consumption, indicates the courts' outlook. Striking is the fact that many observers were livid that a company would "give up" the income from rentable space. Steuer's assertion that an owner "guilty" of this "conspicuous waste" wished to "impress observers with [his] pecuniary strength" was contested by the public and the press. It can be said, nonetheless, what the company paid in real estate taxes it gained in reputation.[38]

While looking through a lens backward changes our view, looking at the recent past through the lens of contemporary experience tends to distort the view plane. It is difficult in a world of mega-developers and star-architects to grasp the fact that architecture was not a cultural concern in the 1950s despite almost two decades of exhibitions on the "new art" of architecture at the Museum of Modern Art. Real estate developers and commercial architects entered a new era, and it is useful to recall that Seagram itself initially contracted for space in a mega-developer building. Eyes were still blind to the sea change that had come with the construction of the glass curtain–walled United Nations Headquarters and Lever House. On the other hand, awareness of urban preservation was not yet part of the scene. In 1955, the *New York Times* supported William Zeckendorf's proposal to replace Pennsylvania Station's magnificent turn-of-the-century steel-and-glass concourse with a high-tech Palace of Progress, "to make more profitable use of valuable real estate holdings."[39] *Not a word of protest was uttered.* As one critic put it: "Whatever preservation-oriented concerns lurked in the hearts of New Yorkers did not register on the public screen."[40] Only in the following decade would municipal and state agencies, the press, and the public begin to recognize the value of architecture old and new and of public space. As the municipality expressed a new concern for the well-being of the individual through incentive zoning, the public rose up to protest the taxes levied on Seagram and the destruction of one of the great monuments of the metropolis, Penn Station. Seagram thus attended to the rebirth in New York of a civic consciousness of architecture's importance to the res publica, playing a central role in bringing about paradigmatic change in the meaning of the city for New Yorkers—individual citizens, the press, government, and private patrons. In an increasingly bureaucratized society, the difficulty lies in the act of maintaining the democratic balance.

Seagram was at the fulcrum of a general shift of attitude made manifest in the 1961 Zoning Resolution and in the public reaction to the extraordinary tax assessment levied on the building and plaza. Between 1961 and 1963, a virtual uproar in favor of preventing the demolition of the great unfolding steel-and-glass vaults of McKim, Mead and White's Pennsylvania Station launched a cause célèbre that helped lead to the establishment of the New York City Landmark Preservation Law of 1965.[41] This only deepened the paradoxical citation of the Seagram plaza as an example of conspicuous waste. From the platform of her newly created role as architecture critic for the *New York Times,* Ada Louise Huxtable presciently made clear that "the impassioned pleas for the cultural and architectural values of the city" were incapable of saving the monumental Penn Station because the city planning commission had no power to do so.[42] In a reversal of its 1955 stance, in May 1962 the *New York Times* published an editorial decrying "the ultimate tragedy [to be] that such architectural nobility has become economically obsolete, so that we must destroy [Pennsylvania Station] for [the] shoddier buildings and lesser values" that would surely replace it.[43]

The Seagram taxation case elicited broad press coverage across the United States. The outcome of litigation over the real estate tax assessment for an office building with so many remarkable features was awaited with great interest and concern owing to the effect it could have on architecture. Public opinion raged against the position taken by the city and the state. The *Architectural Forum* sounded the clarion call in May 1963 with the editorial "How to Ban Architecture," protesting the "grotesque ruling by the New York State Appellate Division," which has, "in effect, just empowered the City of New York to levy a special tax on architectural quality.... Instead of appraising the [Seagram] building in the usual way, the city decided to penalize it for being something quite special—a *prestige* structure. And now the city has been upheld [by the State Appellate Court] in this culturally illiterate decision.... The power to tax architecture on its quality is the power to prevent [architectural quality]."[44]

The *New York Times* editorial published on June 13, 1964, headlined as "A Blow for Architecture," continued this tone: "When it serves society badly, there is something wrong with the law.... Joseph E. Seagram & Sons is to be penalized in the form of higher taxes for building an extravagantly handsome structure that has become one of the city's chief ornaments. For New York this decision is a catastrophe.... Whatever its legal rationalization, this is a tax on architectural excellence, and the result, inevitably, will be to outlaw it."[45] *Newsweek* posed the question, "Is this admittedly extravagant use of expensive space an example of conspicuous waste, or a manifestation of corporate restraint and a demonstration of civic responsibility?"[46] The *Reader's Digest* weighed in.[47] The *New York Herald Tribune* published a "study of this anti-aesthetic, quality-penalizing tax" in its Sunday magazine section.[48]

Of the many letters to the editor addressing the contested tax assessment, I have found only one that supported the court's decision. It was written by the president of the Mexican Institute of Appraisers, Mariano Alcocer, who felt that New York City should not be "responsible for the mistake of an unbalanced Seagram's investment" and that "no nation, city, or country can sacrifice real estate taxes on account of the private construction of rental buildings with the purpose of creating their own prestige."[49] In contrast, the *Real Estate Forum* found difficulty "in reconciling the City's avowed intent, expressed in the new zoning law just passed, to create more open space, more plazas and arcades, with a taxing system that simultaneously punishes the performance of this desirable end."[50] A significant point was made in a letter to the editor of *Progressive Architecture* in late 1963, observing that the parklike plaza surrounding Seagram not only was a setting for the building but also "provides a value to the surrounding buildings and to the City—a value that is as real as tax dollars."[51] However, soon after Seagram was completed, an article in the July 1959 issue of *Architectural Forum* had raised the issue of business strategy, asking: "Can a custom-built, luxury skyscraper like the Seagram building . . . be made to pay its way in today's commercial market?" Preliminary figures indicated that the building might well pay its way, and also earn a modest profit. But, wrote the authors, "even if the building were not to 'pay off' in dollars and cents at all, even if all the profit had to be taken in good will, even then [the] investment would be a sound one."[52] It is useful to explore the value to the *urbs New Yorkensis* of the building's public space.

According to New York rules, the site was underdeveloped; its zoning envelope could accommodate another building the size of the Seagram tower. The original intention of zoning to bring light and air into the streets was perverted by the evolving concept of "highest and best use" of land,[53] determined by the competitive forces within the market, resulting in maximum profitability, so that underbuilding became a threat to those who did so. I learned much about such vulnerability in Chicago.

When the Seagram building and plaza were finished and the Four Seasons Restaurant opened in late July 1959, I returned to school to study architecture. While I had been lucky in my initial instincts about architecture, it was evident to me that I needed solid training in mathematics and design. At the outset, Yale, where both Lou Kahn and Joseph Albers were teaching, seemed ideal, but after two years I was hungry for a more fundamental understanding of architecture than discussing whether a campanile should be placed at the end of a campus or envisioning city planning as city beautiful, painting designs on the oil tanks at the harbor entrance to New Haven to dissimulate them. After spending a summer working in Mies's office in Chicago, I transferred to the Illinois Institute of Technology (IIT), where I completed my professional degree in 1963.

Staying on in Chicago until 1971, I re-enrolled at IIT to take courses in regional planning and the ecological basis of planning (which I then taught for a year at Malcolm X College of Chicago). In 1968, a continuing interest in the urban realm led me to work on a project for the federal government's Model Cities Program in Chicago's Douglas community area, joined by Antonis Tritsis, an architect, planner, and fellow graduate student at IIT.[54] The objective was to develop an alternative urban renewal process in order to revitalize the deteriorated Douglas Community, better known as the Gap or Bronzeville neighborhoods, formerly a notorious section of Chicago's Black Belt south of the IIT campus.[55] Demolition of important buildings menaced Chicago during these years: the fight to save Louis Sullivan's Garrick Theater ended in demolition; Frank Lloyd Wright's Francis Apartments were demolished; and Wright's Robie House and H. H. Richardson's Glessner House (where I learned my first lessons in fighting for preservation) were threatened with demolition. All of this helped to prepare me for the preservation battles I would later engage in Montreal. But it was New York City and Seagram that were on my mind after graduation in 1963, when I took a small office at 230 East Ohio Street (the building in which Mies's office was located) to work on my first commission, to design the Saidye Bronfman Centre in Montreal.[56]

It was from my Ohio Street base that I started gathering information pertaining to development pressures created by the unused air rights (now called development rights) of the Seagram building and plaza—a matter that had long worried me. As already noted, according to the existing 1961 Zoning Resolution, a structure almost double the size of Mies's building could have occupied the Seagram site. This meant that some 500,000 square feet of floor area had gone undeveloped. If the total block were considered, including the YWCA headquarters contiguous with Seagram at the eastern end of the block, the potential built volume of the full block would have been calculated at roughly a third more, or another 325,000 square feet. From my vantage point in Chicago I was well aware of the pressures that could be imposed on underbuilt property, given that the scandal surrounding the move to demolish one of Chicago's finest nineteenth-century buildings, Sullivan & Adler's 1893–94 Stock Exchange, was being played out at that very time. In 1972 this historic building was torn down to make way for a structure two or three times its bulk. This occurred even though it would have been possible to build on the adjacent property and to transfer to that site the unused air rights from the Stock Exchange building.[57]

The transfer of air rights was being studied in New York at the time by a former fellow Yale student, Jaquelin Robertson, who had become the director of New York's Office of Midtown Planning and Development (OMPD). Created by John Lindsay after he was elected mayor in 1965, the OMPD was a division of the mayor's office and functioned in parallel with the city planning department, but its mandate was to develop new solutions to New York's physical impasse. In the meantime, I had moved my office to the North

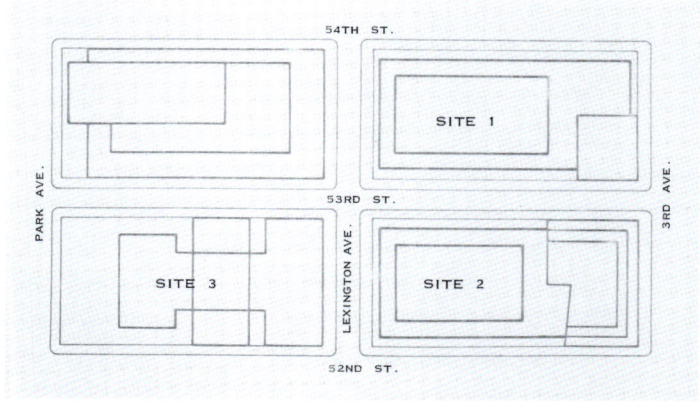

159 Phyllis Lambert and David Fix, principals, Pier Associates, Inc., architects and planners, Plan identifying sites considered in the "Lexington Avenue Development: 52nd Street to 54th Street Feasibility Studies," July 27, 1970.

160 Phyllis Lambert and David Fix, principals, Pier Associates, Inc., architects and planners, model, Scheme A, "Lexington Avenue Development: 52nd Street to 54th Street Feasibility Studies," July 27, 1970, as of right, without transfer of Seagram air rights. Photograph: Pier Associates, Inc., 1970.

Pier Terminal at 403–409 East Illinois Street in Chicago, converting a section of a large warehouse, and named my firm Pier Associates, Inc., Architects and Planners. I was joined by David Fix, another former Yale classmate. Fix and I worked together on the problem of Seagram's air rights and developed a scheme to replace the two YWCA buildings on Lexington Avenue. Named "Seagram East," our proposal dated March 31, 1970, consisted of a ten-story building (the same height as Mies's bustle) connected to the Seagram building through a passage at the ground floor.[58]

When we presented the project to Robertson, we discovered that the OMPD envisioned something beyond our scheme, something much larger that had the potential to achieve a comprehensive plan for the area, "with design control resting in the hands of Seagram and its representatives."[59] This was crucial since the transfer of air rights would be eligible under the City Planning Commission legislation, Section 74-74 for "Commercial Development Extending into More Than One Block," but *only* if all zoning lots in question were under control of a single party.[60] Thus, the transfer of air rights to the two blocks immediately east of Seagram and its neighbor, the First National Bank of New York (between Lexington and Third Avenues and Fifty-Fourth and Fifty-Second Streets), required joint ownership of a minimum of 20,000 square feet by Seagram and a third party, or joint ownership by Seagram and the bank.

Seagram East was exploratory on my part. I wanted to find a solution to the problem before it became one. Armed with documentation provided by the OMPD,[61] Fix and I undertook feasibility studies for solutions to the transfer of Seagram's air rights to the two blocks in question. Working before the computer era to make the calculations for the different possibilities, on July 27, 1970, we produced the "Lexington Avenue Development 52nd to 54th Street Feasibility Studies," showing various solutions:[62] Scheme A, an "Independent Development," established thirty-seven-floor towers rising from an eight-floor base, accommodating totals of 1,059,000 and 1,321,000 square feet, which could be built "as of right" on the subject blocks without the transfer of air rights (figs. 159, 160). Scheme B, a "Large Scale Development," transferred 580,000 square feet of air rights from Seagram

161 Phyllis Lambert and David Fix, principals, Pier Associates, Inc., architects and planners, model, Scheme B, "Lexington Avenue Development: 52nd Street to 54th Street Feasibility Studies," July 27, 1970, with transfer of Seagram air rights to site 2, directly east of Seagram. Photograph: Pier Associates, Inc., 1970.

IRONIES IN THE PUBLIC LIFE OF ARCHITECTURE

162 Phyllis Lambert and David Fix, principals, Pier Associates, Inc., architects and planners, model, Scheme C, "Lexington Avenue Development: 52nd Street to 54th Street Feasibility Studies," July 27, 1970, with transfer of Seagram air rights to site 1, north of Fifty-Third Street. Photograph: Pier Associates, Inc., 1970.

(site 3) to site 2, resulting in a sheer tower of fifty-six floors at 28,000 square feet per floor, totaling 1,641,100 square feet, which would stand some eighteen stories higher than the Seagram tower and directly behind it (fig. 161). Scheme C, a "Large Scale Development," similarly transferred 580,000 square feet from Seagram (site 3), but northward to site 1, resulting in a fifty-seven-floor tower at 33,000 square feet per floor, totaling 1,921,000 square feet, similar in height to the Citicorp building subsequently erected on this site in 1978 (fig. 162).

The situation in which two contiguous blocks of the city could be developed at the same time was, if not unique, extremely rare, as I emphasized in a memorandum to SB in October 1970, urging Seagram to acquire control of the block directly east of Lexington Avenue (between Fifty-Second and Fifty-Third Streets) so that it would be a party to planning these blocks: "[The two blocks] are especially important because of the subway confluence, and the city will zone here for mixed development of retail, housing and offices."[63] Perhaps it was not possible for those who were not aware of the importance of subway interconnections in city planning to understand that such situations call for increased density. Where such nodes of mass transit do occur, the surrounding area in New York City is highly developed, not only in theory but in actuality, as the areas surrounding Times Square and Bloomingdale's department store showed. Equally important at the time was the new commitment on the city's part to legislate "mixed use," breaking with the Industrial Revolution–inspired Zoning Resolution of 1916, which separated residential commercial and industrial usage into different districts, a separation brought into focus by Jane Jacobs when she argued for the chaos and diversity of city streets in her *Death and Life of Great American Cities* of 1961. However, I considered Jacobs's plea for a low-rise city to be backward-looking and saw the new legislation as a way of creating the desired diversity in a high-rise downtown. By the time I had expressed these ideas in the memorandum to SB, the First National Bank had become a major player in the area. Soon to be renamed Citibank, it relocated from Wall Street to Park Avenue one block north of Seagram to occupy a building completed in 1961,⁶⁴ and by 1970, for its own expansion, had procured almost all of the land on the block immediately to the east (between Fifty-Third and Fifty-Fourth Streets) bounded by Lexington and Third Avenues, as well as owning or controlling key parcels in the block immediately east of Seagram.

The possibilities for removing a threat to the Seagram building were thereby severely reduced. In the memorandum of October 1970 to Samuel Bronfman et alia, I emphasized the problem:

> This will be a new type of development in New York City—a new centre if the two blocks are developed together—[but if not, the area] can only be mediocre and the Seagram building [will be] in a cavern. . . . I consider the Seagram building to be in the dangerous position of being blocked from all future possibilities of selling air rights if it does not control the block to the east at this point. Negotiation for a third party who would develop this block would take some time at best, and for the moment there is no third party.⁶⁵

I was convinced that planning involving more than one block would gain traction in major cities. In New York, ground had been broken for the Lincoln Center for the Performing Arts in 1959, and in Montreal, Place Ville Marie (I. M. Pei and Henry Cobb, Architects) was completed between 1962 and 1964.⁶⁶ In Toronto, a number of blocks had been assembled for the Toronto Dominion Centre, completed in 1969 to the design of Mies van der Rohe, an undertaking of the bank itself in collaboration with Fairview, the development arm of my family. Inconsistently, Fairview turned down the project which I proposed for New York in 1969 and another for Chicago in the following year.⁶⁷ (Either they did not understand such markets in the United States or I did not know how to fight for my own projects.)

Ominously, the issue of Seagram's unused air rights remained unresolved until it was taken up again in the late 1970s. This time, the Seagram company became involved, but so slowly that the economic situation changed. And above all, it was already too late. Between 1976 and 1978, Citibank had proceeded to build the fifty-nine-story Citicorp Center designed by Hugh Stubbins between Lexington and Third Avenues, incorporating St. Peter's Lutheran Church (see fig. 163).⁶⁸ In February 1978, at my request Pasanella + Klein documented changes to the zoning resolution over the last fifteen years and their consequences for building on the YWCA site adjacent to the Seagram building.⁶⁹ The document was copied to Joe Blunt, Seagram vice president for administration. Two years later, I received from Lou Goldberg, Seagram vice president for human resources, the pro forma report Cushman & Wakefield had prepared for him concerning an office building on the YWCA site, including the possibility that YWCA would relocate.⁷⁰ Again a year later, in February 1981, Philip Johnson's partner John Burgee, whom I consulted on zoning issues, advised that a building of 385,000 square feet could be built there, but to erect a large building on such a small site would require waivers the city planning commission was not inclined to give at that time. Transferring air rights to the Citibank site across Lexington would be more practical owing to the larger site area, but it involved transfer of air rights from one community board to another, because Lexington Avenue is the dividing line: "One Community Board is very reluctant to accept the bulk in one area to reduce the bulk in an adjacent area, as you can imagine."⁷¹ Nevertheless, Seagram attempted to approach Citibank through its law firm, but there seemed to be no appetite for the project. The lawyers suggested that "the bottom line may well be that the only absolute protection for Seagram is to approach the 'Y' to discuss whether Seagram could acquire the property. It is our feeling that with or without special legislation, 'something' will be built sooner or later on the Y parcel."[72] The trail left off here; the matter would be taken up in the next century.

The decade of the 1970s was crucial in terms of testing the tools of urban planning in an atmosphere fraught with stress. Despite the glowing view of the economy and its future expressed in 1954 by Seagram president General Schwengel, as early as 1959, *Newsweek* ran a story on New York entitled "Metropolis in a Mess."[73] The exposé pointed to widespread slums, high crime rates, racial tensions, declining social services and infrastructure, and the flight of the middle class to the suburbs. A sweeping indictment of the city, based on six months of investigative research, was published by the *New York Herald Tribune* in a series of articles beginning on January 25, 1965, with "Indictment: Reasons for Outrage and Reasons to Act." The collected articles were later republished as *New York City in Crisis*.[74] Most of the outrage was related to the ineptitude of the city's leadership and fiscal scandals involving federal programs, such as the scandalously administered urban renewal projects and the War on Poverty. Both initiatives were intended to address, however inconsistently, the massive influx of unskilled or semiskilled workers who in great numbers replaced the middle class as it fled the city. *Time* reported in February 1967 that "New York City (pop 7,500,000) showed symptoms of shrinkage. Though the city is beefing up its effort to attract new industries, it drives old ones away by reason of costs and congestion, smog and stick-ups, traffic and taxes that rise in a wry ratio with strikes and relief rolls."[75] The same article also reported that "seven of the U.S.'s largest companies had opted out of Fun City . . . within a year," and "14 more corporations with 11,500 employees are also studying whether to take their head offices out of Manhattan." In 1971, at least once a month from January through April, a major story on the flight of corporations from Manhattan appeared in either the *New York Times* or *Time* magazine.[76] By October 1975, the city was on the brink of bankruptcy, a trauma Governor Hugh Carey redressed by creating an agency to provide the city with ready access to credit.[77] With the protracted Vietnam War, the oil crises of 1973 and 1974, and unprecedented rampant inflation coupled with slow economic growth known as "stagflation," the national mood in the United States was morose.

Against this background of municipal crisis and the country's loss of self-confidence, the Seagram company suffered a steady decline from its pinnacle of dominating the spirits market in 1955 and 1956.[78] A momentous event further destabilized the company: the legendary Samuel Bronfman, president of Distillers Corporation–Seagrams Limited, my father, died on July 10, 1971. His eldest son, Edgar M. Bronfman, who had been elected president and chief executive officer of Joseph E. Seagram & Sons, Ltd., in 1957, now took full charge of all Seagram enterprises.[79] After years of suffering what he termed his father's "veto management," rather than feeling a sense of relief at his new authority, he later admitted to being thrown off balance: "In the aftermath of Father's death my personal life quickly went askew. Indeed for much of the next fifteen years I rode an emotional roller coaster, struggling with difficult relationships and painful separations."[80] The turmoil, he wrote, "took its toll on my stewardship of Seagram, at times keeping me from operating on all cylinders. However I was able to prioritize and concentrate on getting the big picture right."[81] My brother's top priority was expansion of the company's foreign operations, but his stewardship of the Seagram building wavered through the decade of the 1970s.

While SB was still alive, during the 1960s Edgar quite sensibly put to rest SB's ambitions to create a Seagram empire of buildings in Chicago and Los Angeles, in addition to New York, commenting that "Father's idiosyncratic nature sometimes led him to pursue ridiculous notions."[82] Edgar simply declared that Seagram was not in the business of real estate. The Los Angeles venture remained a concept that never took root. In Chicago, however, Mies van der Rohe's office had made an initial study in 1958 of a site along Michigan Avenue between Chestnut and Pearson, which Seagram had purchased in 1954 (see chapter 1). The parcel adjoined two historic Chicago landmarks, the only survivors of the Great Chicago Fire of 1871: the 1869 Water Tower pumping station immediately to the south and, across from it on Michigan Avenue, the picturesque Water Tower of the same date. In 1960, Edgar wrote to Mies to inform him that Seagram's board had accepted an offer for the land and would not proceed with the plan to build in Chicago.[83] Although the sale was not consummated, interest in both the site and area were such that the one-hundred-story Hancock Center built on the block north of the Seagram site was announced at the end of February 1965, and studies of the site for the "Upper Michigan Avenue Project" by Skidmore, Owings & Merrill in joint venture with the Office of Mies van der Rohe were completed in October 1969, the year Mies died.[84] In connection with the Michigan Avenue report prepared by a group of real estate developers and managers,[85] I wrote to SB with a development proposal by Chicago realtors Draper and Kramer, Inc., in association with Philip Klutznick, arguing that dynamic interest in the area indicated that it was time to act.[86] However, the real estate arm of the family holdings again demurred.[87]

A series of architectural projects initiated by Edgar followed. The first one involved moving the Seagram offices out of New York City. Seagram had been a major initiator of the office building boom that took hold in Midtown Manhattan and then on Wall Street, making New York the headquarters of 25 percent of *Fortune*'s five hundred largest American corporations.[88] Paradoxically, with this boom still in full swing in the mid-1960s, Seagram considered a move to Connecticut or Westchester, in keeping with the current trend toward corporations leaving New York. A move to Danbury was proposed, and I was asked to assess the new corporate campuses in the vicinity. The notion of leaving New York seemed to me to have been pulled out of the thin air of received ideas, but rather than oppose such an unthinkable abandonment of the Seagram building outright, I thought it wiser to remain in the picture and possibly influence the outcome—especially since I assumed the move would somehow be averted. I toured the Danbury area, made my investigation, and became convinced that executives who had two martinis for luncheon in the city would double the count in the country.

A relocation report was commissioned by the company in 1968 and completed by Seagram's treasurer, Thomas P. Hawe, in early 1972.[89] Known as the "Hawe Report," the study was occasioned not by New York City's perilous condition but by corporate growth requiring a basic rearrangement of the company's office facilities. Two solutions were considered: building a new company headquarters outside New York or retaining 375 Park Avenue for executive corporate and sales offices while moving other departments outside the city or to a new location within it. The report noted that in 1972 the company occupied 172,000 square feet in the Seagram building, which amounted to 75 percent of the company's rental space in Midtown. The report also recommended that Seagram obtain relief from the inequitable real estate tax that Seagram had taken all the way to the state's highest court in the 1960s, losing its case at every step.[90] Surveys were conducted with staff and executives. Hawe concluded that the future of the city was the key to any decision about whether to remain in New York. He pointed to trends indicating that the city would not deteriorate further. Among the indices Hawe cited was the continuing expansion of commercial construction.[91] Furthermore, the rich cultural life of the city, the high levels of creativity it engendered, the intensity of interpersonal urban interaction, and the city's superior educational facilities would all, he felt, count heavily in the long-term effectiveness of the Seagram company.[92] The second option of the Hawe report, to move large, space-consuming functions out of the Seagram building, was adopted and acted on immediately.[93]

Seagram's corporate and sales executives remained at 375 Park Avenue, but in March 1973, Seagram moved 600 members of a workforce of 983 employees from 375 Park to less expensive quarters at nearby 800 Third Avenue.[94] At my recommendation, design of the offices at 800 Third Avenue and the concomitant revisions of the offices at 375 Park were undertaken by the office of Pasanella + Klein. They became, in effect, Seagram's architects responsible for stewardship, and in 1973–74 the firm produced a working document titled "Seagram Interior Design Guidelines," to be revised as needed in order "to establish a basic design philosophy for offices and associated areas at all levels. The objectives of such a program are to provide a consistent level of aesthetic and practical design throughout the company."[95] The guidelines laid out specifications for all furniture at 375 Park Avenue, 800 Third Avenue, and the new Seagram facilities at Des Plaines, Illinois, which Pasanella + Klein had designed. Pasanella explained that although the occupants of an office may change, the furnishings in a space belong to the space and not to the person occupying it, and consequently that the offices should be kept as constant as possible.[96]

Then, in 1974–75, Edgar Bronfman commissioned the Darnley Bottling Plant near Paisley in Scotland. It was thoughtfully designed by British architect Peter Carter, who had been responsible for major projects in Mies's office. Carter was concerned, as always, about landscape and working conditions, asking why those currently working in the bottling hall did not have a view of the beautiful countryside. In his design for a new facility, Carter proposed glazing one end of a large room sited with a view out onto the sloping grounds, for which, with the help of the borough's landscape engineer, he designed a meticulously detailed landscape plan incorporating the native flora. The Darnley plant was never built.[97]

Another unbuilt project followed: In 1979, Pasanella + Klein was chosen from a list of candidates to draw up plans for an office building and hangar at Westchester County Airport.[98] According to Edgar, it was not intended be a fly-in meeting place, as one might assume; rather, he was thinking ahead of his time: "I was thinking about computers and the heat they generate and using that to heat office space."[99] In his opinion, "the building at the airport should have been built. It would have been much more efficient than leasing that space in Westchester we eventually did."[100] My involvement in these projects was limited to advising on the selection of architects. Above all and foremost during this period, I remained focused on the maintenance and conservation of the building and plaza at 375 Park Avenue.

In November 1976, on behalf of Seagram's board of directors, Edgar appealed to Mayor Abraham D. Beame, who succeeded John Lindsay in New York City, for early activation of the city's landmarking legislation for Seagram. The building was then only twenty years old, a decade shy of the thirty required by the New York City Landmarks Law.[101] Three days later, Beame replied to Edgar that he had asked the landmarks preservation commissioner to contact Seagram and look into the matter.[102] The subject received the immediate attention of the press. Paul Goldberger, architecture critic for the *New York Times,* a highly respected voice, commented that Seagram's request reversed the frequent practice of landlords *opposing* landmark designation: "The prestige of the tower has translated itself at least somewhat into monetary terms. Even at the low point of New York City office market, the thirty-four floors that Seagram rents to other tenants are ninety-eight percent occupied at rents substantially higher than those charged at neighboring buildings."[103] Seagram officials met with those of the Landmarks Preservation Commission. However, more than half a year passed without a word from the mayor, at which point Edgar, somewhat exasperated, wrote another "Dear Abe" letter dated May 3, 1977: "Almost seven months ago I proposed that the scope of the Landmarks Preservation Law be enlarged.... Our suggestion received an avalanche of support from virtually every civic and preservation institution, from the press and a collection of preservation, academic and architectural notables.... In fact, the only strong, not opposition, but obstacle to our suggestion has been that nothing has happened to implement it."[104] Amending such legislation would have opened it up to possible negative or counterproductive amendments, and as my brother noted in his letter, the officials responsible for implementation "agreeably but unavailingly told us of the vortex of complexities surrounding any innovation in the landmarks designation. They have proposed that we go away and turn to the Federal Government." Edgar continued that he had no intention of lobbying or politicizing acceptance of the project and added somewhat coercively: "Our initiative too will fade away in discouragement unless some action to a conclusion is taken on it.... So I respectfully suggest to you and your Administration, solely in the interest of the City's welfare, not to look *this* particular gift horse in the mouth and send it limping to the boneyard of irresolution."[105]

In the economic turmoil of the city, how disingenuous was Seagram's request for landmarking? In his first letter to Beame at the end of 1976, Edgar had noted that several offers had been received from investors expressing an interest in buying the building at an "attractive price" with a long-term lease-back of the space occupied by the Seagram company. He continued: "Since we are not primarily in the real estate business, our board did discuss such offers but in the end rejected them. We have not and do not have any intention of transferring ownership of the building. But times and circumstances change and the very suggestion has increased our resolve to preserve for New York City, in perpetuity, the building's architectural and aesthetic integrity."[106] Furthermore the *Architectural Record* had wryly suggested that "taxation may also have a role in the resolution: Seagram, which is taxed on the value of its prestigious architecture, may be taking advantage of recent Federal legislation favoring historical buildings."[107] The issues of economics and landmarking and sustaining architectural culture—the subjects of the next chapter—carry the account of *Building Seagram* into the 1980s and 1990s and, finally, into the new century.

7

SUSTAINING ARCHITECTURAL CULTURE

The Seagram Company agreed to sell its building on May 31, 1979, for eighty-five million dollars.¹ The sale had been under discussion for more than a year, when the exhibition I had prepared, *The Seagram Plaza: Its Design and Use,* was installed in the Seagram Gallery on the fourth floor of the building, and I remember thinking of the bitter irony of the situation. At the time I wrote to Edward Saxe, then deputy director and general manager of the Museum of Modern Art, that the very idea was "chilling."² In March 1979, three weeks after the building was placed on the market, the *New York Times* published an editorial entitled "Selling a Vintage Building" in which Seagram's exacting conditions were outlined:

> As the builder, owner and occupant, in part, of the city's finest postwar skyscraper, Seagram does not want to relinquish the space or style to which it has become accustomed or the luster that this landmark structure adds to its name. The sale is therefore being handled as an "invitational offering" with a lot of strings. A minimum price of $75 million . . . is being proposed to a select group of well-heeled institutional buyers. Numerous guarantees to preserve and protect the building's landmark quality are being required. Seagram had already applied for landmark designation, although the building is still technically too young for that distinction. And the company has no plans to leave; it would lease back its offices for an extended period.³

Seagram's fate was thus already a matter of considerable public concern just two decades after its completion in 1959. The building and the plaza were universally recognized for their essential properties of space, proportions, luster, and elegance, but it must be said that Seagram spared no effort to protect and guarantee those qualities.

The oasis in New York City formed by the Seagram building and plaza was not conceived by Mies as a product to be used, transformed, and discarded. As a deeply thought-through work of art and a singular symbol of twentieth-century culture, it continues to remind us of what the celebrated tenor Dietrich Fischer-Dieskau called "the splendid duty of sustaining the life of the treasury left us by the masters . . . whose great musical works require immaculate performance."[4] Architecture demands an equivalent commitment in the domain of stewardship, a form of watching over that carries a high degree of moral responsibility for managing the built and natural environment and that embraces the total architectural project—from the initial intent to build to the selection of the architect, the realization of the building project, and the long-term maintenance essential to sustaining the life of the "treasury."

Commissioning and building ambitious architecture is one thing; guaranteeing its fate is another. Once an outstanding architect has been selected, once the client or owner has ensured that the building gives tangible form to the significance of the architectural idea, to what extent can a building's fate be "guaranteed" against the unknowable and uncontrollable future? Whose responsibility is it, ultimately, to make sure that buildings like Seagram will be protected and maintained, restored and "preserved," so that the original architectural idea continues to be communicated to the public as a marker in the evolution of a shared culture? Amid the chaos and conflict of public and private interests, this responsibility ultimately falls to the agencies of municipal, state, and federal governments. However, the act of guaranteeing a work of architecture in the public realm begins with ownership. What does being an owner and a patron entail? And even more, what is responsible stewardship? In both cases, ironically, citizens are ultimately the real and effective arbiters.

Numerous instances in the story of building Seagram point to the company's stewardship from the beginning, from the commitment to build in the best possible way for its time to choosing and supporting the architect, realizing Mies's architectural idea to its fullest, creating a new kind of public space for New York, and fostering the public role of the building, plaza, and art programs. This commitment was fully articulated in the mid-1950s, but could it be sustained in the face of inevitable changes of management and ownership within the Seagram company itself? Changes in the municipal administration? Or social and economic change at local, national, and even international levels? As the Seagram story unfolded, it became clear that development pressures could put the building at risk and that historical preservation and landmarking, which also inspired owners and municipalities to create new tools, would eventually play an essential role in safeguarding the building's identity and character.[5]

It is possible to say that "times" and "circumstances" had already begun to reverse New York's fortunes from the beleaguered 1970s. A long article entitled "New York Bounces Back" appeared in *Time* in August 1978, applauding "a remarkable renewal of energy and morale" in the city. Noting that "the romance with the countryside did not always work out," the authors pointed to the transformation of the city, which after seven years of losses showed evidence of significant improvement—more new jobs, revitalized cultural life, and reduced crime.[6] The slowdown of the corporate exodus was trumped by a billion dollars in financed construction of buildings of high quality to be erected near the Seagram building and plaza. Already in place were Hugh Stubbins's 915-foot-high Citicorp Center (1978, now Citigroup Center) on Lexington Avenue between Fifty-Third and Fifty-Fourth Streets (fig. 163) and Edward Larabee Barnes's 603-foot-high IBM building at Fifty-Seventh and Madison (1983), now 590 Madison Avenue (fig. 164). Philip Johnson's 647-foot AT&T

163 Hugh Stubbins and Associates, architects, Citicorp Center, 153 East Fifty-Third Street, New York, 1974–77. Photograph: Norman McGrath, 1978.

building (1984), now the Sony Tower (fig. 165), is at 550 Madison Avenue. Johnson arrogantly anticipated that it would be "a landmark headquarters, hopefully for this generation what the Seagram building was for a generation ago."[7] The companies commissioning these buildings made an effort to engage good architects and demanded more than a standard commercial endeavor. Sited in the "backwater" of Park Avenue, on Lexington or Third Avenue, these buildings made their mark by being considerably taller than Seagram, having benefited from the 1961 Zoning Resolution.[8] To make the most of their less-than-luminary sites, both had sensational characteristics. In order to accommodate St. Peter's Church, the architects and engineers of Citicorp set their fifty-nine-story tower on four massive 114-foot columns positioned at the center of each side, rather than at the corners. This design allowed the northwest corner of the building on Lexington to cantilever seventy-two feet over the new church. The "Chippendale" top of Philip Johnson's granite-clad AT&T building was notorious, but its cavernous open-air public arcade along Madison Avenue, with

164 Edward Larrabee Barnes and Associates, architects, IBM Building (now 590 Madison), 590 Madison Avenue, New York, 1975–83. Photographer unknown, c. 1983–84.

165 Philip Johnson and John Burgee, architects, AT&T Building (now Sony Tower), 550 Madison Avenue, New York, 1978–84, detail. Photograph: Wolfgang Hoyt, 1984.

sixty-foot-high granite-faced columns, movable chairs and tables, and wooden planters that provided open space in a dense shopping area, weighed heavily in the permitting of a much larger building than would have been possible before 1961. Within six years and in the hands of a new occupant, Sony, however, the arcade would be enclosed and turned into shops. Two blocks further north on Madison, the IBM building commands greater visibility by being sited at the corner of the wider and more prominent crosstown Fifty-Seventh Street. The entrance is dramatically placed under a deep cantilever formed by the forty-five-degree angle cutaway corner encompassing both thoroughfares. This covered, open space, together with a midblock atrium off Fifty-Sixth Street dedicated as public space, also figured into permitting a much larger structure under the new zoning law.

Another structure profiting from the 1961 Zoning Resolution potentially had a negative impact on the Seagram building. On December 27, 1977, I received a letter from Hal K. Negbaur, chairman of the Borough of Manhattan Community Board No. 5, informing me of a project for which Fisher Brothers, a commercial development firm, was seeking special permits and a change in the text of the zoning resolution in order to construct a midblock forty-five-story office building of just under a million square feet between Fifty-Second and Fifty-Third Streets and Madison and Park Avenues. "To be more specific the property is immediately behind the Racquet & Tennis Club."[9] Negbaur wrote to me: "It is because of this rather large size for a mid-block building that I think you would be interested in the property." But of course the real issue was its location. The building would face Seagram across Park Avenue (see fig. 172).

The Racquet and Tennis Club was of such urban and spatial significance to Seagram and its plaza that I was concerned about the relationship of the new tower to both the club and Seagram. It was reassuring to know that Skidmore, Owings & Merrill were the architects. As I was living in Montreal at the time, I asked Pasanella + Klein to follow the project closely for Seagram. Arvid Klein recommended that Seagram support the project due to its good massing and sufficient assurance that the Racquet and Tennis Club would remain in its present form for the foreseeable future.[10] The zoning permit was finally granted for the project, which became Park Avenue Plaza when completed in 1981. According to the allowable floor area ratio, the tower has twice the volume of Seagram, but is only five stories higher. The club was finally protected on being granted landmark designation in May 1979.

Paradoxically, at the same time that Seagram was planning to sell its building, enlightened clients were commissioning office buildings by architects of note in the surrounding blocks. These new office buildings were strong indicators of the reemergence of a seller's market. Seagram executives would have been keenly aware of the resurgence of construction in the area, even though some of the buildings weren't completed until 1983 and 1984. IBM obtained planning permission in 1973, AT&T acquired its site in 1974–75,[11] construction of Citicorp was highly visible between 1975 and 1978, and Johnson's building was already a news item by the summer of 1977. The market was ready, and the influx of funds that would come with the building's sale was attractive to Seagram, which had stagnated as a consequence of remaining firm in its commitment to blended whiskies (apparently oblivious to changes in taste) and no longer dominated the industry.[12] Seagram executives must have begun formulating an offer of sale soon after Edgar Bronfman's first letter to Mayor Beame, at the end of 1976, and about a year later, in February 1978, in the letter to Edward Saxe of MoMA concerning the sale of the Seagram Building, where I had written, "Just the idea is chilling," I continued: "However business practices mitigate for this both in the way depreciation can be taken and the structuring of tax laws. It seems that good business practice—where and how a company's assets are committed—also supports this action *if* the building can be properly protected."[13]

Shocking as it was to me, I recognized that if the building were to be sold, it needed to be protected. It was not difficult to convince Seagram executives to safeguard the building bearing the company's name, even after transfer to another owner. I asked architects Pasanella + Klein to work with Seagram's lawyers and with me to develop a rigorous and coherent set of guidelines for maintaining the building in its original condition. These were incorporated as part of Seagram's lease agreement.[14] As the major tenant, Seagram could stipulate controls over the building's future so long as it continued to be the major tenant. And thus, Article 26 of the lease agreement attached to the Deed of Sale was drawn up over some time and activated when Teachers Insurance and Annuity Association of America (TIAA) became the owner of the Seagram building on February 15, 1980.

Under the title *Tenant's Exclusive Rights*, the preamble to Article 26 of the lease agreement established the importance of the proper and correct maintenance of the Seagram "Site":

> The name "Seagram" has been associated with the Site from the date the Building was completed and it is to be reasonably anticipated that the general public will continue to associate the name "Seagram" with the Site, notwithstanding the sale thereof by Tenant

[Seagram] to Landlord [TIAA]. It is therefore of extreme economic importance and significance to Tenant that the Site continue to be maintained in its present architectural state in accordance with the high quality standards adopted and perpetuated by Tenant during the period of its fee ownership.[15]

The premises occupied by Joseph E. Seagram & Sons, Inc., consisted of the entire fourth to seventh floors, as well as space on other floors and in the basement, a total of 128,387 square feet.[16] The initial fifteen-year lease would expire at midnight on February 14, 1995, but the long view was taken: In accordance with Article 24, the lease could be renewed for three successive terms of ten years each, for all or part of the space, providing that the "Tenant or any successor corporation or any related corporation . . . are separately or collectively occupying not less than 22,500 square feet of space in the Building."[17] Under these terms it would have been in full force until 2025, but as will be seen, the lease was extinguished well before that date, and the terms of the lease also became fuel for TIAA when it contested the landmarking of the Four Seasons Restaurant.

Article 26 is the most substantive section of the lease agreement, as well as its essence. Whereas most of the thirty-five articles of the lease agreement are one to two pages in length, Article 26, comprising two sections, constitutes almost 20 percent of the document. The first section, 26.01, covers the most important issues, modification and maintenance: "Modifications"—changes that may or may not be made to the building—cover five pages; "Maintenance" of the building is specified in six pages. The other sections of Article 26.01 govern the use of the "Building Name," "Remedying Dangerous Conditions," the "Use" of the plaza, the factors and procedures of any "Authorization" required, and the "Records" that are to be kept.[18] In effect, Seagram established draconian control.

"Modifications" were defined as "alterations, reconstruction or demolition of any part of the site." The document states flatly that "no aspect of the site shall be modified without Tenant's prior written authorization." The factors governing authorization are spelled out as the consideration by the Tenant (Seagram) "of the effect of the proposed work in changing, destroying or affecting the exterior of the building."[19] Similar to the requirements of New York's Landmarks Preservation Commission, this requirement is highly effective in precluding hasty unilateral action by convening the best minds to find solutions to problems. However, significantly, and differing from New York City landmark laws, as will be seen, Article 26 sets standards for all interior public spaces on all floors: all elevator lobbies, all public corridors, and all men's and women's toilets. I was relieved that we could now establish these standards after twenty years without them, for some public spaces in the building, notably the public corridors on most floors, had become chaotic. On the thirty-fifth floor, for instance, where the Seagram curator had her office, one was immediately affronted, on turning from the elevator into the corridor, by what would be called today a "monster" doorway: two oversized, heavily molded dark wooden doors with oversized molded-brass knobs. Article 26 allowed Seagram to redress lacunae of standards with a specifically drafted document entitled "Public Areas Design Standards," which was annexed to the lease agreement.[20] Among other stipulations, doors on public corridors were returned to the original gray painted metal or comb-cut American oak, finishes that complemented the elegantly restrained travertine walls and dark green terrazzo floors of the elevator lobbies.[21]

Remarkably, under "Modifications," transparency of the glass curtain wall was taken into account. Because glass walls permit two-way vision, seeing in and seeing out, the definition of a glass wall must consider the interior surfaces seen through the exterior wall. New York's high-rise buildings lose a sense of unity owing to the discordant patterns of fluorescent tube ceiling fixtures, but Article 26 protected the luminous ceiling to a depth of three modules, amounting to sixteen feet around the entire building perimeter. Protection against modification also applied to the inside face of the exterior wall: No changes could be made to the bronze frame, the air distribution enclosure, the venetian blinds, or the way partitions meet the outside wall: they can be located only on the module line at the back of the mullions and are limited to a width of three and one half inches. Another category governing "Modifications" applied to such operational features as the mechanical and electrical systems, which over time would be subject to change. In such cases the landlord was given permission to undertake the required changes, but only with Seagram's written authorization.

"Maintenance" focuses on protecting the building for the long term. Maintenance of the "Site" was to be accomplished according to an explicit schedule in strict accordance with the specifications. While historic building preservation professionals use photographs, drawings, and architectural and historical analysis in order to define what must be protected, this work does not involve the "how" of maintenance. In protecting the building for the long term, under the rubric of "Maintenance," Article 26 spells out periodic care according to the time and the manner in which such action is to be carried out and how. Because the procedures covered in Article 26 give a sense of what is involved in preserving the character of a building, I list them here in some detail. Lighting was to be maintained according to a complex lamping schedule: Exhibit D1 includes fluorescent lamps maintained on a group relay basis; incandescent lamps replaced on failure with a maximum interval of twenty-four hours after failure and before replacement. Dimmer control settings for the lobby were to be maintained according to Exhibit D2. The timing and manner of maintenance is similarly stipulated for all lighting, sweeping, cleaning, and maintenance or repair of the granite of the plaza, the granite caulking, the exterior travertine, the interior travertine, the exterior bronze, the lobby bronze, steps, pools and sidewalks. And graffiti of whatever nature was to be promptly removed, beginning within five business days of written notice by the Tenant.

Service contracts were included: the maintenance of proprietary equipment as well as cleaning and security operations could not be modified, cancelled, or permitted to lapse without the prior written authorization of the Tenant. The procedures were specified in the exhibits: Exhibit D4a, interior bronze; Exhibit D4b, elevators; Exhibit D4c, mechanical systems, including control and the treatment of the air-conditioning circulating water; Exhibit D4d, window-washing equipment, security guards, elevator starters and operators, and porters and cleaning women; Exhibits D4f and D5, landscaping contracts for the English ivy and gingkoes on the plaza and the Park Avenue mall; Exhibit D6, Christmas decorations;[22] Exhibit D7, cleaning; and Exhibit D8, the Four Seasons Restaurant, regardless of the Tenant. The Landlord could extend bidding to a firm other than the existing contractor, but only on approval by the Tenant. In Article 26, the section on "Periodic Maintenance" specified a schedule for wiping down surfaces of the building and plaza: the *verde* antique marble benches, every spring; the serpentine marble sheer wall panels, every five years. The plaza granite and the pools were to be cleaned every two years; the horizontal surfaces of the plaza and steps, every year; and all vertical surfaces, every five years. Exhibit D3 specified that "the exterior bronze shall be cleaned and oiled, in its entirety, every year starting in April and continuing until completed, but not later than October of the same year."[23]

The basic terms of Article 26, based on many years of experience at Seagram, were drafted by Seagram's lawyers, architects, and executives without a purchaser in mind. Once the purchaser was known, revisions made in the final drafts show the main preoccupation to have been clarification of the Tenant-Landlord relationship, in order to ensure that the roles, responsibilities, and sequence of decision-making processes would be understood and agreed upon by both sides. The most substantial changes in the final version came about during negotiations with the future owner of the building, TIAA. One such change addressed "air rights," or "development rights," as expressed in the city's 1961 Zoning Resolution. The Tenant's approval of transferring air rights, initially set at two square blocks in all directions around the site, was extended to four blocks, giving the new owner greater flexibility. Transfer of the Four Seasons and Brasserie restaurant leases was subject to all the terms governing "Modifications," but a new clause addressed responsibility in the event the restaurant operators would change or the restaurant were vacated: the Landlord would be responsible for identifying a new operator. However, should the Landlord fail within a certain period of time, the Tenant (Seagram or its successors) would have 120 days to find an operator, and should that fail, the Landlord would be allowed to lease the space for another use having the "quality and standards" of the building. Furthermore, should the restaurant be abandoned, Seagram reserved the right to require the Landlord, at Seagram's expense, to seal off entrances to it from the lobby of the building. TIAA later used these clauses as arguments in its fight against the landmark designation of the Four Seasons Restaurant. Some changes made in the final stages of the negotiation gave Seagram more control, particularly in ensuring increased protection for "Picasso Alley" in order to maintain a constant environment for *Le Tricorne* by specifying that the "Landlord will not do, or permit to be done, any work in Picasso Alley, other than routine/custodial maintenance."[24]

In negotiating the lease, Seagram clearly was intent on claiming the right to protect the works of art it had placed in the public spaces, reserving for itself the exclusive right to place them and organize art programs on the plaza and other public spaces of the property. Incidents such as a car displayed on the plaza or a tenant wishing to display sculpture from its president's private collection in this public space led Seagram to stipulate control of the plaza's use so that no objects of art would be placed in or about the plaza or other public areas without the written approval of the Museum of Modern Art. The principle of establishing objective standards of what could be placed on the plaza or within the lobby was for judgment on any works proposed to "be made by an entity involved in establishing and nurturing standards in the visual arts—in sum, a museum."[25] The Landlord was equally intent on avoiding responsibility for, and the costs associated with, these artworks and programs. The lease specified that Seagram was to repay the Landlord for maintenance of the mechanical systems for "Picasso Alley" (or undertake the maintenance itself), and together with Seagram's right to use the plaza for art exhibits and public events, Seagram agreed to reimburse the Landlord "for all expenses, damages or fines incurred or suffered by Landlord, and for which Landlord has not been and will not be reimbursed by insurance, by reason of any injury or damage to persons or property resulting from any such use by Tenant [Seagram] of the plaza."[26]

The lease agreement between Seagram and TIAA also contains a statement relating to the continuation of Seagram's "policy of genial permissiveness" (in contrast to heavy-handed security measures) to ensure public enjoyment of the plaza and public spaces of the building.[27] In his testimony at the public hearing about landmarking Seagram in 1988, William H. Whyte pointed to the "genial permissiveness" with which the building was operated, and as he commented elsewhere: "If you stick your hand in one of the pools, as people like to do, guards won't come running up to make you desist. If a bag woman sits on a ledge and sits there—as a matter of fact, for quite some time . . . [she is] not harassed."[28] (As a consequence of the terrorist attack on Lower Manhattan of September 11, 2001, the free flow of movement through the Seagram building lobby was impeded, forcing visitors to pass through security controls. With placement of such barriers, and others, throughout the city, New York's civility has faded.)

The second section of Article 26, Article 26.02, outlined penalties for violation, by the Landlord, of prohibitions described in Section 26.01. Seagram and TIAA both acknowledged the importance of the Landlord's strict performance of, and compliance with, obligations described under Section 26.01, and they both recognized "that the damage to Tenant resulting from any breach of Landlord's obligations thereunder will be irreparable, and far greater than the cost of Tenant's remedying such breach, and impossible of accurate measurement."[29] The Tenant would be repaid for all reimbursable expenses accrued, included going to court, remedying the violation by undertaking the corrective work itself, and offsetting the costs against the rent due each month until the situation was satisfactorily resolved. The building was the carrot; legal contestation and withholding rent were the stick. Because standards of maintenance are subject to legitimate differences of opinion, Article 27 established arbitration procedures. Although penalties were considered, these clauses were never invoked. Significantly, Article 28 required the Landlord to seek landmark designation when the building became eligible.

The final iteration of the "Agreement of Purchase and Sale" between Seagram and TIAA is dated May 31, 1979. The lease agreement, with its provisions to protect the integrity of the design and to properly maintain the Seagram building and its public spaces, was signed on February 15, 1980. The articles of the lease, incorporating Seagram's years of managing the building, were safeguards. Clearly, the new owners, who paid more for the building than the asking price, felt that it was in their interest to do so. In fact, the restrictions aimed at protecting the building would ensure its future value. TIAA's real estate officer stated:

> The Seagram Building is perhaps the most distinguished asset in our nationwide portfolio of investment properties. We acquired the building from Joseph E. Seagram & Sons, Inc., with the understanding that the property would be maintained and preserved by us with the same sense of diligent preservation exhibited by Seagram. Since we are responsible for the economic security of so many people, Teachers must invest in properties which represent the finest architectural, economic and social attributes.[30]

Seagram executives and their architects continued to hold regular, semimonthly coordination meetings concerned with maintenance, which now included representatives of TIAA. The archival records show that the most frequent subjects of discussion and contention were plantings on the plaza and the Park Avenue mall, controlling the environment of "Picasso Alley," and the ever-present issue of maintaining the standard of the color of the bronze in the lobby.[31] The architects remember controversies over the treatment of surfaces, particularly overcleaning of the granite and marble and the lobby bronze with the arrival of each new property manager whose ambition was to make the property look like new. The architects also recall doing a great deal of work to enhance access for the handicapped that finally was dropped as well as a flurry of placing barriers at the edge of the pools, which also went away.[32] In the second decade of the twenty-first century, when Article 26 is no longer in force, the maintenance officers of the current owners still speak of its terms with awe.[33]

A degree of comfort between owner and tenant was cultivated in making the proper decisions, and the process worked reasonably well until November 1989, when TIAA objected to the installation of Mark di Suvero's sculpture *Mozart's Birthday* on the plaza.

TIAA claimed that the size and scope of the piece could cause structural damage during installation; it postulated the potential of permanent rust stains on the granite; it demanded the written consent of the Landmarks Preservation Commission for this installation and stated that, in its "professional" opinion, the presence of the sculpture on the plaza would impair its efforts to market the building. Furthermore, TIAA noted concerns expressed by some tenants regarding restrictions on the use of the plaza during recent charitable events, which led to its fear that the installation of a work of this size would aggravate the situation.[34] Seagram took exception to TIAA's charges.[35] Curator Carla Ash felt that permitting TIAA to make aesthetic or marketing judgments on each work to be installed could completely disrupt Seagram's efforts. Seagram's vice president of Management Services and Corporate Logistics was prepared to take action as he wrote to TIAA's agent: "Teachers response was not a reasonable one, as required under Article 26 of the Lease; and we intend to exercise our right to implement the sculpture program in the future."[36] In the end, because of the size of the sculpture and complaints concerning disruption and access to the plaza, Seagram's legal department and executive staff advised against the installation of *Mozart's Birthday*.[37]

One might well ask why, after years of working mostly smoothly with Seagram and its architectural consultant on issues pertaining to the maintenance of the building and its public spaces, TIAA balked when Seagram proposed to install di Suvero's sculpture on the plaza. In compliance with Article 27 of the sale document, in February 1988, TIAA had applied for landmark designation, and perhaps it was uncomfortable entering new terrain. The use of the plaza and the building's public spaces had for thirty years been the sole purview of Seagram, and the provisions of Article 26 of the lease agreement guaranteed that it would remain so. After landmarking, the roles of the players changed; from that point forward, TIAA would deal directly with the Landmarks Preservation Commission. "Flexing its muscles" with a newfound feeling of empowerment and wary of what it might entail, TIAA tested the possibilities.

The Landmarks Preservation Commission's public hearing on designating Seagram was held on May 17, 1988. On that occasion Martin Lord, TIAA's real estate officer, declared: "Starting today, we look forward to working closely with you [the commission] to define what the public interest in the Seagram Building will be." He continued grandly: "Let us go forward with the spirit of the enlightened creators of the Seagram Building and preserve its heritage for future generations to appreciate."[38] Nonetheless, TIAA would take exception to numerous proposals put forward at the public hearings staged around Seagram's landmarking.

Gene A. Norman, chairman of the commission, presented three aspects of the Seagram building for possible designation. "The building itself, including the plaza and the [out]side of the building. We'll be discussing as an interior designation the lobby spaces on the first floor. Then, finally, we'll be discussing for possible designation the Four Seasons Restaurant, one of the tenant spaces adjacent to the lobby."[39] Those representing the building owner were the first to speak. Martin Lord, of TIAA, and Paul Byard, architectural adviser and special counsel to TIAA, both emphasized the quality of the building and its superb maintenance, which makes it "such a wonderful public asset."[40] They had sought letters from "luminaries that would simply be witnesses of the many different interests that people have in this building."[41] As director of planning for the Seagram building, I submitted Article 26 to the commission for its records. In outlining its provisions, I noted that it offered greater protection to the building and plaza than did the provisions of the Landmarks Law, and not only would incorporating Article 26 into the landmark designation of the Seagram building be desirable but it might well be applicable to buildings landmarked in the future.[42]

Philip Johnson's presentation was brief. Four years after completing AT&T, which he considered to have challenged Seagram, he seemed interested in denigrating Mies. Incongruously, he praised me as his "beloved employer" for many years and avoided mention of Mies, in effect substituting me and himself for Mies. Philip qualified the building "as the finest building of a commercial nature of the 20th century, and I'm extremely proud, after all these years, and her leadership, to have it be considered a landmark and I recommend sincerely that you do so." On being asked if there was not some factual anecdotal remembrance that he would share, Philip talked of the bronze, attributing its use to SB, whom he quoted as saying, "'I don't know why we don't make a building of that material,' and Mies, of course, did exactly that." Philip then explained his own role in advancing the use of bronze for the building: "People in the industry told me they could not have—they had no facilities for making bronze in that shape or size. I said, 'Gentlemen, go out and make a machine,' which they did. It was a great day."[43] Thus spoke Philip on the day in 1988 when he testified before the Landmarks Preservation Commission.

Giovanni Pasanella, Seagram's architectural consultant, proposed that the commission incorporate three conditions of Article 26 that were not covered by the Landmarks Law. One was transparency: he asked the commission to designate the interior three-bay depth of the luminous ceiling that is visible from the outside "and gives the building its characteristic glow." The second recommendation pertained to the technical dimensions of maintenance, "requiring certain recurring actions on the owner's part, as opposed to merely permitting them," citing the yearly oiling required to prevent the bronze skin from oxidizing, retaining a uniform lamping schedule and lighting maintenance, and requiring "attention to the dimming system [in the lobby] that maintains the visual transparency under different lighting conditions." Pasanella also asked the commission for consideration to be given to defining the activities allowed to take place in the plaza, "a public place in the context of the City."[44] Chairman Gene Norman expressed interest in these issues, which would be very useful in examining the proposal for landmark designation.[45]

During the May hearing, numerous speakers approved the proposal to designate Seagram: the building exterior and plaza, the lobby interior, and the Four Seasons interior.[46] In all, twenty-one witnesses spoke in favor of landmark designation of Seagram. No witnesses spoke in opposition.

Some speakers remarked on the conviviality of the hearing.[47] Margot Gayle, president of the Friends of Cast Iron Architecture, summed up the hearing's ambience as "a celebration of excellence."[48] Chairman Norman mentioned how satisfying it was to witness the outpouring of support for the designation of the Seagram building as a landmark.[49] A note of concern about the theoretical consequences of landmarking, however, was struck by Frank Sanchez, representing the National Trust for Historic Preservation. After declaring support for designating the Seagram building, its lobby, and the Four Seasons Restaurant as landmarks, Sanchez wondered "out loud" about the relationship of new buildings to city design: He asked how would the commission, were it in existence when Seagram was in design, have reacted to its proposed construction in that particular stretch of Park Avenue, which could possibly have been a designated district with "distinctive qualities of uniform height, [the] use of similar masonry materials and [an] unbroken street wall?" Commissioner Todd replied, "I'm very interested in your remarks, Mr. Sanchez, you are touching on something broader than this one building. . . . Had this been the case in this particular stretch of Park Avenue, this building might not ever have existed."[50]

Then came the turning point in the hearing. The Friends of the Upper East Side Historic District, which supported landmark designation of all three parts of Seagram, nevertheless asked why the restaurant was included in the hearing at this time.[51] Norman responded that once the Seagram building was on the agenda and a request to designate the restaurant was received, it made sense to examine the three parts: the building exterior and plaza, the interior of the lobby, and the interior of the restaurant.[52] The question of the Four Seasons Restaurant was about to become the cause célèbre of Seagram's landmarking process. I, for one, had not known that the restaurant was to be discussed and therefore did not speak to it, but the wonderfully bespoken Brendan Gill, chairman emeritus of the New York Landmarks Conservancy, declared, "The restaurant is by no means merely a part of the whole; it is, rather, a treasure within a treasure, worthy of designation in its own delectable right."[53]

However, when a partner of Lord Day & Lord, Barrett Smith, the law firm representing the Four Seasons Restaurant, issued the "gentle, hopefully gentle comment" concerned with ensuring that the restaurant operators would have sufficient flexibility to continue to run the restaurant if the components of the restaurant were designated ("wall surfaces, floor surfaces, ceiling surfaces, hanging sculpture, metal draperies, so forth"),[54] it signaled a level of trouble to come, which was followed by another when a member of the commission's staff asked about the ownership and fixity of some of the artworks in the restaurant. Much discussion followed,[55] but because no one was prepared to answer these questions during the proceedings, the hearing concluded on the first two issues, the proposed designation of the building and plaza and interior designation for the lobby, and discussion of the third, designation of the interior of the Four Seasons Restaurant, was postponed. The record was left open for a period of ninety days to allow additional information to be added to the record and to continue the hearing for the Four Seasons designation.[56]

In the months following the May 17 hearing, the commission's staff grappled with Giovanni Pasanella's requests. Regarding "transparency," they wondered about how far jurisdiction extended: Although they could not designate private interior spaces, internal elements that contribute to the external effect could be included as part of the exterior designation, and they were inclined to find a way of doing so. The staff strongly supported designating the plaza but pondered the issue of its use: they opposed a permanent installation of sculpture that would require landmarking but questioned the pragmatics of their ability to manage the rotation of artworks on the plaza.[57] TIAA also responded to Pasanella's recommendations. More than a year after the May 17 hearing, in a letter to the commission, TIAA categorically *told* the commission that its statutes did not allow the commission to apply these recommendations. TIAA made various objections, claiming that specifying maintenance procedures would exceed the commission's authority; that its statutes prohibited the commission from regulating the use of a landmark and therefore from defining activities permissible on the plaza; and, regarding transparency, that Landmarks Law § 25-302g declared architectural exteriors to be limited to the "outer surfaces of an improvement," and not the interior surfaces enclosed by the exterior surfaces.[58] Ultimately, these issues did not factor in the designation of the Seagram building and plaza.

If the May 17 hearing was a veritable love-in, imbued with an aura of sweetness and light, the subsequent hearing on July 12, 1988, held specifically to consider the Four Seasons Restaurant, became a contradiction in itself—like the name of Jack London's protagonist in the novel *White Fang*, where the "pure" and "honest" connotations of the color white are tied to the treacherous notion of *fang*, "the long perforated tooth of a poisonous serpent." The battle of the Four Seasons had begun. New stances were taken. A vice president of TIAA confirmed support for landmarking the Seagram building and plaza and the lobby as an interior space but asserted that TIAA had a corporate responsibility to its policyholders to oppose the designation of the Four Seasons, which could adversely affect the economic value of the space. The TIAA adviser, Paul Byard, raised four jurisdictional issues.[59] First, he argued, "the restaurant was not public space in a legal sense, but rather more like a club than a theater." Second, under New York law, the commission's authority was limited to real property and fixtures. Third, he raised the question of eligibility under the thirty-year law, claiming, incorrectly, that the original certificate of occupancy dated to the fall of 1959. Fourth, he asserted, if the restaurant were not eligible by reason of age, the commission was acting outside its authority. Byard reinforced the second point, saying that the main interest was not in the architecture but rather in the art, for if what he termed "pretty glitter" were removed, what was left for the commission to designate?[60] Or, as Byard scathingly put it in a letter to TIAA in which he summed up his testimony:

> The Four Seasons itself is somewhat of a puzzle as a potential landmark. . . . Almost all the elements which give it its character—the furnishings and equipment designed by Mies and the Huxtables, the Lippolds, the Picasso, the plants, the relatively recent "shattered glass" screens, the bar, the would-be Viennese cafe curtains—can be readily removed, if not simply wheeled away. If they were removed, the space that would remain would be a void, perhaps with some paneling and possibly with a pool but without any particular architectural character. The space does not, for example, appear to have a readily appreciable set of proportions like a double or triple cube room nor does it have a fixed structural configuration like a theater. It does not seem even to qualify as a particularly good example of the Miesian "universal" space since it lacks the sense of carefully modulated lateral expansiveness associated with the best of those.[61]

In July, a month before the date of Byard's letter, Gordon J. Davis of Lord Day & Lord, Barrett Smith wrote to Chairman Norman, responding to the commissioner's request for suggestions as to what part of the restaurant should or should not be included in landmark designation. He proposed, as a practical measure, excluding components subject to the greatest risk of deterioration over time. These were the floor and wall coverings of the mezzanine of the Pool Room, the leather coverings of the south wall of the Pool Room, all floor areas that were then carpeted, and the parquet floor surrounding the walnut bar in the Bar/Grill Room.[62]

Seagram itself opposed the designation of artworks as landmarks. A memorandum on the subject referred to Section 17 of the Agreement of Purchase and Sale of Seagram to TIAA, in which it was specifically stated that Seagram was to retain all "art work and/or fine arts located in the Brasserie and Four Seasons restaurants."[63] In addition, according to case law determining whether an object is personal property, and thus removable, or a fixture attached to the property, the Seagram memo stated: The Lippold, "suspended from the ceiling by means of wires,"[64] could be removed at any time, and the Picasso, like other wall hangings, could easily be moved to another location. Moreover, Article 29 of the lease agreement provided that Picasso's *Le Tricorne* is and "shall remain the property of Tenant [Seagram] and may be removed by Tenant at any time."[65] Seagram concluded, "Under New York law, '*Le Tricorne*' and the two Lippold sculptures are not fixtures appurtenant [attached] to the Seagram Building and, thus, cannot and should not be designated as interior architectural features of the Building."[66]

Richard Lippold countered Byard's negative assessment of the restaurant space: "The proportions of the rooms are faultless. Without their furnishings they would be as 'meaningless' as the empty hall of Versaille [sic] or Monticello." His sculptures, he added, were inseparable from the Four Seasons, in that they "are built into the room and technically virtually impossible to reinstall elsewhere. Their materials, proportions and scale are as closely related to the materials, scale and proportions of the room as are the sculptures of Chartres cathedral." He hoped also that Seagram would relinquish its interest in his artwork at the Four Seasons.[67] Within three weeks after Lippold's plea, Seagram agreed, on my recommendation, to pledge that the sculptures would remain permanently on display in the Grill Room, "so long as the Four Seasons remains a designated landmark."[68] Constitutional questions of due process under the Fifth Amendment and other jurisdictional issues were raised at the July hearing by TIAA: Was the restaurant a public space? What was the commission's authority regarding movable property versus "fixture"? Was the quality of the space appropriate for landmarking? Did the Four Seasons qualify under the thirty-year rule? The questions were debated in letters addressed to the Landmarks Preservation Commission, in other hearings, and in petitions, from August 10, 1988, through the hearing of October 3, 1989, and beyond.[69]

The hearing of October 3, 1989, was the third and final hearing before the Landmarks Preservation Commission in the process of landmarking Seagram. Three separate motions were to be voted on. The first motion, to designate the exterior (the Seagram building and plaza) had been unanimously approved at the hearing of May 17, 1988, and therefore designation was immediately granted without discussion. The second, "A Motion to Designate the Seagram Building First Floor Interior," was read by Commissioner Adolf Placzek.[70] In the preamble, Placzek emphasized the unity between the plaza and lobby, achieved through the use of common materials, continuous horizontal planes, and the transparency of glazed exterior walls, as well as the fact that the design of the lobby is inherently bound to the tower: bronze-clad columns along with other carefully crafted materials common to both. The motion was passed unanimously. Placzek and I had known each other for some twenty years, so his insistence on presenting the motion was especially meaningful to him, as it was to me.[71] In his preamble Placzek credited Philip Johnson and a "coalition of talented consultants" with the design of the lobby. The bronze mesh panels of the elevators cabs singled out were indeed Philip's, the lighting was a combination of Philip and Kelly, but the structure of the space and the materials were Mies's.

The third motion for the third part of Seagram to be designated that day, the chairman pronounced, has "to do with what is called the Four Seasons Restaurant," and he went on: "I should say that there has been some opposition to this by the owners of the building, we as commissioners have received a great deal of material from learned counsel and also counsel from Seagram's family or organization and Bronfman family and from the tenants."[72] The material included the lengthy presentations by TIAA attorneys, using case law based on precedents to prove that the Four Seasons was not eligible for landmarking and its space unworthy of designation. TIAA further claimed that designation would cause it harm by limiting the operations of the premises to the operations of a restaurant, even though the space could be adaptable to other use.[73] The components of the Four Seasons Restaurant to be designated were as follows:

> The Four Seasons Restaurant, ground floor interior consisting of the entrance lobby and the staircase leading from the entrance lobby to the first floor interior; first floor interior consisting of the restaurant lobby including the freestanding piers, the Pool Room vestibule, the Pool Room (dining room), including the marble pool, the staircase leading to the mezzanine dining room, the mezzanine dining room, the Bar Room/

BELOW

166 Four Seasons Restaurant, Grill Room, photograph made for comparative study, showing furnishings and sculpture, submitted by TIAA to the Landmarks Preservation Commission, August 1989.

OPPOSITE

167 Four Seasons Restaurant, Grill Room, photograph altered to remove furnishings and sculpture, submitted by TIAA to the Landmarks Preservation Commission, August 1989.

168 Four Seasons Restaurant, Grill Room, photograph made for comparative study, showing bar and Lippold sculpture, submitted by TIAA to the Landmarks Preservation Commission, August 1989.

169 Four Seasons Restaurant, Grill Room, photograph altered to remove Lippold sculpture and bar, submitted by TIAA to the Landmarks Preservation Commission, August 1989.

Grill Room vestibule, the Bar Room/Grill Room (dining room) including the bar, the staircases leading to the balcony level, and the balcony, and the balcony level dining rooms; and the fixtures and interior components of these spaces, including but not limited to, wall surfaces, floor surfaces, ceiling surfaces, doors, railings, hanging sculptures, and metal draperies."[74]

"The bar . . . ceiling surfaces, doors, railings, hanging sculptures, and metal draperies" lay at the heart of TIAA's continuing objection to landmarking the Four Seasons. As far as TIAA was concerned, these were personal property not attached to the building, and if what Byard had called "pretty glitter" were to be removed, nothing would remain to designate. In what it must have considered an ingenious and dramatic move to prove its point, TIAA presented six before-and-after photographs of the Four Seasons, three views showing the rooms in their present state and the same views from which everything they considered to be personal (movable) property was expunged—furniture, the bar, the Lippold sculptures, the ceiling (considered a "trade fixture"), the railings of the stairs leading from the Fifty-Second Street lobby, and the metal curtains (figs. 166–71).[75] Chairman David Todd spoke to the absurdity of the allegation: "With respect say to omitting railings, which obviously are required by law, simply because they were well-designed and simply because they were sculpted to conform to the character of the space, somehow making a claim that these were therefore personal [proper]ty, I find verging on—the strongest polite word I could find—nonsense."[76] Nor did Todd let slip Commissioner Landau's qualification of the Four Seasons Restaurant as one of "New York's premier dining spaces . . . with an exceptional culinary reputation." He corrected Landau: "I think dining is somewhat incidental. It is one of the finest spaces that happens to be used for dining but the modifier is secondary."[77] With this cautionary adjustment, anticipating further challenges to the commission's ruling, the Four Seasons Restaurant was unanimously designated an interior landmark, on

225

October 3, 1989, in the entirety of its three parts—one exterior, two interiors. Seagram was now officially a new New York City landmark.

The final step in the landmarking procedure was review of the commission's decree by the New York City Board of Estimate, the city agency responsible for budget and land use and the last body to act in the designation process.[78] On January 25, 1990, the commission's ruling in the case of Seagram came before the Board of Estimate.[79] I had been exceedingly worried that TIAA's arguments might find favor with the board, and knowing that wide

170 Four Seasons Restaurant, Pool Room, photograph made for comparative study, showing furnishings and pool, submitted by TIAA to the Landmarks Preservation Commission, August 1989.

171 Four Seasons Restaurant, Pool Room, photograph altered to remove all furnishings except pool, submitted by TIAA to the Landmarks Preservation Commission, August 1989.

backing was essential, I joined forces with the Municipal Arts Society to encourage everyone we knew to write letters of support. Support came by letter and in person, as in the commission's first hearing in May 1988. Distinguished architects, historians, and directors of institutions eloquently presented the case for landmark designation.[80] I still recall the tension that filled the relatively small, square room where the board, composed of Mayor David Dinkins, the president of the city council, the city comptroller, and the presidents all five boroughs of New York, sat at a long table elevated at one side of the room.

Ruth Messinger, president of the Borough of Manhattan and chair, called on those in opposition to speak first. TIAA asked the Board of Estimate to exercise its review on a variety of grounds, and this time a number of members of TIAA's group were called on to bear witness: beyond the Real Estate Board, all those who testified against upholding the designation were in TIAA's employ.[81] By the time of the hearing, TIAA's associate general counsel and in-house lawyer both acknowledged that other uses were contemplated in the lease document between the restaurateurs and TIAA.[82] With little imagination or logic, TIAA repeated its argument that interior designation would effectively prevent future adaptation of the space (for retail, a bank, offices, or as an automobile showroom), because designation of "the bar, the pool, the metal drapes, the Lippold ceiling structure, the raised platform in the Grill Room, the railings and other features" effectively locked them into restaurant use.[83]

Deborah Beck of the Real Estate Board of New York (a body that does not normally comment on individual landmark designations) intervened, fearing that designation of the Four Seasons would set a "harmful precedent" by preserving the use of space as well as designating pieces of removable property as part of the landmark. She argued that such a precedent would cause landlords to discourage their tenants from creating beautiful or notable interiors. For Beck, the broad issue was whether designation should be implemented to preserve a use. "Unlike lobbies, auditoriums and other public spaces, which up to now have been exclusively the recipients of interior designations, restaurants, stores and other commercial uses are not intrinsic to the function and operation of the buildings they are located in."[84] The testimony of Peter Ashkenazi, owner of New York's first designated interior, the hundred-year-old Brooklyn restaurant Gage and Tollner, disproved Beck's contention. Landmarking, he said, never interrupted the restaurant's ability to transact business or to make slight modification in paintings or other elements where Landmarks Preservation Commission approvals were required, nor had landmark designation restricted or diminished the number of people interested in purchasing the property.[85]

Chairwoman Messinger pointed to seventy-six other designated interiors; in some instances these comprised theater seats, wall sconces, and all kinds of other interior furnishings. Consequently, designation of the pool, the bar, the sculpture, and the curtains at the Four Seasons was, in her judgment, no different.[86] Commenting on the before-and-after photographs presented by TIAA, Messinger spoke forcefully: "Let me say that the space, in my judgment, is spectacular even as pictured stripped of all its tables and non-designated furnishings." Stating that "for thirty years, the restaurant and the space it occupies have served as a sparkling highlight in the cultural life of this City," the chair announced that she was voting for designation.[87] With the unanimous vote of the presidents of all the other New York boroughs for the designation of the building, the interior, and the space occupied by the Four Seasons Restaurant, landmark designation of Seagram was complete.

A public hearing of the Board of Estimate on January 25, 1990, approved the landmark designation. TIAA then challenged the legality of landmarking the Four Seasons by bringing its case before the New York state courts (as Seagram had, in the matter of taxation, thirty years earlier). TIAA pursued its battle and kept it going into the last decade of the twentieth century. On April 27, 1990, its lawyers launched a petition against the City of New York, the New York City Board of Estimate, and New York's Landmarks Preservation Commission; the petition was brought before the Supreme Court of the State of New York (the state's civil trial court, but not its upper court), Justice Beatrice J. Shainswit presiding. In challenging the designation of the Four Seasons Restaurant, TIAA set forth another elaborate memorandum—this one sixty-eight pages long—in support of its claims, formulating nine causes.[88]

In response, six months later, in sixteen pages, Judge Shainswit began the court session by placing the challenge to the commission's ruling in the context of the legislation whereby the state of New York empowered the city "'for the protection, enhancement [and] perpetuation' of 'buildings . . . and other objects having a special character or special historical or aesthetic or value,' provided, however, that 'such measures, if adopted in the exercise of the police power, shall be reasonable and appropriate to the purpose, or if constituting a taking of private property shall provide for due compensation.'"[89] Crucially, the judge contended that the exercise of this power was vested in the commission subject to the City Charter and the Landmarks Law and written into the New York City Administrative Code, which declares "as a matter of public policy that the protection, enhancement, perpetuation and use of improvements and landscape features of special character or special historical or aesthetic interest or value is a public necessity and is required in the interest of the health, prosperity, safety, and welfare of the people."[90]

Furthermore, Judge Shainswit asserted the status of interior landmarks. These had been specifically authorized in an amendment to the Landmarks Law in 1973, designating as interior landmarks those interiors that are thirty years old, "customarily open or accessible to the public, or to which the public is customarily invited."[91] Interior architectural features are defined as "the architectural style, design, general arrangement and components of an interior, including, but not limited to, the kind, color and texture of the building material and the type and style of all windows, doors, lights, signs, and other fixtures appurtenant to such interior."[92] Judge Shainswit took up each of TIAA's causes, the first four being statutory, established by the state legislature, the remaining five having been authorized by the US Constitution. On the first cause, in which the petitioner wished to upset a landmark designation, the role of the court was to review the record to see if the challenged action had a rational basis and was not arbitrary or capricious. The designation of the Four Seasons as an interior landmark was supported by individuals and organizations with expertise and parallel prior designations of interior landmarks; the judge read into the record the names of many notable architects and architectural firms, historians, and members of the art world who registered support, as well as associations and institutions. The proponents greatly outnumbered the opposition, which was essentially confined to the real estate community. Designation of the Four Seasons was shown to be consistent with precedent: "The record also attests that there are scores of other interior designations in New York City."[93] Judge Shainswit concluded: "It is apparent that the designation of the Four Seasons falls within the flow of interior landmark designations that the Commission has pursued in carrying out its authorized functions."[94]

In the second cause, TIAA attacked the commission as being subservient to the "city's elite, who have managed to protect one of its favorite watering holes at the expense of more than a million individual policy holders whose pension fund owns the building." The judge's response was clear-cut: "The short answer . . . is: the interior landmark designation is not the fruit of class warfare."[95]

TIAA insisted again on the commission's limitation in designating real property only, and not personal property (the bar, the railings, the metal chain curtains, the Lippold, and so on). Judge Shainswit noted merely that New York's Landmarks Law does not distinguish between real and personal property. This simple, anticlimactic response was breathtaking, considering the reams of paper, the disputation, and the attention of talented minds that had been wasted on what was, in effect, a nonissue. Reasserting that the commission's jurisdiction extended to interior architectural features that include "fixtures appurtenant to such interiors," the judge asserted: "The special aegis of the Commission [is] to supply its own interpretation and application."[96]

In the fifth cause, TIAA claimed designation of the Four Seasons to be inconsistent with due process, considering this action to be a "taking"—that is, confiscation without compensation—because it did not substantially advance a legitimate governmental purpose. Repeating that the Four Seasons catered to an elite clientele, TIAA supported this claim by highlighting the requirement that patrons wear a jacket, to which Judge Shainswit replied: "The enforcement of a dress code is not a taking of property."[97] She was again at pains to explain the position of historic preservation as an accepted, legitimate, and important government concern, finding that the landmark designation of the Four Seasons fell "within the cultural fabric fostered by the Landmarks Preservation Law," which "does not bring in its wake any due process violation."[98] This, like the following claims, was a constitutional question.

In the sixth cause, TIAA was concerned with what its economic position might be in 1999, when the lease would expire and it would be forced to choose between closing the space or allowing it to operate as a restaurant, which could result in hardship for them. The judgment stated that the court need not enter into the "thicket of [economic] uncertainty," and there was no support for this cause.[99]

The seventh cause of action regarded designation of the Lippold sculptures, notwithstanding Seagram's ownership, claiming that they would confiscate TIAA's right to possession of the space occupied by the two hanging sculptures. Because Seagram had agreed that the works would remain in situ for as long as the Four Seasons remained a designated landmark, the judge considered the argument "much too ephemeral to serve as a prop for a constitutional claim."[100]

In the eighth cause, TIAA pled that designation had illegally impaired its right to remove movable property (the bar, for example). Again the judge affirmed this cause to be within the jurisdictional sphere of the commission, which, "on a full record, has rationally drawn a nexus between such items and the overall cultural impact of the Four Seasons."[101]

Last, the ninth clause of action claimed that TIAA's right to freedom of expression and privacy had been violated by the designation: "The design and appearance of interior space is intimately associated with the owner; it is an inherently personal decision that should be left to the owner."[102] Again Judge Shainswit deferred to the primacy of the Landmarks Law: "Any limit on freedom of expression flows from the Landmarks Preservation Law itself. Since that law has passed constitutional muster, there is no violation of any protected First Amendment right. The intent of the Landmarks Preservation Law is not to restrict free speech, but to further a substantial governmental interest—historic preservation."[103] In conclusion, Judge Shainswit determined that TIAA's claims did not rise to the level of infringements of constitutional rights, and she issued a judgment of dismissal for each cause of action on October 16, 1990. The Supreme Court, Appellate Division, First Department, concurred on July 30, 1992.[104] Dropping its constitutional claims, TIAA then brought its statutory case before the state's highest court, the New York Court of Appeals, where on October 19, 1993, Chief Judge Judith S. Kaye agreed with the opinion of the Appellate Division, deciding that it "should be affirmed."[105] TIAA's case could go no further, and the court's ruling that the Landmarks Preservation Commission had the authority to include specific interior furnishings in such a designation, whether they were movable or not, was considered by the Preservation League of New York State to be a strong legal affirmation of an important section of the city's Landmarks Law, which up until then had not been seriously challenged.[106]

This brief account (which some might consider too long) of the challenges to landmarking the Four Seasons Restaurant as part of the landmarking process for the Seagram building illuminates ideas and processes inherent in urban preservation and fundamental to the culture of architecture and the city. I was struck on reading the record (no mean task) by how jurisprudence can be abused. The absurdity of the arguments put forward by a major corporation is inexcusable in its self-reference, lack of vision, and wrong-headedness, not to mention the waste of precious time and effort demanded of so many people in order to uphold the initial decision to fully landmark Seagram.

EPILOGUE
CHANGING HANDS

Building in New York in the decade after World War II belonged to a simpler and more forward-looking time—one might even say utopian, and certainly so relative to today. Taking up its unfulfilled prewar promise of becoming the most public expression of civilization, architecture assumed a new face and new intentions. The United Nations established its world headquarters in New York, bringing with it the ideal of one world. Its new buildings, designed by major international architects, represented this new vision. New attitudes about city building were adopted as services succeeded manufacturing, and zoning changes took advantage of a dormant prewar zoning amendment, so that office buildings were brought to Midtown Manhattan and integrated among residential and commercial buildings.

The first postwar corporate building in New York of any urban ambition, Lever House, was erected in this part of town, and it challenged the norm of filling the envelope—that is, the three-dimensional legal volume within which a structure could be built. Even the real estate professionals, architects, and builders who produced the "Skytop" study to provide Seagram with options for what could be built on its site did not consider justifying every square foot of the zoning envelope. Doing so would soon become gospel in real estate, as money would become in the business world. And in effect, the two corporate headquarters, Seagram and Lever House, on Park Avenue, diagonally across from each other, changed the outlook on New York's urban form. Representing the most advanced architectural thought, they nourished a revolution in the attitude toward regulating building in the city, replacing the original rules in which urban form was a by-product of zoning, with incentive zoning aimed at shaping the city through architecture.¹ The advent of landmarking also signaled a new vision of architecture: buildings could now be understood as cultural benefits, overcoming, or at least challenging, their common assessment as objects of consumption.

Into the 1970s, the concept of outstanding architecture was embraced by a few major corporations—Citicorp, CBS, IBM, and AT&T—in this same Midtown area. Facing Seagram across Park Avenue, Skidmore, Owings & Merrill designed the Park Avenue Plaza, for the Fisher Brothers, a large real estate partnership, behind the Racquet and Tennis Club (fig. 172). The fate of buildings was linked to the real estate market, which reflected the national economy. With the recession of the 1970s, the real estate market was such that the major buildings by outstanding architects commissioned by iconic American companies near Seagram were sold within a few years after completion. By 1987, vacancy rates in Midtown had hit double digits, yet lenders continued to provide financing for new projects until the recession of the early 1990s left Manhattan landlords with bankrupt skyscrapers.² It was at this time that the Seagram building itself was sold, twenty years after it opened.

With the exception of Seagram, whose sale in 1980 was accompanied by rigorous lease conditions protecting its fabric and use, change of ownership brought the obliteration or downgrading of the public spaces that under "incentive zoning" had allowed new construction a quid pro quo of built space for open space. In 1992, eight years after its completion, Johnson and Burgee's AT&T building changed hands to become Sony's US headquarters (with a twenty-year lease); the public arcade was enclosed and turned into Sony shops. IBM

172 Skidmore, Owings & Merrill, architects, Park Avenue Plaza, 55 East Fifty-Second Street, New York, 1979–81. Photographer unknown.

sold its tower to E. J. Minskoff Equities, Inc., in 1994, eleven years after the building opened, and the the amenities installed by IBM were downgraded or entirely removed.[3] These abrogations of legislation, which brought greater income to the owners and therefore greater tax revenue to the city, were not punished, as had been the creation of open space before 1961.

One must conclude that architecture fared infinitely better before real estate developers pervasively took hold; their presence, according to a respected confrère, "was not very high profile until the late 70's, early 80's," which is to say, they flourished in New York City after the economically disastrous 1970s.[4] The corporations who commissioned proud buildings in New York to signify their eminence in the world of business and finance (and who, by this gesture, contributed to the quality of the city), gave way to the real estate families for whom building was simply business. Private real-estate professionals emerged, wielding power in the city and earning very high return on investments (20 percent was considered normal, and that was compounded). Real estate investors received a variety of government-sponsored tax breaks. An unnamed partner in a well-known Wall Street firm enumerated some of the many ways money could be made: losses could be deducted at the highest rates and the earnings from rent kept; losses could be sold to other wealthy individuals; or, when a building's value rose, the owners could borrow against it and then deduct the payments on loans from their taxes. In addition, the federal tax reforms of 1986 altered the playing field, and large institutions began to play an increasing role.[5] After half a century, the families of developers who swung into action after World War II were deemed to be royalty: they were to New York what the oil barons were to Houston.[6] In the summer of 1997, an article in the *New York Times Magazine*, "The Real-Estate Royals: End of Line?" featured the Rudins, Dursts, Roses, Fishers, Tishmans, and Resnicks, commenting on their durability and influence:

> With a few additions and subtractions, these are the same families that dominated the city's real-estate market 40 years ago. They have survived the assaults of the big insurance companies of the 60's, the near-bankruptcy of the city in the 70's, the entry into the market in the 80's of well-capitalized foreign giants like Sumitomo and Ladbroke and Olympia & York. They have expanded their fortunes as arriviste competitors have come and gone. They are as close to a stable ruling class as New York has enjoyed since the beginning of the century, when Manhattan was owned by the Astors and the Rhinelanders.[7]

When these families attended the 101st annual banquet of the Real Estate Board of New York in August 1997, they had much to celebrate: "Manhattan's $90 billion real-estate market [is] in the first flush of exuberance. New construction is up. Midtown vacancies are down near the single digits."[8] And when the elegant new Midtown buildings near Seagram, and Seagram itself, changed hands because of their owners' financial problems, so did others—remarkably, Rockefeller Center and the Chrysler building, which had long been symbols of New York City and of American capitalism. In 1989, the Japanese conglomerate Mitsubishi purchased 51 percent interest in Rockefeller Center and, in 1990 and 1991, another 29 percent, for a total of 80 percent of what a reporter for the *New York Times* called "the Hope diamond of world real estate."[9] By 1995, Rockefeller Center was bankrupt. The major problem was the low rents of longtime tenants: more than 95 percent of the commercial space in the original Rockefeller Center buildings was cheaply rented under long-term leases negotiated during the mid-1970s, when New York's economy was abysmal. Since at least one-third of the leases were set to terminate in 1994, Mitsubishi had expected to realize much greater income by increasing rents, but the New York real estate market collapsed again at the end of the 1980s. A group led by Goldman Sachs and Jerry Speyer of Tishman Speyer acquired the center in 1996. The following year, the headline "A New Owner to Take Over an Old Classic" appeared in *New York Times*. The "Classic" was the Chrysler Building, and Jerry Speyer, who had first tried to buy it twenty years earlier, was the winning bidder.[10]

In 1998 Unilever sold Lever House to Aby Rosen and Michael Fuchs, who had moved to New York from Germany ten years earlier. Their firm, RFR Holding LLC, negotiated a lease-back arrangement allowing Unilever to remain on the top four floors. Immediately following the acquisition, RFR announced a twenty-five-million-dollar capital improvement program.[11] In December 1998 the Woolworth building, at which two-thirds of the leases in the 932,000-square-foot building were about to come up for renewal, was sold to a group of investors by the company that had built it in 1914.[12] In what was still considered a hot real estate market in 2000, the black Canadian granite CBS tower known as the Black Rock, designed by Eero Saarinen and completed in 1965, was to be sold when the media conglomerate Viacom acquired CBS. CBS had put its fully rented building on the market the year before, but the bids were too low, so the company began moving its employees out of the building, for as the *New York Times* reported, "if the building were sold with CBS continuing to occupy half of it, the sale price would be significantly reduced."[13]

In the furor of this market, the Seagram building and plaza again came up for sale. At the end of August 2000, Warren Wechsler, first senior vice president of the Real Estate Board of New York was enthralled: "This latest posting further demonstrates New York's stature as the most important real estate market in the world. Some of the buildings up for sale are among the most distinguished in New York. They are of unprecedented worth."[14] In October, a *New York Times* headline ran: "On Park Avenue, Another Trophy Changes Hands." The story reads: "The iconic bronze and topaz glass skyscraper on Park Avenue joins other prime properties as Rockefeller Center, the Chrysler Building, the World Trade Center, and CBS's Black Rock on what has become a crowded auction block."[15] Three days later, the same reporter, Charles V. Bagli, wrote: "With the New York market sizzling, landlords and investors have been putting some of the world's best-known real estate trophies on the block, from Rockefeller Center to the World Trade Center, in the hopes of scoring big before the boom peters out. The first to go was the Seagram Building . . . which was snapped up by a pair of German developers for a cool $379 million."[16] The final price on closing, December 14, 2000, was $375 million. The purchasers, Aby Rosen and Michael Fuchs of RFR, who had purchased Lever House fourteen months earlier, won an intense bidding war for the Seagram building; Jerry Speyer was the underbidder, reportedly by more than twelve million dollars.[17]

The high market went hand in hand with profits that could be exacted by raising the rent of long-below-market leases that were soon to expire, as was the case for Rockefeller Center, the Chrysler Building, CBS, Woolworth, and others. At Seagram, it was reported, three quarters of the tenants paid rents that were then half the average of those in Midtown, but with leases that would expire within five years, the owners could expect to raise the rents.[18] TIAA sold Seagram because it was reluctant to spend the estimated forty to fifty million dollars necessary to modernize 375 Park Avenue, or so it was reported.[19] TIAA was already somewhat restive under the strictures of Article 26, and the cost of replacing the luminous ceiling had been discussed.[20] But in its press release of December 15, 2000, announcing the sale that became official on December 14, TIAA expressed pride in having the building "considered by many to be the finest office building in the world" in its portfolio.[21]

The perception of Seagram as a "trophy," "part of a portfolio," or "in keeping with construction in the city since the 1970s," was disappointingly prosaic. One article does refer to Seagram's "architectural pedigree" as a reason for purchasing the building,[22] and Aby Rosen inferred this: "For us, this is a value-added play, and we are known as value-added investors. Based on the property's central location and superior design, we believe the building will always attract credit-worthy corporate tenants regardless of the ups and downs of the real estate market."[23] But RFR had another reason to acquire Seagram that was not yet divulged, or perhaps not yet planned—Seagram's air rights. In the winter of 2005, five years after RFR's acquisition of the Seagram building and plaza, the firm purchased 610 Lexington Avenue, adjoining the Seagram building.[24] The site was the northern half of the block's frontage on Lexington at Fifty-Third Street, where the nine-story YWCA building was still standing. The southern half of the Lexington Avenue frontage had been a nine-story YWCA headquarters building until 1984, when it was replaced by a thirty-six-story black glass structure designed by the ubiquitous Emery Roth.[25] Owning the adjacent site, RFR could transfer the Seagram air rights to 610 Lexington Avenue. Rosen planned an

173 Foster + Partners, architects, 610 Lexington Avenue, New York, rendering showing tower, to be erected immediately to the east of the Seagram building, c. 2008 (unbuilt).

EPILOGUE: CHANGING HANDS

incredibly thin tower: ninety feet east-west by forty-nine feet north-south (fig. 173). At 709 feet high, it would soar two hundred feet above the Seagram tower, distanced from it by a few feet more than the depth of Seagram's east wing. A resolution to allow this was narrowly passed by Community Board 5 on November 10, 2005.[26]

As the owner of Seagram and Lever House, Rosen was clearly conscious of the architectural stakes in this new building. He commissioned the recently knighted British architect Norman Foster. Posthaste, with the twelve-day-old community board's approval in hand, together with a group of associates, they appeared before the Landmarks Preservation Commission on November 22, 2005, to ask for support for a special permit waiving setback and height regulations for the transfer of air rights from Seagram to a 709-foot-high tower to house condominiums and a hotel. The meeting was concerned primarily with the visual impact of the new tower on the "iconic" view of Seagram at street level, from across Park Avenue in front of the Racquet and Tennis Club, where the architects demonstrated that it would not be visible, and from the Fifty-Third Street corner, where "it would only be slightly visible and not appear higher than the 515-foot-high Seagram building."[27]

While the Municipal Arts Society and the New York Chapter of the AIA supported Foster's project at the Landmarks Preservation Commission meeting, a spokesperson for the Historic Districts Council reminded the commission that on Lexington Avenue it would have "a negative impact," looming over the Seagram building. I, too, was troubled by the height, commenting: "Foster is capable of making a very beautiful building [but] the height is of concern and the engineering of such a tall, thin building [will be] problematic."[28] Again, I hoped that the specter would go away. However, as I think about the issue years later, it seems to me that the pencil spear of the asymmetrically placed tower would be incidental as it appeared to shift with the movement of the viewer. Most important, it would absorb all but a few feet of Seagram's transferable 200,965 square feet of unused floor area. In addition, the commission's approval of the air-rights transfer would require the developer to establish a covenant with the New York Landmarks Conservancy for continued maintenance and restoration of the landmark. One recalls Giovanni Pasanella asking the Landmarks Preservation Commission to adopt such a requirement for landmarking in general and specifically for Seagram. Such requirements had existed under Article 26. RFR struck an agreement with Shangri-La Hotels by May 2007. Building permission was obtained from the City Planning Commission July 2, 2008,[29] and the YWCA building was demolished. However, by spring 2009, in the economic climate following the new recession recognized to have taken hold in December 2007,[30] the project was no longer viable. The air-rights issue remains a moot point.

With or without Foster's or another tower, the area around the Seagram building has changed drastically (compare figs. 174 and 175). The 1960s had seen replacement of structures on Park Avenue immediately to the north and south of Seagram. Because the new buildings profited from the 1961 Zoning Resolution, they were not completely constructed to the property line on the avenue and thus enclose Seagram plaza, as Mies had assumed they would. To the north and to the south, both properties were designed and built with unsympathetic, small open public spaces facing Seagram that are negative rather than positive additions to the public realm (see fig. 175). The area to the east had built up over the final years of the twentieth century. Even so, the proportions of the severe yet gentle bronze tower overcome this disparity from a distance. Walking or driving north, the "wow" of the serene plaza is there, and on top of the granite parapet walls, the massive *verde* antique benches hold the space of the plaza.

In June 2000, when I was in Venice for the Seventh International Architecture Biennale,[31] a French journalist invited me for a drink on the terrace of the Hotel Monaco and Grand Canal. As we sat down, she said, "Vivendi, tell me about Vivendi." What was she talking about? I had never heard this word before. Soon I was to learn that it spelled the end of Seagram—the company. I was stunned as both came at once, the change of the building's ownership and that of the corporation, and I couldn't untangle the two. Ironically, just as the exhibition I curated on the design and use of Seagram plaza was installed in the Seagram Gallery in 1978, the building was sold the first time to TIAA; when both the building *and* the company were being sold in 2000, I had been concentrating for some time on curating the exhibition *Mies in America*.[32] On asking, I was told that Seagram was interested in entertainment because the corporation had a duty to maximize shareholder value; DuPont would be increasingly regulated in concert with environmental concerns, whereas expanding values lay with the film and music business. In writing this account I have become aware that shareholder value was a credo—a mantra, an *idée reçue*—of the corporate world, fueling the hostile corporate takeovers of the 1980s (such as Seagram's takeover of Conoco) and leading to the extravagant rise in executive pay that fueled the Enron era.[33] And then the dot-com bubble peaked in March 2000. The Vivendi-Seagram deal was formally announced June 20, 2000.

There is considerable coverage on the takeover of the distiller and its transformation into an entertainment company by a French water utility that was transforming itself into a telecommunications and entertainment conglomerate.[34] The salient facts relate to generational changes. The French Compagnie Générale des Eaux, formed in 1853 under Napoléon III, diversified into telecommunications and mass media in the 1980s and changed its name to Vivendi in 1998; Seagram, founded in 1857, incorporated by Samuel Bronfman in 1926, and diversified by him first with the acquisition of the small Canadian oil company Royalite in 1950, followed in 1963 with the purchase of Texas Pacific Coal & Oil; in 1980, led by Edgar M. Bronfman, Seagram purchased the Conoco oil company, becoming in the process the largest shareholder of E. I. du Pont de Nemours.[35] With the approval of the board of directors, Edgar Bronfman, Jr., appointed CEO of Seagram in 1994, sold most of Seagram's shares in DuPont in order to buy 80 percent of MCA/Universal from Matsushita Electric in 1995. In June 2000, Vivendi acquired controlling shares of Seagram, creating Vivendi Universal. The new company sold off Seagram's spirits businesses in its bid to be a major entertainment conglomerate. Then Vivendi Universal collapsed in March 2001; mismanagement on the part of its CEO, Jean-Marie Messier, led to his dismissal as the value of the company's stock dropped from seventy-seven dollars to less than twenty-five dollars per share.[36]

Seagram's executive offices, designed by Philip Johnson, were destroyed by Vivendi, and changes in management in New York led me to write to Edgar Bronfman, Jr., on July 31, 2002:

> A number of problems arise: Vivendi inherits Article 26 by virtue of occupancy. If that occupancy decreases Article 26 will probably not be applicable. Seagram monitored the application of Article 26, in consultation with me through P + K. With the change to Vivendi this process is not secured and problems have arisen, and there are many ongoing issues, and projects in the works. The building has a new owner: the owner was always part of the building monitoring team. . . . Thus many new chefs are in the kitchen, and none of them are part of the culture, or even knowledgeable about the ingredients. This is a recipe for disaster.[37]

But Seagram didn't live here anymore. And very soon, neither would Vivendi Universal. It failed, like a few highly visible foreign companies that briefly captured American real estate and entertainment companies in the same general economic environment in which, crazed with hubris, the CEO of Vivendi Universal bet on his ability to create a media empire.[38] In the spring of 2006, withdrawing its listing from the New York Stock Exchange and reverting to the name Vivendi, the company Vivendi Universal ceased to exist.

The Seagram companies were sold, the collections of drinking vessels, photographs, prints, and paintings were dispersed at auction,[39] and the corpus of *Drawings by Sculptors* was purchased by a collector. I mourned but held fast to my determination to retain Picasso's curtain,[40] as the point of arrival on the glorious trajectory from the Racquet and Tennis Club, across Park Avenue, up a few steps and across the Seagram plaza, through the lobby with its passage of elevator cores, and up the broad steps to the entrance of the Four Seasons Restaurant. A gala dinner simultaneously celebrating the opening of the exhibitions *Mies in Berlin* at the Museum of Modern Art and *Mies in America* at the Whitney Museum of American Art took place on Seagram plaza—the plaza that had opened the prospect of clearings in the forest of the city—the evening of June 20, 2001. From the dais set on the plaza, facing the bronze tower, I recollected how, when the building was under construction, I would stride down Park Avenue in Seven League Boots, knowing what a wonderful thing we were doing.

174 Aerial view of the Seagram building within built context. Photograph: Tommy Weber, June 1958.

OPPOSITE

175 High view of the Seagram building and immediate surroundings. Photograph: Ezra Stoller, 1991.

APPENDIX 1
PHYLLIS LAMBERT TO SAMUEL BRONFMAN, JUNE 28, 1954

Paris, June 28, 1954

Dearest Daddy,

Received your letter when in London and a day later found what you call the building report and I, a plan of the building. To find a plan of a building rather surprised me as I thought that you were going to have a consultant first and then go about choosing an architect. Well now I will set about writing the letter about which I have been thinking for a few days and this letter starts with one word repeated very emphatically NO NO NO NO NO. You will forgive me if sometimes I use rather strong terms and sound angry but I am very disturbed and find nothing whatsoever commendable in this preliminary-as-it-may-be-plan for a Seagram's building. Further I refuse to use the term "Renaissance Modernized" and therein lies the crux of the whole thing. When I talked to you of the Renaissance the point that I wanted to emphasize above all is that to the man of the Renaissance the idea of creating a beautiful building was the idea of creating a beautiful way of life. It was a renaissance or a rebirth of ideas, a refinding rather a rediscovery of a noble society which, to the man of the renaissance, represented the very high ideals of a society and a way of life and culture. Through the new scholarship of the 15th century (called in Italy the Quatrocento) the high level of Greek culture in every field of endeavour was rediscovered and the place of man in the universe was put into new relief. Man was now the centre of the universe and God was to be apprehended no longer through mystical ideas but through mathematical symbols, perfection in proportions and harmony and man being a reflection of god perfect in his proportions and able through his intellect to understand the mathematecical basis of the world and search for that harmony which was all important. Thus man was conceived as a noble creature physically and morally and intellectually as he had been considered according to the thinkers of the Quatrocento in that admirable civilization of the Greeks. The Greek civilization is not under discussion and as history is only the way one age looks at another, what is important and tells us the thought of any given period, is how it interprets other periods. There are, of course, documents to go by and certain recorded facts, but then again it is always the interpretation of these facts and documents that is important...what is emphasized and what is not. Now then, the great document of the architect of the quatrocento was a book on architecture written by a Greek, Vitruvius. In his third book on Temples Vitruvius supplied the answer as to what sacred buildings should be like and when the parts were properly harmonized and proportioned and that is upon analyzing the proportions of the human figure, (and here again the manner in which the proportions of the human figure are analyzed are indicative of a way of thought, but I shall not go into that here) the harmonies and perfections of the human figure should be applied to the harmony and proportions of the temple. Thus the temple, or to extend it, any architectural unit was to reflect the perfections of man, which meant the perfections of harmony and thus pythagoras was carefully studied and the mathematical progressions and relationships in musical harmony. It was Alberti, the advisor to patrons and artists who set down verbally the tennents of architecture of the Renaissance. It was a mathematical definition, based on Vitruvius stating that beauty consists in a rational integration of the proportions of all the

[Handwritten margin note:] You can't modernise the Renaissance — you can only learn from it understand what it meant & why their buildings were beautiful. By analysing what is beautiful in the past one can analyse what is beautiful in the present but by the different conception and a different vocabulary —

[Handwritten bottom note:] — modernizing the Renaissance is like modernizing Shakespeare — it would mean absolutely nothing

parts of a building, in such a way that every part has its absolutely fixed
size and shape and nothing could be added or taken away without destroying
the harmony of the whole. This man created harmony was a visible echo of a
celestial and universally valid harmony. Now through this harmony of
mathematical proportions expressing God and found in his noble creation, man,
Alberti wanted to reimbue this philosophy of the nobility of man, the
"virtus" of the Greek civilization, into men, and thus by creating
buildings based on this harmony, men who would perceive this harmony either
intellectually and or intuitively and become more noble and strive towards that
perfection which he was intended to arrive at. I have talked of all this
to point out what seems to me most important, and that is that there was
a conscious philosophy, aimed at the betterment of Man, underlying the
which formed the architecture of the renaissance and of every period in
which architecture has been dynamic expression of a dynamic society. It
is a society that has nothing to say for itself, that is living vegetable
like that copies other periods, and it is the misguided and uninstructed
and unintelligent man that in a dynamic society copies other periods, or
just helter skelter, ignoring the philosophy of his time and the very
urgent basic need to construct with a full understanding of the ideas that
he wants to express and the means at his disposal to attain his end.
As Professor Pevsner points out in his excellent book on European Architecture
no other art acts upon us as incessently and so ubiquitously as architecture.
"We can avoid intercourse with what peole call the Fine Arts, but we cannot
escape buildings3" And the philosphy that a building expresses seeps into
a society and helps to mould it at the same time that it expresses it (the
society). Now in putting up a building in NY you are erecting a *monument* (you have two clauses — first, building)
which is just a place to work in with no specific appeal to men's imagination
or intelligence or agreement, and in this case as long as your building is
sound, and functional, and fairly agreable, it does not much matter what
it looks like because it will just be another vaguely modernized skyscraper
office building like so many others and you won't be effecting anyone
much one way or the other. This is not what you plan to do, but if you do
not plan to do this you have one alternative and one alternative only; you
must put up a building which expresses the best of the society in which you
live, and at the same time your hope's for the betterment of this society.
You have a great resposibility and your building is not only for the people
of your companies, it is much more for all people, in NY and the rest of the
world and unless you think of it that way there is no sense going on unless you
just do what I outlined in the first alternative. And you are creating an
everlasting monument to yourself. No one much thinks of the business prowess
of the Medici although it is probably the most brilliant of any time.
But who does not know the name of the Medici (I am not thinking of the later
decadent descendants which unfortunately the name symbolizes for too many
people) but the magnificent monuments errected by them. It just happens to turn
out that most great men in history (that is those who were not philosophers or
writers, or painters or soldiers) happen to get forgotten by the mass of men
unless there is a meaningful monument ever present before men's eyes. These last few
sentences are just asides that came to me upon writing. In the meantime
I have had my lunch and mistakenly made the mistake of looking at the proposed
building at this time as it certainly did not aid my digestive processes and
certainly raised my bloodpressure. I first looked at the plan at 11:30 PM
on returning from London. Since I had nightmares that night (literally). Since then I have
analyzed the building and at lunch I did a ground plan of it which just made
matters worse. I try to be calm about the whole thing but every time
I lokk at the plan or think about it I just get angrier. Sorry, I can't help it.

* I doubt we can learning from other periods — thus we must all learn from what has gone before us.

I shall not waste your energies or mine to tell you what I think of Messers
Pereira and Luckman...that will be quite clear by the time I give you my
analysis of the building. For the present, suffice it to say that there are
architects in the United States who know what they are doing, who have
culture and knowledge, who have studied and understood the history of the
past and through this, and being conscient of the society in which they live
are trying in the noblest of terms, a vital and dynamic expression of a vital
and dynamic society which owes so much to the past but which is creating
the present and moulding the future. I'll get back to this later.
Under discussion for the moment is the Seagram's building, prediminary study
by the firm of Pereira and Luckman, New York -Los Angeles. Knock them
between the eyes boys, that's the way. Show'em you can do sumpthing new
sumpthing terrific. Yup a nice big high skyscraper popping up to the sky
without letting it stop. Accentuate the verticals so that she goes streaking
up like a comet...nothin' to stop her...good and futuristic...a Flash Gordon
job...that's it flashy...real rich materials...make the man in the street
realize what youve got there...bowl hime over...impress him with your power
your wealth;;.keep him out of it...make him scared to go in...all that lower
part good and simple, just a mass of polished marble...no-one can penetrate
that except those that know that they go in there and belong so show them
where they got to go....that's it...three huge emblems like seignorial
shields crushing down over liile breaks in the front which must be the way
to get in...you dare go in...well jets lets take a gander...can't do us no
harm. By golly its dark in here;..oh there was a storm and the electricity
went off for a moment...but gee look at it now;..by gum its huge...hey look
you can almost see yourself like in a mirror those polished marble walls are
sure sumpthin'. And all those elevators dashin' up and down...I'm getting a bit
dizzy...hey, don't you want to go up in them elevators and maybe see something
upstairs;..naw - they're all offices and who cares about that anyway they'd
never let you in and I'm dog tired...lets get out into the street for some fresh
air and real light. Out in the street again...whats them funny sort of tower
things going up the side? - dunno sorta looks like silos but aint this the
Seagram's building?- make whisky, guess that's where they store their grain.
At this point an employee of Seagram's overheard our two friends and decided
that he would enlighten them and so he expained that these were the executive
offices, that is suites, on the four corners of the building. Our friends,
having been enlightened discussed the matter further. By golly they got an
awful lot of them executives...yup pretty important poeple to be takin up all
that place, why them towers just cut off all the light from the rest
of the building but I guess it don't make much difference where the ordinary
people live work, they gotta work some place...Hey what d'you think them
blank places in the building cover up...guess they don't want you to have the
chance to see all that goes on (snide laughter). Enough of my little joke *
but it covers the criticism of the building quite thoroughly. Where is
there any sense of a noble well proportioned building which delights people
in a democratic society (what could be more anti-democratic than your executive
suites), and uglier to boot? In this mechanical hum drumm dashing new York
where is there any sense of peacefulness, of relaxation, of drawing people off
the street to relax in pleasant surroundings. Where is there any humanization
of the monster, the sky scraper? It crushes people, makes them feel insignifigant and hopeless. There is not ONE REDEEMING FEATURE. It is a CHEAP
product of a mind that has learnt to approach everything from the point of
view of Sensationalism. ixxxmxxx It makes me too sick to go on but just as
a last word to Messers Pereira and Luckman I defy them to make a plausible
ground plan out of this bit of vulgarity which they have dared to
present to you.

* only a joke in the manner of presentation - I mean it quite seriously as a criticism -

4

I am sorry that I cannot be constructive in my criticism, that is have more of an idea of what modern architecture is up to. I am rather new at this game as you know and have been trying to learn...as a matter of fact I am so fascinated thAT I am considering really learning about architecture (by going to a school or working with an architect) but I have to look into all this. I also feel a bit guilty about this "Renaissance Modernized" business as I was the one who talked to you about the Renaissance and I did not make clear to you what I meant. I have used the renaissance as an example as it happens to be the one period in architecture that I know a little about and also about the most fascinating period of general culture and creativeness from every point of view and what has interested me most is that a building or a painting or a statue is never an isolated "work of art" but part of a whole society of a way of life of a philosphy and in this period the artist did not have that rediculous impotent rôle that he had in the nineteenth century and which, thank heavens he is losing, the romantic figure starving in the garret, a bohemian outside of society producing "art for art's sake" the most huge bit of nonsense to have been conceived of and most indicative of an unhealthy society lacking life force. The artist (architect etc.) of the renaissance was equally as important as the businessman, the philosopher, the scholar, the mathematician, the scientist: in fact he was all these things. But none of the works of the men of the rennaisance were bits of fancy...the foundations were rigously learnt in every field of endeavor (and the guilds controlled the standards which were of the highest). The past was studied carefully, Pythagoras, Plato, to mention two names and the old buildings found in the Forum were carefully measured and studied and Vitruvius studied so that the best of the past inspired men and they understood that the Greeks and the Romans who followed them had a well planned system of proportions and they analyzed why a given form was more pleasing than another, why a column had the height of 15 times its diameter and that this was more pleasing for a certain building type than the column having a height of nine times its diameter, or 14 and a half. A painting of Raphael was just mere fancy but the whole problem of composition carefully worked out on a mathematical basis and new ways of rendering space for a society that had a new conception of space, were all worked out with the highest degree of understanding of the science of the period. But they were not copying the past...they were learning from it and transforming it according to their ideas and understanding and this study of the past lead to new discoveries of the present. But any real appreciation and understanding of one period of the other and the integrity of the present can only come from just saying this pleases me, but if it does WHY does it and through the analysis comes the understanding of WHY and WHAT and HOW. There are architects now who are very concerned with these problems and really thinking about it, knowing what the are up to. The sky scraper and office buildings (the great buildings used to be palaces and churches) modern technology and modern conception of space (evolving from the painters, the cubists) all pose new problems in architecture and very exciting that is. I wish that I could suggest some architect or say more about modern architecture. I am just beggining to study it. But some of the great modern architects I can name although my list will not be comprehensive. There is Wright Mies van der Rohe, Walter Gropius, Le Corbousier, Lescaze, but I do not really know much about their work and plan to study it. The more I think of it, the more I am convinced that there are two very exciting new buildings in New York...the UN building and Lever Brothers. I might have scoffed at them and it easy to scoff at something that quite changes what we are used to and what we have considered quite comfortable. New conceptions are putink the flesh and sometimes quite violently change our way of looking at things and we take a while to even

APPENDIX 1

be able to look at these "new" things and it is hard sometimes to judge right away. But what are we trying to judge? *Is it beautiful?* Whether the concretization of these new conceptions (these buildings or paintings or statues or music, or way of doing business...) are really sincere and valid and well thought out and planned or do they just aim at shocking us, surprising us and pretend to represent a new philosophy. The Pereira Luckman plan is unhappily of the later breed. I am not touching on whether the philosophy underlying any endeavour be true and good ; I must assume that it is so for otherwise I will have to go off into all sorts of philosophical discussions.

Now what must be the idea behind a building in NY, an office building that is. I have not written an outline of what I think that this building should represent and the functions that it should fill so please forgive what will probably be not too orderly a presentation. Before building a building we must know its purpose; what will it be used for? An office building can be of two types : a general office building for various firms and companies or a building for the use of one company only, such as the Lever Brothers Building. The latter is probably an easier and more agreeable problem to handle as one organizes it solely to fit the needs and functions of a given firm and thus the planning of the building as a whole can be devided according to the various depts etc and the recreation facilities planned for people who are all working together. However this can all be worked out in a general building in which Seagrams, for eg, reserves part of the building for its own company and can organize that part of the building quite as functionally, fitting its own needs, as can the one company building. The real advantage in the one company building is that it is smaller. But why is its smallness, in comparison an advantage? Because an office building is for people and thus must be as agreeable as possible . One cannot humanly stick people into these immense work units which are so out of scale with the human being that he is crushed and insignifigant in the face of it, where he is just a number, where he trudges through a dreary entrance (usually quite out of scale with the rest of the building because it is like a pin hole opening) into a huge dreary hall with ugly flooring just because so many people will trudge across it, as it is made dark and pebbled (which is not at all necessary) and usually staring him in the face are long alphebetized lists telling who is where, and then those clanging elevators whizzing up and down. Electric light to lead his dreary way and all so mechanized. Then into cubby hole offices, and as often as not the lower salari group and secretaries work in halls that are inside with no windows and so they are all shut in in their work cells...what a nightmare to work in an a closed-in room without windows, and live all day by electric light. There are no recreation facilities, only small or not so small washrooms...no place to relax for a few moments and realize that one is not a machine but a person living in a world that was originally quite beautiful until cement and steel banished the green and the trees from our cities. (Man must make something beautiful to replace the beauty he has banished.) Thus a small building like Lever's , just because it is a one company building, takes the sting off much of this coldness and impersonalness of these big buildings, and it is more like a big family home ...the people that work there must have a feeling of this being "our" building and must be proud of it. An incentive to work better . But your plan as far as I know also to have offices which you will rent and the pleasant and necessary working conditions mentioned above can with ingenuity and intelligent planning be worked out. However the larger the building, the harder and one very important problem in this not so big versus big building, is the actual architecture of it, the aesthetics of it if you will but I don't much like that word. *the beauty of it.*

244 APPENDIX 1

On Park avenue there are no immensely high buildings and one must think of
the surroundings of a building and not have it too much out of proportion
with its surroundings. The question of city planning is important.
I guess that your building won't be one of these skyscrapingskyscrapers
for if I understand correctly, these extremely tall buildings no longer
make financial sense.
The building, as I have said, being for humans, must be humanized. The
I have already mentioned, or touched on the question of recreation, facilities
light, real daylight, contact with the world. Now the sense of a narrow building
such as the UN and Lever buildings becomes quite clear. You have all your rooms on two surfaces (U.N.) or all around (Lever) and then no rooms on the inside which do not have daylight. Maybe a ground plan would show this more easily

vaguely the UN plan with elevator core in the middle — I think — anyway a possibility

corridor & elevators

Offices — Rooms to be disposed of as one wishes

in the Lever brothers building I am not sure either and so won't

do my plan, the elevators are further towards one end and on the floor that I saw the whole front end, the area shadowed in this sketch → was one big room housing secretaries & people at desks in general (I don't remember what the organization of that floor was as far as the work done there is concerned) and executive ~~suite~~ offices off the corridor — The big room had light from 3 sides which however posed problems as the ~~light~~ sun as it moved caused such strong shadows that the electric light was used to counteract — but at least all the secretaries were "out in the air" — had a lovely view and the whole colour scheme & acoustics of the room made a calm & orderly place of what is in other buildings a Bedlamic nightmare —

executive suites

I would also like to mention here, should have been earlier when I talked of
recreation, that there is an attractive staff dining room so that this terrible
hustle bustle for secretaries is solved...they can have a longer lunch period
because they don't waste time going out, looking for a restaurant and waiting,
and they are out of the madding crush in the streets, of everybody out to eat
at the same time. Off the dining room is the terrace so that they may get
fresh air and walk around a bit after lunch. There are also lounges on
different floors where the personnel may agreeably take a few minutes off.
(They aren't very attractive as I remember, but that is my taste...but the
idea is a fine one.)

The part of the building that people see most is what is on the street level.
I will again point to the Lever building. I don't consider it completely
successful but I like very much what they tried to do. You want to invite
people into your building and afford them a pleasant place to take a few
minutes breather...a beautiful attractix calm entrance hall with the elevators
not dominating the scene but as discreet as possible, with daylight again
so that it is gay and bright (electric light is always depressing)
and with a lovely vista so that the eye can rove and is not blocked and
confined. In the Luckman plan you have this heavy tomblike façade which
not only makes the heart heavy but keeps you firmly out. The use of the
stilts or columns in the Lever Building (something which has long been used
by Le Corbousier) forms a modern arcade (the term not used architecturally)
and then the use of glass as walls lets you see right through and go in
without any barrier and so you create a real and an optical volume which
in itself is a fascinating thing to play with. And because your walls are of
glass, you have daylight. The little garden outside which forms part of
the ground floor, is a lovely idea, if not completely successful and something
that could be improved upon. Unfortunately Lever's make a bad display job in
their wall window. Also, they have used no wall decoration at
all and a mosaic might have been a lovely idea for the West Wall of an unpleasant
dark marble, and defines the solid confines of the garden-patio. I am
just suggesting possibilities here.

As to a building in glass I am not quite sure what I think but I rather think
that I like it. At first my reaction was that maybe it was wrong to make
a building which weighs tons look as if it floats and to make the walls not
quite definite because they are always changing. But Why Have a building
crushing down on us...in the best architecture the aim has always been for
lightness for elegance and we don't have to be reminded that a
skyscraper is a huge heavy ungainly monster. And is there anything wrong in
having the interest in a surface due largely to changing reflections ...I
think not at all as long as your partitions separating and joining the sheets
of glass are in the right proportion one to the other and each to the
whole. And one has a mosaic out of this lovely pattern of many pannels
of glass and colour through the light reflecting on each section and the
reflection of the sky and other buildings in the glass, and of course, the
basic field of colour from the glass itself. One great advantage of the glass
wall is that it does not become grime infested and streaked with the years.
The attraction of some of the newer apt; houses in NY comes from their lovely
whiteness and yet how dreary will they be a few years from now when all the
dirt and fumes greys and streaks them and this is inevitable in any modern
city. The white temple was fine in Greece when no grease and dirt and
fumes besmirched them. And so with a glass building, at the same time that
you have clean lines and the play of volumes in space (which is the modern
approach to spatial problems,) you have as your decoration through your pattern

of glass and your reflection...how wonderfully simple, how elegant, how lovely.

As I have written this letter and thought about these problems I am more and more convinced that the Lever building points the way. I would even urge very strongly calling on the architects of the Lever Building. In leafing through one of my books just a few minutes ago I came across what I was formulating to say to you very well stated by one of the most intelligent and delightful writers (writer-critic) ~~John~~ on architecture and the arts in general, the ~~19xxhe~~ 19th Century Englishman, John Ruskin. "~~Architecture is the decoration~~

"So long as any given styles are in practice all that is left for the individual imagination to accomplish must be within the scope of those styles, not in the invention of a new one. For who is to come after you, clustered Columbuses? to what fortunate islands of styles are your architectural descendents to sail, avaricious of new lands? <u>When your desired style is invented, will not the best we can all do be simply to build in it?</u> and cannot you now do that in styles that are known?"

(underlinings by me)

This new style seen in Lever and UN buildings has been growing for a long time, the Bauhaus in Dessau (germany) being about the first impetus as far as I know and that was after the 1st world war, (now) Walter Gropius was the architect. But now I will study all this ~~and~~ now, what definite direction my inquiries will take. I will ask Regina Slatkin to get me all the material she can on the UN and Lever buildings. I have been two days writing this letter and so I will end it now and so send it to you. There is lots more I could say, but that will be for another day. I would appreciate if you could have a copy of this letter made for me, as I did not use a carbon, and as I was developing my thoughts as I wrote I would like to know what I had to say! I am of course very anxious to know of your reaction to all that I have written and suggested. I will take it for granted at any rate that no further plans will be forthcoming from Messers Pereira and Luckman...you can't make a silk purse out of a sows ear, an architect out of a huxster, nor can people who presented such a plan ever produce anything worthwhile as it is all vulgar surface with absolutely nothing behind it and I'm being extremely generous in saying as little as that.✱ You will probably go to various firms who will give you different plans. I think that the best person to ~~speak~~ consult on who the best architects are is Lewis Mumford, who has written many books on architecture and city planning in the US and who writes about the newest buildings erected in the US and abroad, in the New Yorker. Would you like me to write to him now? It would be better to talk to him, and if you wanted me to fly over for a few days to do so I should be delighted. Also may I suggest that it would be better to lay the corner stone in '57 than to put up a bad building because time presses; one cannot chose between a couple of years and imortality. I shall also be a bit fresh in making such a statement to my Pappa but shall risk any ire that it may provoke for the moment and that is PLEASE PLEASE PLEASE turn a deaf ear to the Slaters and Wachtels etc...as far as these things go they just don't know. Think quickly of that awful portrait of you by Slaters friend...I think you konw what I mean and agree with me but don't get waylaid <u>please</u>. Hoping to hear from you very soon, much love Phyllis.

✱ It is quiet elegance, harmony, sobriety - humility that makes beauty not flashiness —

APPENDIX 2
SEAGRAM PLAZA INSTALLATIONS AND SEAGRAM GALLERY EXHIBITIONS

Dates in this appendix are drawn from two lists prepared by the Seagram Curator's Office (Records of the Seagram Curator's Office, Fonds Seagram Building, boxes 134-021 and 134-026, CCA) and from other documentation in the Curator's Office records.

INSTALLATIONS ON SEAGRAM PLAZA

Olmec Head, 5th century
Spring 1965 (May 18–c. June 1, 1965)

Barnett Newman
Broken Obelisk, 1963–67
Fall 1967 (September 27–October 31, 1967)

Easter Island Head, date unknown
Fall 1968 (October 21–November 21, 1968)

Louise Nevelson
Atmosphere and Environment XII, 1970
Winter 1971 (January 26–c. March 9, 1971)

Marvin Torffield
Listen for the Narrow Beam, 1973
Fall 1973 (October 4–20, 1973)

Jean Dubuffet
Milord la Chamarre, 1973–74
Fall/Winter 1974–75 (November 14, 1974–c. January 15, 1975)

Mark di Suvero
Praise for Elohim Adonai, 1966
Fall/Winter 1975–76 (October 23, 1975–February 12, 1976)

Horia Damian
The Hill, 1976
Fall 1976 (October 13–29, 1976)

Michael Heizer
Guenette, 1977–78
Summer/Fall 1979 (June 11–October 27, 1979)

Carl Andre
Fermion, 1981
Summer/Fall 1981 (July 31–October 30, 1981)

Don Gummer
Spiral Crown, 1982
Spring/Summer 1982 (May 16–August 6, 1982)

Willem de Kooning
Seated Woman, 1969–81
Spring/Summer 1983 (April 26–August 2, 1983)

John Chamberlain
American Tableau, 1984
Fall 1984 (September 12–November 5, 1984)

Alexander Calder
Tom's, 1974
Spring/Summer 1985 (April 27–September 7, 1985)

Joel Shapiro
Untitled, 1974–75
Fall 1986 (October 16–November 26, 1986)

Julian Schnabel
Ozymandias, 1986–90
Spring/Summer 1990 (May 5–August 4, 1990)

Claes Oldenburg
Monument to the Last Horse, 1990–91
Spring/Summer 1991 (June 1–August 24, 1991)

Keith Haring
Headstand, 1988
Summer/Fall 1997 (June 14–October 11, 1997)

Tony Smith
Light Up, 1971
Summer 1998 (July 1–September 22, 1998)

Richard Long
Brownstone Circle, 2000
Spring 2000 (April 8–June 24, 2000)

SEAGRAM GALLERY EXHIBITIONS

The Court Houses of Indiana
Summer/Fall 1975 (August 20–c. November 20, 1975)
Curator, Richard Pare

The United States County Court House Project
Winter 1975–76 (December 10, 1975–c. March 10, 1976)
Curator, Richard Pare

The County Court House in the United States
Spring 1976 (April 12–c. July 12, 1976)
Curator, Richard Pare

The County Court House in the United States IV
Summer 1976 (July 14–c. October 1, 1976)
Curator, Richard Pare

The County Court House in the United States V
Fall/Winter 1976–77 (October 5, 1976–c. January 5, 1977)
Curator, Richard Pare

The Romanesque Revival and the Early Courthouses of Virginia
Spring 1977 (March 7–c. June 7, 1977)
Curator, Richard Pare

The Seagram Plaza: Its Design and Use
Fall/Winter 1977–78 (November 22, 1977–March 1, 1978)
Curator, Phyllis Lambert, in collaboration with Ludwig Glaeser

Animals: Drawings and Photographs
Spring 1978 (March 7–June 7, 1978)
Curator, Martha Beck

After Court House
Fall/Winter 1978–79 (October 20, 1978–c. January 20, 1979)
Curator, Richard Pare

Contemporary Landscape
Winter/Spring 1979 (January 31–April 26, 1979)
Curator, Martha Beck

Acquisitions, 1977–1979
Summer 1979 (June 18–September 7, 1979)
Curator, Richard Pare

Nature Arranged: Modern Still Lifes
Fall/Winter 1979–80 (October 5, 1979–January 3, 1980)
Curator, Martha Beck

Winter: An Exhibition of Photographs
Winter/Spring 1980 (February 1, 1980–May 1, 1980)
Curator, Richard Pare

Self Portraits
Spring/Summer 1980 (May 19–August 8, 1980)
Curator, Martha Beck

Photographs by Richard Pare, Summer 1980
Winter/Spring 1980–81 (December 15, 1980–March 30, 1981)
Curator, Richard Pare

Dreams and Fantasies
Spring 1981 (April 2–June 30, 1981)
Curator, Martha Beck, with assistance by Marie Keller

The Second Avenue Court House: An Architectural Transformation
Summer/Fall 1981 (July 22–October 22, 1981)
Curator, Raimund Abraham

Recent Acquisitions from the Seagram Collection
Winter/Spring 1981–82 (December 4, 1981–March 31, 1982)
Curator, Richard Pare

New York: Visions of the City
Spring/Summer 1982 (April 26–July 22, 1982)
Curator, Martha Beck, with assistance by Marie Keller

Incidents and Events
Summer/Fall 1982 (July 28–October 28, 1982)
Curator, Marie Keller

Contemporary Watercolors
Fall/Winter 1982–83 (November 10, 1982–February 11, 1983)
Curator, Marie Keller

Interiors
Winter/Spring 1983 (February 28–May 26, 1983)
Curator, Martha Beck and Marie Keller

Photographs from the Seagram Collection: People in an Urban Environment
Summer 1983 (June 16–September 16, 1983)
Curator, Carla Caccamise Ash

"O, Write My Name": American Portraits, Harlem Heroes
Fall 1983 (September 29–December 19, 1983)
Organized by Carla Caccamise Ash in collaboration with the Eakins Press Foundation

Signs of the Times: Storefronts and Billboards: Photographs from the Seagram Collection
Winter/Spring 1984 (January 10–April 12, 1984)
Curator, Carla Caccamise Ash

Drawings by Sculptors: Two Decades of Non-Objective Art in the Seagram Collection—Part I
Winter 1984–85 (December 12, 1984–February 8, 1985)
Curator, David Bellman

Drawings by Sculptors: Two Decades of Non-Objective Art in the Seagram Collection—Part II
Winter/Spring 1985 (February 20–April 19, 1985)
Curator, David Bellman

Home: Photographs from the Seagram Collection
Fall/Winter 1985–86 (November 12, 1985–February 12, 1986)
Curator, Carla Caccamise Ash

Garry Winogrand, 1928 to 1984: Photographs from the Seagram Collection
Spring/Summer 1986 (April 1–July 25, 1986)
Curator, Carla Caccamise Ash

Locomotion, Past and Present: Photographs from the Seagram Collection
Winter 1986–87 (December 15, 1986–March 13, 1987)
Curator, Carla Caccamise Ash

The Streets of New York: Photographs from the Seagram Collection
Spring/Summer 1987 (April 15–July 15, 1987)
Curator, Carla Caccamise Ash

Simple Pleasures: Photographs from the Seagram Collection
Summer/Fall 1987 (August 24–December 3, 1987)
Curator, Carla Caccamise Ash

The Working Life: Photographs from the Seagram Collection
Winter 1987–88 (December 11, 1987–April 1, 1988)
Curator, Carla Caccamise Ash

Windows on the World: Photographs from the Seagram Collection
Summer/Fall 1988 (August 1–November 6, 1988)
Curator, Carla Caccamise Ash

Women/Men: Photographs from the Seagram Collection
Winter/Spring 1988–89 (December 5, 1988–April 20, 1989)
Curator, Carla Caccamise Ash

Shadows and Silhouettes: Chiaroscuro in Photographic Images
Spring/Fall 1989 (May 8–October 26, 1989)
Curator, Carla Caccamise Ash

Photographs of the Fifties: The Decade of the Seagram Building
Fall/Spring 1989–90 (November 8, 1989–April 9, 1990)
Curator, Carla Caccamise Ash

Prints from the Early Seagram Collection
Spring/Fall 1990 (May 1–October 31, 1990)
Curator, Carla Caccamise Ash

The Seagram Building, 1958: Photographs by Ezra Stoller
Fall/Winter 1990–91 (November 15, 1990–January 25, 1991)
Curator, Carla Caccamise Ash

The City Life of Flora and Fauna: Photographs from the Seagram Collection
Summer 1991 (June 3–September 6, 1991)
Curator, Carla Caccamise Ash

Night Lights: Photographs from the Seagram Collection
Fall/Winter 1991–92 (October 15, 1991–February 14, 1992)
Curator, Carla Caccamise Ash

Little Pictures: Photographs from the Seagram Collection
Winter/Spring 1992 (February 26–May 29, 1992)
Curator, Carla Caccamise Ash

Summer Pastimes: Photographs from the Seagram Collection
Summer/Fall 1992 (June 15–October 16, 1992)
Curator, Carla Caccamise Ash

Art and Archives from the Seagram Museum
Fall/Winter 1992–93 (November 2, 1992–March 4, 1993)
Curator, Carla Caccamise Ash, in conjunction with staff from the Seagram Museum, Waterloo, Ontario

Other Places: America Beyond New York City: Photographs from the Seagram Collection
Spring/Summer 1993 (March 22–July 9, 1993)
Curator, Carla Caccamise Ash

California Photography from a Seventies Perspective: Part I
Summer/Fall 1993 (August 5–December 22, 1993)
Curator, Carla Caccamise Ash

California Photography from a Seventies Perspective: Part II
Winter/Spring 1994 (January 10–June 3, 1994)
Curator, Carla Caccamise Ash

Americana: Symbols and Images
Summer/Fall 1994 (July 14–November 18, 1994)
Curator, Carla Caccamise Ash

Landmarks of New York
Winter 1994–95 (December 5, 1994–March 24, 1995)
Curator, Carla Caccamise Ash

Faces: Photographs from the Seagram Collection
Spring/Summer 1995 (April 10, 1995–August 4, 1995)
Curator, Carla Caccamise Ash

Up/Down: Varied Viewpoints: Photographs from the Seagram Collection
Summer/Fall 1995 (August 28–December 29, 1995)
Curator, Carla Caccamise Ash

Moments in Black History
Winter/Spring 1996 (January 29–May 10, 1996)
Curator, Carla Caccamise Ash

California Photography from a Seventies Perspective: Part III
Spring/Summer 1996 (May 28–September 10, 1996)
Curator, Carla Caccamise Ash

Court House: Revisiting Seagram's Bicentennial Project
Fall/Winter 1996–97 (October 1, 1996–January 17, 1997)
Curator, Carla Caccamise Ash

African to American Pioneers
Winter/Spring 1997 (February 3–June 9, 1997)
Curator, Carla Caccamise Ash

Keith Haring: Prints 1982 to 1989
Summer/Fall 1997 (June 17–October 3, 1997)
Curator, Carla Caccamise Ash

Photographs from the Archives of Universal Studios, Inc.
Fall/Winter 1997–98 (November 17, 1997–March 13, 1998)
Curator, Carla Caccamise Ash

Photogravures: From Pictorialism to Strand
Spring/Summer 1998 (April 6, 1998–July 1, 1998)
Curator, Carla Caccamise Ash

Tony Smith Sculpture: Through Drawings and Photographs
Summer/Fall 1998 (July 6–September 30, 1998)
Curator, Carla Caccamise Ash

Contrasts: Photographs from the Seagram Collections
Fall/Winter 1998–99 (October 19, 1998–March 5, 1999)
Curator, Carla Caccamise Ash

Fleeting Moments: Photographs from the Seagram Collections
Spring/Summer 1999 (March 29–August 6, 1999)
Curator, Carla Caccamise Ash

Past Attractions: Lobby Cards from the Laemmle Era at Universal Studios, 1920 to 1936
Summer/Fall 1999 (August 30–December 3, 1999)
Curators, Carla Caccamise Ash and Jan-Christopher Horak

Structures: The Bechers' Photographs and Contrasting Images
Winter/Spring 2000 (February 7–March 31, 2000)
Curator, Carla Caccamise Ash

Richard Long: Photography and Text Works
Spring/Summer 2000 (April 10–August 10, 2000)
Curator, Richard Long

Classics from the Seagram Collection
Winter/Spring 2001 (February 12–May 22, 2001)
Curator, Carla Caccamise Ash

OTHER LOCATIONS

City Scenes: Photographs from the Seagram Collection
Montclair Art Museum, Montclair, New Jersey
Fall/Winter 1997–98 (September 27, 1997–January 4, 1998)
Curator, Carla Caccamise Ash

APPENDIX 3

SOME CONSERVATION ISSUES AS REMEMBERED BY ARVID KLEIN AND TOM STETZ OF PASANELLA + KLEIN

CORRIDOR CARPETING

Almost from day one, TIAA asked approval for carpeting the public corridors. For them, it was a business decision, they said, rather than an aesthetic one. They argued that every first-class office building had carpeted corridors, and therefore that was what prospective tenants expected. They implied that TIAA was in some way losing money by not being able to offer that level of amenity. We could not convince them that the vinyl tile flooring was "classic" and an integral part of the charm of Seagram's corridors.

As for the vinyl flooring, of course the original material had been unavailable for a long time, and when the *Corridors Restoration Project* was undertaken after the sale of the building, we had used the readily available product that most closely approximated the original; it was similar, but the color was a bit off. Eventually we found a rubber tile manufacturer who was willing to manufacture tiles in the custom gray color (but not the original nine-by-nine-inch size) in small batches, and those were used until TIAA prevailed upon Phyllis Lambert to consider a carpeting option, which was ultimately chosen by Philip Johnson's office.

PLAZA ELEVATOR

This came up, I believe, when someone in a wheelchair sued the Four Seasons Restaurant after having been routed through the loading dock and the kitchens to get to their table, and definitely did not like the experience. The city of New York joined in the suit, upholding the tenets of the Americans with Disabilities Act (ADA) of 1990, but the suit was ultimately dropped. (We were told that this was due to the city having exhausted the funds they had budgeted for the suit.) As a result of all this, TIAA's legal department was energized into considering the access issue for the building as a whole, since wheelchair access had become a legal requirement. We looked at various ramp schemes, ostensibly the easiest way to overcome the three steps up to the plaza, but it was clear that all such schemes would be visually objectionable and intrusive, as they would most certainly all involve extensive railings. TIAA was surprised that there would be any objections to such a simple solution.

So we developed an elevator scheme that would have inserted a "stealth elevator" near the Fifty-Second Street entry stairs. This design was carried through contract drawings, including engineering drawings, and costed out. (I believe that it was on the order of a million dollars.) At that point TIAA made the (legal) argument that this would constitute a financial hardship, which was one of the loopholes offered in the ADA legislation, and the project died—much to everyone's relief. The access issue was dealt with by a bell that would summon a lobby attendant to bring out a temporary ramp. Signage was placed to direct the handicapped to that call bell.

SAFETY MEASURES FOR THE PLAZA POOLS

Probably as a spin-off of the handicap access issue, TIAA's legal counsel came up with the idea that the plaza pools needed some sort of "protection" that would keep blind people from falling into them, and suing not only for damages (which had always been a risk for the building) but for civil rights damages through the ADA. We never could decide whether they were actually serious about this project or why anyone would have even imagined such a thing, but TIAA did keep after it like a terrier with a bone. Perhaps they saw Article 26 as essentially a mechanism to discourage changes and that by invoking some authority higher than that lease condition—that is, a federal law—they might abrogate Article 26 in some way and recapture some of their freedom of action as owners of the property.

Possible solutions to the pool issue involved some sort of tactile warning strip, similar to what one encounters along subway and rail platforms: raised discs that the blind person's cane would sense. The commonly available glued-down version was ruled out as too tacky, even by TIAA: indeed, they seemed to be willing to consider remaking or retooling the granite pavers at the pool edges with integral raised granite discs, at a huge cost. One problem with this was that the ADA standard that had been promulgated had gone through a few refinements and changes, and nobody could seem to pin down what would legally satisfy both the ADA and New York City's own requirements. Next, of course, railings were proposed, either similar to the other plaza railings, which in such a location would have been visually unacceptable, or, at one point, glass railings, which were characterized as "invisible" (!). As an interim measure, Building Management was instructed by TIAA to place movable stanchions and ropes around the pools, which they did—only to discover that they were causing rust stains on the pavers. The problem was finally "solved," and I don't quite remember by whom, by arguing that the noise of the fountains should be considered a sufficient cue to alert a blind person of danger. And the stanchions were removed (but put back in place whenever the fountains were not working).

NIGHT LIGHTING

We kept asking Building Management to try to find a way to revive the original night-lighting setup, which had been deactivated during the 1970s energy crisis and never revived. The Building Manager maintained that over the years, the various lighting circuits devoted to the lighting system (which was completely separate from the general luminous ceiling lighting) had been "robbed" to service other electrical uses, as the demand for power in the building had grown over the years. Arvid Klein wanted them to just "throw the switch" and see what happened, but TIAA was always leery of that, fearing the worst, and nothing much ever came of the idea, though it was often revived.

On the subject of the luminous ceiling, toward the end of the whole period it seemed that TIAA, or at least Building Management, might be interested in some complete rethinking and replacement of the luminous ceiling lighting itself. Aside from aesthetic issues (some tenants really simply hated the look), it was expensive to maintain, especially as the components were inherently custom made. The Mylar panels had to be replaced regularly, as they would turn yellow, and they had to be handmade. Also, sprinkler piping had been retrofitted through the whole ceiling construction, which made plan changes more complex than before that work was done. The energy savings of a new luminous ceiling would be, one might argue, substantial. And so on. But that idea got nowhere as soon as someone at TIAA would consider the costs, and any concrete idea about what would be an acceptable replacement was lacking.

OVERMAINTENANCE

With the arrival of each new property manager at TIAA, it seemed that the first order of business was the desire to make the building "look like new," to sparkle from increased maintenance. It would bother them that surfaces were showing their age: this was thought to make the building less appealing to potential new tenants. The word *patina* was definitely not in their vocabulary. We encountered this thinking applied especially to the ground-floor areas, the places that are most highly visible, and each surface had to be defended from overmaintenance.

Plaza/Lobby Granite: There was a long history of confusion and ad hoc cleaning methods. On the plaza, when the original snow-melting system failed, salt had to be used in the winter, and the result by springtime was a white residue on the granite, which had to be cleaned away. There was a lot of back-and-forth sniping, such as, for instance, whether muriatic (hydrochloric) acid should be used, or indeed ever had been used, with denials or defensiveness as seemed appropriate. I [Tom Stetz] remember that Earl Fries, the Seagram facilities man, once secured a sample of the cleaning material ostensibly for his own personal use and then had it analyzed—to find that it did in fact contain an acid. At that point Seagram threatened to hold TIAA in violation of Article 26, and therefore the whole lease agreement, which demonstrated to TIAA how seriously these issues were to be taken. In the case of the granite lobby floor, the situation was complicated because it seemed that a small amount of liquid wax was typically added to the washing water, the result over time being wax buildup and yellowing. I'm not sure that any of these issues was ever really resolved, except to make Building Management more circumspect but probably more willing to use gentler cleaning methods.

Plaza Resurfacing: At one point, the more general issue of resurfacing the plaza came up, a one-time procedure that had been written into Article 26 for the new owner to undertake at a certain point. TIAA was agreeable to doing something, as it worked into their principle of maintaining the building "like new." The problem was that there was no easy answer as to how that was to be accomplished. Certainly not through sandblasting, which would alter the surface of the originally hand-tooled stone. Removing the stones to a shop for resurfacing? Hardly feasible. Various consultants were brought in, various trials made, and again no real conclusion.

Marble Benches: Since these were subject to deterioration from exposure to the elements, and also from physical abuse, especially after skateboards and inline skates became popular, a spring restoration always seemed necessary. It was only with some difficulty that Building Management was finally dissuaded from the yearly polyurethaning, which was supposed to simulate a high polish but which usually yellowed after a time. Various patching techniques were tried, including the "preservationist" approach favored by the Landmarks Law (using patching material that did not try to blend into the marble fabric, in the interest of "honesty"), and ultimately TIAA agreed that there should be a one-time grinding down and repolishing of the benches, and from then on more moderate patching procedures.

Bronze: I won't go into the long and inconclusive story of attempts to deal with the buildup of cleaning oils and soot on the facade and the progressive "greening" of the upper reaches, because TIAA was in agreement that *something* ought to be done and was cooperative. Again, with each new property manager, the idea of completely stripping the surface to make it look new again would recur. The idea had to be combated, and ultimately it would founder with the realization that the costs would be enormous and the techniques to be used undetermined.

One source of continuing strife between Seagram and TIAA was the way that the lower or "lobby" bronze was treated versus that of the superstructure. The former always received more attention and was several times stripped, reoxidized, and reoiled. The issue was that, in so doing, it could, and sometimes did, look different from the upper bronze work, which was of course not wanted. TIAA maintained that the lobby bronze was highly visible and had to be kept pristine, etc., etc. Again, no real resolution was ever reached, other than to harangue TIAA every year about overdoing the lobby bronze.

NOTES

Abbreviations Used in Notes

BSRC	*Building Seagram* Research Collection, Canadian Centre for Architecture, Montreal
CCA	Canadian Centre for Architecture, Montreal
CSC	Collection Seagram Company, Ltd., Hagley Museum and Library, Wilmington
EMB	Edgar M. Bronfman
FPL	Fonds Phyllis Lambert, Canadian Centre for Architecture, Montreal
FSB	Fonds Seagram Building, Canadian Centre for Architecture, Montreal
PL	Phyllis Lambert
MoMA	Museum of Modern Art, New York
RG	record group
SB	Samuel Bronfman

PROLOGUE. UNLIKELY CONVERGENCES

1. Samuel Bronfman, b. 1889, aboard ship; d. 1971, Montreal, Quebec. He changed the date of his birth to 1891, wishing to claim Canadian citizenship by birth. See Michael Marrus, *Mr. Sam: The Life and Times of Samuel Bronfman* (Toronto: Viking, 1991), 21ff.
2. SB contracted with Wathen Knebelkamp, scion of the distinguished distilling family in Kentucky, assisted by an engineer, to build the most modern contemporary distilling plant, and also to learn from him "everything I could to make sure we made good whisky." Ibid., 116ff.
3. The similarity between the names of the two companies, Distillers Company Limited and Distillers Corporation Limited, is interesting. The Scottish Distillers Company Limited (DCL) had been formed in 1877 and by 1925 DCL's new accessions included three aristocrat-headed distillers that are the still-great names in whisky: John Haig & Company, Buchanan-Dewar, and John Walker & Sons, Ltd. Looking to expand to North America, the DCL chairman studied whisky production in Canada—Gooderham and Worts of Toronto, Hiram Walker and Sons of Walkerville, and Corby's at Belleville, as well as the LaSalle plant, which they found to be less at risk for obsolescence. See Marrus, *Mr. Sam,* esp. 116–22. The Bronfman management style and forthrightness inspired confidence, and a director explained: "We liked Sam and our people recognized the cogency of his case. He had opened our eyes to wider fields and since we knew him better than anybody else in Canada, there was no real point in us seeking to do business elsewhere." Ibid., 123.
4. Joseph E. Seagram & Sons, Ltd., named after Joseph Emm Seagram (1841–1919), was founded in 1883 when he became sole proprietor.
5. David J. Spence, b. 1873, Louisville, Kentucky; d. 1955, Montreal, Quebec. The building exterior has not visibly changed streetside since 1931. Over time, numerous spaces were changed on the interior, but the offices of Samuel and Allan Bronfman are preserved. See assessment report by Susan Bronson, *Seagram Building, Montreal: Heritage Study for Seagram Canada* (Montreal: N.p., 1999). The building was transferred to McGill University in 2002 and renamed Martlet House.
6. The hotel was by the MIT-trained Canadian architects George Allen Ross and Robert Henry Macdonald. The firm Ross & Macdonald (active 1913–44) had already realized impressive buildings in the immediate vicinity: to the north, the grand turreted Château Apartments building (1924–26); to the east, the Beaux-Arts Eaton's department store (1925–27); and just down the street, their full-block Beaux-Arts commercial office complex, the Dominion Square building, was erected at the same time that 1430 Peel was under construction.
7. Horses are heraldic "supporters" that traditionally signify readiness for deployment for king and country; in the Scottish tradition, only royals and peers and certain heads of considerable families are entitled to deploy supporters; sheaves of grain and oak, on the other hand, are devices related to Seagram's distilling industry.
8. Joseph E. Seagram & Sons, Inc., was incorporated on October 23, 1933. The Twenty-First Amendment to the US Constitution repealed the Eighteenth Amendment of 1919, giving states the right to legislate the sale and use of alcohol. In New York, a huge majority voted for repeal, but not everywhere did it happen overnight: Mississippi, where alcohol had been illegal since 1907, became the last state to repeal Prohibition in 1966.

9. In 1933, DC-SL took over a distillery in Indiana and acquired a second distillery from the Calvert company in Maryland. DC-SL set up Calvert as a second US subsidiary. The Seagram and Calvert companies formed the core of DC-SL's expansion in the United States between 1934 and 1945. During that period, the Seagram companies absorbed eighteen firms, principally whisky distilleries. See Graham D. Taylor, "'From Shirtsleeves to Shirtless': The Bronfman Dynasty and the Seagram Empire," *Business and Economic History On-Line* 4 (2006): 8–9, http://www.h-net.org/~business/bhcweb/publications/BEHonline/2006/taylor.pdf.

10. House of Seagram print ad, October 1934, reprinted in *Responsible Drinking: A Seagram History of Commitment,* Seagram Company, Ltd., booklet [1994], FPL, box 08-L-753. Also republished in *Responsible Drinking* were other Seagram ads that proscribed drinking and driving ("We who make whiskey say: 'Drinking and Driving Do Not Mix,'" August 1937) and the misuse of drinking ("Some men should not drink," November 1938), as well as ads promoting the film *The Lost Weekend* in newspapers throughout the United States in January 1946. The 1945 film by Billy Wilder, starring Ray Milland and Jane Wyman, was based on a novel of the same title by Charles R. Jackson about a writer who drinks heavily and goes on an alcoholic weekend binge.

11. Marrus, *Mr. Sam,* 231ff. One must beware when advertising is interpreted to support literary devices by historians who play (or compose) with evidential information. In a recent example, Benjamin Flowers in *Skyscraper: The Politics and Power of Building New York City in the Twentieth Century* (Philadelphia: University of Pennsylvania Press, 2009) compares the 1930s, focusing on the Empire State Building, with the 1950s, focusing on Seagram. On page 96, Flowers comes to the easy conclusion of the thesis that he set up: "In the 1950s, Seagram once again turned to modern architecture to enlarge and refine the company's reputation." Yes, but very much no.

12. Marrus, *Mr. Sam,* 235.

13. See Terence Robertson, "Bronfman: The Life and Times of Samuel Bronfman, Esq.," unpublished manuscript [1969], 491–92, Jack McClelland Fonds, William Ready Division of Archives and Research Collections, box 19, McMaster University. Also quoted in Marrus, *Mr. Sam,* 240–41.

14. See John McDonald, "Seagram in the Chips," *Fortune,* September 1948, 99, 166; also quoted in Marrus, *Mr. Sam,* 244.

15. John Bassett, president of the Gazette Print Company and the *Montreal Gazette,* invited Stephen Leacock—better known as a humorist and author than as the longtime chair of McGill University's Department of Economics and Political Science—to write the book at SB's request: 165,000 copies were distributed by 1967. *Canada: The Foundations of Its Future* (Montreal: House of Seagram and Gazette Print, 1941).

16. Samuel Bronfman, foreword, ibid., unpaged [1].

17. Jean Béraud, "Canada: The Foundation of Its Future," typescript, trans. R. Page, originally published in *La Presse,* February 6, 1943; Seagram Museum Collection, acc. 2173, ser. III, box 68, Hagley Museum and Library (hereafter cited as Seagram Museum Collection). For its halted distribution, see Carl Spadoni, *A Bibliography of Stephen Leacock* (Toronto: ECW Press, 1998), 336.

18. The exhibition was organized and curated by Robert Pilot and A. J. Casson, president and immediate past president of the Royal Canadian Academy, respectively. *Cities of Canada: Reproductions from the Seagram Collection of Paintings,* commentary by Bernard K. Sandwell, privately published by the House of Seagram (Toronto: Sampson-Matthews, 1953), unpaged, CCA Library. Bronfman discussed the traveling exhibition in a radio interview with Neil Le Roy, Toronto, September 1954, Seagram Museum Collection, acc. 2173, ser. III, box 83.

19. The exhibition's advertising role was made more explicit in Seagram's 1953 Annual Report, which under the rubric "Seagram Sells Canada" declared, "It is a matter of good corporate citizenship that a business organization trading in world markets should do its full share in selling its *country* as well as its own *products* abroad. This has long been the philosophy of the House of Seagram." 1953 Annual Report, Distillers Corporation–Seagrams Limited, 22, Imprints Department, Hagley Museum and Library. That attitude, like Seagram's advertising campaigns urging temperance, was unusual half a century ago. In 1953, 1954, 1955, and 1957 the company continued to inform its readers about the development of Canada and its connections with the American economy in abundantly illustrated forty-page supplements to the annual reports. All Seagram annual reports are held in the Imprints Department, Hagley Museum and Library.

20. Morris Lapidus to Alan [sic] Bronfman, July 9, 1954, FPL, box 08-L-515.

21. Morris Lapidus, *Too Much Is Never Enough* (New York: Rizzoli, 1996), 183–84.

22. Ibid., 116. Lapidus also characterized the style of Seagram's offices of 1934 as "Elizabethan"; John C. Cook and Heinrich Klotz, *Conversations with Architects* (New York: Praeger, 1973), 166–67. "For Seagram, newly arrived in the Chrysler Building, I wanted to convey a feeling of age in a most distinguished way." That he was able to design in a historical style was due to the eclectic training of architects at Columbia University in the mid-1920s, which he said allowed the students to "reproduce any style in history without any research. If a client wanted a Louis XIV French villa, there was no problem. A colonial town hall? Presto, and there it was. A little English Gothic church? You name it, and you got it." Lapidus quoted in Martina Düttmann, *Morris Lapidus: Architect of the American Dream* (Basel: Birkhäuser, 1992), 9.

23. Lapidus, *Too Much Is Never Enough,* 116.
24. Lapidus stated that the only place that he could "cut loose" from historical style in designing the Seagram offices "was in the bar, where I was expressing my feeling of what contemporary good living with liquor might be. I took the chance in the bar, and I went as far as I knew how to go using my own idiom." Quoted in Cook and Klotz, *Conversations with Architects,* 168. Evan M. Frankel, partner in Ross-Frankel, Inc. (1902–1991), an acquaintance of Bronfman, was peripherally involved in the acquisition of 375 Park Avenue. See Anton Trunk to James E. Friel, March 17, 1950, CSC, acc. 2126, RG 2, ser. X, box 844; and Robert G. Morgan, Douglas Gibbons & Co., Inc., to SB, May 24, 1950, ibid., box 845. On the wall above the banquettes, muralist Stuyvesant Van Veen depicted the production and tasting of spirits. These features were enhanced by a sophisticated use of indirect fluorescent lighting that Lapidus deployed in his shops, in a signature theatrical effect that could "effectively seduce the prospective customer"; Düttmann, *Lapidus,* 10.
25. The pavilion was sponsored by the four major companies—Seagram, Schenley, National Distillers, and Hiram Walker—and was intended to legitimize the industry by demonstrating that a great deal of American history was attributable to distilling.
26. Lapidus, stretching the concept, later claimed his idea to be a precursor of Lever House. Writing to Seagram in 1954, he boasted that his 1941 scheme "includes many features which predate Lever house by fifteen years. At that time I was thinking of the gardens within the building and an approach very similar to the one which was eventually used." Lapidus to Alan [*sic*] Bronfman, July 9, 1954, FPL, box 08-L-515.
27. These included spring exhibitions at the Art Association of Montreal (later the Montreal Museum of Fine Arts): March 20–April 15, 1940, *Kids;* March 20–April 13, 1941, *Five and a Half;* April 1–30, 1942, *Missing the Bus;* April 1–30, 1943, *Miss Helen MacDonald;* April 28–May 28, 1944, *Oenone;* April 5–29, 1945, *Lindy Lou* and *Composition;* and fall exhibitions at the Royal Canadian Academy, November 6–December 4, 1941, *Study of a Head;* the Art Gallery of Toronto, November 6–December 6, 1942, *Study of a Head* and *Helen MacDonald;* the Musée de la Province de Québec, Quebec City, October 5–26, 1943, *My Mother;* the Art Association of Montreal, November 5–27, 1943, *My Mother;* and the Art Gallery of Toronto, November 17–December 7, 1944, *Lindy Lou.*
28. The 1948 Vassar Arts Conference is discussed in chapter 5.
29. See Phyllis Lambert, "In Memoriam: Richard Krautheimer (1897–1994)," *Journal of the Society of Architectural Historians* 54, no. 1 (March 1995): 4–7, 115–21.
30. Foreword to the official catalogue of the Werkbund exhibition *Die Wohnung,* Stuttgart (1927); quoted in Fritz Neumeyer, *The Artless Word: Mies van der Rohe on the Building Art,* trans. Mark Jarzombek (Cambridge, MA: MIT Press, 1991), 258; originally published as *Mies van der Rohe: Das kunstlose Wort; Gedanken zur Baukunst* (Berlin: Wolf Jobst Siedler, 1986).
31. "Wherever technology reaches its real fulfillment, it transcends into architecture. . . . Architecture has nothing to do with the invention of forms. It is not the playground for children, young or old. Architecture is the real battleground of the spirit." Mies van der Rohe, "Architecture and Technology," *Arts and Architecture* 67, no. 10 (1950): 30, quoted in Neumeyer, *Artless Word,* 324. For Mies, spiritual problems were cultural: "In its simplest form architecture is entirely rooted in practical considerations, but can reach up through all degrees of value to the highest realm of spiritual existence, into the realm of the sensuously apprehendable, and into the pure sphere of art." Mies van der Rohe, Address as Director of Architecture, November 20, 1938, translation published in Philip Johnson, *Mies van der Rohe* (New York: Museum of Modern Art, 1947), 192, quoted in Neumeyer, *Artless Word,* 316.
32. Johnson was director of the department from 1932 to 1934 and from 1946 to 1954.
33. According to Joseph Fujikawa, a key architect in the office of Mies van der Rohe, Johnson had "been in and out of Mies's office ever since we were in the Champlain Building. He'd come walking in Monday morning. 'Well, what's new, boys?' Then he'd go around where each of us was working and ask questions. 'What are you doing?' I guess he picked up quite a bit of information which he then ran back to New York and used." Transcript of interview with Kevin Harrington, April 10, 1996, CCA, tape 3, side 1, p. 38. By 1946, Johnson was preparing his exhibition on Mies at MoMA.
34. Christian Norberg-Schulz, "A Talk with Mies van der Rohe," *Baukunst und Werkform* 11, no. 11 (1958): 615–18. Quoted in Neumeyer, *Artless Word,* 339.
35. Mies's bequest of the drawings to MoMA's Architecture and Design Collection is documented in a letter of July 19, 1963. The Mies van der Rohe Archive at MoMA was established in 1968. See Arthur Drexler, "Introduction," *The Mies van der Rohe Archive,* ed. Arthur Drexler, 9 vols. (New York: Garland, 1986–92), 1:xi.
36. The Chicago Architects Oral History Project was begun in 1983 by the Art Institute of Chicago to document the contributions of architects to Chicago in the twentieth century. The CCA archives and collections contain documents pertaining to Mies, Mies and his American colleagues, and Oral History Archives created between 1996 and 2000.
37. Phyllis Lambert, "Farnsworth on Mars, or on the Stewardship of Buildings," lecture presented at the Berlage Institute, Rotterdam, April 17, 2005, and published in *Hunch* 10 (Summer 2006): 72–83.
38. The sale was finalized in February 1980. See Closing Memo-

randum: Sale of Seagram Building, February 15, 1980, FPL, box 08-L-649.

CHAPTER 1.
A SITE AND AN ARCHITECT FOR SEAGRAM

1. The brothers Percy and John Uris, who began developing residential real estate in the 1920s, focused on construction and financial aspects of commercial development after World War II. In 1960, they created Uris Building Corporation, a real estate investment firm.
2. According to the Lease Agreement between Uris Building Corporation and Joseph E. Seagram & Sons, Inc., dated October 26, 1951, and signed by both parties, Seagram rented the sixth, seventh, and eighteenth through the twenty-first floors for a total of $615,000 per annum, for a period of ten years and four months. Seagram Corporate Records, Vivendi S.A., New York (hereafter cited as Seagram Corporate Records). Six months later, Seagram asked Cross & Brown, rental agents, to inform Uris that Seagram would not occupy the six floors at 380 Madison. Terribly shocked, Uris suggested a payment of $750,000 to buy a clean release on the space. In a memorandum to file dated April 23, 1952, James E. Friel indicated that this was too much and urged Seagram executives to act quickly so that Uris could rent out his space. CSC, acc. 2126, RG 2, ser. X, box 844. On November 28, 1952, Uris Building, Inc., and Joseph E. Seagram and Sons, Inc., agreed on a possible cancellation of the lease and, on March 18, 1953, to termination of the lease. Seagram was to pay $98,750 to Uris, having already paid $51,250 on signing the original lease agreement. Seagram Corporate Records.
3. John McDonald, "Seagram in the Chips," *Fortune,* September 1948, 96f. In a later *Fortune* article Seagram was acknowledged to be the industry leader since 1947, outpacing its rival, Schenley. Philip Siekman, "The Bronfmans: An Instinct for Dynasty, Part I," *Fortune,* November 1966, 202. For the early association and rivalry between Schenley Industries' Lewis Solon Rosenstiel and Bronfman, see Michael R. Marrus, *Mr. Sam: The Life and Times of Samuel Bronfman* (Toronto: Viking, 1991).
4. Anton L. Trunk to James E. Friel, March 17, 1950, CSC, acc. 2126, RG 2, ser. X, box 844. Trunk also stated that Mayor O'Dwyer's suggested changes to the property rental law would make it possible "to secure possession of most any of the Park Avenue Apartment House Sites." This became a political football between city and state, Democrats and Republicans, and although a rent law favoring owners was not passed as the mayor had hoped, this did not stop the acquisition of Park Avenue apartment house sites.
5. The partnership of W. L. Rouse and L. A. Goldstone was at its height between 1909 and 1917, when it had 119 jobs in progress and erected forty-seven apartment houses. They were the architects of the first Delphi Theatre in New York (1914), and the year after the partnership was dissolved, in 1927, Lafayette Goldstone was appointed architect for the house of Ogden Mills Reid, editor of the *New York Herald Tribune.* Today it houses the New York University Institute for the Study of the Ancient World.
6. See James Barron, "Henry Z. Steinway, Piano Maker, Dies at 93," *New York Times*, September 19, 2008.
7. Christopher Gray, "Is It Time to Redevelop Park Avenue Again?" *New York Times,* May 14, 1989.
8. James Trager, *Park Avenue: Street of Dreams* (New York: Atheneum, 1990), 189.
9. James E. Friel, "Park Avenue Real Estate," memorandum to file, July 24, 1950, CSC, acc. 2126, RG 2, ser. X, box 845.
10. It was listed on the National Register of Historic Places in 1983.
11. See Leland Roth, *McKim, Mead & White, Architects* (New York: Harper and Row, 1983), 343.
12. Robert G. Morgan to SB, May 24, 1950, CSC, acc. 2126, RG 2, ser. X, box 845. The letter was accompanied by a well-documented sketch of the area and assessed value of each of the buildings on the proposed site. Trunk to Friel, May 25, 1950, ibid., box 844.
13. Joseph P. Kennedy, Sr., as a distributor of whiskies, knew SB. In 1933 his company, Somerset Importers, became the exclusive American agent for Gordon's Gin and Dewar's Scotch. Kennedy greatly admired SB, likening him to Napoleon, and gave him an attaché case that Napoleon supposedly had carried. The case was always on the table where SB sat in the library of his Montreal residence.
14. William Zeckendorf, Sr. (1905–1976), was moving fast into the position of a major developer. He had worked briefly with his uncle, a well-established real estate investor-builder, until 1939, when he accepted a partnership in the "reputable if not very profitable" property management company Webb & Knapp, which under his leadership acquired the United Nations site and the Chrysler building, among other properties. Zeckendorf's role in the company grew steadily, and because of his preferences, Webb & Knapp moved into construction work in the early 1950s and began developing such multiuse complexes as the Mile High Center in Denver (completed in 1956) and Place Ville-Marie in Montreal (completed in 1962). See William Zeckendorf with Edward A. McCreary, *Zeckendorf—The Autobiography of William Zeckendorf* (New York: Holt, Rinehart and Winston, 1970).
15. Trunk to Friel, July 19, 1950; memorandum from Trunk (no recipient), copy to SB, September 25, 1950; Trunk to Ellis D. Slater, November 9, 1950; all CSC, acc. 2126, RG 2, ser. X, box 845.
16. Trunk to Slater, November 9, 1950.
17. Trunk to G. Richard Davis, January 19, 1951, CSC, acc. 2126, RG 2, ser. X, box 844.

18. Resolution adopted by the board of directors of Joseph E. Seagram & Sons, Inc., at the meeting on April 26, 1951, CSC, acc. 2126, RG 2, ser. X, box 845.
19. F. E. Desmond, memorandum to file Re: 373 Park Avenue Corporation, file, May 28, 1951, CSC, acc. 2126, RG 2, ser. III, box 376.
20. "Suggested Outline of Program for Development of Building to House the Seagram Companies," memorandum, July 16, 1951, CSC, acc. 2126, RG 2, ser. X, box 844.
21. Relevant documents include: Joseph Willard, White & Case, to SB, August 13, 1951, FPL, box 08-L-515; and James L. Robertson to Slater, January 7, 1952; and Slater to Friel, January 31, 1952, both in CSC, acc. 2126, RG 2, ser. X, box 844. An unsigned memorandum from an officer of the Bankers Trust Company to James E. Friel of Seagram dated February 8, 1952, contains a list of architects and buildings "of possible interest." Records of the Seagram Curator's Office, FSB, box 134-007.
22. George A. Fuller Company, Kahn and Jacobs, Cushman and Wakefield, "Project 'Skytop': Studies of Various Schemes Showing Allowable Building Size and Comparable Financial Setup, March 24, 1952," CSC, acc. 2126, RG 2, ser. X, box 844; the Skytop study is also held in Records of the Seagram Curator's Office, FSB, box 134-043.
23. See lease between Seagram ("Landlord") and The Parlex Corporation ("Tenant"), April 1, 1952, 2–3, BSRC.
24. The New York firm of Ely Jacques Kahn (1884–1972) and Albert Buchanan was in practice from 1917 to 1930: the Squibb Building (1930) was their best-known work. Kahn's practice changed from a Beaux-Arts expression to a language of Modernism after 1940 when he formed a new partnership with Robert Allan Jacobs (1905–1993), who had worked with Le Corbusier in Paris and Wallace K. Harrison in New York. The firm's remarkable 1944 Municipal Asphalt Plant, a freestanding concrete parabolic disk at the FDR Drive between Ninetieth and Ninety-First Streets, is now known as Asphalt Green and is a community center. During the late 1940s and the first half of the 1950s they were considered to be among the most competent architects producing high-rise commercial structures in the city. See chapter 2.
25. See chapter 6 and the Epilogue on air rights issues.
26. See chapter 6 on taxation issues.
27. The original questionnaire has not surfaced. See letters and schedules from Cushman & Wakefield to Lou R. Crandall, April 29, 1952; Cross & Brown to Crandall, May 8, 1952; and Charles F. Noyes to Crandall, May 8, 1952, all in CSC, acc. 2126, RG 2, ser. X, box 844. The real estate companies replied with complex schedules accompanied by various comments: J. Clydesdale Cushman, president of the company, was positive that given the tremendous demand for office space, with thirty-four new office and commercial buildings constructed in the past five years, high absorption rates in old buildings, and only five new office buildings in Manhattan that would be ready for occupancy in 1955, many prominent corporations housed in old buildings would want to move to such space. With caveats, Noyes concurred. Cross & Brown were for a bulk building: "We do not believe in a tower building because of the present construction costs; the cost of up-keep; the cost of operation and the higher rentals that must be obtained to make it a paying proposition.... If your clients wish a building for their own use solely and bring in special promotional ideas, then they might desire to do something like the Lever Bros. building and produce a tower type edifice."
28. "Skytop" Project: Recapitulation of the real estate survey made by Cross & Brown, Charles F. Noyes, and Cushman & Wakefield on a hypothetical forty-story and three-basement building for Seagram-Distillers Corporation at 375 Park Avenue, May 21, 1952. CSC, acc. 2126, RG 2, ser. X, box 844.
29. See "Leases New York," "Floor Space New York," and "Floor Space Summary," dated December 31, 1954, Records of the Seagram Curator's Office, FSB, box 134-007.
30. Memorandum reporting a telephone conversation between Gibson Fuller Dailey and Edmund Wagner, president of General Realty & Utilities Corporation, regarding the surveys of Cushman & Wakefield, Charles F. Noyes and Cross & Brown, attached to "Skytop" Project: Recapitulation, May 21, 1952, CSC, acc. 2126, RG 2, ser. X, box 844; see n. 28, above.
31. To SB's mortification, the Bronfman name was brought up during the investigations, but "Nothing for us" was the conclusion of the investigator who interviewed SB in March 1951. See Marrus, *Mr. Sam,* 343–54.
32. Members were: General Frank R. Schwengel, president of Joseph E. Seagram & Sons, Inc., the US holding company; Victor A. Fischel, president of Seagram-Distillers Corporation; James E. Friel, vice president and treasurer; Ellis D. Slater, president of Frankfort Distillers Corporation; William Wendell Wachtel, president of Calvert Distillers. Members of the staff were: John A. Handy, Jr., acting secretary; Herbert P. Brown, controller; Joseph G. Friel, treasurer; Frederick J. Lind, legal counsel.
33. Minutes of the Meeting of the Advisory Committee, May 27, 1952, CSC, acc. 2126, RG 2, ser. III, box 376.
34. Minutes of the Meeting of the Advisory Committee, January 12, 1953, CSC, acc. 2126, RG 2, ser. III, box 376. The museum suggestion dates from March 9, 1953.
35. David Tishman, Tishman Realty & Construction Co., Inc., to SB, August 14, 1953, CSC, acc. 2126, RG 2, ser. X, box 844. However, Tishman was not an altruist: three days later, he enclosed a copy of the August 14 letter in his letter to Victor A. Fischel recommending that SB consider taking space in Tishman's 99 Park Avenue building, which could be named after Seagram. Ibid.
36. Minutes of the Meeting of the Advisory Committee, Novem-

ber 9, 1953, CSC, acc. 2126, RG 2, ser. III, box 376.

37. Minutes of the Advisory Committee Meeting, December 14, 1953, CSC, acc. 2126, RG 2, ser. III, box 376.

38. Quoted by Marrus, *Mr. Sam,* 122.

39. Minutes of the Advisory Committee Meeting, June 11, 1953, CSC, acc. 2126, RG 2, ser. III, box 376. Royalite Oil Company, Ltd., was an Alberta company; its subsidiary, Royalite Oil Company, Inc., a Delaware company, was party to the bid.

40. Minutes of the Advisory Committee Meeting, December 14, 1953.

41. See Memorandum of Meeting on Building Held on April 15, 1954, from "JAH" (John A. Handy, Jr.) to Victor A. Fischel, James E. Friel, John A. Handy, Jr., Ellis D. Slater, and William Wendell Wachtel, CSC, acc. 2126, RG 2, ser. X, box 844. The subcommittee was called "our building committee" in a memorandum from Seagram president Frank R. Schwengel to the Board of Directors dated April 26, 1954, FPL, box 08-L-515. It was referred to as one of our subcommittees in the Minutes of the Advisory Committee Meeting, April 26, 1954, item C.1: "New Buildings—New York—Chicago," CSC, acc. 2126, RG 2, ser. III, box 376.

42. Minutes of the Advisory Committee Meeting, April 26, 1954, CSC, acc. 2126, RG 2, ser. III, box 376.

43. Bankers Trust Company to Friel, unsigned memorandum, February 8, 1952 (discussed in n. 21, above). Friel forwarded this material accompanied with a memorandum to SB, Allan Bronfman, Victor A. Fischel, Frank R. Schwengel, Ellis D. Slater, and William Wendell Wachtel on February 11, 1952. Both documents are held in Records of the Seagram Curator's Office, FSB, box 134-007. "Awards Offered to Identify Buildings," *New York Times,* October 2, 1951, dates the prize contest to early October. On December 11, 1951, the *Times* ran "Railroad Man Wins Identification Prize."

44. Ironically, Universal, which Seagram acquired when it purchased controlling interest in MCA in 1995, was the instrument of Seagram's undoing.

45. James E. Friel to SB, Allan Bronfman, Victor A Fischel, Frank R. Schwengel, Ellis D. Slater, and William Wendell Wachtel, memorandum, February 11, 1952, Records of the Seagram Curator's Office, FSB, box 134-007.

46. Robert A. M. Stern, Thomas Mellins, and David Fishman, *New York, 1960: Architecture and Urbanism Between the Second World War and the Bicentennial* (New York: Monacelli Press, 1995), 416.

47. In the 1950s and 1960s, Emery Roth & Sons became the most influential architectural firm in New York and contributed substantially to changing the appearance of Midtown and Lower Manhattan. Their speculative office buildings with glass and metal facades, especially in the east Midtown area of Manhattan, became a ubiquitous feature of the city. They designed thirty-seven buildings between 1946 and 1957—that is, an average of three and a half large buildings a year. See Stern, Mellins, and Fishman, *New York, 1960,* 51; and Richard Roth, "High-Rise Down to Earth," *Progressive Architecture* 38, no. 6 (June 1957): 199.

48. Bien had designed the distinguished Art Deco Carlyle Hotel, which opened in 1930.

49. See Stern, Mellins, and Fishman, *New York, 1960,* 419.

50. Although officially credited to the United Nations Board of Design, headed by Director of Planning Wallace K. Harrison, the thirty-nine-story slab for the secretariat and the horizontal box for the assembly halls are largely, but not wholly, based on Le Corbusier's initial proposals of 1947. United Nations Secretary General Trygve Lie had New Yorker Harrison nominated as director of the Board of Design Consultants, whose members were Le Corbusier for France, the Australian Gyle Soilleux, the Belgian Gaston Brunfaut, the Brazilian Oscar Niemeyer, the Englishman Howard Robertson, the Canadian Ernest Cormier, the Chinese Liang Ssu-Ch'eng, the Russian Nikolaï Bassov, the Swede Sven Markelius, and the Uruguayan Julio Vilamajo. For the best history of the fractious design process for the United Nations Headquarters, see Jean-Louis Cohen, "Introduction," *United Nations Headquarters for Le Corbusier: Plans,* vol. 9, DVD-ROM (Paris: Fondation Le Corbusier, 2009).

51. Wright's daughter Catherine married Kenneth Baxter; their daughter was the actress Anne Baxter.

52. Frank Lloyd Wright to Alan [*sic*] Bronfman, April 19, 1952, 1–2, Frank Lloyd Wright Archives, Frank Lloyd Wright Foundation.

53. Ibid., 2.

54. "Am I to suppose that brother Sam is perhaps a kind of a stumbling block in that way because I am *your* man"; ibid.

55. Wright to Kenneth Baxter, March 17, 1954, CCA Library.

56. According to H. Allen Brooks, "Wright apparently claimed that he had been thinking about designing a very tall building for many years but the earliest extant, dated drawing for the Mile High is dated August 10, 1956." H. Allen Brooks to Roberta Prevost, November 3, 2002, BSRC. This date is confirmed in Bruce Brooks Pfeiffer, director of the Frank Lloyd Wright Archives, to PL, June 14, 2002: "Wright's conceptual sketch was made and dated by him on August 10, 1956." FPL, 08-L-804.

57. Wright to Bronfman, April 19, 1952, 3.

58. Ellis D. Slater, interoffice memorandum, March 11, 1952, CSC, acc. 2126, RG 2, ser. X, box 844.

59. The auto showroom was installed on the ground floor of Warren and Wetmore's 1916 apartment house at 430 Park Avenue, which was stripped down to its steel frame and wrapped with a curtain wall by Emery Roth & Sons in 1954, resulting in a taller building without setbacks than would have been permitted for a new building under existing zoning regulations. See "Total Reconditioning: 430 Park Avenue," *Progressive Architecture* 35, no. 5 (May 1954): 106–9.

Wright's showroom is now occupied by Mercedes-Benz; it was renovated in 1982 and 2007.

60. See Memorandum of Meeting on Building Held on April 15, 1954. Sylvan Bien and Walker & Poor, who were included in the 1952 list (Bankers Trust Company to Friel, memorandum, February 8, 1952), were dropped, and the firms Voorhees Walker Foley & Smith, Eggers & Higgins, and O'Connor & Kilham emerged. William Lescaze, who gained renown as a young modernist working with George Howe on the PSFS in 1930–32 and made his mark with a design for 2 Broadway on the site of the New York Produce Exchange, was included in the list along with Skidmore, Owings & Merrill and Pereira & Luckman. On Lescaze, see "The Impact of Mechanical Equipment on Design," *Architectural Record* 115, no. 4 (April 1954): 195–99.

61. List of Current Work of George A. Fuller Company, as of September 1, 1954, Records of the Seagram Curator's Office, FSB, box 134-007. Projects are listed by state.

62. Charles Luckman, *Twice in a Lifetime: From Soap to Skyscrapers* (New York: W. W. Norton, 1988), 124.

63. Ibid., 323ff.

64. Voisin was one of New York's preeminent restaurants. *New York Times,* July 13, 1954.

65. Seagram-Distillers Corporation Public Relations department press release, July 12, 1954, BSRC.

66. "Repeat Performance," in "The Talk of the Town," *New Yorker,* August 28, 1954, 16.

67. "New Peak on Park," *Newsweek,* July 26, 1954, 66f.

68. William Hamby, Fordyce & Hamby Associates, Architecture and Engineering, to SB, June 9, 1954, FPL, box 08-L-515. The architects had presented a model and concept to members of the board of directors of the opera, who expressed interest. At the June 14, 1954, meeting of the Advisory Committee, Victor Fischel "outlined . . . the interview which was held with the architects, Fordyce & Hamby. He explained in detail the events which led up to the unauthorized release in the newspapers relating to the Metropolitan Opera project." Minutes of the Advisory Committee Meeting, June 14, 1954, 2, CSC, acc. 2126, RG 2, ser. III, box 376.

69. "Park Ave. to Get New Skyscraper," *New York Times,* July 13, 1954. Ironically, as I was working on an early draft of this chapter during the first week of October 2008, the US Congress voted in support of a seven-hundred-billion-dollar bailout, which did not stanch the flow of bank failures due to overextension of real estate loans.

70. See appendix 1 in this volume; FPL, box 08-L-515.

71. See Eli Bronfman, "A Timely Landmark: A Contextual History of the Seagram Building," typescript, 2011, 9, BSRC.

72. PL to Lewis Mumford, August 22, 1954, Lewis Mumford Papers, Rare Book and Manuscript Library, University of Pennsylvania (hereafter cited as Mumford Papers).

73. Minutes of the Advisory Committee Meeting, August 30, 1954, 1, CSC, acc. 2126, RG 2, ser. III, box 376.

74. PL to Eve Borsook, [c. mid-August 1954], quoted in Phyllis Lambert, "How a Building Gets Built," *Vassar Alumnae Magazine,* February 1959, 14.

75. I also talked to Peter Blake, then writing for *Architectural Forum,* and Douglas Haskell, its editor.

76. See Lambert, "How a Building Gets Built," 14. From my letter to Mumford of August 22, 1954, I have been able to reconstruct the last part of my visits to architects: August 23, Boston "to meet Belluschi (as head of MIT), and with Gropius' group—unfortunately Gropius is away"; Thursday, August 26, "Philadelphia to see the Howe-Lescaze building and to meet George Howe"; "On Monday a week [August 30] I am off to Chicago where there is much for me to see— to meet Mies. I shall also go to Racine and on Friday [September 3] of the same week, I shall go to Detroit. Then the first week in September [this must be the first full week] to Paris to see Breuer and put my house in order." Mumford Papers.

77. See Aline B. Saarinen, "Our Cultural Pattern: 1929—and Today," *New York Times Magazine,* October 17, 1954, in which she characterizes the contemporary cultural scene as one in which progressive art dominates, perceiving a need for consolidation after "so many new corners were turned in the first three decades of the twentieth century."

78. Only Saarinen and Gropius made appointments with me in which they made direct proposals. Saarinen described a building that would be entered on a sunken plaza, and its skin would be much more sculptural than Mies's 860 Lake Shore Drive. He eventually completed such a building for the CBS headquarters on 51 West Fifty-Second Street in New York in 1964. I was intrigued by Saarinen and gave myself the option of considering him for the Chicago building. Walter Gropius asked to meet me on his return from Japan when I was about certain that Mies should be the architect, and I told him so. I was extremely disconcerted when, as I left him at LaGuardia Airport, having visited with him a house in Long Island that TAC had designed, he pleaded with me to let him design the building.

79. PL to Borsook, October 30, 1954, quoted in Lambert, "How a Building Gets Built," 14, 16.

80. I recall that Father was immediately convinced, and reported that the reaction of Seagram executives to Mies being appointed architect was less than enthusiastic, but imputing to them his own turnaround, he said they would soon declare that they were the ones who championed Mies.

81. Luckman to SB, October 4, 1954, FPL, box 08-L-515.

82. SB to Luckman, November 3, 1954 (copy), FPL, box 08-L-515. SB continued, "You will recall you offered to leave this material with me the last time we met; but I indicated that I did not feel that we should have it because it is possible that some small detail or other of our new building might resemble something in your sketches and that this might result in some feeling on your part." There are two drafts

for this letter, copies, undated, with slightly differing texts. With the drafts is a copy of published A.I.A. Standards, with emphasis mark next to section II.2: "An Architect shall not render professional services without compensation." Presumably, Luckman had been compensated for his services before the date of this letter.

83. Philip Johnson's fascist sympathies and activities of the 1930s were immediately communicated to me by my sister's former Smith College classmate, Ann Resor (daughter of Helen Resor, who commissioned Mies to design the house that first brought Mies to America). I can only think that my father, active in international Jewish affairs, passed over this information because he did not wish to upset the project for building Seagram in which he had become fully invested, and in addition, did not take these long-past affiliations seriously.

84. This was changed when Mies's application for a license in New York was not accepted, and reinstated later when it was.

85. PL to Borsook, December 1, 1954, quoted in Lambert, "How a Building Gets Built," 16.

86. In ibid. Seagram executives moved into the building in December 1957; however, the company housewarming receptions took place only in May 1958, and the Four Seasons opened only in July 1959. I left my full-time position at Seagram on beginning architecture school in the fall of 1958.

CHAPTER 2.
MIES VAN DER ROHE'S UR-BUILDING

1. While the Neue Nationalgalerie in Berlin was under construction, Mies commented to his grandson Dirk Lohan that he was tired. To Lohan's response, "I was in the field all day and you have been in your room doing nothing; why are you tired?" Mies replied, "*Ja*, I was not doing nothing, I was thinking." This was told to me by Lohan some years ago.

2. Gene Summers to PL, e-mail, June 29, 2009. Gene R. Summers (1928–2011) joined the office of Mies van der Rohe in 1950. After service in Korea he returned to Mies's office to work on the Seagram building, and in 1956 he became architect in charge of all nonresidential work. He left Mies's office in 1966, becoming partner in charge of design at C. F. Murphy Associates, Chicago, in 1967. He then partnered with Phyllis Lambert at Ridgway Ltd., Newport Beach, California, 1974–78, and after five years in France as artist and furniture designer, Summers was dean of the College of Architecture, IIT, 1989–93. He then returned to private practice in California.

3. Mies asked to see the engineers or technicians instead of manufacturers' salesmen.

4. PL to Eve Borsook, August 1–2, 1955, FPL, box 08-L-309.

5. Johnson in John C. Cook and Heinrich Klotz, *Conversations with Architects* (New York: Praeger, 1973), 19, 21.

6. Ibid., 21.

7. When Mies arrived at the Bauhaus, the local authorities asked him to report a teacher who was considered to have strong leftist leanings. According to Mies, he asked Klee, who waved away the question not wishing to have anything to do with such inquiries, while Kandinsky, trained as a lawyer, rubbed his hands together with relish. Mies indicated his strong dislike for Kandinsky's reaction.

8. Franz Schulze, *Mies van der Rohe: A Critical Biography* (Chicago: University of Chicago Press, 1985), 15–16.

9. Until Philip withdrew from practice in 2004, Manley remained with him. See Gene Summers, transcript of interview with Kevin Harrington, June 24, 1996, CCA, tape 3, side B, p. 84.

10. For Haid, see the Fonds David Haid, CCA.

11. While still a graduate student, he detailed the cabinetry for the Farnsworth House, and after graduation, he supervised construction of the IIT Chapel, and then was given the responsibility for the development of Mies's Commons building at IIT.

12. Cullinan Hall, Museum of Fine Arts, Houston (1954–58).

13. Summers to PL, e-mail, January 8, 2009; Summers, transcript of interview with Harrington, June 24, 1996, tape 3, side B, p. 83. See also Phyllis Lambert, ed., *Mies in America* (Montreal: Canadian Centre for Architecture, and New York: Whitney Museum of American Art and Harry N. Abrams, 2001); transcript of Pauline A. Saliga's interview with Gene Summers, "Oral History of Gene Summers," compiled under the auspices of *The Chicago Architects Oral History Project,* The Ernest R. Graham Study Center for Architectural Drawings, Department of Architecture, The Art Institute of Chicago (Chicago: Art Institute of Chicago, 1993); and Gene Summers, "On Mies/The Architectural Experience," in Werner Blaser, *Gene Summers Art/Architecture* (Basel: Birkhauser, 2003).

14. Summers, transcript of interview with Harrington, June 25, 1996, tape 3, side B, p. 84.

15. Richard Foster, typescript of "Draft, July 18, 1986," unpaged [3–4], FPL, box 08-L-796. In the first paragraph of the document, Foster explains, "I've been asked from time to time what my contribution was toward the building of the Seagram's [*sic*] Building, and whether I had worked with Mies van der Rohe." The document was kindly sent to me in June 2009, by Joseph Disponzio, the landscape architect Foster consulted on the ginkgo trees for Seagram plaza. See Sandra Radosh Kuhns, Richard Foster Associates, to Joseph Disponzio, June 1, 1988, FPL, box 08-L-796.

16. L'Huillier Sheaff (1902–1995), who served as vice president and also president of Cushman & Wakefield, Inc., before becoming chairman of the company in 1960, was a key consultant for Seagram on New York office building requirements and eventually also took charge of identifying tenants and leasing space in the building.

17. Foster, typescript of "Draft, July 18, 1986," [2].
18. Ibid., [3].
19. Kazys Varnelis, ed., *The Philip Johnson Tapes: Interviews by Robert A. M. Stern* (New York: Monacelli, 2008), 144.
20. Ellis D. Slater was referred to as chairman of the Building Committee in a questionnaire sent to Seagram employees by Frank R. Schwengel asking for suggestions regarding the new building, in which he wrote: "It can be made a center of public interest and public enlightenment. For New Yorkers and for visitors to New York, it can become a new New York landmark—a Mecca for all." Draft of questionnaire to all employees of affiliated Seagram companies re: new building, January 10, 1955, FPL, box 08-L-515.
21. The members of the Building Committee were named in a press release dated March 30, 1955, carrying the news that "the design for Seagram Park Avenue, the new 38-story skyscraper to be erected for Joseph E. Seagram & Sons, Inc., was revealed today with the filing of plans by Seagram with the New York City Building Department." Records of the Seagram Curators Office, FSB, box 134-029.
22. PL to Borsook, December 1, 1954, quoted in Lambert, "How a Building Gets Built," 18.
23. PL to Borsook, August 1–2, 1955, 1–2.
24. Varnelis, *Philip Johnson Tapes*, 139.
25. Transcript of summary statements made in the final session of the meeting, May 3, 1955, 13, Records of the Seagram Curator's Office, FSB, box 134-007. George R. Bailey was a Chicago real estate man, president of G. R. Bailey & Company. The other ten members of the Building Planning Service were preponderantly from Texas and the Midwest, functioning as officers in charge of new construction, or operating or buildings managers. Members from New York included the chief officer in charge of the Empire State building and the building manager of the New York Life Insurance Company who had supervised the air-conditioning and new elevators for this one-million-square-foot building. See Cushman & Wakefield, Inc., Committee list "Building Planning Service Meeting; Seagram Park Avenue (Building)," stamped "Received April [25], 1955," Records of the Seagram Curators Office, FSB, box 134-007.
26. Mies van der Rohe to Cameron Alread, Edow Davidson, Edgar Marshall, and Louis Thomas, May 11, 1960, Ludwig Mies van der Rohe Papers, container 54, Manuscript Division, Library of Congress (hereafter cited as Mies Papers).
27. PL to Borsook, December 1, 1954, 16–17.
28. I experienced this behavior when in the summer of 1960 I worked for a few weeks in Mies's office on the Home Federal Savings and Loan Association building in Des Moines, Iowa (1959–62), and then on a student project for the School of Architecture at Yale, with Mies as my mentor. The project was for a hypothetical school. In order to carve out from the center an auditorium and gymnasium with a series of bents twelve feet on center, I proposed using six exoskeletal girders above the roof in order to remove the center row of columns. Mies sat at my table, looked for a long while, and then said, "*Ja*, why don't you use just one girder running in the other direction." Six girders twelve feet apart was certainly excessive, but when one of the architects in Mies's office viewed my elegant and reasonable one-girder scheme, he burst out, "Wherever did you get that idea!"
29. PL to Borsook, December 1, 1954, 18.
30. Mies found the multidirectional plan of square high-rise buildings to be confusing as one never knew which way to turn.
31. I had visited Borsook in Rome the previous Easter, living at the foot of the Spanish Steps in Piazza di Spagna, hence my enthusiasm for steps and piazzas.
32. PL to Borsook, December 1, 1954, 17.
33. Ibid., 18.
34. Minutes of the Advisory Committee Meeting, December 8, 1954, 2, CSC, acc. 2126, RG 2, ser. III, box 376.
35. See "Floor Space Summary" for Seagram, December 31, 1954, Records of the Seagram Curator's Office, FSB, box 134-007. The company at this time occupied 81,000 square feet of space in the Chrysler building, 26,000 of which were on the original fifteenth floor. An additional 27,000 were located in four other buildings in the city.
36. The date is known from Edward Duckett to Myron Goldsmith, February 17, 1955: "We have made one exhibition model in which we milled the struts or mullions out of plates of jeweler's bronze." Fonds Myron Goldsmith, box 32-001T, CCA. The cardboard model was a massing model and thus ephemeral; the brass presentation model was eventually given by the Seagram Company and Philip Johnson to MoMA.
37. Mies often talked of the effectiveness of large drawings, and the drawings he made for his five theoretical projects of the 1920s were very large: Friedrichstrasse Skyscaper Project, 1921, 68¼ × 48 in.; Glass Skyscraper Project, 1922, 54¼ × 32¾ in.; Concrete Country House Project, 1923, 33¾ × 90 in.; Concrete Office Building Project, 1923, 54½ × 113¾ in.; and Brick Country House Project, 1924, 30 × 40 in.
38. Edward Duckett, interview with Kevin Harrington, September 25, 1996, CCA, tape 7, side 1, pp. 171–72.
39. "The building front is stupendous! The whole project is accepted. My father is in thralls of delight—a minor miracle." PL to Anthony and Caroline Benn, March 18, 1955, FPL, box 08-L-309.
40. This contrasts with approaches by Saarinen, for example, who believed that each building must relate to its function and site and prided himself on exploiting particular situations.
41. Mies van der Rohe, transcript of interview with John Peter, 1955, 4. Interviews with Ludwig Mies van der Rohe, Mies Papers, container 62.

42. Mies van der Rohe, *G,* no. 1 (July 1923): 3, in Fritz Neumeyer, *The Artless Word: Mies van der Rohe and the Building Art,* trans. Mark Jarzombek (Cambridge, MA: MIT Press, 1991), 241. Mies wrote, "Supporting girder construction with a nonsupporting wall. That means skin and bone structures."

43. The curtain wall was first developed in the United States in 1918. The first example is the still-standing Hallidie building in San Francisco by Willis Polk. Polk designed a true curtain wall, a continuous membrane free of structural members in the facade plane. But it was an isolated example: there was no connection to Mies's project for a glass skyscraper of 1921, nor was Mies's project related to Polk's. In 1924, Frank Lloyd Wright drew high-rise towers with an all-glass skin for the proposed National Life Insurance Company Office Building in Chicago.

44. "Mies van der Rohe Considered and Interviewed by Graeme Shankland," *Listener,* October 15, 1959, 622.

45. See Phyllis Lambert, "Forging a Language," 277–312, and "High Rise," 354–367 in *Mies in America.*

46. Learning from one building to the next was continual in Mies's office. The need to restrain steel plates that would expand and contract with changes in temperature from summer to winter was understood from Alumni Memorial Hall. "Shortly after that was built, we noticed the plaster ceilings in the four corners of the building were cracking, mainly due to this fascia plate exposed on the exterior that was expanding out and then contracting. It cracked the ceiling in the corners. So since then, we've added shear studs to resist that horizontal movement." Joseph Y. Fujikawa, transcript of interview with Kevin Harrington, May 1, 1996, CCA, tape 6, side 2, p. 98. The solution to this was later applied at 860–880 Lake Shore Drive: "At twenty-six stories high, the steel plate on the column had to be welded solid or else the rain would get in, so the problem came up of how to keep the steel from expanding and moving up and down, and also possibly buckling. So there's a system of restraint, with shear bolts every so often, up the whole height of the building, cast into the concrete fireproofing. These shear bolts sort of lock the steel in place to keep it from moving independently of the building, both vertically and horizontally, so everything is locked together" (ibid., 97, 98).

47. Fujikawa, transcript of interview with Harrington, April 10, 1996, CCA, tape 1, side 2, p. 15.

48. I am grateful to Dirk Lohan for the Sullivan reference.

49. Fujikawa, transcript of interview with Harrington, April 10, 1996, tape 1, side 2, p. 16.

50. Fujikawa also noted that, after Promontory, the Chicago Housing Authority (CHA) built exposed concrete frame apartments. Fujikawa, transcript of interview with Harrington, April 24, 1996, CCA, tape 3, side 2, p. 53.

51. "Sometime during this [time] . . . Mies asked me to make a sketch of it with those exterior mullions. . . . I think he was really unsatisfied with Promontory, and was thinking he could do better, and was thinking already with mullions." Myron Goldsmith, transcript of interview with Kevin Harrington, May 29, 1996, CCA, tape 5, sides 1 and 2, p. 71.

52. Mies van der Rohe, *Frühlicht* 1, no. 4 (1922): 122–24; cited in Neumeyer, *Artless Word,* 240.

53. The towers were actually located at 900–910 North Lake Shore Drive; they were first called 900 Esplanade and today are known as the Esplanade Apartments.

54. Fujikawa also noted that, although the subject of air-conditioning had been given serious consideration, Mies's 860–880 Lake Shore Drive towers were not air-conditioned because the developers felt that the additional cost "might jeopardize the entire project." But by the mid-1950s, there was no such hesitation. Fujikawa concluded that, with 900 Esplanade, "We feel strongly that developments in the design of heating and cooling systems must keep pace with advances in architectural and structural design." Both citations are from Joseph Y. Fujikawa to Robert W. Roose, December 10, 1956, Mies van der Rohe Archive, Professional Papers, MoMA.

55. Fujikawa, transcript of interview with Harrington, April 24, 1996, tape 3, side 2, p. 51. (Mies's Commonwealth Promenade apartment buildings in Chicago were designed 1953–55.)

56. Mies van der Rohe, transcript of interview with John Peter, 1955, 7. Interviews with Ludwig Mies van der Rohe, Mies Papers, container 62.

57. Before the construction of 900 Esplanade, the only available heat-absorbing glass had been the green used in Lever House. The gray glass that later became available prompted Mies to talk with relish of the various shades of tinted glass he had used at Barcelona. Mies investigated the problems of large areas of glass in buildings early on. In June 1940, he wrote to the Libbey-Owens-Ford Company regarding the latest research on how to exclude the radiant heat of the sun on un-shaded glass and the latest information on heat-absorbing plate glass (including cost information). Mies van der Rohe to Mr. Alexander, June 10, 1940, Mies van der Rohe Archive, Professional Papers, Office Material Folder 2, MoMA.

58. Fujikawa, transcript of interview with Harrington, April 24, 1996, tape 3, side 2, p. 51.

59. Ibid., 52.

60. Making an experiment in order to evaluate this effect, Mies used natural silver-colored aluminum for his Commonwealth Promenade apartment buildings at the same time that the black aluminum tower was being erected at 900 Esplanade. Black aluminum presented technical problems, however. The black anodizing at 900 Esplanade did not hold up, and eventually the metal surfaces had to be painted. Joe Fujikawa talked of black dye: "In '49, the only color we could get aluminum in was this silvery color. There was no color

anodizing then. That came later when aluminum became really popular, and people were getting tired of the silvery color; and that's when industry went into dyes and things to make it different. Although when we were working on 900 and Commonwealth, 900 was supposed to be black dye, permanent; but it turned red in a few years, so it wasn't successful." Fujikawa, transcript of interview with Harrington, May 1, 1996, tape 6, side 2, p. 94.

61. Architecturally ambitious office structures of the time were designed with large bays: at the United Nations building and Lever House, they spanned twenty-eight feet in the long dimensions of the building, but were variable in the other direction. The modules were, respectively, four feet and four feet, eight inches. See "Evolution of the High-Rise Office Building," based on a study prepared by Robert P. Sitzenstock, *Progressive Architecture* 44, no. 9 (September 1963): 146–57.

62. Summers, transcript of interview with Harrington, June 24, 1996, tape 3, side B, pp. 89–90. Summers continued: "Four-foot six is a little small. But there are a number of buildings that have been done with four-foot six. Five feet is a little bit too much—I mean if you want to get to the real efficiency of laying out."

63. Mies van der Rohe to Myron Goldsmith, December 28, 1954, Fonds Myron Goldsmith, box 32-001T.

64. Goldsmith to Mies van der Rohe, January 18, 1955, Fonds Myron Goldsmith, box 32-001T. Goldsmith (1919–1996), Mies's most brilliant student, worked for him from 1946 until 1953, when he was awarded a Fulbright grant to work with Pier Luigi Nervi (1891–1979) at the University of Rome. Nervi and Goldsmith were both masters of concrete design.

65. There was much talk of using the H. H. Robertson Q-Floor's steel cellular in-floor cable distribution system introduced in 1931, but finally, the under-floor ducts carrying electrical and telephone lines, low-voltage intercom, and closed-circuit television were embedded in the fill of the four-inch poured-in-place concrete floors.

66. Summers explained that Mies's office would take "extreme care to see that we had a very clear bay system." But Severud wanted to interpose a column at the end of the elevator core toward Park Avenue, the width of one elevator, which is approximately ten feet. In Summers's words: "Well, that was putting in another column in between the bay[s]. . . . It was clear that it was an advantage structurally to have it there, because within the core, along the column line between two banks of elevators, that is where you put cross-bracing or sheer walls out of concrete even in order to stiffen the building up against lateral loads. . . . And that made sense. But it did, in fact, put a steel column in a place that we would not normally like to have a steel column. So we got Kornacker to study it, and he, of course, said, 'Yes, you can do it without it.' [He] came up with some figures and some steel sizes and everything. . . . And we sat down with Severud, the engineer, his firm, and we talked to them about it. They acknowledged the fact that, yes, you can do it. But it's going to cost more money to do that because you're going to have make much heavier cross bracing. . . . They acknowledged the fact that, yes, you can do it under these circumstances. Mies said, 'It's okay. We'll keep the column.' So the column was put in. And it's still there. But he did satisfy himself that it could be done [without the extra column]." Summers, transcript of interview with Harrington, June 25, 1996, tape 4, side A, pp. 95–96.

67. See PL to Mumford, September 23, 1958, 3–4, Mumford Papers.

68. Mies van der Rohe, transcript of interview, February 12, 1958, 8, Interviews with Ludwig Mies van der Rohe, Mies Papers, container 62.

69. Philip Johnson in Cook and Klotz, *Conversations with Architects*, 19. A similar issue disturbed members of Mies's office during the design of 860–880 Lake Shore Drive. The issue was the mullion on the column, which Myron Goldsmith discussed: "Always I think aesthetics, beauty, that tricky word. . . . But I think, above all, the aesthetic aspects were always uppermost in his [Mies's] mind. [He] just could not stomach something that turned out ugly or not very nice, no matter what the real reasons. By the way, I think he used the real reason one of the first times when he was speaking of 860 and this extra mullion on the column. The office was very upset about it, and I don't know if they kept bringing it up—that mullion was clearly superfluous. He said it helps stiffen the plate, but the real reason is that it needs it aesthetically, it breaks the rhythm if you leave it out." Goldsmith, transcript of interview with Harrington, June 10, 1996, tape 9, side 2, p. 123.

70. Fred N. Severud and Anthony F. Merrill, *The Bomb, Survival, and You: Protection for People, Buildings, Equipment* (New York: Reinhold, 1954); "Concrete Spine Designed by Severud-Elstad-Krueger Firm," *New York Times,* April 7, 1957.

71. Jaros, Baum & Bolles (JB&B) mechanical engineers were the only members of the Seagram team who were also involved in the design of the World Trade Center. Worthington, Skilling, Helle & Jackson were the structural engineers for the Twin Towers, and Tishman Realty & Construction Company was the general contractor. In the context of a Pratt Institute symposium on April 9, 2001, in which Barry Bergdoll and I participated, Joan Ockman stretched historic fact and imagination when she proposed that the bomb shelter at Seagram was in some way related to Mies, Germany, and World War II. JB&B designed a deicing system for the central portion of Seagram plaza to facilitate melting snow and ice that would accumulate there. Galvanized pipe conduits laid in the concrete bedding beneath the granite were to contain a light, quick-heating oil. See "Ice, Snow Doomed in Seagram Plaza," *New York Times,* December 9, 1956. This

was another "security issue" with which neither Philip nor Mies was involved. I recall discussion of the plaza being heated, but finally the system was not installed.

72. The term *air conditioning* was used as early as April 1906 in a patent claim filed by textile engineer Stuart W. Cramer. See Margaret Ingels, *Willis Haviland Carrier, Father of Air Conditioning* (Garden City, NJ: Country Life, 1952), 26. However, as Reyner Banham pointed out in *The Architecture of the Well-Tempered Environment* (Chicago: University of Chicago Press, 1969), the engineer-inventor Willis Haviland Carrier "has as good a right to be known as the father of his art," even though his corporation continued to use the term *man-made weather* until 1933, long after air-conditioning was more or less common parlance (171ff.). Carrier's equipment was used in the first fully air-conditioned office building, the Milam building in San Antonio (1928), as well as in the Philadelphia Savings Fund building (1932), the United Nations building (1947–53), and Lever House (1952).

73. Building ordinances legislated that for residential units, fresh air must be obtained via a direct opening to the exterior (some form of window); office desks tended to be placed close to window walls, which, when opened, caused papers to fly helter-skelter in the blowing gale twenty stories or so up. I remember that as a child, this very effect amused me on visits to Seagram's offices in the Chrysler building.

74. Summers, transcript of interview with Harrington, June 25, 1996, tape 4, side A, p. 98.

75. Speaking of certain aesthetic decisions without accounting for the overall concept (columns spacing, mullions per bay, and so on), according to another member of the office, Joe Fujikawa, the proportions of 860 Lake Shore Drive were dictated by necessity: "I think people believe that Mies really studied the proportions of the curtain wall on 860. But in reality, they were pretty much a consequence of the givens. The floor thickness—as I said, we ended up with about an 18-inch slab, so the exterior cladding over the floor I think was something like 21 inches, or something on that order, because we had to have a lip coming down below and a lip coming up to catch the window frames at the floors. The column widths were pretty much what Frank Kornacker's structural steel plus the concrete fireproofing required, and adding to that with a 1-inch lip to catch the windows. I think they were about the same, similar dimension of 21 or 22 inches wide. So they were practical considerations and not a question of how wide those face dimensions should be visually." Fujikawa, transcript of interview with Harrington, April 10, 1996, tape 1, side 1, p. 97.

76. See Phyllis Lambert, "Mies Klassizisimus: Some Notes," in *Architecture and the Classical Tradition from Pliny to Posterity: Essays in Honour of Pierre Du Prey*, ed. Matthew M. Reeve (New York: Harvey Miller, 2013).

77. See Lauren Stadler, "Air, Light, and Air-Conditioning," trans. Jill Denton, *Grey Room* 40 (Summer 2010): 85–99.

78. This calculation made by George R. Bailey (see n. 25, above) is cited in Banham, *Architecture of the Well-Tempered Environment,* 182.

79. "The Adam Building," Mies to Firm S. Adam, July 2, 1928 (draft), in Neumeyer, *Artless Word,* 305. See also Lambert, *Mies in America,* 431, 353, fig. 4.184. Berlin was light-advertising-mad at this time. In 1928 the city held a light festival, *Berlin im Licht* (Berlin in light), for which, among other light works, all major stores had *Lichtreklame* installed. Ludwig Hilberseimer wrote: "Mies van der Rohe has presented the possibility of *Lichtreklame* independently from horizontal bands in his latest design for commercial buildings. The entire façade consists of a skin of plate glass held by a metal structure, on which advertisement can be placed independently from the architectural structure." Quoted in Dietrich Neumann, ed., *Architecture of the Night: The Illuminated Building* (Munich: Prestel, 2002), 40.

80. In 1952 Kelly had created a luminous ceiling in an office building in New York City by Landis Gores, ex-partner of Philip Johnson (1919–1991). Quite primitive, it was composed of incandescent light in a building with no air-conditioning. "Building Engineering," *Architectural Forum* 98, no. 1 (January 1953): 150. In the 1920s, Germany had been highly inventive in the art of architectural lighting; in 1929 Walter Gropius created a modular glazed ceiling in the main hall of the Dessau Labor Exchange; and throughout the 1920s Felix Mendelssohn was responsible for advanced ideas in lighting for the interiors as well as exteriors of theaters and department stores, which Philip must have known about. Margaret Maile Petty refers to Kelly's lighting program for Richard Neutra's Kaufmann House of 1947, in which he used a luminous ceiling in the entry as well as a luminous partition for the bathroom. See Margaret Maile Petty, "Illuminating the Glass Box: The Lighting Designs of Richard Kelly," *Journal of the Society of Architectural Historians* 66, no. 2 (June 2007): 198. Dietrich Neumann discusses and illustrates a luminous Shell gas station made of six-inch-square German tiles in 1933–34 by John Eberson on 124th Street in New York City, where in 1934 William Lescaze used solid glass blocks to illuminate part of the facade of his own house at 21 East Forty-Eighth Street. Neumann, *Architecture of the Night,* 62–63.

81. See Appendix 3, "Some Conservation Issues, as Remembered by Arvid Klein and Tom Stetz of Pasanella + Klein," in this volume.

82. "New Progress in Light," *Architectural Forum* 106, no. 2 (February 1957): 155.

83. Rem Koolhaas, "Eno/abling Architecture," in *Autonomy and Ideology: Positioning an Avant-Garde in America,* ed. Robert E. Somol (New York: Monacelli, 1997), 297.

84. Mies had sheathed the columns of the Tugendhat house in bronze (chromed) and proposed sheathing the cross columns of the Resor house in bronze. Peter Palumbo, inspired

by Seagram, commissioned Mies to design Mansion House Square in London, in 1967, which was to have a bronze skin, but the project was never executed. See Peter Carter, *Mies van der Rohe at Work* (London: Pall Mall, 1974). Philip Johnson used mullions of bronze and flat bronze rings from which shallow domes rise to form the roof supported by cylindrical columns sheathed in Illinois Agatan marble for the Dumbarton Oaks museum, which he began to design in 1959. However, his use of metal in this case was purely ornamental. Mies very much liked this beautifully made pavilion.

85. Summers stated that Mies took a much more active role in designing Seagram than even the National Gallery, Berlin: "He did stay quite close to the Berlin Museum but in New York, first he was very anxious to see that be done as well as it could be done. And second, it was the only building being worked on." Summers, transcript of interview with Harrington, June 25, 1996, tape 5, side 2, p. 139.

86. Summers, transcript of interview with Harrington, June 24, 1996, tape 3, side B, p. 88.

87. In the theory and practice of the strength of materials, the material farthest from the neutral access (at the center) gives the greatest strength to a beam, hence the H- or I-sections.

88. Cook and Klotz, *Conversations with Architects,* 18.

89. Summers, transcript of interview with Harrington, June 24, 1996, tape 3, p. 89.

90. Foster, typescript of "Draft, July 18, 1986," [5].

91. Summers, transcript of interview with Harrington, June 24, 1996, tape 3, side B, pp. 88–89.

92. Varnelis, *Philip Johnson Tapes,* 140. The rest of the story as recounted by Philip is self-aggrandizing and shows his animosity toward Mies. First, Summers was the person who detailed the skin, not Johnson. Furthermore, Philip makes the highly unlikely claim that "I tried to explain to him that there were certain processes in making the thing and his detail just didn't work. But I couldn't explain it to him" (ibid.).

93. Summers, transcript of interview with Harrington, June 24, 1996, tape 3, side B, p. 91.

94. Foster, typescript of "Draft, July 18, 1986," [5].

95. Summers, transcript of interview with Harrington, June 24, 1996, tape 3, side B, p. 92. In the same interview, Summers tells a wonderful story about the patina, Mies, and Alexander Calder. "Calder had telephoned Mies . . . and he said, 'Mies, how do you get this patina on the bronze like on the Seagram Building?' And so Mies said, 'You've got to write a letter to Gene Summers in my office, and he'll tell you all about it.' . . . as Calder would do. . . [he wrote] with a brush. And it was in black ink and written with a brush. And he was very nice. 'Dear Mr. Summers . . . Mies asked me to write to you. And I'm doing work in bronze and, you know, how did you get the patina with the Seagram Building?' So I told him that we used ferric nitrate as the principal chemical, and then used lemon oil to finish it off and to hold it for as long as you can hold it. The patina—once you put that material out in the weather, you know, it changes" (ibid.).

96. See "First Bronze Panels Are Placed," *Engineering News-Record,* November 8, 1956, 24.

97. General Bronze Corporation advertisement in "A Special Report on 375 Park Avenue: An International Address of Distinction; The World's First Bronze Skyscraper," *New York Times,* April 7, 1957.

98. "'Hurricane' Used to Test First Bronze Skyscraper," in "A Special Report on 375 Park Avenue." See also photos of Mies at General Bronze Corporation, Garden City, NY, July 1956, by Frank Scherschel, Time Life & Pictures, licensed by Getty Images.

99. After Seagram, a process of flame-cutting replaced hand-cutting to texture granite.

100. PL to Borsook, August 1–2, 1955, 3.

101. This model was remade in New York for the exhibition *Buildings for Business and Government* at MoMA, 1957. After the exhibition it was donated to MoMA, where because of its large size and impermanent material it perished in storage.

102. The partnership agreement of October 18, 1954, between Mies, Johnson, and Seagram was dissolved on December 31, 1955, and a contract with Johnson as sole partner was signed December 12, 1955. The original partnership agreement of October 18, 1954, was reinstated on February 8, 1957. See copy of signed letter of agreement between Seagram and the partnership of Mies and Johnson, dated January 10, 1957, accepted by Joseph E. Seagram & Sons, Inc., February 8, 1957, Records of the Seagram's Curator's Office, FSB, box 134-007. Mies reapplied to the Board of Regents and was granted his license in June 1956, but not without the help of Henry T. Heald (1904–1975), president of the Ford Foundation 1956–65, president of New York University 1952–56, and president of the Armour Institute of Technology (AIT), which became Illinois Institute of Technology (IIT), 1938–52. I also asked the help of New York senator Herbert H. Lehman, former governor of New York, whose aide Carolin A. Flexner wrote to me on July 20, 1956, saying: "Certainly [Mies] should have had his license at the beginning, and it should not have taken you and all the people involved this length of time to have proved to the State of New York that he is one of the outstanding architects in the world." Flexner told me that the situation was endemic among professionals of all stripes in New York, fearful of competition from the flood of émigrés from Europe. See correspondence between PL and Carolin A. Flexner (letters dated July 1956), FPL, box 08-L-515. See also correspondence between PL and Henry T. Heald (letters dated July 1956), FPL, box 08-L-536.

103. PL to Donald R. F. Harleman, who was an assistant professor in the Hydrodynamics Laboratory at MIT, February 27, 1996, FPL, box 08-L-790.

104. Varnelis, *Philip Johnson Tapes,* 141.

105. See Harleman to PL, January 9, 1996, FPL, box 08-L-790. "Both Ippen and I had done our doctoral theses on high

velocity (supercritical flows) [*sic*] that characteristically display sudden and rather unstable changes in depth. Ippen assigned me to supervise the design, construction and operation of the model fountain and to assist the graduate student, William B. Davis, who eventually wrote an SM thesis on the study." The thesis was titled "Transition Phenomena in Radial Free Surface Flow" (MIT, 1958), BSRC.

106. Summers, transcript of interview with Harrington, June 25, 1996, tape 4, side A, pp. 99–100.
107. Ibid., 100.
108. The exhibition *Buildings for Business and Government* was installed at MoMA from February 25 to April 28, 1957. The buildings were either under construction or recently completed. In addition to the Seagram building, they included the United States Embassy in New Delhi, Edward D. Stone, architect; the United States Air Force Academy, Colorado Springs, Skidmore, Owings & Merrill, architects; the Technical Center for General Motors, Warren Michigan, Eero Saarinen & Associates, architects; the office building for Chase Manhattan Bank, New York City, Skidmore, Owings & Merrill, architects; the Terminal building for Lambert Field, St. Louis, Missouri, Helmuth, Yamasaki & Leinweber, architects.
109. Summers, transcript of interview with Harrington, June 25, 1996, tape 4, side A, p. 100.
110. See chapter 5 in this volume for the sculpture proposals for the plaza.
111. Varnelis, *Philip Johnson Tapes,* 141.
112. PL to Mumford, September 23, 1958, 5, Mumford Papers.
113. In the same spirit as Mies's choice of weeping beeches, landscape architect Karl Linn chose ginkgos "not only because there is no insect or disease to which they are susceptible, nor because they are tolerant of city conditions, but also because of their shape and foliage. We needed a tree, I feel, which will not be bulky in its foliage but will reveal an interesting branch formation in silhouette against its background." Karl Linn to Richard Foster, May 18, 1959, Records of the Seagram Curator's Office, FSB, box 134-007.
114. Summers, transcript of interview with Harrington, June 25, 1996, tape 4, side A, pp. 100–101.
115. The quarry near North Berwick, Maine, has been closed for many years. David Duford to PL, e-mail, July 28, 2010.
116. The setback at Fifty-Third Street is one foot, two and five-eighths inches, and at Fifty-Second Street, one foot, nine inches. The ownership of this area is marked at Park and Fifty-Third by two bronze strips embedded in the sidewalk delimiting the property lines and a bronze plaque inscribed with the following message: "Private Property: Crossing and Use Subject to Permission by the Owner and at the Risk of the User."
117. The mounds are necessary to provide enough soil for the trees to flourish. See Cathrin M. Brun to C. W. Tuttle, November 3, 1959, Records of the Seagram Curator's Office, FSB, box 134-007. Six ginkgos of eleven to thirteen inches' caliper and about forty feet high, selected by landscape architect Karl Linn, were planted in the first week of November 1959. See Linn to Foster, May 18, 1959, Records of the Seagram Curator's Office, FSB, box 134–007; and John C. Devlin, "Park Ave. Plaza Gets New Trees," *New York Times,* October 29, 1959.
118. Summers, transcript of interview with Harrington, June 24, 1996, tape 2, side B, p. 49.
119. Johnson in Cook and Klotz, *Conversations with Architects,* 43. N.B.: Johnson had no input into the ultimate design of the benches and their relationship to the pools.
120. Summers, transcript of interview with Harrington, June 25, 1996, tape 4, side A, p. 101.
121. After the first installation of the trees in 1959, in 1960 Seagram's public relations department wanted to use colored lights, but we convinced them of the necessity of establishing a tradition.
122. "The Talk of the Town: For Joy," *New Yorker,* December 26, 1959, 14. Philip Johnson commissioned Gene Moore, a designer who created Christmas displays for department stores. See also "Park Ave. Building Aglow with Lights in Yuletide Display," *New York Times,* December 4, 1958, in which a photograph is reproduced.
123. Harleman recalled: "I have very distinct memories of several visits to the lab by you, Philip Johnson and Mies van der Rohe. We had great fun demonstrating the varied water configurations. I also recall that all of you seemed enthusiastic about having a truly unusual fountain." Harleman to PL, January 9, 1996, FPL, box 08-L-790. In another letter, Harleman commented on the two separate projects: "I do not believe the MIT fountain and the large water plaza were one and the same. My recollection is that there were to be two of the MIT type fountains in rather small square, shallow enclosures. The MIT model basins were 8ft by 8ft by 6" deep and I thought they were about half or a quarter of the prototype size. It would be interesting to know the size of the present vertical jet basins on either side of the front plaza. I think our fountains were to be in those locations." Harleman to PL, March 7, 1996, FPL, box 08-L-790.
124. Anemometers recording the wind speed were added to signal controls that would lower the spray on windy days.
125. See chapter 5 in this volume.
126. Summers, transcript of interview with Harrington, June 25, 1996, tape 4, side B, pp. 108–9.
127. Varnelis, *Philip Johnson Tapes,* 143–44.
128. Three months earlier, J. Gordon Carr, an architect working with the Seagram Internal Planning Office, conducted a tour of the building's second to ninth floors. Finishing work on the building was in the final stages: ductwork, plumbing, and hung ceilings were advancing on the basement concourses A and B, the elevator lobbies had been finished on the other floors, and the washrooms were almost all finished except on the fifth floor. The fifth floor also lagged behind the others in the installation of the block work for corridor walls,

but the luminous ceiling was installed there first. The report from Carr's office also shows that tenant work on the rest of the floors was just beginning. It is clear that tight coordination was needed to complete all the floors: Carr notes that on Friday, September 13, Seagram's approval of the layout of the ninth floor was received, and the drawing was issued to Fuller and filed with the Building Department of the City of New York on September 16, 1957. Norman Green to C. Isaacson, September 16, 1957, Records of the Seagram Curator's Office, FSB, box 134-007. A contract between Seagram and Carr was signed August 15, 1955, "for full professional services [to be provided] in planning, designing and furnishing of your contemplated offices in Seagram Park Avenue," CSC, acc. 2126, RG 2, ser. X, box 845. All design and standards for Seagram and tenant spaces were set by Philip Johnson's office. For the complete file on Carr, see CSC, acc. 2126, RG 2, ser. X, box 845.

129. See N.Y. App., 1st Dept., Respondent's Brief, In the Matter of Joseph E. Seagram & Sons, Inc., against The Tax Commission of the City of New York, December 19, 1962, 9. The total rentable floor area amounts to 626,069 square feet. The "Final Certificate of Occupancy" was issued in October 1959.

130. John F. Mariani, with Alex von Bidder, *The Four Seasons: A History of America's Premier Restaurant* (New York: Crown, 1994), 39.

131. Seagram's in-house public relations people, whose programs in the early days of this field were preposterous or crude, proposed an extravaganza exhibition that could never have taken place: "The first known Rembrandt will be available [from Paris]. . . . Germany is working on original scores of Beethoven, Bach, etc." A. A. Schechter to Harry N. Bulow, memorandum, July 7, 1958, CSC, acc. 2126, RG 2, ser. VIII, box 798.

132. See Proceedings of *The Future of Man,* September 29, 1959, 3, BSRC; another copy of the proceedings is held with the Bertrand Russell Papers at McMaster University, Hamilton, ON, along with the script and recording of Bertrand Russell's five-minute broadcast to the symposium. See also "Talk of the Town," *New Yorker,* October 10, 1959, 33–34, in which the event was captured in considerable detail.

133. Proceedings of *The Future of Man,* 8. *The Future of Man* was preceded by an earlier symposium, *The Next Hundred Years: A Scientific Symposium* (November 22, 1957), organized by Joseph E. Seagram & Sons, Inc., to commemorate the one hundredth anniversary of the company. It was chaired by Dr. Detlev W. Bronk, president of the Rockefeller Institute. Participants included Dr. Albert Szent-Gyorgyi, Dr. Harrison Brown, Dr. Clifford C. Furnas, Dr. James Bonner, Dr. Hermann J. Muller, Dr. John Weir, and Dr. Wernher von Braun, and major television anchormen made up an interview panel that included Jon Daley, Chet Huntley, and Edward R. Murrow. The proceedings were moderated by William L. Laurence, science editor for the *New York Times.* This event focused on the necessity of communication between the sciences and society—a theme recently addressed by C. P. Snow's famous lecture entitled "Two Cultures," published in the *New Statesman* a little more than a year earlier, October 6, 1956. A copy of the Proceedings of *The Next Hundred Years: A Scientific Symposium* is in BSRC.

134. Mies van der Rohe, "Lecture," first draft of unpublished ms, March 17, 1926, collection of Dirk Lohan, Chicago; Neumeyer, *Artless Word,* 253.

135. The openness of the eastern section follows through the additional six floors of the intermediate level, and when that drops off, the T-shaped tower rises twenty-nine more floors, while the escape stairs and washrooms fold into the tower core, where two banks of elevators are no longer needed.

136. Contrarian and nonstructuralist, Philip Johnson said the most difficult problems were stairs, chairs, and public squares.

137. See Peter Eisenman, "miMISes READING: does not mean A THING," in *Mies Reconsidered: His Career, Legacy, and Disciples,* ed. John Zukowsky (Chicago: Art Institute of Chicago and New York: Rizzoli, 1986), 86–98; reprinted in Peter Eisenman, *Eisenman Inside Out: Selected Writings, 1963–1988* (New Haven: Yale University Press, 2004), 189–201. See also Eisenman, "Mies and the Figuring of Absence," in Lambert, *Mies in America,* 712–14.

138. "Philip Johnson on Ludwig Mies van der Rohe," in John Peter, *The Oral History of Modern Architecture* (New York: Harry N. Abrams, 1994), 175.

PORTFOLIO

Note to epigraphs: Ludwig Mies van der Rohe, "What Would Concrete, What Would Steel Be Without Plate Glass," unpublished text for a prospectus of the Association of German Plate Glass Manufacturers, March 13, 1933; quoted in Fritz Neumeyer, *The Artless Word: Mies van der Rohe on the Building Art,* trans. Mark Jarzombek (Cambridge, MA: MIT Press, 1991), 314; Mies van der Rohe, "Skyscrapers," published without title in *Frühlicht* 1, no. 4 (1922); quoted in Neumeyer, *Artless Word,* 240.

CHAPTER 3.
UNION OF BUILDING AND PLAZA IN THE URBAN LANDSCAPE

Note: This chapter is developed from the lecture entitled "Ludwig Mies van der Rohe and the Landscape of the City," presented as the Dudley Memorial Lecture, delivered on May 8, 2007, at the Corcoran Gallery of Art, Washington, DC.

1. In Behrens's office Mies asked the question, "What is architecture?" He said that he read "to find out. That was the

reason I read." Quoted in John Peter, *The Oral History of Modern Architecture: Interviews with the Greatest Architects of the Twentieth Century* (New York: Harry N. Abrams, 1994), 156. In the same text Mies said: "I was interested in the philosophy of values and problems of the spirit. I was also very much interested in astronomy and natural sciences. I asked myself the question, 'What is the truth? What is the truth?' until I stopped at Thomas Aquinas, I found my answer there" (ibid., 158). Mies's private library, which contained close to eight hundred volumes at the time of his death, is for the most part held in Special Collections at the University of Illinois. In "Einzigartigkeit: Mies van der Rohes philosophisch-kultureller Hintergrund," *Mies van der Rohe: Vorbild und Vermächtnis,* exh. cat. (Stuttgart: Ernst Klett, 1986), 71–83, Francesco Dal Co argues that the writings of Catholic reformers Romano Guardini, Jacques Maritain, and Max Scheler constituted the philosophical basis of Miesian thought. My thanks to CCA Visiting Scholar Panos Mantziaras for mention of this in his presentation, "The City Landscape from H. Thünen's *Isolierte Staat* (1826) to R. Schwarz's *Von der Bebauung der Erde* (1949)," at CCA Study Center Seminar, October 19, 2001.

2. The year 1986 marks the earliest publication on archival and bibliographical sources: Arthur Drexler, ed. (vols. 1–4), and Franz Schulze, ed. (vols. 5–20), *The Mies van der Rohe Archive* (New York: Garland, 1986–92), which was made possible by Mies's donation of his architectural drawings to MoMA in the late 1960s. Fritz Neumeyer's fundamental work *The Artless Word: Mies van der Rohe and the Building Art,* trans. Mark Jarzombek (Cambridge, MA: MIT Press, 1991), is concerned with Mies's thought as expressed in his writings. Mies's correspondence and texts were given to the Manuscript Division, Library of Congress, in 1971 and 1973. The CCA archives and collections contain documents pertaining to Mies, Mies and his American colleagues, and Oral History Archives created between 1996 and 2000.

3. The exhibition was mounted in the Seagram Gallery from November 22, 1977, to March 1, 1978. The Seagram Gallery is discussed in chapter 5 of this volume.

4. "The Seagram Plaza: Its Design and Use," unpaged [4], typescript, FPL, 08-L-190.

5. Ibid., [5].

6. Christian Norberg-Schulz, "A Talk with Mies van der Rohe," *Baukunst und Werkform* 11, no. 11 (1958): 615–18; quoted in Neumeyer, *Artless Word,* 339. Myron Goldsmith, who worked closely with Mies on the Farnsworth house, the clear-span steel-and-glass pavilion that he poised lightly on the prairie grass, reminds us that Mies personally staked out the location of the pavilion and its terrace in relation to the giant linden that stood near the river. The site, Goldsmith said, gave the house its distinct form, referring to the requirement that it be lifted off the ground because the river regularly flooded its banks: "Of course, then it led to the terrace, the stair and all that. So maybe you could have cut the cost by a third by moving it up." Myron Goldsmith, transcript of interview with Kevin Harrington, June 7, 1996, CCA, tape 6, side 2, p. 85. The solution seemed logical, even banal, but to my knowledge, it has not been discussed as an example of Mies's relating building form to site. Other examples are Joseph Fujikawa's discussion of the siting of 860–880 Lake Shore Drive in Chicago and Gene Summers's discussion of siting the Chicago Federal buildings and the Toronto-Dominion Centre as more pragmatic than philosophical. See Joseph Fujikawa, transcript of interview with Kevin Harrington, May 1, 1996, CCA, tape 5, side 2, pp. 80–84 passim; Phyllis Lambert, "Space and Structure," in *Mies in America,* ed. Phyllis Lambert (Montreal: Canadian Centre for Architecture, and New York: Whitney Museum of American Art and Harry N. Abrams, 2001), 409; and Gene Summers, transcript of interview with Kevin Harrington, June 26, 1996, CCA, tape 8, side 1, p. 202.

7. See Barry Bergdoll, "The Nature of Mies's Space," in *Mies in Berlin,* ed. Terence Riley and Barry Bergdoll (New York: Museum of Modern Art, 2001), 67–105.

8. Ibid., 71.

9. Ibid., 68.

10. Hermann Muthesius, *Landhaus und Garten* (Munich: F. Bruckman, 1907); quoted in Bergdoll, "Nature of Mies's Space," 70.

11. *Um 1800: Architektur und Handwerk im letzten Jahrhundert ihrer tradizionellen Entwicklung,* ed. Paul Mebes, 2 vols. (Munich: F. Bruckmann, 1908), which covered the Biedermeier period, was influential for Mies.

12. Hermann Muthesius, *Landhaus und Garten* (Munich: F. Bruckmann, 1910), xxv; quoted in Bergdoll, "Nature of Mies's Space," 72. The house fulfills the call of the reformers for a tight relationship between gardens and interiors, including naming functions in their garden plans as in their floor plans. There was to be a play garden for children, and the gendered interior rooms, the gentlemen's room or library and the ladies' parlor, were to have a corresponding conversation garden and a rose garden. Riehl's library deliberately faces out onto an enclosed garden court, and the parlor onto the rose garden.

13. Bergdoll, "Nature of Mies's Space," 74. Mies worked in Behrens's studio from October 1908 to early 1912, but with a year's absence from late 1909 to late 1910. See Franz Schulze, *Mies van der Rohe: A Critical Biography* (Chicago: University of Chicago Press, 1989), 41.

14. Peter Behrens, "Der moderne Garten," *Berliner Tagblatt* 40, no. 291 (June 10, 1911): 8–9; quoted in Bergdoll, "Nature of Mies's Space," 74–75.

15. Alois Riehl, *Zur Einführung in die Philosophie der Gegenwart: Acht Vorträge* (Leipzig: B. G. Teubner, 1908), 270; quoted in Fritz Neumeyer, "Space for Reflection: Block versus Pavilion," in *Mies van der Rohe: Critical Essays,* ed.

Franz Schulze (New York: Museum of Modern Art, and Cambridge, MA: MIT Press, 1989), 153, 171n13.

16. Mies van der Rohe, "Baukunst unserer Zeit," foreword to Werner Blaser, *Mies van der Rohe: Die Kunst der Struktur/ The Art of Structure* (Zurich: Artemis Verlag für Architektur, 1965), 6; also quoted Neumeyer, "Space for Reflection," 153, 171n15.

17. Terence Riley, "Making History: Mies van der Rohe and the Museum of Modern Art," in Riley and Bergdoll, *Mies in Berlin*, 10–23; note in the same essay Riley's mention of other early houses Mies did not acknowledge, esp. 14.

18. "Architekt Ludwig Mies: Villa des Herrn Geheimer Regierungsrat Prof. Dr. Riehl in Neu-Babelsberg," *Moderne Bauformen* vol. 9 (1910): 20–24; noted by Neumeyer, in "Space for Reflection," 154, 171n21.

19. Sergius Ruegenberg, Mies's coworker between 1925 and 1931, recalled that the large folio *Sommerresidenz des russischen Zaren in Orianda auf der Krim*, drawn in 1838 and published in 1878, lay on Mies's table "forever and was never removed." See Neumeyer, *Artless Word*, 129, 361–62n56.

20. "In later years Mies recalled the occasions when he and the rest of the Neubabelsburg [studio] staff were conducted by [Behrens] on pilgrimages through the Berlin area to visit Schinkel sites." Schulze, *Mies van der Rohe: A Critical Biography*, 42.

21. Karl Friedrich Schinkel, "The Charlottenhof near Potsdam," in *Collection of Architectural Designs: Including Designs Which Have Been Executed and Objects Whose Execution Was Intended* (Chicago: Exedra Books, 1981), 48.

22. Bergdoll, "Nature of Mies's Space," 73.

23. The exedral bench, so powerful at the end of the artificial terrace of the Schloss Charlottenhof, was invoked by Mies as the terminus of gardens for Haus Werner (1913–15) and Haus Urbig (1915–17), and also as an element of furniture on the upper terrace of Tugendhat; it morphs into the powerful benches at Seagram, as well as benches at the Federal Center in Chicago (1967).

24. Schinkel, "Charlottenhof near Potsdam," 48.

25. Mies also created openings in the massive retaining wall of his last work, the New National Gallery in Berlin, where the podium houses the permanent collection, opening onto the sculpture garden.

26. Schinkel in Detlef Mertins, "Living in a Jungle," in Lambert, *Mies in America*, 594.

27. "Nasci" issue of *Merz* no. 8–9 (April–July 1924): 81–82. Raoul Francé (1874–1943), botanist and popular science writer, whose discussion ranged freely from botany to aesthetics, epistemology, and technology and whose many publications Mies avidly collected given his strong interest in the organic unfolding of architectural form.

28. Mertins, "Living in a Jungle," 598.

29. Katharine Kuh, "Mies van der Rohe: Modern Classicist," *Saturday Review*, January 23, 1965, 22–23.

30. Inaugural address as director of architecture at AIT, 1938; quoted in Neumeyer, *Artless Word*, 317.

31. August Endell, *Die Schönheit der grossen Stadt* (Stuttgart: Strecker und Schröder, 1908), 59–60; quoted in Neumeyer, *Artless Word*, 182–83. Endell imagined the urban effect of the glass structure as it appeared above the surrounding houses: "luminous . . . like a high, red-shining mountain . . . enflamed to glaring fire by the evening sun" (ibid., 182).

32. Mies van der Rohe, untitled, *Frühlicht* 1, no. 4 (1922): 124; quoted in Neumeyer, *Artless Word*, 240.

33. Bruno Taut, "Nieder der Seriosismus!" *Frühlicht* 1 (January 1920): 13; quoted in Fritz Neumeyer, "Nexus of the Modern: The New Architecture in Berlin," in *Berlin, 1900–1933: Architecture and Design; Architektur und Design,* ed. Tilmann Buddensieg (New York: Cooper-Hewitt Museum and Berlin: Gebr. Mann Verlag, 1987), 54, 80n42. *Frühlicht* was published as a section of *Stadtbaukunst alter und neuer Zeit* in vols. 1–14 and then became an independent periodical under the same title in autumn 1921; Taut published Mies's "Skyscrapers" in *Frühlicht* 1, no. 4 (Summer 1922): 122–24.

34. Mies van der Rohe, unpublished ms, March 13, 1933, Ludwig Mies van der Rohe Papers, Manuscript Division, Library of Congress; quoted in Neumeyer, *Artless Word*, 314; originally published as *Mies van der Rohe: Das Kunstlose Wort; Gedanken zur Baukunst* (Berlin: Wolf Jost Siedler, 1986).

35. See Dietrich Neumann, "Friedrichstrasse Skyscraper Project, Berlin-Mitte, 1921," in Riley and Bergdoll, *Mies in Berlin*, 180–83. Neumann's description takes inspiration from August Endell. Neumann refers to the use of glass for the "curtain wall" facade of Bernhard Sehring Tietz's department store in Berlin (1900), as well as large expanses of glass being used in the construction of the Friedrichstrasse railway station. However, the first skyscraper in which large plate-glass windows composed the greater part of a building's surface was Daniel Burnham's Reliance building in Chicago, built 1890–95.

36. Mies van der Rohe, untitled, *Frühlicht* 1, no. 4 (1922): 124; quoted in Neumeyer, *Artless Word*, 240.

37. Sergius Ruegenberg, *Caricature of Mies van der Rohe with Model of 1922 Glass Skyscraper*, c. 1925, © Berlinische Galerie, Berlin.

38. Mies van der Rohe, untitled, *Frühlicht* 1, no. 4 (1922): 124; quoted in Neumeyer, *Artless Word*, 240.

39. Peter Behrens, *Berlins dritte Dimension*, ed. Alfred Dambitsch (Berlin: Ullstein, 1912), 10–11; quoted in Jean-Louis Cohen, "German Desires of America: Mies's Urban Visions," in Riley and Bergdoll, *Mies in Berlin*, 363.

40. A photograph made at the opening of the First International Dada Fair on June 30, 1920, shows the architect Johannes Baader drawing Mies's attention to the cover *of Neue-Jugend* (June 17, 1920), which featured Daniel Burnham's triangular Flatiron building in New York; reprinted in Detlef Mertins, "Architectures of Becoming: Mies van der Rohe and the

Avant-Garde," in Riley and Bergdoll, *Mies in Berlin,* 106.
41. Neumeyer, "Nexus of the Modern," 46.
42. Bruno Taut, *Der Weltbaumeister: Architekturschauspiel für symphonische Musik* (Hagen, Westfalen: Folkwang Verlag, 1920); Taut, *Die Stadtkrone* (Jena: E. Diedrichs, 1919), 59–60; both quoted in Neumeyer, "Nexus of the Modern," 46, 79n30, 50, 80n36.
43. Paul Scheerbart, *Glasarchitektur* (Berlin: Verlag der Sturm, 1914), published in English as *Glass Architecture, by Paul Scheerbart* (trans. James Palmes) and *Alpine Architecture, by Bruno Taut* (trans. Shirley Palmer), ed. with intro. Dennis Sharp (New York: Praeger, 1972).
44. Bruno Taut, *Alpine Architektur* (Hagen, Westfalen: Folkwang Verlag, 1919); see note 43, above, for English edition information.
45. "Dandanah, the fairy palace," a richly colored, solid-glass building-block toy that Taut designed, was made available in 1915–16. Phyllis Lambert Collection, CCA.
46. Scheerbart, *Glass Architecture*, 14. Author's translation of this phrase.
47. Ibid.
48. See Detlef Mertins, "The Enticing and Threatening Face of Prehistory: Walter Benjamin and the Utopia of Glass," *Assemblage* 29 (April 1996): 14–16.
49. See Mertins, "Enticing and Threatening Face of Prehistory," 22n39.
50. Mies van der Rohe, "While we want to stand with both feet firmly on the ground, we want to reach with our head to the clouds," ms, June 19, 1924, Collection of Dirk Lohan, Chicago; quoted in Neumeyer, *Artless Word,* 250.
51. Mies van der Rohe, "Bürohaus," *G* 1 (July 1923): 3. In lieu of the translation published in Neumeyer, *Artless Word,* 241, I have used that of Neumeyer in "Nexus of the Modern," 57.
52. Mies van der Rohe, "Bürohaus," 3; quoted in Neumeyer, *Artless Word,* 241.
53. Scheerbart, *Glass Architecture,* 46, 42. Mies frequently referred to the structure of Gothic cathedral; see Phyllis Lambert, "Mies Immersion: Introduction," in Lambert, *Mies in America,* 217.
54. Scheerbart, *Glass Architecture,* 41.
55. Ibid., 41, 51. Scheerbart also noted from experience at the Botanical Gardens at Dahlem the high cost of heating single glazed structures, and he further discussed double glass walls, light, heating, and cooling (ibid., 41). But as noted above in chapter 2, Mies, whose practice in America was coincident with the development of air-conditioning, considered the problem of heat loss and heat gain to be a problem of physics that could be solved. He was also aware that the prohibitive cost of double glazing at the time, and the limits it set on glass size, would have shattered his dream of glass architecture.
56. Philip Johnson describes the materials in *Mies van der Rohe* (New York: Museum of Modern Art, 1947), 67. The Glass Room that Mies designed with Lilly Reich for the Werkbund at Stuttgart in 1927 had freestanding walls made of clear, etched, and tinted mouse gray and olive green plate-glass. See also Detlef Mertins, "Architectures of Becoming: Mies van der Rohe and the Avant-Garde," in Riley and Bergdoll, *Mies in Berlin,* 128.
57. Scheerbart, *Glass Architecture,* 42, 43.
58. The placement of the furniture at the Tugendhat house may be seen as illustrations for Scheerbart's chapter eight in which he wrote, "Furniture [is to be placed] in the middle of the room," not against the glass walls, and tables and chairs are to be made of glass and metal, "if the whole environment is to convey a sense of unity" (ibid., 43).
59. Ibid., 46.
60. Reyner Banham, "The Glass Paradise," *Architectural Review* 125, no. 745 (February 1959): 87–89; republished in *A Critic Writes,* ed. Mary Banham et al. (Berkeley: University of California Press, 1996), 38.
61. Mies wrote this in relation to the Seagram building: Mies van der Rohe to Cameron Alread, Edow Davidson, Edgar Marshall, and Louis Thomas, May 11, 1960, Ludwig Mies van der Rohe Papers, container 54, Manuscript Division, Library of Congress (hereafter cited as Mies Papers). In a 1955 interview with John Peter, Mies qualified his work: "What I do . . . what they call . . . my kind of architecture, they should just call it . . . a structural approach." Transcript of interview with John Peter, 1955, 10. Interviews with Ludwig Mies van der Rohe, Mies Papers, container 62.
62. See Phyllis Lambert, "Learning a Language," in Lambert, *Mies in America,* 222–330.
63. Kurt W. Forster, "The Seagram Building Reconsidered," *Skyline,* February 1982, 29.
64. Herbert Muschamp, "Opposites Attract," *New York Times Magazine,* April 18, 1999.
65. K. Michael Hays, "Critical Architecture: Between Culture and Form," *Perspecta* 21 (1984): 22. Hays otherwise essentially expanded on Manfredo Tafuri's well-known reading of the Seagram building as "disenchanted" skyscraper, "silent" and "asemantic." See, e.g., Manfredo Tafuri, *Architecture and Utopia: Design and Capitalist Development* (Cambridge, MA: MIT Press, 1976), trans. Barbara Luigia La Penta (Bari, Italy: Giuseppe Laterza e Figli, 1973).
66. Transcript of interview with John Peter, 1955, 14–15.
67. Mertins, "Living in a Jungle," 633.
68. Ludwig Hilberseimer, "Gesellschaft und Städtebau," typescript, c. late 1937–early 1938, which became the basis of *The New City: Principles of Planning* (Chicago: Paul Theobald, 1944), 174; quoted in Richard Pommer, "More a Necropolis Than a Metropolis," *Ludwig Hilberseimer: Architect, Educator, and Urban Planner* (Chicago: Art Institute of Chicago and Rizzoli International, 1988), 45.
69. See Phyllis Lambert, "Mies Immersion," 209–11.
70. Max Schmidt, *Das Bismarck-Nationaldenkmal auf der*

Elisenhöhe bei Bingerbrück (Hundert Entwürfe aus dem Wettbewerb) (Düsseldorf: Düsseldorfer Verlags-Anstalt, 1911), cited in Adrian V. Sudhalter, "Ludwig Mies van der Rohe and Photomontage in the 1920s" (seminar paper, Institute of Fine Arts, New York University, 1997), 5; see also Lambert, "Mies Immersion," 220n37.

71. Sudhalter, "Ludwig Mies van der Rohe and Photomontage in the 1920s," 12.
72. For Mies's connections to montage and film, see Lambert, "Mies Immersion," 204–11.
73. For the complete sequence and key plan, see Lambert, *Mies in America,* 252–55.
74. Krauss refers to the critic Kasha Linville. See Rosalind Krauss, "The Grid, the /Cloud/, and the Detail," in *The Presence of Mies,* ed. Detlef Mertins (New York: Princeton Architectural Press, 1994), 140–41.
75. Mies made the montages with George Danforth and William Priestley, members of his office, in 1939, during the later stages of the unbuilt project.
76. The collage was made with George Danforth. See Phyllis Lambert, "Project for a Museum for a Small City (1943)," in Lambert, *Mies in America,* 426–29.
77. Mies van der Rohe, "Museum for a Small City," *Architectural Forum* 78, no. 5 (May 1943): 84–85; quoted in Neumeyer, *Artless Word,* 322.
78. Mumford, "The Lesson of the Master," *New Yorker,* September 13, 1958, 147.
79. Russell Lynes, "Space No Land Waste; Added Tax on Seagram Building for Providing Square Assailed," *New York Times,* May 21, 1963.

CHAPTER 4.
LIGHT: PHILIP JOHNSON'S *STIMMUNG*

Note: Part of this chapter was developed for a lecture presented on February 24, 2004, to the Collins/Kaufmann Forum on Modern Architecture at Columbia University, at the invitation of Barry Bergdoll. It was published in an edited version as "*Stimmung* at Seagram: Philip Johnson Counters Mies van der Rohe," *Grey Room* 20 (Summer 2005): 38–59. A related piece with different emphasis has been published as "Light Changes: Philip Johnson, Richard Kelly, and *Stimmung* at Seagram," in *The Structure of Light: Richard Kelly and the Illumination of Modern Architecture,* ed. Dietrich Neumann (New Haven: Yale University Press, 2010), 80–95.

1. Philip Johnson in conversation with PL, late 1954.
2. Quoted in Sybil Gordon Kantor, *Alfred H. Barr, Jr., and the Intellectual Origins of the Museum of Modern Art* (Cambridge, MA: MIT Press, 2002), 303.
3. For this and subsequent quotations from this article, see "Seagram's Custom Look: 13 New Ideas for Better Skyscraper Design," *Architectural Forum* 109, no. 1 (July 1958): 72–75.

4. B. H. Friedman, "The Most Expensive Restaurant Ever Built," *Evergreen Review* 3, no. 10 (November–December 1959): 112.
5. In *The Structure of Light,* Neumann positioned Kelly, showing how he "belonged to a second generation of lighting designers, building on the work of Bassett Jones, Stanley McCandless and many others." Neumann to PL, e-mail, September 25, 2009.
6. Lewis Mumford, "The Lesson of the Master," *New Yorker,* September 13, 1958, 147.
7. Ibid., 142.
8. PL to Lewis Mumford, September 23, 1958, 4–5, Lewis Mumford Papers, Rare Book and Manuscript Library, University of Pennsylvania.
9. See chapter 2, n. 102, above.
10. Philip Johnson to Gene R. Summers, January 17, 1957, Manuscript Division, Library of Congress.
11. See Henry-Russell Hitchcock, "Introduction," in *Philip Johnson: Architecture, 1949–1965* (New York: Holt, Rinehart and Winston, 1966), 10.
12. Quoted in Hilary Lewis and John O'Connor, *Philip Johnson: The Architect in His Own Words* (New York: Rizzoli, 1994), 37.
13. Ibid. Experience frequently generates theory. In the course of discussions about reworking the interior of the guest house, Kelly and Johnson visited Johnson's Hodgson house, which was in construction across the road. With the roof but not the walls in place, temporary walls were erected about a foot outside the roof and a little higher. Kelly recounts his epiphany: "When Phil and I stepped inside the effect was magic. Light from the sky, which was invisible to us, reflected from the temporary walls and gave the feeling of great space. We decided this was it." Arnold Nicholson, "Mr. Kelly's Magic Lights," *Saturday Evening Post,* July 5, 1958, 64.
14. Lewis and O'Connor, *Philip Johnson,* 37.
15. Philip Johnson, "House at New Canaan, Connecticut," *Architectural Review* 108, no. 645 (September 1950): 152–59.
16. Ibid., 154.
17. Ludwig Mies van der Rohe, interview by Graeme Shankland, published as "Architect of 'the Clear and Reasonable,'" *Listener,* October 15, 1959, 622.
18. Mies van der Rohe, "Mies in Berlin," transcript of October 1964 interview by Horst Eifler and Ulrich Conrads, recorded by Radio in the American Sector, Berlin, 8. Ludwig Mies van der Rohe Papers, container 62, Manuscript Division, Library of Congress.
19. "Richard Kelly was probably the first to introduce those bulky dimmers, which had been in use for stage lighting for quite some time, into his domestic lighting designs." Neumann to PL, e-mail, September 25, 2009.
20. Florentine Dietrich for Dr. Burkhardt Goeres, Schlösser und Sammlungen, to Renata Guttman of the CCA Library, e-mail, September 23, 2004, confirmed that the 1921 and

1927 editions of the Baedeker guidebook, *Berlin und Umgebung,* both list Schloss Charlottenburg and refer to rooms including the bedroom of Queen Luise, which is also mentioned in a 1937 guide to the museum as having been renovated in the 1930s. I wish to express my gratitude to Wallis Miller, who put me in touch with the archives at the Schlösser und Sammlungen in order to ascertain whether the room was visible when Johnson was in Berlin. I also wish to thank Denise Bratton, who, when I read to her my description of the Brick House guest room, made the connection to Queen Luise.

21. Barry Bergdoll, *Karl Friedrich Schinkel: An Architect for Prussia* (New York: Rizzoli, 1994), 31.
22. Designed in 1954 with Richard Kelly and Edison Price, this became known as the "Glass House floor lamp."
23. Philip Johnson, "Schinkel and Mies," in *Philip Johnson Writings* (New York: Oxford University Press, 1979), 165. Johnson originally presented this text as a lecture at Congress Hall, Berlin, on March 13, 1961.
24. See Kurt W. Forster, "'Only Things That Stir the Imagination': Schinkel as a Scenographer," in *Karl Friedrich Schinkel, 1781–1841: The Drama of Architecture,* ed. John Zukowsky (Chicago: Art Institute of Chicago, and Tübingen: Wasmuth, 1994), 18–35.
25. Johnson, "Schinkel and Mies," 177.
26. Peter Blake, "A Conversation with Mies," in *Four Great Makers of Modern Architecture: Gropius, Le Corbusier, Mies van der Rohe, Wright; A Verbatim Record of a Symposium Held at the School of Architecture from March to May 1961* (New York: Columbia University, School of Architecture, 1963), 94.
27. Ludwig Mies van der Rohe, "Miscellaneous Notes to Lectures (Around 1950)," in Fritz Neumeyer, *The Artless Word: Mies van der Rohe on the Building Art,* trans. Mark Jarzombek (Cambridge, MA: MIT Press, 1991), 328; originally published as *Das kunstlose Wort: Gedanken zur Baukunst* (Berlin: Wolf Jobst Siedler, 1986).
28. Philip Johnson, "Introduction," *Karl Friedrich Schinkel: Collection of Architectural Designs* (1866; reprint ed., Chicago: Exedra Books, 1981), 1.
29. Philip Johnson, "Philip Johnson Remembers Richard Kelly," *Lighting Design and Application* 9 (June 1979): 49.
30. Ibid.
31. Richard Kelly, "The Better to See . . . ," *House and Garden* 90, no. 6 (December 1946): 152.
32. Richard Kelly, "Focus on Light . . . New Techniques Inspire Exciting Use in Decor," *Flair* 1 (February 1950): 66.
33. Ibid., 68.
34. Ibid., 69.
35. Ibid., 67.
36. Forster, "'Only Things That Stir the Imagination,'" 24.
37. The 1950 Rockefeller Guest House in New York was Kelly and Johnson's first collaboration, followed by the Hodgson house (1951) and the Wiley house (1953).
38. See Margaret Maile Petty, "Illuminating the Glass Box: The Lighting Designs of Richard Kelly," *Journal of the Society of Architectural Historians* 66, no. 2 (June 2007): 216n19. See Elliot Noyes to Richard Kelly, November 23, 1945, Richard Kelly Papers, Manuscripts and Archives, Yale University Library.
39. Stanley McCandless, *A Method of Lighting the Stage* (New York: Theatre Arts Books, 1932); later editions followed in 1939 and 1947; an emended and revised edition appeared in 1958.
40. Ibid., 9.
41. Ibid., 16.
42. Richard Kelly, "Lighting as an Integral Part of Architecture," *College Art Journal* 12, no. 1 (Fall 1952): 26. I have corrected Kelly's incorrect French transcription; the English translation is from Jean-Louis Cohen, *Toward an Architecture* (Los Angeles: Getty Research Institute, 2007), 102.
43. McCandless, *Method of Lighting the Stage,* 50.
44. Richard Kelly, "Good Lighting Is Part of Good Living," *House and Garden* 101, no. 3 (March 1952): 192.
45. Kelly, "Lighting as an Integral Part of Architecture," 24.
46. Kelly, "Good Lighting Is Part of Good Living," 138.
47. See "The Basic Scheme Was to Wash Walls with Light from Invisible Sources," in Olga Gueft, "Four Seasons Restaurant, by Philip Johnson," *Interiors Magazine* 119, no. 5 (December 1959): 168.
48. The PAR lamp was developed by Dick Thayer in 1937, when he experimented with sealed-beam lamps. These were first used in automobiles in 1940.
49. "The Light Changes," *Vogue* (January 1, 1957): 136–39, in which the columnist wrote: "In this New York *pied-à-terre* designed by Philip Johnson and lighted by Richard Kelly, the effect is all lightness and light—a warm surrounding luminescence that bathes everything (and everybody) in the room, seeming to come from no particular source. There are no 'islands,' no 'pools' of light surrounded by darkness . . . rather, there is a total ambiance that can be brightened or dimmed at the owner's will."
50. "Seagram's Custom Look," 75.
51. Minutes of the Advisory Committee Meeting, June 1, 1955, 2, CSC, acc. 2126, RG 2, ser. III, box 376.
52. See George W. Seaton, *Cue's Guide to New York City* (New York: Prentice-Hall, 1940), 100.
53. See http://www.nyc-architecture.com/ARCH/Notes-1930_Restaurants.htm.
54. PL to Eve Borsook (copy), June 6, 1955, 1–2, FPL, box 08-L-309.
55. Ibid., 2.
56. Two telegrams and a binder titled "The Barberry Room," dated September 1956, are evidence of activity focused on locating a restaurant in the new Seagram building. A Western Union telegram from Bill Conlan to Harry Bulow,

Seagrams [*sic*] Distillers, Chrysler building, September 23, 1956, referred to "plans" to locate the Barberry Room in the House of Seagram. Bulow was Seagram's public relations officer; Conlan was unknown to me, as were the "plans." The telegram reads: "Complete prospectus submitted to financial backers on the Barberry Room for House of Seagram is now available Normal [*sic*] Bel-Geddes returning from Spain October 1 to meet with staff and commence interior designs based on two level layout drafted by Kniffen and Demarest. Plans for room include revival of Algonquin Round Table discussions which Alexander Woollcott initiated in Elbow-Barberry Room in 1938. Also Danton Walker and Inez Robb will do a half-hour radio discussion program from the room each week." Records of the Seagram Curators Office, FSB, box 134-007. I have found no follow-up to these documents.

57. John F. Mariani, with Alex von Bidder, *The Four Seasons: A History of America's Premier Restaurant* (New York: Crown, 1994), 22.

58. Ibid., 22–23.

59. Ibid., 23.

60. The "Agreement of Lease" between Joseph E. Seagram & Sons, Inc., referred to as "Landlord," and 375 Park Avenue Restaurant Corporation, referred to as "Tenant," with an attached rider, was dated February 1, 1957; BSRC.

61. Mariani and von Bidder, *The Four Seasons*, 25. According to Article 38 of the rider, the sum of $25,000 was to be paid from January to December 1958, and thereafter, a rental referred to as "Minimum Rental" was to commence January 1, 1959, and for the balance of the lease, the annual rental was $50,000. A further rental, sometimes referred to as a "Percentage Rental," was equal to the entire excess over the minimal rental in a fiscal year: 6 percent of the first $1,500,000 of gross income; 5.5 percent of the next $500,000; 5 percent and then 4.5 percent of the next two amounts of $500,000 in excess of gross income; and finally 4 percent of all gross income in excess of $3,000,000. Rider attached to "Agreement of Lease," between Joseph E. Seagram & Sons, Inc. and 375 Park Avenue Restaurant Corporation, February 1, 1957, 2.

62. Rider attached to "Agreement of Lease" between Joseph E. Seagram & Sons, Inc. and 375 Park Avenue Restaurant Corporation, February 1, 1957, 6.

63. Mariani and von Bidder, *The Four Seasons*, 15.

64. Geoffrey T. Hellman, "Profiles: Directed to the Product," *New Yorker*, October 17, 1964, 81. Hellman wrote that the Newarker would become famous for its generous portions: the oysters were so large they had to be eaten with a knife and fork, and Baum would add a seventh on a separate plate for orders of a half-dozen. He also added a third claw to lobster orders. Baum displayed a flair that earned him the moniker "the Cecil B. De Mille of restaurateurs"; later he was responsible for all 222 restaurants in the World Trade Center and the Windows on the World, which he designed.

65. Baum probably read *Cooking and Dining in Imperial Rome; A Bibliography, Critical Review and Translation of the Ancient Book Known as* Apicius de re coquinaria, *Now for the First Time Rendered into English,* trans. and ed. Joseph Dommers Vehling (New York: W. M. Hill, 1936), a chef's, rather than a classicist's, translation.

66. Mariani and von Bidder attributed the origin of the term "New American Cuisine" to Silas Spitzer in an article he wrote on Stockli, the Four Seasons' first chef and RA's executive chef, published in *Holiday* magazine, December 1959. Mariani and von Bidder, *The Four Seasons*, 45.

67. *Philip Johnson Tapes,* 142. Mies had designed the Arts Club, where one entered, mounting what became a famous staircase, to access exhibition spaces and a restaurant within an existing building in Chicago (1948–51). Drawings show that he was concerned with defining the flow of space and the scale of the restaurant; the problems involved were minor compared with those of the Four Seasons.

68. The Forum opened December 21, 1957. William Pahlmann (1900–1987) was a highly influential interior decorator who gained fame in creating audacious design for high society. In 1936, after his return from Parsons Paris School of Art and Design, his rooms at Lord and Taylor in New York brought him international attention among the interior design profession. In 1946 Pahlmann founded William Pahlmann Associates, continuing to design residential interiors but increasingly designing hotels, offices, and upscale retail stores such as Bonwit Teller and Tiffany and Co. His syndicated newspaper column, "A Matter of Taste," distributed three times a week by the Hall Syndicate from 1962 to 1973, played a major role in establishing the field of interior design in postwar America. His archives are held at the Hagley Museum and Library.

69. I applied this lesson when RA proposed a retrospective scheme for the Brasserie in the Seagram building, the entry of which is cut into the podium at Fifty-Third Street; I turned down the scheme on the grounds that it was not in Seagram's best interest (see Article 26); I proposed three architects and left the choice to them. The Brasserie, which RA still managed, was originally designed by Philip Johnson, but a fire in a ceiling duct put it out of commission in 1995. One of the architects proposed reinstalling Philip's scheme, which was never a strong design, but RA chose the forward-looking proposal of Diller + Scofidio, in which the art was integral and not applied as it had been before.

70. Mariani and von Bidder, *The Four Seasons*, 27.

71. *Philip Johnson Tapes,* 145.

72. Mariani and von Bidder, *The Four Seasons*, 33.

73. Ibid., 30.

74. Ibid.

75. Edison Avery Price (1918–1997), who had an intense, fey quality, almost that of the mad genius, worked in the studio

of Cleon Throckmorton in the 1940s helping Isamu Noguchi build sets for Martha Graham ballets, and eventually took over the operation of the studio. Buckminster Fuller's tensegrity mast shown at MoMA in 1959 was made in his studio. Price also made the ceilings for the Saidye Bronfman Centre, Montreal (Phyllis Lambert, architect, 1967). His obituary by Robert McG. Thomas, Jr., for the *New York Times,* published on October 17, 1997, described Price as "the inventive lighting master whose innovative fixture designs give minimalist modern interiors their unobtrusive glow and shed new hidden light on old masters and other museum art.... He was seventy-nine and widely recognized as the originator of the entire modern lighting consulting industry." See also Stanley Abercrombie, "Edison Price: His Name Is No Accident," *Architecture Plus* 1, no. 7 (August 1973): 34–43.

76. Mariani and von Bidder, *The Four Seasons,* 32. The authors also claim that Johnson first proposed silk curtains, which would have deteriorated quickly from exposure to the sun.

77. Restoration of the rooms, ongoing since 2009, continues. The architect in charge, Belmont Freeman, having identified the manufacturers of the chains, the Federal Chain Company of Providence, found that the company went out of business in the 1970s. The anodizing process requires three steps: First, the aluminum is dipped in a solution to oxidize it, which leaves it with a coating of aluminum oxide, which is porous; then it can be dipped into a dye solution. Last, the metal is immersed in boiling water, which fixes the dye. Looking at the curtains today, Freeman notes that the gold and copper colors dominate in the lower reaches of the curtains. The original mix was slightly different, but von Bidder bought out the company's remaining stock (some two thousand feet of chain), and all they had left was the gold and the copper, so years of replacing chain has altered the color mix. Belmont Freeman to PL, e-mail, May 10, 2010.

78. Quoted by Mariani and von Bidder, *The Four Seasons,* 33.

79. Bergdoll, *Karl Friedrich Schinkel,* 31.

80. Richard Lippold, "Sculpture: Richard Lippold, The Four Seasons: Collaboration for Elegance," *Progressive Architecture* 40, no. 12 (December 1959): 144.

81. Lippold sought to "repeat without redundancy the virtues of [Mies's] architecture, and so make an inseparable entity of the two." "I feel," he continued, "the sculpture would surely lose most of its meaning without the building. Unless this is so I have not succeeded." Ibid.

82. See S. H., "On and Off the Avenue: About the House," *New Yorker,* April 4, 1959, 132.

83. *Philip Johnson Tapes,* 145.

84. Mariani and von Bidder, *The Four Seasons,* 35.

85. He purchased his *Number Ten* (1950) for MoMA in 1952, making it the first Rothko to enter the permanent collection.

86. In the last few years, the shelter canopy of large, heavy leaves of the original seventeen-foot *Ficus decora* has been replaced by artificial foliage, owing to the difficulty of providing enough light for the plants to survive.

87. The lack of a strong masterwork in the Pool Room has become manifest in recent years; conscious of the deprivation, the restaurateurs have experimented with placing borrowed works on the south wall paneling, which tarnishes the room's architectural integrity.

88. Karl Linn, "Planting: Karl Linn, The Four Seasons: Collaboration for Elegance," *Progressive Architecture* 40, no. 12 (December 1959): 142.

89. Blake, "Conversation with Mies," 94.

CHAPTER 5.
ARCHITECTURE AND ART ALLIED

1. See *Business Buys American Art,* exh. cat. (New York: Whitney Museum of American Art, 1960); and *Directory of Corporate Art Collections,* ed. Shirley Reiff Howarth (Largo, FL: International Art Alliance, 1983), with revised editions. The *Directory* rarely provides dates for the acquisition of different works or groups of work within a collection.

2. French Impressionist and Postimpressionist collections included Cantor Fitzgerald Securities Corporation, New York, 1945, and Reader's Digest Association, Pleasantville, NY, 1950. Pre-Columbian art was collected by the Nasher Company, Dallas, 1950. Prehistoric, historic Amerindian, and Inuit ethnographic works were collected by Fayette Bank and Trust Co., Union Town, PA, 1957, and Herco, Inc., Hershey, PA, as of 1937.

3. Until Lincoln Center opened in the mid-1960s, Rockefeller Center, with its promenade and sunken plaza, as well as other public areas above- and belowground, was the only other major public open space in the city's commercial and social core. See chapter 6 and Epilogue in this volume on the development of private public spaces inspired by the example of Seagram.

4. Sir John Soane, *Description of the House and Museum on the North Side of Lincoln's Inn Fields, the Residence of Sir John Soane* (1835–36), "Exordium," vii, Library, Sir John Soane's Museum, London.

5. The lack of art allied to modernist buildings was a constant lament in postwar America. Some voices advocated "Pedestrians' sculpture," an idea advanced by Thomas B. Hess based on an expression coined by the sculptor Philip Pavia, who was a powerful force among the New York avant-garde.

6. J. Gordon Carr, architect, Seagram Internal Planning Office, to C. Isaacson, Joseph E. Seagram & Sons, Inc., September 16, 1957. The letter concerns building progress, after a tour of the building's second to ninth floors, concourses "A" and "C" inclusive. Records of the Seagram Curator's Office, FSB, box 134-007.

7. See *Vassar Miscellany News,* February 4, 1948, 3. The title of the exhibition, co-curated with Eve Borsook, was incorrectly published in the Conference Program as "Modern Design: Architecture and Advertising." Panelists included painter Ben Shahn and composer John Cage; other participants included playwright Irwin Shaw and dancer and choreographer Merce Cunningham. *Vassar Miscellany News,* February 25, 1948, 3. Also influential was the formidable Agnes Rindge Claflin's notoriously daunting course on modern art, and later I got to know better some of her fabulous circle, including Lincoln Kirstein and art dealer Kirk Askew. See Phyllis Lambert, "Kirstein's Circle: Cambridge, Hartford, New York, 1927–1931," in *Autonomy and Ideology: Positioning an Avant-Garde in America,* ed. Robert E. Somol (New York: Monacelli, 1997), 32–39. I met Kirstein in the 1950s with Philip Johnson, who was later to design Kirstein's New York State Theater at Lincoln Center, which opened in 1964.

8. PL to Borsook, August 1–2, 1955, 4, FPL, box 08-L-309. Nelson Rockefeller arrived in the studio with his wife led by Dorothea Speyer, sister of the Chicago architect and museum curator A. James Speyer. As I moved to leave, Brancusi urged me to stay. We drank champagne after the visitors left.

9. H. P. Roché to PL, August 13, 1955, author's translation, FPL, box 08-L-515. Henri-Pierre Roché (1879–1959) was an art collector, adviser, and dealer; a writer; and a guide for the American Industry Mission when it visited France. He received an award for his novel *Jules et Jim* at the age of seventy-four, and both this novel and *Les Deux Anglaises et le continent* were made into films by François Truffaut. The Harry Ransom Center at the University of Texas at Austin, holds his papers. I knew none of this history in the 1950s.

10. Roché to PL, September 1, 1955, FPL, box 08-L-515.

11. Roché to PL, November 16, 1955, FPL, box 08-L-515.

12. I do not recall discussing sculpture for plaza with Mies, which seems strange now, but at that time I was not aware of Mies as a collector or that he visited the galleries in New York with Gene Summers while working on Seagram. See Vivian Endicott Barnett, "The Architect as Art Collector," in *Mies in America,* ed. Phyllis Lambert (Montreal: Canadian Centre for Architecture, and New York: Whitney Museum of American Art and Harry N. Abrams, 2001), 90–131.

13. See "Vue d'atelier, les Coqs, vers 1941–1944," in *Brancusi Photographer: Photographs Introduced and Selected by Marielle Tabart and Isabelle Monod-Fontaine* (New York: Agrinde, 1979), 55.

14. Richard Lippold (1915–2002) had his first one-man show at the Willard Gallery in 1947. The contract, on the letterhead of the Willard Gallery in New York, "between Mr. Joseph E. Seagram [sic] and Richard Lippold" to construct "two pieces to hang in the Bar and Grill of the Seagram Building at 375 Park Avenue, N.Y.C, for the sum of: $40,000," was drawn up in February 1958 and signed on April 21, 1958. FPL, box 08-L-515. See "Richard Lippold Exhibition Checklist," in Curtis L. Carter, Jack W. Burnham, and Edward Lucie-Smith, *Richard Lippold Sculpture* (Milwaukee, WI: Patrick and Beatrice Haggerty Museum of Art, Marquette University, 1990), 37. The date of 1957 is confirmed in Richard Lippold, "Sculpture: Richard Lippold, The Four Seasons: Collaboration for Elegance," *Progressive Architecture* 40, no. 12 (December 1959), in which Lippold is quoted saying that he was asked "to consider the design and execution of two works . . . about a year and a half before its completion" (144).

15. Richard Lippold, transcript of testimony before the Board of Estimate Hearing on the Seagram Building, Plaza, Interiors and Four Seasons Restaurant, Calendar Nos. 40 and 41, January 25, 1990, New York, 42–44, Records of the Office of Facilities and Office Services, FSB, box 134-OF-004.

16. See John Mariani and Alex von Bidder, *The Four Seasons: A History of America's Premier Restaurant* (New York: Crown, 1994), 32.

17. The curtain is signed in the lower right corner "Picasso *Pinxit* 1919."

18. Nesta Macdonald, "Pablo's Curtain Call," *Observer,* November 2, 1986, 36–39. See also correspondence between Macdonald and PL, February and March 1994, FPL, box 08-L-550.

19. In London he made an increasing number of portraits; he sketched Olga many times, as well as Massine, Diaghilev, André Derain (designer of *La Boutique fantasque*), Edwin Evans (a music critic), Alfred Seligsburg (lawyer for the company's backer, Otto Kahn), Kahn himself, and the dancers Lydia Lopokova, Vera Nemtchinova, and Felix Fernandez, the Spanish flamenco dancer they brought to London to teach the company.

20. Museo Picasso, Málaga, Spain.

21. PL and John Richardson, telephone conversation, January 10, 2003. See also *A Life of Picasso: The Triumphant Years, 1917–1932* (New York: Alfred A. Knopf, 2007), in which Richardson wrote: "I am unable to agree with her identification of the figures in the curtain" (522n48).

22. Vladmir Polunin and Cyril W. Beaumont, eds., *The Continental Method of Scene Painting* (London: C. W. Beaumont, 1927), 55.

23. Sacheverell Sitwell is quoted in Richardson, *Life of Picasso,* 121.

24. Douglas Cooper, *Picasso Theatre* (London: Weidenfeld and Nicholson, 1967), 40. Cooper comments that Manuel de Falla's overture, which included trumpets and drums accompanied by the noise of heel-tapping, castanets, and lustily shouted "Olés," was composed during the last days of rehearsals in London.

25. Richardson, *Life of Picasso,* 121.

26. Three are in the collection of the Musée Picasso, MPP: 1661, 1660, 1630; a fourth belongs to the Picasso Estate, catalogued by the Online Picasso Project as OPP.19:283.

27. Musée Picasso, MPP: 1657.
28. Richardson, *Life of Picasso,* 121.
29. Cooper, *Picasso Theatre,* 40.
30. Roland Penrose, *Picasso: His Life and Work* (London: Victor Gollancz, 1958), 210. Pierre Daix considered *Parade* to be a rejection of Cubism; comparing the two curtains, Daix found in *Le Tricorne* the assertion of a stronger mastery of composition, and suggested that the ballet itself offered Picasso "a fine opportunity for inventiveness . . . using the occasion to produce a manifesto of sorts"; see Pierrre Daix, *Picasso, Life and Art,* trans. Olivia Emmet (New York: Icon Editions, 1993), 161, 169.
31. Cooper, *Picasso Theatre,* 42.
32. Richardson, *Life of Picasso,* 123. Daix considers the years 1917 to 1923 as the period of Picasso's "single driving determination." Whether it be classicism, classic Cubism, constructions, or ballets, "his ambition was to encompass and become the modern point of convergence of Poussin, Cézanne, and Ingres" (*Picasso, Life and Art,* 162).
33. Richardson, *Life of Picasso,* 123.
34. In 1953 S. L. Grigoriev, registrar of the Ballets Russes, recalled Diaghilev's decision: "'No, I must sell it. So will you please produce it . . . tomorrow? I'll do the cutting myself.' The 'cutting out' he referred to was what made the sale of the *Tricorne* picture possible; for it had been painted as a comparatively small panel in the center of a huge cloth. Diaghilev would have liked also to sell Picasso's curtain for *Parade*. . . . But the design in that case covered the whole expanse of [the cloth]; and no-one could be found to buy anything so vast." S. L. Grigoriev, *The Diaghilev Ballet, 1909–1929,* trans. Vera Bowen (Harmondsworth, UK: Penguin, 1960), 224; quoted in Richardson, *Life of Picasso,* 123. Reber was one of Paul Rosenberg's major clients. In 1929 Max Beckmann painted his portrait, titled *Dr. G. F. Reber,* now in the collection of the Wallraf-Richartz Museum in Cologne.
35. Barr declined, noting: "Phoned [Forest] Saturday 17th. Wouldn't give price on phone. Don't like piece—too large, too dry. Avoided interview. B." Handwritten note by Barr, c. January 15, 1948, Alfred H. Barr, Jr., Papers, "Picasso proposed acquisitions: c. 1945–c. 1949 correspondence," ser. 12, subseries VII.A, The Museum of Modern Art Archives, New York. I wish to thank Anya Domlesky for finding the Forest-Barr connection and for bringing together most of the documents pertaining to *Le Tricorne*.
36. See Léonide Massine to Monroe Wheeler, December 16, 1956, in which Massine refers to his earlier letter of November 7, 1956, on the same subject. FPL, box 08-L-515.
37. Alfred H. Barr to Philip Johnson, March 5, 1957, FPL, box 08-L-515.
38. Klaus G. Perls to Johnson, March 18, 1957, FPL, box 08-L-515.
39. PL to Perls, telegram, July 12, 1957, Perls Galleries Records, 1937–97, box 24, Archives of American Art, Smithsonian Institution.
40. PL to Perls, July 17, 1957. Perls Galleries Records, 1937–97, box 24.
41. Perls to PL, July 20, 1957, FPL, box 08-L-515.
42. "Ce rideau du *Tricorne* est de ma main et a été peint à Londres l'an 1919 Picasso/Cannes (A.M.)/le 20.2.1957."
43. Perls to PL, February 7, 1958. Perls Galleries Records 1937–97, box 24. The "certificate" is held in FPL, box 08-L-758.
44. See notation attached to abovementioned letter from Perls to Lambert, February 7, 1958, Perls Galleries Records 1937–97, box 24.
45. As recorded in the catalogue record of the Seagram Curator's Office, FPL, box 08-L-648.
46. Lambert to Picasso, undated [summer 1957] (draft, author's translation), FPL, box 08-L-515.
47. Johnson to Marie Cuttoli, January 3, 1958, FPL, box 08-L-515.
48. Mark Rothko, "Notes on the Seagram Mural Commission," in *Rothko: The Late Series,* ed. Achim Borchardt-Hume (London: Tate, 2008), 95. Kind thanks to the artist's son, Christopher Rothko, for providing a copy of the original notes.
49. Ibid. An editorial note on the same page assigns the date of 1960 to these reflections, as some of the sheets contain inventory lists related to selection of works for the Rothko retrospective at MoMA in 1961. This document has been ignored by those close to Rothko who have put forward the idea that the room was to be an employees' restaurant. See also James E. B. Breslin, *Mark Rothko: A Biography* (Chicago: University of Chicago Press, 1993), 375.
50. Sidney Janis to PL, June 6, 1958, FPL, box 08-L-811.
51. Breslin, *Mark Rothko,* 381.
52. Rothko, "Notes on the Seagram Mural Commission," 95.
53. John Fischer, "Mark Rothko: Portrait of the Artist as an Angry Man," *Harper's Magazine,* July 1970, 16; reprinted in *Writings on Art: Mark Rothko,* ed. Miguel López-Remiro (New Haven: Yale University Press, 2006), 130–38.
54. Michael Compton, "Mark Rothko: The Subjects of the Artist," in *Mark Rothko, 1903–1970* (London: The Tate Gallery, 1987), 60.
55. Breslin, *Mark Rothko,* 382.
56. Michael Compton, "Introduction to the Seagram Mural Project," in Thomas Kellein, *Mark Rothko: Kaaba in New York* (Basel: Kunsthalle, 1989), 15.
57. Arnold Glimcher, "Interview with Dan Rice," in ibid., 26.
58. Rothko, "Notes on the Seagram Mural Commission," 95.
59. Quoted in Breslin, *Mark Rothko,* 373.
60. Fischer, "Mark Rothko," 16–23.
61. Ibid., 16.
62. Ibid., 20.
63. Ibid.
64. Ibid., 22.
65. Ibid.
66. Mark Rothko, "A Symposium on How to Combine Architecture, Painting and Sculpture," MoMA, New York, March

19, 1951, published in *Interiors* 110, no. 10 (May 1951): 104; quoted in López-Remiro, *Writings on Art: Mark Rothko,* 74.

67. Ibid.

68. Rothko, "Notes on the Seagram Mural Commission," 95. Willem de Kooning remembered Rothko's happiness just after he had signed the contract for the Seagram murals: "I had never seen him so happy about his work. . . . The reason why he was happy—he made a contract; he was very careful. He made a contract so he could get out of it"; quoted in Breslin, *Mark Rothko,* 373.

69. Rothko, "Notes on the Seagram Mural Commission," 95.

70. Ibid.

71. Three of the images used (from left, the second, fourth, and fifth) are those in the Rothko Room at the Tate Modern in London, which correspond with the dimensions of the mezzanine walls. The others in the montage are held by the Kawamura Memorial Museum of Art, Sakura City, Japan (first from left), and the National Gallery of Art, Washington, DC (third from left).

72. "Instructions for Exhibition at the Whitechapel Art Gallery, 1961; Suggestions from Mr. Rothko Regarding Installation of His Paintings," Whitechapel Art Gallery Archive, London, in *Rothko: The Late Series,* ed. Achim Borchardt-Hume (London: Tate, 2008), 96–97. See also photographs of installations of the Seagram murals at: Tate Modern, London, 2008; Kawamura Memorial Museum of Art, Sakura City, 2008; and National Gallery of Art, Washington, DC, 2005, in ibid., 98–99.

73. In the MoMA catalogue of 1961, curator Peter Selz wrote: "Like much of Rothko's work, these murals really seem to ask for a special place apart, a kind of sanctuary, where they may perform what is essentially a sacramental function." Peter Selz, *Mark Rothko* (New York: Museum of Modern Art, 1961), 14. See also Breslin, *Mark Rothko,* 376.

74. I had met Cuttoli (1879–1973) two years earlier through Dorothy Liebes, the preeminent textile designer and weaver of American modernism. See Virginia Gardner Troy, "Marie Cuttoli: Patron of Modern Textiles," in *Textile Narratives + Conversations: Textile Society of America 10th Biennial Symposium 2006,* CD-ROM (Earleville, MD: Textile Society of America, 2007).

75. Johnson to Cuttoli, January 3, 1958, FPL, box 08-L-515. See Dorothy Liebes Morin to PL, December 5, 1955, FPL, box 08-L-515.

76. Aimé Maeght, to Cuttoli, March 11, 1958, FPL, box 08-L-515. Aimé Maeght of Galerie Maeght, Paris, was Miró's dealer and adviser, or "Marchand-conseiller," asking them to put into writing their conditions for the commission of seven tapestries.

77. Cuttoli to Johnson, January 11, 1958, FPL, box 08-L-515. I acquired the two Mirós she had mentioned, plus a third one, *Composition,* for Seagram. Janis to PL, May 9, 1958, FPL, box 08-L-472.

78. Contract on the letterhead of the Willard Gallery, New York, between Mr. [sic] Joseph E. Seagram and Richard Lippold to construct "two pieces to hang in the Bar and Grill of the Seagram Building at 375 Park Avenue, N.Y.C.," February 20, 1958, FPL, box 08-L-515.

79. Sidney Janis Gallery, New York, to PL (with copy to Mark Rothko), on behalf of the artist, to confirm the details of the commission, following his conversation with Philip Johnson, June 6, 1958, FPL, box 08-L-811.

80. Minutes of the Internal Planning Committee, November 19, 1957, CSC, acc. 2126, RG 2, ser. II, box 225.

81. The White Horse Tavern, named after the same famous Scottish pub as one of Seagram's brands, was installed on the seventh floor of the Seagram building. Completely outside my purview, it had originated as a traveling exhibition created by a Seagram-affiliated wine company, Browne-Vintners, whose eighteenth- and nineteenth-century tavern artifacts and furniture consisted of pewter measures and plates, pottery ale mugs, flasks, bottles, and decanters, candle boxes and sconces, gateway tables and early Georgian benches, as well as related prints. The tavern served as a meeting place and was used for staff functions. I was also completely unaware that the CEO of Paul Masson Vineyards, another division of Joseph E. Seagram & Sons, Inc., had commissioned his neighbor Ansel Adams in 1960 to make a photographic document titled *The Story of a Winery.* Some thirty of these images were shown at the Smithsonian Institution, and the exhibition traveled between 1963 and 1966.

82. PL to Pierre Bernard, June 11, 1957, referring to the collection *l'art de boire:* "Seagram is moving (into building) on 15 November [1957] and we await lists and photographs of objects so we can begin ordering them." FPL, box 08-L-515. "Itemized receipts of payment," Pierre G. Bernard, antiquarian, Paris, December 9, 1957, FPL, box 08-L-515. The objects dating principally from the seventeenth and eighteenth centuries include wine containers and drinking vessels, labels, corkscrews, alcohol weights, and an English edition of André Jullien's *Manuel du sommelier* (London: W. Anderson, 1825). An invoice of November 14, 1957, records the purchase of prints depicting the history of distilling from Denis Diderot's *Encyclopédie.* See Historical Presentations and Research to Seagram Distillers Company, invoice, November 14, 1957, for a collection on the history of distilling, including forty prints, as well as books, pamphlets, and documents, 3 pp., FPL, box 08-L-515.

83. PL to William Lieberman, December 27, 1957, FPL, box 08-L-515. I mention that Herbert Matter had been provided with a set of about thirty photographs of the process. Matter was then preparing the mural of the distilling process for the fifth-floor reception area.

84. "To recapitulate our conversation of this afternoon, we agreed that [Reginald Murray] Pollack . . . will be commissioned to make prints connected with the distilling and wine

industries for the Seagram building." Ibid. See attestation of originality of twenty prints signed Reginald Pollack, Paris, April 14, 1958, FPL, box 08-L-515. A Memorandum from Jane Perin of my office to Cohen notes that Pollack was paid on May 2, 1958. See my memorandum, also dated December 27, 1957, on "Last minute directives," which references offices to be paneled in English oak and plants to be ordered for different types of offices and workspaces, and includes a "Special note to Murray Cohen," in which I asked him to explain that although they would not be received for two months, prints had been "commissioned for Seagram by six leading print makers . . . working especially for Seagram because of the building, etc. etc." In this same memo I confirmed that the program of commissioned prints (discussed with Lieberman that day) had been approved and that we were also acquiring "prints already in existence by [André] Masson and [Antonio] Frasconi," including Frasconi's woodcut *The Winery* (c. 1955). FPL, box 08-L-515.

85. PL to Nelly van Doesburg, April 9, 1958, and van Doesburg to PL, April 14, 1958, FPL, box 08-L-515. The tapestries measure, respectively: six feet, six and three-quarters inches, by seven feet, two and a half inches; six feet, six and three-quarters inches, by eight feet, one and a half inches; and seven feet, ten and a half inches, by nine feet, ten inches. I had met Nelly at a New York party given by Frederick Kiesler.

86. At the end of 1974, Seagram had eight tapestries and fourteen wall hangings and decorative carpets valued at $118,000 by Christie's. Insurance valuation prepared by Christie's for Joseph E. Seagram & Sons, Inc., December 18, 1974, Records of the Seagram Curator's Office, FSB, box 134-007.

87. LeWitt had initially proposed drawings but chose "to make silkscreens because of the intensity of the color, and the graphic quality possible in the medium." Naomi Spector to Noel Manfre, May 17, 1975, FPL, box 08-L-518; attached are two manuscript pages by Sol LeWitt, one on the scheme and edition of "Sol LeWitt/Lines & Color/1975," composed of "all combinations of line (straight, not straight, and broken) and space using black, white, yellow, red and blue," the other showing layout for each wall. Ibid.

88. See appendix 2, "Seagram Plaza Installations and Seagram Gallery Exhibitions," in this volume.

89. I commissioned the mural and also the Seagram seal, which Matter transposed to form a cast bronze sculpture mounted on the fourth wall of the area, behind the reception desk leading to the top executive offices along Park Avenue. See PL to Herbert Matter, August 20, 1957, FPL, box 08-L-515. Matter was already working on a design for the Seagram seal by this date. The mural is now owned by Aby Rosen of RFR Holding, the realty company that purchased the Seagram building in 2000, and is currently installed at Four Stamford Plaza in Stamford, CT. It is one of only two painted by Matter; the other was created for the Grosse Pointe Public Library, Grosse Point, MI. The whereabouts of the seal are unknown.

90. See invoices from Galerie Chalette, Peter H. Deitsch, and Saidenberg Gallery, to PL, April 18–June 18, 1958, providing titles of lithographs and etchings, with their individual prices; FPL, box 08-L-515. In a 2002 inventory of Seagram collections, at least forty-nine graphic works dating from the late 1940s to the 1950s were recorded. See Barry M. Winiker's "Inventory of art in the [Seagram] collection," as described by cover letter dated October 16, 2002, FPL, box 08-L-826. Winiker's inventory lists a total of 293 graphic works. The posters eventually acquired were listed in Winiker's inventory under "New York (Posters)."

91. In the 1970s and 1980s the major acquisitions made by the Seagram curator consisted of portfolios and multiple prints by the artists Richard Estes, Sol LeWitt, Frank Stella, Roy Lichtenstein, and Donald Judd. The focus then shifted to "Drawings by Sculptors."

92. See list of "Art on Display at Seagram Building" on fourth, fifth, and thirty-seventh floors, and the amount paid for each work, attached to which is a list of "Galleries in New York City" on which is noted by hand "job file 3/30/59." The page dealing with art on the thirty-seventh floor is titled "Philip Johnson–Phyllis Lambert Offices." Thanks to the Department of Architecture and Design, Museum of Modern Art, for supplying this document, copy now held in BSRC.

93. Designers and manufacturers of executive office furnishings, except as noted in the text, were as follows: executive desks with leather tops of different colors, designed by Jens Risom, were produced by Knoll Associates, with input from Philip Johnson; Risom and Knoll also produced ebonized oak desks and credenzas. An example of the latter, as well as the Eero Saarinen desk chair together with Mies van der Rohe's "Brno" armchair and "Barcelona" chair, are seen in fig. 126. I selected the Hans Wegner side chair for the executive offices because of the refined sculptural quality of their wood frame (see fig. 125). Low seating was by Knoll. Some examples of furniture from the Seagram executive offices are in the collection of the Montreal Museum of Fine Arts, gift of Phyllis Lambert.

94. Enthusiasm for printmaking in the United States was stimulated by the formations of master printing houses, notably, on the East Coast, Universal Art Editions (ULAE), founded by Tatyana Grossman in West Islip, NY; and on the West Coast, Gemini G.E.L. and Tamarind Lithograph Workshop, founded in Los Angeles, respectively, in 1965 and 1960.

95. Olga Raggio (1925–2009) was at that time assistant curator of Western European arts at the Metropolitan Museum of Art and required permission to act for a collector outside the museum. The director of the museum, James Rorimer, in this case encouraged her, since assuming the responsibility for forming, managing, documenting, and installing a

collection of decorative arts was considered training for a young curator. On her activity for the collection, see FPL, box 08-L-515. See PL to Derek C. Davis, April 29, 1961 (drafted by Olga Raggio), and Raggio to PL, March 27, 1966, FPL, box 08-L-516.

96. Olga Raggio compiled and annotated two catalogue files on the collection: "The Seagram Collection of European and American Drinking Vessels—Catalogue File," typescript, n.d., and "The Seagram Collection of European and American Drinking Vessels and Related Objects—Inventory File," typescript, n.d. Both are held with Records of the Seagram Curator's Office, FSB, box 134-045. The illustrated catalogue *Ancienne Collection Seagram: Verrerie et objets d'art européens* (Paris: Artcurial, 2005), documents Seagram's European drinking vessels, which were sold at the Hôtel Dassault, Paris, on March 15, 2005, FPL, box 08-L-722.

97. The position was first held by a member of Seagram's staff, Noel Manfre, from 1972 to 1977. The immediate mandates were to manage and document acquisitions, to place artworks in the new offices in consultation with the occupants, to oversee the conservation of works in Seagram collections, and to monitor the artwork belonging to Seagram installed in the Four Seasons Restaurant. By the time Manfre was succeeded by art historian Carla Ash, in 1977, the curator's responsibilities intensified. Ash worked directly with acquisitions for and the holdings of Seagram's offices in Connecticut, Illinois, and California, managing loans from the collections to various museum exhibitions, making small donations to arts organizations, and managing new collections. As curator, she was also responsible for exhibitions in the Seagram Gallery from 1977, the majority of which she curated, and coordinating sculpture proposed for the Seagram plaza and the installation of the works agreed to.

98. See C. Joseph Blunt to Pierre Apraxine, August 6, 1973, which refers to an agreement between Seagram and MoMA drawn up on February 16, 1973, FPL, box 08-L-518.

99. Following Apraxine's experience working with the Seagram collection, in 1977, he became director of the Gilman Paper Company Collection and thus, ironically, competed with Seagram and the nascent CCA in the acquisition of photographs.

100. Richard Pare, "Introduction," *The Seagram Collection of Photographs, April 25–26, 2003, New York* (New York: Phillips, de Pury & Luxembourg, 2003), 4. Pare refers to a tendency that inspired the 1975 exhibition *New Topographics: Photographs of a Man-Altered Landscape* at the George Eastman House, which was reconstituted as *New Topographics*, co-organized by the Center for Creative Photography at the University of Arizona and the George Eastman House International Museum of Photography and Film in Rochester, NY, in 2009–12; an accompanying publication by the same title was copublished by Steidl Publishers and the Center for Creative Photography in cooperation with the George Eastman House, also in 2009.

101. Phyllis Lambert, "The Record of Buildings as Evidence," in *Court House: A Photographic Document,* ed. Richard Pare (New York: Horizon, 1978), 10. I have edited the text slightly.

102. Statement by Richard Pare projecting the scope and intent of the United States County Court House Project for Joseph E. Seagram & Sons, Ltd., November 4, 1974, 2, FPL, box 08-L-354. Approximately six thousand negatives, seven thousand contact proofs, and some eight thousand prints were produced.

103. Edited by Richard Pare, conceived and directed by Phyllis Lambert, with contributions by Phyllis Lambert, Richard Pare, The Honorable Paul C. Reardon, Calvin Trillin, and Henry-Russell Hitchcock & William Seale; and the photographers of *Court House,* Harold Allen, Lewis Baltz, Richard Bartlett, Douglas Baz, Caldecot Chubb, William Clift, Jim Dow, Frank Gohlke, Allen Hess, Pirkle Jones, Lewis Kostiner, Ellen Land-Weber, Patrick Linehan, Nicholas Nixon, Ira Nowinski, Tod Papageorge, Richard Pare, Stephen Shore, Bob Thall, Jerry Thompson, Charles H. Traub, Paul Vanderbilt, Laura Volkerding, Geoff Winningham (New York: Horizon, 1978).

104. Comprising two sets of 120 photographs each, the exhibitions were organized by the American Federation of Arts in collaboration with the National Trust for Historic Preservation. The first of these was displayed at Colonial Williamsburg, March 10–April 16, 1978, in connection with the Second National Conference for the Judiciary held in Williamsburg and attended by some five hundred judicial leaders, including the chief justices of all major English-speaking countries and all the states and territories. Subsequently, thirty-two venues across North America presented the exhibition, including the Art Institute of Chicago, the Amon Carter Museum of Western Art at Fort Worth, Texas, the San Francisco Art Institute in California, and, in Canada, the University of Calgary, Alberta.

105. Gene Thornton, "Photography View; A Strong Sense of Grass-Roots America," *New York Times,* July 18, 1976.

106. Wolf von Eckardt, "The Sites of Justice: A Sweeping Photographic Documentary," *Washington Post,* May 10, 1978.

107. Seagram fully catalogued the documents collected, including the photographers' correspondence and the master prints and negatives donated to the Library of Congress in 1980. The Dunlap Society presented prints of all unique negatives that were presented in a 180-microform edition, *County Court Houses of the United States: The Seagram County Court House Archives and Other Photographic Collections in the Library of Congress,* 2 vols. (Essex, NY: Dunlap Society, 1981).

108. *Drawings by Sculptors* was at the Montreal Museum of Fine Arts, May 3–June 10, 1984. It then traveled to the Vancouver Art Gallery, August 10–September 23, 1984; the Nickle Arts Museum, Calgary, October 5–November 18, 1984; Seagram Gallery, New York, December 12, 1984–February 10, 1985,

109. and February 20–April 19, 1985; and London Regional Art Gallery, London, ON, May 24–June 30, 1985.
109. Richard Pare, untitled document on the fifth *Court House* exhibition, October 5, 1976, FPL, box 08-L-519.
110. Richard Pare, "After Court House," October 20, 1978, 2, FPL, box 08-L-519.
111. With the graphic designer Massimo Vignelli, Glaeser prepared a maquette for an elegant little publication that was, unfortunately, never realized. The CCA Archives holds the maquette together with the texts by the curators. FPL, box 08-L-190.
112. See William H. Whyte, *The Social Life of Small Urban Spaces* (Washington, DC: Conservation Foundation, 1980), 69. The film has been digitized and is held in the archives of the Project for Public Spaces, New York.
113. See Carla Ash, Exhibition Handout, Records of the Seagram Curator's Office, FSB, box 134-023.
114. A. D. Coleman, "Images of Faded Times Square Theaters Summon Up Recollections of Another Era," *New York Observer,* January 28, 1991.
115. Howard Thompson, "Going Out Guide: Oasis on Park," *New York Times,* August 2, 1979.
116. John Russell, "Art: Collective Paradoxes for the Summer Season," *New York Times,* June 20, 1980. Martha Beck, who founded the remarkable Drawing Center in Soho in 1977, curated numerous exhibitions in the early years of the Seagram Gallery. See appendix 2, "Seagram Plaza Installations and Seagram Gallery Exhibitions," in this volume.
117. Richard F. Shepard, "Going Out Guide: Spaces," *New York Times,* August 30, 1982.
118. Ibid.
119. Frank O'Hara, "Personal Poem," in *Lunch Poems* (San Francisco: City Lights Books, 1964), 32. I thank Brian Hatton for bringing this poem to my attention.
120. PL to Borsook, August 1–2, 1955, 3–4.
121. The montage is held in the Mies van der Rohe Archive at MoMA.
122. PL to Edgar M. Bronfman, April 30, 1969, FPL, box 08-L-518.
123. Olga Gueft, "The Ballplayer on the Plaza," *Interiors Magazine* 124 (July 1965): 59.
124. Ibid.
125. See *Boston Herald Traveler,* November 10, 1968; the *Indianapolis Star* reported that "its shipment to New York is sponsored by the Chilean Education Ministry and the International Fund for the Preservation of Ancient Monuments," November 10, 1968; articles on the Easter Island head from New York papers include: "Head's Up on Park Av.," *New York Post,* October 21, 1968, which included a photograph; Grace Glueck, "5-Ton Head from Easter Island Is Put on a Pedestal," *New York Times,* October 22, 1968, including a photograph; and "A Big, Old Head Makes the Park Avenue Scene," *New York Daily News,* October 22, 1968, also including a photograph. Articles appeared during October and November 1968 in major newspapers across the United States, including the *Washington Daily News, Chicago Tribune, Chicago Sun-Times, Boston Herald Traveler,* Annapolis, MD, *Capital,* Eau Claire, WI, *Leader,* and *Fresno Bee.* Records of the Seagram Curator's Office, FSB, 134-026.
126. See appendix 2, "Seagram Plaza Installations and Seagram Gallery Exhibitions," in this volume, which gives the chronology for sculpture installations on Seagram plaza.
127. Roberta Smith, "Richard Long," *New York Times,* April 28, 2000. In conjunction with the plaza installation, Carla Ash, curator of the Seagram collections, mounted the exhibition *Richard Long: Photography and Text Works, 1987–1988,* in the Seagram Gallery. Records of the Seagram Curator's Office, FSB, box 134-028.
128. Ash to PL, e-mail, January 12, 2006, BSRC. Ash wrote: "I had a budget of $5,000 per installation which mainly went toward paying the engineer Seagram hired to study the safety of the installation plans and work with the artist to make any necessary adjustments and, for the more difficult pieces, to pay for him to be on site during the installation. Rarely, if ever, did any money actually go to the artist. His expenses were paid by his gallery, and in some cases by the artist himself or, I suspect, a private patron. I remember that the Heizer installation, for instance, cost well over $100,000 and Seagram did not pay for any of it, including the engineer."
129. Lynn Langway and Mary Rourke, "Corporations: The New Medicis," *Newsweek,* November 15, 1976, 95.
130. I purchased this photograph for the CCA collection. Made with a 35mm camera at the corner of Fifty-Second Street looking north, it derives from the Seagram Collection and sold at the auction *The Seagram Collection of Photographs, April 25–26, 2003, New York* (New York: Phillips, de Pury & Luxembourg, 2003), illustrated on p. 31 of the catalogue.
131. William H. Whyte, *The Social Life of Small Urban Spaces* (Washington, DC: Conservation Foundation, 1980), 14; Whyte, *The Organization Man* (New York: Simon and Schuster, 1956).
132. Jerold S. Kayden, *Privately Owned Public Space: The New York Experience* (New York: New York City Department of City Planning and Municipal Art Society of New York, 2000), 44–45, table 1.
133. Whyte, *Social Life of Small Urban Spaces,* 14. The high economic benefit in comparison with the cost of the plazas, and the lineup of three continuous blocks between Forty-Seventh and Fiftieth Streets on the west side of Sixth Avenue, which resulted in a windswept stretch of the city, motivated the reform of the 1961 Zoning Resolution. See Kayden, *Privately Owned Public Space,* 16, 45, 90.
134. William H. Whyte, "The Best Street Life in the World: Why Shmoozing, Smooching, Noshing, Ogling Are Getting Better All the Time," *New York,* July 15, 1974, 27.
135. This would become part of the new Zoning Resolution of 1975.

136. William H. Whyte in conversation with PL, quoted in Phyllis Lambert and Ludwig Glaeser, "The Seagram Plaza: Its Design and Use," undated typescript prepared for the 1977 exhibition by the same name, curated by Lambert in collaboration with Glaeser, p. [9], FPL, box 08-L-190.
137. Whyte, *Social Life of Small Urban Spaces,* 50.
138. Ibid., 60.
139. Ibid., 63.
140. William H. Whyte, "Please, Just a Nice Place to Sit," *New York Times,* December 3, 1972.

CHAPTER 6.
IRONIES IN THE PUBLIC LIFE OF ARCHITECTURE

Note: This chapter is based on a lecture entitled "Ironies in the Public Life of Architecture: The Seagram Building, 1954–1958," delivered January 19, 2006, on acceptance of the Vincent J. Scully Prize at the National Building Museum in Washington, DC. A related lecture, "The Social, Esthetic, Cultural, and Financial Significance of 'Wasted' Space: The Seagram Building, 1954–58," was delivered on November 9, 2006, as the Second Annual Eleanore Pettersen Lecture at the Irwin S. Chanin School of Architecture of the Cooper Union.

1. Lewis Mumford, "The Lesson of the Master," *New Yorker,* September 13, 1958, 141.
2. William H. Jordy, "Seagram Assessed," *Architectural Review* 124, no. 743 (December 1958): 376.
3. The City Planning Commission was formed between 1934 and 1935, in the first years of the administration of Mayor Fiorello La Guardia (1934–45). Initiated by revision of the 1936 City Charter, it was financially dependent on the Board of Estimate of the City of New York.
4. The Zoning Resolution of 1916 was enacted after the Equitable Building, rising forty-two stories without a setback, ignited concerns about the loss of light and air in the streets of lower Manhattan. Remarkably in parallel, Seagram, in turn, inspired the 1961 revision of the 1916 zoning law: similarly, it rose straight from the ground plane but was set back from the sidewalk. In 1926 the Supreme Court in *Village of Euclid v. Ambler* recognized that zoning tied to a comprehensive plan is an appropriate extension of the community's authority to pass laws related to protecting the public health, safety, morals, and general welfare.
5. Highlights of Wagner's administration include the institution of the Community Board system for neighborhood representation; the establishment of New York University; the enactment of landmark preservation legislation; the expansion of public housing stock for poor and middle-class residents; and the expansion of the hospital system.
6. Voorhees Walker Smith & Smith, *Zoning New York City: A Proposal for a Zoning Resolution for the City of New York Submitted to the City Planning Commission,* August 1958, 128.
7. Ibid. Similarly, see "Bonuses for Building Area Increase as a Reward for Building of Plazas (Introduced to the World of Zoning by the Seagram Building of 1958), Arcade Spaces and Other Public Amenities Increased the FAR [Floor Area Ratio]," http://www.in-arch.net/NYC/nycadd.html. See the website for the New York City Department of City Planning/Zoning-Zoning History, http://www.nyc.gov/html/dcp/html/zone/zonehis.shtml.
8. Voorhees et al., *Zoning New York City,* 128.
9. N.Y. Supreme Court, App. Div., 1st Dept., Brief of Petitioner-Appellant, undated [c. fall 1962], in the matter of Joseph E. Seagram & Sons, Inc., Petitioner-Appellant, v. The Tax Commission of the City of New York, Respondent, 25, New York State Library, copy in BSRC.
10. N.Y. Supreme Court, App. Div., 1st Dept., Respondent's Brief, December 19, 1962, 27, New York State Library, copy in BSRC.
11. Cited in ibid., 21–22. Two years later, the court noted: "Since this practice [of erecting prestige buildings] is becoming a common feature of urban areas, such investment has ceased to be idiosyncratic and is undoubtedly translatable into market value terms." Court of Appeals, State of N.Y., "Petitioner's Contentions," in Respondents' Brief, March 17, 1964, 8, New York State Library, copy in BSRC.
12. N.Y. Supreme Court, App. Div., 1st Dept., Respondent's Brief, December 19, 1962, 4.
13. Ibid., 4–5.
14. Ibid., 72.
15. N.Y. Supreme Court, App. Div., Reply Brief of Petitioner-Appellant, in late December 1962 or January 1963, 8, New York State Library, copy in BSRC.
16. Judge Aaron Steuer wrote the opinion of the court on the issues of land value and tenant improvements as an expense item. Judges Breitel, Earger, and Valente concurred with his opinion on these two issues, and Judge Stevens concurred as a result. Judge Steuer's opinion also treated the issue of building value. Court of Appeals, State of N.Y., Respondents' Brief, March 17, 1964, 5.
17. "New York Courts Uphold Tax on Quality," *Architectural Forum* 118, no. 5 (May 1963): 5, 7.
18. Steuer quoted in Edith Evans Asbury, "Seagram Tower to Appeal on Tax," *New York Times,* May 17, 1963.
19. Court of Appeals, State of N.Y., Respondents' Brief, March 17, 1964, 9–10.
20. Counselor at law Timothy T. More finds the case to be interesting from a legal perspective, given the legal issues that were raised, "because the facts made it difficult for the judges to agree on the legal reasoning to support their decisions and because of the (generally misinformed) publicity regarding the decisions." Timothy T. More to PL, memoran-

dum, August 19, 2010, *Building Seagram* Research Collection, CCA. More also commented: "Seagrams [*sic*] achieved a huge public relations coup because of the wording of the lower court decision which critics could read as imposing a tax on quality and the plaza and because of the reporting that the final decision was 4–3, inferring that there was a strong dissent." More to PL, e-mail, August 3, 2010, BSRC.

21. Peter Collins wrote that the three judges' dissent was on a point of law. This was to the effect that it was "erroneous to consider the cost of construction as prima facie evidence of the value of a newly-erected structure, when that structure was built especially for prestige and advertising value as well as for the headquarters of its owner." Peter Collins, *Architectural Judgement* (Montreal: McGill-Queen's University Press, 1971), 199. Collins, professor of architecture at McGill, studied law at Yale University to research his book. Thanks to Robert Graham for this reference.

22. Court of Appeals, State of N.Y., "Petitioner's Contentions" in Respondents' Brief, March 17, 1964, 12–13.

23. Ibid., 13.

24. Ibid.

25. Court of Appeals, State of N.Y., Respondents' Brief, March 17, 1964; the argument is succinctly summarized in the table of contents.

26. The lawyers of the Tax Commission of the City of New York argued that cost was a better approach, since the building was new and using this capitalized-income method could very well result in an assessed value of $21 million if one used a rent for Seagram's space and the Four Seasons Restaurant, which reflected the unusually high cost of the leasehold improvements. The courts consistently added $3 million to the $14 million that Seagram asserted was the capitalized income value, on the grounds that certain claimed expenses should be disallowed. As to the difference between the $17 million and the $21 million, the majority opinion said that Seagram had not correctly assessed the rent for its space because its name was associated with the building and naming rights would ordinarily result in a higher rent.

27. More to Phyllis Lambert, e-mail, August 23, 2010, BSRC.

28. The Fine Arts Federation of New York was composed of: the National Academy of Design, Architectural League of New York, National Institute for Architectural Education, National Sculpture Society, National Society of Mural Painters, Brooklyn Chapter of the American Institute of Architects, Associates of the Art Commission, Inc., New York Chapter of the American Society of Landscape Architects, New York State Chapter of the American Institute of Interior Designers, and American Watercolor Society.

29. Court of Appeals, State of N.Y., Brief of *Amici Curiae,* March 16, 1964, 2, prepared by attorney Paul Windels as part of the case involving Joseph E. Seagram & Sons, Inc., and the Tax Commission of the City of New York; New York State Library, copy in BSRC.

30. Ibid., 4.

31. Court of Appeals, State of N.Y., Respondents' Brief in Reply to Brief of *Amici Curiae,* April 24, 1964, New York State Library, copy in BSRC. The brief clearly states with explanations: (1) the Appellate Division did not adopt a novel method of assessment; (2) the alleged "excess cost" was not incurred for "aesthetic" reasons; and (3) the Appellate Division did not create a new classification of "prestige buildings."

32. Ibid., 4.

33. "Seagram Building Denied Tax Credit by Appeals Court," *New York Times,* June 11, 1964.

34. More to PL, memorandum, August 19, 2010.

35. "N. Y. Court Upholds Tax on Seagram Tower," *Architectural Forum* 121, no. 1 (July 1964): 5. In the words of the Supreme Court: "The building as a whole bearing the name of its owner includes a real property value not reflected in commercial rental income." Cited in Court of Appeals, State of N.Y., Respondents' Brief, March 17, 1964, 6–8.

36. "By 1964 when the decision was written, the minority opinion could say with some assurance that prestige buildings with plazas were becoming the norm. Indeed, a discernible trend in modern prestige building, for at least a quarter of a century, may make construction to the building line an inadequate improvement—economically. Exclusively utilitarian construction may produce more 'rentable' space, but not more valuable space." Timothy T. More, "An Assessment of the Seagram Building" (unpublished paper, Brown University, 2003), "Appendix," 2, FPL, box 08-L-804. More noted that, as reported in the press, the four-to-three decision of the court of appeals concerned only the approach to be taken but that the judgment against Seagram was unanimous. In his "Memorandum to File re: Seagrams [*sic*] Building Tax Appeal," April 25, 2003, quoting Seagram & Sons, Inc., against Tax Commission of the City of New York, 238 N.Y.S. 2d 228, 1963, 2, FPL, box 08-L-804.

37. See http://www.nyc.gov/html/dof/html/property/property_val_estimate.shtml under Finance, Property, Estimating Market Value.

38. A half century later it has been noted that "the ultimate irony is that Seagram not only made an acceptable rental return on its extraordinary expenditures in acquiring the site and constructing the building, but also realized a great marketing return on its investment and that the critics uniformly continue to believe incorrectly that the Assessor and the courts treated Seagram unfairly. [Bronfman] made a bold and brilliant decision in building and marketing such an extraordinary building—indeed, in seeing that a great work of architecture could advance the reputation of Seagrams [*sic*] perhaps better than anything else the company could do." More to PL, e-mail, August 3, 2011, BSRC. "The artistic merits and landmark status of the Seagram Building continue to make it a desirable rental. In addition, the

company's boost in recognition and reputation that directly resulted from the construction of the building cannot be overstated.... Bronfman made one of the better decisions of his career." Eli Bronfman, "A Timely Landmark: A Contextual History of the Seagram Building" (unpublished paper, Williams College, 2011), 9, BSRC.

39. Peter Kihss, "'Palace' Is Slated for Penn Station," *New York Times,* June 8, 1955, quoted in Hilary Ballon, *New York's Pennsylvania Stations,* with a photo essay by Norman McGrath and an essay by Marilyn Jordan Taylor (New York: W. W. Norton, 2002), 96.

40. Ballon, *New York's Pennsylvania Stations,* 96.

41. Because of its enormity, Penn Station remains symbolic, but Barry Bergdoll has made a technically precise point: "It is often said that the fact that the destruction of Penn Station gave rise to the founding of the NYC Landmarks Preservation Commission is a myth, it was actually the Brokaw Mansion on Fifth Avenue and 79th Street." Reader's notes on first draft of the manuscript for this book, received May 26, 2010, BSRC.

42. Ada Louise Huxtable, "How to Kill a City," *New York Times,* May 5, 1963.

43. "Kill Him, but Save the Scalp," *New York Times,* March 21, 1962.

44. "How to Ban Architecture," *Architectural Forum* 118, no. 5 (May 1963): 97.

45. "A Blow for Architecture," *New York Times,* June 13, 1964.

46. "Beauty and the Beast," *Newsweek,* June 10, 1963, 75.

47. "Tax on Beauty," *Reader's Digest,* September 1963, 9.

48. This is the language printed in an ad in the *Tribune* of December 15, 1964, announcing the upcoming piece by Anthony Bailey, "Seagram Besieged: The Ugly Tax on Beauty," *New York Herald Tribune,* December 20, 1964.

49. "Why Tax Quality?" comprising five letters to the editor published in *Architectural Forum* 119, no. 1 (July 1963): 17. The letters offer opinions on the assessment of real estate tax on the Seagram building. Neill Smith wrote, "The decision to establish a new tax category for prestige buildings such as Seagram's [sic] in one stroke wipes out 100 years of effort for city betterment," and Mrs. John T. O'Hara asked, "If revenue must be obtained by taxing an intangible such as beauty or quality, why not tax some of Seagram's neighbors for their *lack* of quality, elegance, etc.?"

50. Richard Stanley, "Alice in Wonderland," *Real Estate Forum* 18 (June 1963): 3.

51. Harry E. Rodman, "The Seagram Building and Our Tax Laws," *Progressive Architecture* 44, no. 12 (December 1963): 7.

52. "Seagram's Bet on Elegance," *Architectural Forum* 109, no. 1 (July 1958): 66–67. The article showed that Seagram was not only renting very fast; it was 90 percent rented at the end of May 1958. In addition, it commanded rents well above those of "ordinary" buildings; at Seagram, space was being rented at $7 to $8.30 a square foot as compared with $5 to $5.20 a square foot in "ordinary" buildings.

53. The notion of "highest and best use" is a concept used in land-use valuation and real estate appraisal. It was commonly used during the 1980s, at which time there was a considerable literature on the subject in the fields of economics and finance as well as real estate development. The literature was founded on the theories of prominent economists, including the political economics of David Ricardo and the spatial economics of Johann Heinrich von Thünen. See Mark G. Dotzour et al., "Highest and Best Use: The Evolving Paradigm," *Journal of Real Estate Research* 5, no. 1 (1996): 17–32.

54. The Model Cities Program was authorized under President Lyndon B. Johnson in November 1966 by the Demonstration Cities and Metropolitan Development Act of 1966. The initiative created a new program at the Department of Housing and Urban Development (HUD) that was intended to improve coordination of existing urban programs and provide additional funds for local plans. The program's initial goals emphasized comprehensive planning, involving not only rebuilding but also rehabilitation, social service delivery, and citizen participation. In 1969, the Nixon administration changed course, and HUD retreated from insisting on citizen participation. The program was terminated in 1974 by President Gerald Ford. Antonis Tritsis (1937–1992) completed his doctorate at IIT under Ludwig Hilberseimer. After his return to Athens, Tritsis became involved in politics with the restoration of democracy in 1974, joining the Panhellenic Socialist Movement, becoming minister of the environment (1981), minister of religion and education (1986), and eventually mayor of Athens (1991). His many revitalization projects included planting trees throughout Athens, limiting motor vehicles in the city's center and reintroducing a tram, and unifying the ancient city's archaeological sites.

55. Phyllis Lambert, "Planning Studies for the Douglas Community Organization, Chicago, 1968–69," FPL, box 08-L-353. See also L. Lee Hilary, "From Bronzeville-Gap to Montreal," *Catalyst* (Summer 2001): 11; and Liane Lefaivre, "Phyllis Lambert, Advocacy Planner in the Late 1960s," *Harvard Design Magazine* (Spring–Summer 2004): 83–86.

56. The Saidye Bronfman Centre for the Arts, YM-YWHA, Montreal, 1963–67, Phyllis Lambert, Architect, Menkes and Webb, Associated Architects. See materials held in FPL.

57. When the Stock Exchange building was demolished in 1972, pieces of the building were put up for auction; sections of the Trading Room were reconstructed in 1977 by architects Vinci & Kenny as a permanent installation at the Art Institute of Chicago.

58. See PL, notes from telephone conversation with John White of James Landauer Associates on December 15, 1969, regarding a fee to be paid to Pier Associates for providing an eco-

58. (cont.) nomic feasibility study of the west block front at [600–608] Lexington Avenue between Fifty-Second and Fifty-Third Streets; FPL, box 08-L-356. See also Zoning Computations Schemes I–IV, Max Siegel Associates, December 15–17, 1969, FPL, box 08-L-356.
59. Terrence Williams to David Fix, May 18, 1970, FPL, box 08-L-356.
60. "In this case it would mean that Seagrams [*sic*] could purchase the YWCA properties, lease them for a period of fifty years with 25-year renewal option to a third party who in turn would be responsible for assembling the other properties required under the provisions of Section 74-74. The developer would then lease the Seagram East Building back to Seagrams [*sic*] for whatever period would be deemed appropriate." Ibid.
61. See Stephen Quick to PL, with attached drawings of the subway platform options, Rudin building, and Capital Budget drawings, June 30, 1970; Transmittal of Bromley plates nos. 79 and 85 from Williams to PL and Fix, July 7, 1970; Transmittal from Williams to Pier Associates, July 16, 1970; and Quick Transmittal of 9 Bromley Maps of Central Midtown Area from Williams to PL, July 24, 1970; all FPL, boxes 08-L-356, 08-L-168.
62. Pier Associates, Inc., Architects Planners, "Lexington Avenue Development—52nd Street to 54th Street: Feasibility Studies," Chicago, July 27, 1970, FPL, box 08-L-356.
63. PL to SB, EMB, Jack Yogman, and E. Leo Kolber, memo regarding the Seagram East Property and Lexington Avenue Development, October 28, 1970, FPL, 08-L-356. Yogman was executive vice president of Seagram, and Kolber was head of the Bronfman family's financial arm, CEMP Investments.
64. Citibank's architecturally undistinguished building had been designed as Astor Plaza for Vincent Astor by Carson & Lundin and Kahn and Jacobs, and occupied the total block between Park and Lexington Avenues.
65. PL to SB et al., October 28, 1970.
66. Other such projects included Roy Thompson Hall, designed in 1976 by Arthur Erickson, and the Quartier International de Montréal by Daoust Lestage, principal architects, 1995–2003. A few years later, in 1998, I initiated the CCA Competition for the design of cities. The competition challenged architects from around the world to rethink and redesign a site on the western edge of Manhattan. In February 1999, a jury of eight international architects and city planners selected five finalists from some one hundred nominations from around the world. Of the five finalists—Ben van Berkel and Caroline Bos, Van Berkel & Bos UN Studio, Amsterdam; Peter Eisenman, Eisenman Architects, New York; Thom Mayne, Morphosis, Santa Monica; Cedric Price, Cedric Price Architects, London; and Jesse Reiser and Nanako Umemoto, Reiser + Umemoto RUR Architecture P.C., New York—the jury selected the Eisenman Architects proposal.
67. See below in this chapter.
68. Hugh Stubbins (1912–2006) had realized important commissions: the Kongresshalle in Berlin (1957); the Loeb Drama Center (1960) and Francis A. Countway Library of Medicine (1965) at Harvard University; the Southwest Residential Area, University of Massachusetts, Amherst (1966); the Forsyth Wickes Addition (1968) and George Robert White Wing (1970) of the Museum of Fine Arts, Boston (1970); the Veterans Stadium in Philadelphia (1971); and the Federal Reserve Bank of Boston (1976).
69. Arvid Klein to PL, February 6, 1978, FPL, box 08-L-517.
70. See Cushman & Wakefield, Inc., report, November 25, 1980, FPL, box 08-L-517.
71. John Burgee to PL, February 9, 1981, FPL, box 08-L-516.
72. Sanford Grossman of Simpson Thacher & Bartlett to Richard Karl Goeltz, a financial officer of Seagram, confidential memorandum re: Seagram/"Y", March 17, 1981, FPL, box 08-L-517. By this time, Seagram had been purchased by Teachers Insurance and Annuity Association of America, and Grossman felt that a high-rise structure immediately east of Seagram might not raise the same level of concern as it would to the interested parties at Seagram.
73. "Metropolis in a Mess," *Newsweek,* July 27, 1959, 29–31.
74. "Indictment: Reasons for Outrage and Reasons to Act," *New York Herald Tribune,* January 25, 1965. See also Barry H. Gottehrer, *New York City in Crisis* (New York: David McKay, 1965).
75. "Headquarters: Exodus from Fun City," *Time,* February 24, 1967, 83–84.
76. Marilyn Bender, "After Manhattan's Corporate Exodus, Companies Begin to Look Homeward," *New York Times,* January 10, 1971; Ada Louise Huxtable, "It's So Peaceful in the Country," *New York Times,* January 17, 1971; Richard Reeves, "Loss of Major Companies Conceded by City Official," *New York Times,* February 5, 1971; "Corporations: How Are You Going to Keep Them in Manhattan?" *Time,* March 8, 1971, 73; "Business: Why Companies Are Fleeing the Cities," *Time,* April 26, 1971, 86–88; Richard Reeves, "Concerns in Many Cities Leaving for the Suburbs," *New York Times,* April 28, 1971.
77. Carey created the Municipal Assistance Corporation (MAC) to issue bonds backed by a dedicated portion of the city's sales tax. From 1975 to 1993, MAC was chaired by banker Felix Rohatyn, who suggested that 1970s city planners failed to demonstrate accuracy and transparency in their accounting methods, which made it difficult to navigate the crisis. He discussed the potential for the governor's office to shore up New York's financial viability. See Katie Moore, "Felix Rohatyn Addresses City's Fiscal Crisis in Annual M. Moran Weston Lecture," *Columbia News,* March 31, 2003, http://www.columbia.edu/cu/news/03/03/felixRohatyn.html.
78. See Edgar M. Bronfman, *Good Spirits: The Making of a Businessman* (New York: G. P. Putnam's Sons, 1998), 98, 99.

79. Under the watchful eye of our father, at twenty-eight my brother, Edgar M. Bronfman, replaced General Schwengel as president. As he put it, "I became president *de jure* in 1957 and *de facto* in 1962"; quoted in Nicholas Faith, *The Bronfmans: The Rise and Fall of the House of Seagram* (New York: St. Martin's, 2006), 169. After a five-year battle, in 1962, Edgar eased out the last and major member of his father's old guard.
80. *Good Spirits,* 145.
81. Ibid., 97.
82. Ibid.
83. EMB to Ludwig Mies van der Rohe, March 1, 1960, FPL, box 08-L-353.
84. "Upper Michigan Avenue Project, Site Utilization Report Schemes A, B, and C (plans, elevations, and photographs of models)," and other studies, FPL, box 08-L-184.
85. Murray Wolbach, Jr., to PL, March 18, 1969, FPL, box 08-L-353.
86. PL to SB, March 25, 1969, FPL, box 08-L-353. See also correspondence between PL and Marshall Holleb, Wolbach, Philip M. Klutznick, E. Leo Kolber, and Edward Marcus of Neiman Marcus; memos of meetings involving Mies van der Rohe, Skidmore, Owings & Merrill, and PL; and relevant newspaper clippings, all in FPL, box 08-L-353.
87. Only in 1970 was the matter concluded when Seagram finally sold the property to Klutznick, who immediately and successfully began to develop the site as Water Tower Place (completed 1975), a large, mixed-use development comprising a 758,000-square-foot shopping mall and a seventy-four-story tower housing residential apartments and the Ritz Hotel. See Klutznick to PL, April 10, 1970, and Klutznick to EMB, April 10, 1970, FPL, box 08-L-353. Klutznick was appointed US secretary of commerce by President Jimmy Carter in 1980.
88. Thomas P. Hawe, "Relocation Project," typescript for Joseph E. Seagram & Sons, Inc., February 14, 1972, 21 pp., FPL, box 08-L-516. Hawe indicated that the number of *Fortune* 500 companies located in New York was 118 in 1972, down from 129 in 1959; in "Business: Why Companies Are Fleeing the Cities" the figure 125 is given for 1970. At the time, included among *Fortune* 500 companies were approximately 20 percent of the nation's largest financial institutions, utility and retailing companies, and most of the investment banks.
89. Hawe, "Relocation Project."
90. Ibid., 1.
91. Fifteen million square feet of rentable office space were completed in 1971 alone, and twenty-three million more were scheduled to become available in 1972. Other indicators cited in the report were: the growing awareness of a serious economic problem; the national welfare scheme, which could substantially mitigate the city's welfare burden; and revenue sharing with state and local authorities that would grow. The report expressed hope that monies from the US Highway Trust Fund would be made available for public transportation. Ibid., 14–15.
92. Surprisingly, the section of the report entitled "Corporate Image" made no mention of the importance of the image of 375 Park Avenue, the Seagram building, to the company; on the contrary, in the opinion of the company's executives, the city was no longer "the most prestigious location, and a suburban headquarters would add dignity to the Company." Ibid., 12.
93. In EMB to PL, September 4, 2009, e-mail, my brother noted: "It later occurred to me that it might be all right for a holding company to move to the countryside, but the costs of bringing customers there and back, the lack of electricity in the air in the country, all made me realize that it would have been stupid then, and I still agree with that."
94. "The Rent Was Too High," *Architectural Forum* 136, no. 3 (April 1972): 22.
95. Pasanella + Klein, Introduction, "Seagram Interior Design Guidelines," FPL, box 08-L-516. The design guidelines contain specifications for work stations, desks, cabinets, chairs, and credenzas for Seagram offices at 375 Park Avenue and at 800 Third Avenue, as well as Des Plaines, IL. They include layout plans and photocopied images of furniture used in the new Seagram offices, designed and manufactured by Knoll and Hermann Miller, side chairs by Hans Wegner and executive desks redesigned with Jens Risom, and other manufacturers. In Giovanni Pasanella to Louis S. Goldberg, memorandum with copies to PL and C. J. Blunt, June 1, 1978, "Subject: Interior Design - Furnishings," Pasanella wrote, "When we began to work on Seagram Interiors in 1971–2, there existed several methods for realizing interior design. As we and Phyllis Lambert began to analyze and understand the issues some principles evolved, which were formalized in the Interior Design Guidelines issued 1973–4"; FPL, box 08-L-516. Pasanella + Klein designed the new sixth-floor executive offices of the Seagram building in the early 1980s using the basic layout of the original suites on the fifth floor, including oak paneling and the Jens Risom desks; they added some low tables of their own design, as well as new clerical desks to accommodate data-processing equipment. See Nicholas Polites, "The Seagram Building: Living with a Landmark," *Building Economics* 1, no. 5 (May 1986): 44–53.
96. Pasanella to Goldberg, memorandum, June 1, 1978. Pasanella added that the Interior Design Guidelines did not cover the fifth-floor executive offices at 375 Park Avenue, but since the original design was "quite Miesian, we sought to extend that fact in our renovation work." He added that "in 1976, Edgar Bronfman took a more active role in the furniture selection" (1). This was reflected in changes to three executive offices on the fifth floor; only two offices and the secretarial alcoves on that floor conformed to the original design concept. EMB's office took over his father's partners

desk and some of the Chippendale chairs, but the "olde English" buttoned-leather couches and other furniture he added did not project a forward-looking presence.

97. Unbuilt project for Chivas Brothers Seagram Plant, Darnley, 1975, Peter Carter, architect. See Fonds Peter Carter, project 47-7002, CCA. In Mies's office, which he joined in 1958, Carter worked on the Colonnade Apartments, New Jersey; the Friedrich Krupp Administration Building, Essen; the Chicago Federal Centre; and the Toronto-Dominion Centre, for which he was architect in charge of design and construction; and the Mansion House Square project, London. See also Phyllis Lambert, "Mies and His Colleagues," in *Mies in America,* ed. Phyllis Lambert (Montreal: Canadian Centre for Architecture, and New York: Whitney Museum of American Art and Harry N. Abrams), 574–89.

98. The other architects from whom I requested portfolios were Araldo Casutta, Conklin and Rossant, Michael Graves, Richard Meier, Cesar Pelli, James Stewart Polshek, James Volney Righter, and Arthur Takeuchi. See 1979 Westchester County Facility, notes and correspondence from architects; FPL, box 08-L-355.

99. EMB to PL, e-mail, September 5, 2009.

100. EMB to PL, e-mail, September 4, 2009.

101. EMB to Abraham D. Beame, November 1, 1976, FPL, box 08-L-517. It is possible that my work with the OMPD in early 1970, when the landmarking of Seagram was first explored as a condition of the transfer of air rights, brought this to his attention. In a letter to Mayor Beame, EMB proposed an amendment to the law that would allow landmark status to be granted before the statutory thirty years, providing the owner voluntarily agreed to waive his thirty-year exemption.

102. Beame to EMB, November 5, 1976, FPL, box 08-L-517.

103. Paul Goldberger, "Seagram Building Owners Plan to Seek Landmark Designation," *New York Times,* November 8, 1976.

104. EMB to Beame, May 3, 1977, FPL, box 08-L-517.

105. Ibid.

106. EMB to Beame, November 1, 1976, FPL, box 08-L-517.

107. "The Seagram Company Has Asked New York City to Designate Its Mies-Designed Headquarters Building a Landmark," *Architectural Record* 160, no. 8 (December 1976): 33.

CHAPTER 7.
SUSTAINING ARCHITECTURAL CULTURE

Note: This chapter is developed from part of a lecture entitled "Farnsworth on Mars: Or on the Stewardship of Buildings," presented on May 17, 2005, at the Berlage Institute, Rotterdam. The lecture was published as "Farnsworth on Mars? Or, On the Commissioning and Stewardship of Buildings," *Hunch: The Berlage Institute Report* 10 (Summer 2006): 72–83.

1. See Closing Memorandum: Sale of Seagram Building, February 15, 1980, FPL, box 08-L-649.

2. PL to Edward L. Saxe, February 15, 1978, FPL, box 08-L-517.

3. *New York Times,* March 16, 1979.

4. Dietrich Fischer-Dieskau, quoted by Wolf-Eberhard von Lewinski in "The Artist's Life," trans. Mary Whittall, booklet accompanying the CD Dietrich Fischer-Dieskau, *Mahler: Lieder eines fahrenden Gessellen, Kindertotenlieder, 4 Ruckert-Lieder,* Deutsche Grammophon, 415 191-2 GH.

5. The campaign to save the Pennsylvania State House in Philadelphia (1753) is generally considered to have been the first instance of historic preservation in the United States. For a cogent account of attitudes toward center versus periphery, see Mitchell Schwarzer, "Myths of Permanence and Transience in the Discourse on Historic Preservation in the United States," *Journal of Architectural Education* 48, no. 1 (September 1994): 2–11.

6. "Nation: New York Bounces Back," *Time,* August 21, 1978, 20–23.

7. "Notes on People," *New York Times,* June 17, 1977.

8. These buildings profited from the 1961 Zoning Resolution, using the creation of atria to gain extra height. Trump Tower was built at the same time and on the same block as the IBM building. Martin Filler commented on these new towers and the new zoning regulations, writing, "A complex series of air-rights transfers (from above the Tiffany Building on the southeast corner of 57th Street and Fifth Avenue and from above the new Bonwit Teller Building on 57th Street) combined with zoning variances granted in return for atriums provided by both skyscrapers has permitted the erection of an unbelievable total of some 1,758,000 square feet of space in the 43-story IBM Building and the 58-story Trump Tower." Martin Filler, "High Ruse, Part I," *Art in America* 72 (September 1984): 160.

9. Hal K. Negbaur to PL, December 27, 1977, FPL, box 08-L-517. Having been asked by Negbaur to put forward my ideas, I responded as follows: "I propose four clear courses of action: 1) Ask the City for a planning review of the whole area. The extent of development poses a serious problem for the local infrastructure—for example, the new Citicorp Building has already put a notable strain on the Lexington Avenue Subway. 2) Ask for an evaluation of the use of gallerias; are the citizens getting what they are paying for? [I was referring to W. H. Whyte's observations that most plazas created by the bonus plazas in the 1961 zoning regulation did not work, which led to his studies for 1975 code reform.] There are now enough gallerias to warrant similar evaluation. 3) Board could ask for 'review of air rights in relation to the allocation of such rights from buildings still standing to new projects.' 4) Board could ask that Community Boards have professionals available for consultations." PL to Negbaur, January 13, 1978, FPL, box 08-L-517. Negbaur replied, asking if he could turn over my letter of January 13, 1978,

to the construction committee of his board, indicating that they would need an independent consultant and adding: "I have implemented the first part of your letter that deals with municipal services. The City Planning Commission is hopefully reviewing it. As to the other subjects you have raised, I am slightly at a loss on what to do." Negbaur to PL, February 3, 1978, FPL, box 08-L-517.

10. See J. Arvid Klein to Louis S. Goldberg, with copies to PL, March 13, 1978, January 15, 1979, FPL, box 08-L-517. The through-block galleria allowed extra bulk, according to amendments to the 1961 Zoning Resolution.

11. AT&T hired Philip Johnson to do a feasibility study for a new headquarters building on a site the company owned at Fifty-Fifth Street and Madison Avenue. "AT&T acquired the property, about half a city block, between February 1974 and November 1975." "AT&T Sets Architect's Survey," *Wall Street Journal,* June 21, 1977.

12. See Nicholas Faith, *The Bronfmans: The Rise and Fall of the House of Seagram* (New York: St. Martin's, 2006), 197–211, especially: "During the 1970s, the situation grew ever grimmer, for by then blends accounted for a mere fifth of the market, a drop of two-thirds in twenty years. Joseph E. Seagram & Sons, Inc., the American subsidiary that accounted for 85 percent of the group's total sales, saw its market share fall to less than a fifth, against a peak of 30 percent" (201).

13. PL to Saxe, February 15, 1978.

14. Conditions specified in a lease attached to a deed of sale can, in fact, be powerful tools for conservation, because they have the potential of going far beyond the protection afforded by landmarking legislation and can be applied to a variety of situations. For example, in 1979, in Montreal, conditions specified in a lease attached to a deed of sale were used to stipulate rules governing the maintenance and alienation of a nonprofit cooperative condominium in the Milton-Parc neighborhood. Condominium law permitted establishing the rules and conditions under which low- and middle-income families could remain in the heart of the city's downtown. Clauses in the lease set the social and physical conditions the community wanted and protected their buildings against demolition. See Susan Altschul, "Condominium for Social Purposes," *Journal des Notaires du Québec* 92, no. 3–4 (November 1989): 219.

15. Lease Agreement, February 15, 1980, 56, FPL, box 08-L-649. The contract was prepared with Richard Clurman of E. M. Warburg, Pincus & Co., Inc.

16. Other spaces to be occupied by Seagram, as specified in Article 1 of the lease agreement, were on the second, third, eighteenth, twentieth, thirty-first, and thirty-fifth floors.

17. Article 26, Lease Agreement, February 15, 1980, 56.

18. Article 26.01, Part A. Modifications; Part B. Building Name; Part C. Remedying Dangerous Conditions, allowed immediate correction, without prior review and approval, of dangerous conditions, and mandated restoration of any such conditions contrary to Part A; Part D. Use, limited and defined permissible use of the plaza and public spaces by the public and Landlord; Part E. Maintenance; Part F. Authorization, established mechanics of review and approval process for all work requiring same; Part G, Records, established a system of record maintenance accessible to Joseph E. Seagram & Sons, Inc., governing all works for which authorization is required, including a log; as-built drawings; contract documents; submittals and complete Building Department documents. Ibid.

19. Article 26, Lease Agreement, February 15, 1980, 56–57.

20. "Technical Specifications: Public Areas Design Standards, Exhibit A1," Lease Agreement, February 15, 1980, n.p.

21. The current owners began to institute new design standards for both the corridors and the toilet rooms in 2010, and although they are somewhat too modish, there is considerable value in maintaining standards throughout the building: indeed the value translates itself into the highest office rental in New York.

22. The Christmas decorations designed by Gene Moore at Philip Johnson's request consist of coniferous trees covered with tiny white lights that fill both pools on the plaza. The year after the first installation, Seagram public relations people envisioned the possibility of changing the colors each year, but I saw this as an invitation to kitsch and mandated the lights to be the same every year, knowing that repetition would lead to a tradition.

23. Article 26, Lease Agreement, February 15, 1980, 63, 64, and Exhibit D3.

24. Ibid., 64.

25. PL to Saxe, February 15, 1978. Saxe agreed to our proposal. See Saxe to PL, February 23, 1978, FPL, box 08-L-517.

26. Article 26, Part D. Use, 62.

27. Ibid.

28. Letter from William H. Whyte, read aloud by Gene A. Norman, transcript of the Landmarks Preservation Commission Public Hearing, May 17, 1988, 101, Records of the Seagram Curator's Office, FSB, box 134-008. See also chapter 5 in this volume.

29. Article 26.01, Lease Agreement, February 15, 1980, 71.

30. Martin Lord, real estate officer of TIAA, transcript of the Landmarks Preservation Commission Public Hearing, May 17, 1988, 15.

31. See minutes of meeting and letters pertaining to maintenance of the Seagram building, Records of the Office of Facilities and Office Services, FSB, boxes 134-OF-006 to 134-OF-009.

32. Carla Ash and Tom Stetz of Pasanella + Klein both remember that, in connection with the Americans with Disabilities Act of 1990, TIAA commissioned studies of a very complicated handicapped entry, which finally was abandoned. TIAA tried to invoke the same issue in connection with the plaza steps, but access was actually available through the

delivery ramp on Fifty-Second Street, proceeding through the Four Seasons kitchen. "TIAA had pursued it when Sen. Javits became ill and had to go in that way. But Tom [Stetz] told me that the Senator actually did not mind." Carla Ash to PL, e-mail, November 16, 2009. "[TIAA also wanted to place] railings around the pools, a supposed ADA issue which never went anywhere but they actually put stanchions up for awhile. Also, a television saucer on the roof [proposed by TIAA] never went anywhere." Ash to PL, e-mail, November 4, 2009. See also appendix 3, "Some Conservation Issues, as Remembered by Arvid Klein and Tom Stetz of Pasanella + Klein," in this volume.

33. Meeting with Steve P. Morrows, senior vice president of RFR Realty LLC, December 4, 2009, on the occasion of a visit by the Mies van der Rohe Society of Chicago, led by myself. Because the visit occurred close to Christmas, the RFR managers were engaged with installing the trees and they marveled at the specifications and diagrams for infilling the plaza pools with spruce trees—just so many, of such and such a size, arranged in such and such a manner.

34. Roger H. Kahn to Ash November 21, 1989, FPL, box 08-L-648. In August 1988, in correspondence concerning Seagram's landmarking, Martin Lord noted the importance of the decorum of Seagram plaza, writing that it "is the aspect of the building which is most immediately visible to visitors, tenants and passers-by and which provides a first impression of our property." Martin Lord to Gene A. Norman, August 10, 1988, Records of the Office of Facilities and Office Services, FSB, box 134-OF-010.

35. Curator Carla Ash recalled recently that "their actions took us aback, considering that I had never [experienced] any damage during or after installation and had always worked very closely with a structural engineer through the whole process." Ash commented on the di Suvero: "I do now recall the fiasco and . . . I believe part of their stand was a reaction to some important or influential tenant objecting to any 'impediment' on the plaza. I had heard such statements during and after some installations. And, of course, they also wanted to flex their muscles by strictly interpreting the article and perhaps because, I seem to vaguely recall, on some occasion we had thwarted their proposed activity in the lobby or on the plaza." Ash to PL, e-mail, October 27, 2009.

36. Harold M. Garrett to Kahn, December 11, 1989, FPL, box 08-L-648. See also Ash to Phyllis Lambert, memorandum, November 27, 1989, FPL, box 08-L-648, stating that Seagram's engineers saw no problem with the weight and that gaining approval from the Landmarks Preservation Commission was routine.

37. Ash to PL, memorandum, January 9, 1990, ibid.

38. Transcript of the Landmarks Preservation Commission Public Hearing, May 17, 1988, 16, 17.

39. Ibid., 4.

40. Ibid., 18.

41. Ibid., 19. Paul Spencer Byard (1939–2008) solicited and received letters from architects and others.

42. Ibid., 23–31.

43. Ibid., 32–34.

44. Ibid., 36–40.

45. Ibid., 40.

46. Testimony was given by representatives of the Municipal Arts Society, the Architectural League, the Committee to Save the City, the Historic Building Committee of the New York Chapter of the American Institute of Architects (AIA), and Community Board No. 5, which had adopted a resolution to designate and urged the commission to develop an agreement and plan for maintenance. Testimony was given by representatives who spoke for architects Ricardo Bofill and Dirk Lohan. Ibid., 68, 82. Letters from architects including Gordon Bunshaft, James Stewart Polshek and Partners, and Donald C. Smith of Skidmore, Owings & Merrill, were read aloud; letters from Hugh Hardy, Robert A. M. Stern, Edward Barnes, and Robert Venturi were also referenced. Ibid., 19–20, 98, 103–4. Critics who spoke included Peter Blake, Kenneth Frampton, and William H. Whyte, who referred to his time-lapse film study of people sitting on the plaza. A letter by Donald Trump in favor of designation was read aloud. Letters specifically supporting the restaurant were received from Thomas N. Armstrong, III, director of the Whitney Museum of American Art, architecture critic Martin Filler of *House and Garden* magazine, artist Helen Frankenthaler, and designer Milton Glaser.

47. Halina Rosenthal, president of the Friends of the Upper East Side Historic District, spoke of the harmony that attended the pursuit of Seagram's designation, which she contrasted with the case of Lever House, in which "barricades had to be erected and a battle had to be fought, won perhaps only with a legendary kiss." Ibid., 89.

48. Ibid., 64.

49. Gene A. Norman to Arthur S. Margolin, May 31, 1988, Records of the Seagram Curator's Office, FSB, box 134-008.

50. Transcript of the Landmarks Preservation Commission Public Hearing, May 17, 1988, 56–59.

51. Ibid., 90–91.

52. Ibid., 91–93. The record later shows that the request was made by the operators of the Four Seasons Restaurant.

53. Ibid., 62.

54. Ibid., 47–48.

55. Ibid., 48–51.

56. Ibid., 110–12.

57. John J. Kerr, Jr., Simpson Thacher & Bartlett, Seagram counsel, "Notes of Meeting with Landmarks Preservation Commission on July 28, 1989," transmitted to Harry C. Beatty, Esq., Legal Department, Joseph E. Seagram & Sons, Inc., September 12, 1989, 2, Records of the Seagram Curator's Office, FSB, box 134-008.

58. Lord to Norman, August 10, 1988, Records of the Office

of Facilities and Office Services, FSB, box 134-OF-010. In its arguments against designating maintenance as part of Seagram's landmarking, in this letter, TIAA mentioned the requirements of Article 26 and its own "exemplary record" in complying with them, all the while ignoring the possible actions of future and less diligent owners. TIAA's argument also assumed that Article 26 would always be in place, although it had its limits in time, given that it was a fixed-term lease, and the perpetuity of ownership was in no way guaranteed.

59. See the following documents: Tom Stetz to Earl Fries, memorandum, with copies to PL, J. Arvid Klein, and Giovanni Pasanella, July 13, 1988, summarizing the July 12, 1988, public hearing on the Four Seasons Restaurant, FPL, box 08-L-649; and Harry C. Beatty, "Four Seasons Landmark Meeting," memorandum, July 18, 1988, Records of the Office of Facilities and Office Services, FSB, box 134-OF-010.

60. Beatty, "Four Seasons Landmark Meeting," memorandum, July 18, 1988, 2.

61. Paul Spencer Byard to Lord, August 9, 1988, Records of the Office of Facilities and Office Services, FSB, box 134-OF-010. It is worthy of note that Byard had some standing as a preservation architect. He and others were awarded the Citation of Merit in 1996 by the Metropolitan Chapter of the Victorian Society in America for extensive renovation and system upgrade of the Flushing Town Hall.

62. Gordon J. Davis to Norman, July 5, 1988, Records of the Office of Facilities and Office Services, FSB, box 134-OF-010.

63. Agreement of Purchase and Sale between Joseph E. Seagram & Sons, Inc., as Seller, and Teachers Insurance and Annuity Association of America, as Purchaser, May 31, 1979, Section 17, 14, attached to Memorandum of Joseph E. Seagram & Sons, Inc., concerning the Designation of the Interior Space of the Seagram Building Occupied by the Four Seasons Restaurant, undated [August 19, 1988], 2, 3, FPL, box 08-L-770.

64. Memorandum of Joseph E. Seagram & Sons, Inc., concerning the Designation of the Interior Space of the Seagram Building Occupied by the Four Seasons Restaurant, undated [August 19, 1988], 2.

65. Ibid., 3.

66. Ibid., 10. The memo addresses case law on three factors examined by the New York courts in determining whether an object is personal property, and thus removable, or a fixture appurtenant to the realty: (1) annexation: whether the article is so attached to the realty that its removal would materially damage or decrease either in value; (2) adaption: whether the article is so uniquely adapted to its location that the realty could not be imagined to be used for its present purposes without it; and (3) intent: whether the original owner of that article intended to make a permanent annexation to the freehold.

67. Richard Lippold to the Landmarks Preservation Commission of New York, September 11, 1989, Records of the Office of Facilities and Office Services, FSB, box 134-OF-010.

68. PL to David F. M. Todd, September 28, 1989, Records of the Seagram Curator's Office, FSB, box 134-008.

69. See FPL and FSB, documents and correspondence, c. 1987–96, boxes 08-L-649, 134-OF-10, and 134-008.

70. The components of the first floor interior were listed as: "comprising the lobby, passenger elevator cabs, the fixtures and interior components of [all] faces, including but not limited to, interior piers, wall surfaces, ceiling surfaces, floor surfaces, doors, railings, elevator indicators, and signs." Transcript of Seagram Building Landmark Hearing, October 3, 1989, 2–3, Records of the Seagram Curator's Office, FSB, box 134-008. In his preamble, Adolf Placzek mentioned the steel and bronze mesh panels of the elevators cabs, and that the building was still virtually intact due to the prescient maintenance plan of Joseph E. Seagram & Sons, Inc.; he said that the building and plaza, along with the lobby, have inspired many subsequent designers, affected New York building regulations and taxation procedures, and provided a favorable environment for work and repose.

71. Adolf Placzek (1913–2000) was appointed director of the Avery Library at Columbia University in 1960. On retirement from that post in 1980, Placzek became a much-loved adviser to the Canadian Centre for Architecture in Montreal, where he gave astute direction to our growing collection of materials on architecture and the city.

72. Transcript of Seagram Building Landmark Hearing, October 3, 1989, 3.

73. Michael T. Sillerman to Todd, July 28, 1989, Records of the Seagram Curator's Office, FSB, box 134-008. A twenty-four-page letter signed by Ellen R. Zimmerman, Lord Day & Lord, Barrett Smith, attorneys, Four Seasons Restaurant, to Todd, August 16, 1989, Records of the Seagram Curator's Office, FSB, box 134-008, refuted Sillerman's positions.

74. Landmarks Preservation Commission, October 3, 1989, Designation List 221, LP-1666, 1, Records of the Seagram Curator's Office, FSB, box 134-008.

75. The legal argument involved statutory legal definitions: personal, movable property versus "Fixtures." The definition of *fixture* in landmark law arises in the context of *architectural features*. *Architectural features* are defined as "the Architectural style, design, general arrangement, and components of an interior, including but not limited to the kind, color, and texture of the building material and the type and style of all windows, doors, lights, signs, and other fixture appurtenant to such interior." *Appurtenance,* in property law, is a legal right or privilege attached to a property and inherited with it.

76. Transcript of Seagram Building Landmark Hearing, October 3, 1989, 12. The chairman also commented on the allegation that somehow this is a trade fixture. "I hardly think

that the architect had that in mind when he designed that ceiling."

77. Ibid., 16.
78. The New York City Board of Estimate was a governmental body in New York, responsible for budget and land-use decisions. Under the charter of the newly amalgamated City of Greater New York (passed 1897, effective 1898) the Board of Estimate and Apportionment was composed of eight ex officio members: the mayor of New York City, the New York City comptroller, and the president of the New York City Council, each of whom was elected citywide and had two votes, and the five borough presidents, each having one vote. The La Guardia Reform Charter of 1938 simplified its name and enhanced its powers. In 1989, the US Supreme Court, in *Board of Estimate of City of New York v. Morris,* declared the New York City Board of Estimate unconstitutional on the grounds that the city's most populous borough (Brooklyn) had no greater effective representation on the board than the city's least populous borough (Staten Island), this arrangement being a violation of the Fourteenth Amendment's Equal Protection Clause pursuant to the high court's 1964 "one man, one vote" decision. Under the newly rewritten 1990 City Charter, most of the responsibilities that the Board of Estimate had previously had were delegated to the New York City Council.
79. Transcript, Board of Estimate, Calendar Nos. 40 and 41, hearing on Seagram's designation, January 25, 1990, 89 pp., Records of the Office of Facilities and Office Services, FSB, box 134-OF-004.
80. Among those who testified for landmarking were: Brendan Gill; Tom Margittai, co-owner of the Four Seasons Restaurant and its legal counsel from Lord Day & Lord, Barrett Smith; sculptor Richard Lippold; Kent Barwick of the Municipal Arts Society; Richard Beauford of the New York Landmarks Conservancy; William O'Shaughnessy, president of WBO and WRTN; architectural historian Richard Pommer; architects Lewis Davis of Davis Brody Associates, Robert A. M. Stern; James Polshek; Bernard Tschumi, dean, Columbia Graduate School of Architecture, Planning and Preservation; Steven Holl; and myself. Architects John Hejduk and Dirk Lohan, Mies's grandson, sent letters.
81. In addition to Martin Lord, the following individuals retained by TIAA testified: Paul Byard; Michael Sillerman of Rosenman & Colin, legal counsel; Dean Cole, real estate appraiser; Roger Kahn of Edward S. Gordon, leasing agent for 375 Park Avenue; and Peter Jordan, associate general legal counsel.
82. Transcript, Board of Estimate, Calendar Nos. 40 and 41, hearing on Seagram's designation, January 25, 1990, 83–84.
83. Ibid., 4–5.
84. Ibid., 79–80.
85. Ibid., 35–36.
86. Ibid., 86.
87. Ibid., 85.
88. Petitioner-Plaintiff's memorandum of law, summary judgment on its constitutional claims, Supreme Court of the State of New York, County of New York, Teachers Insurance and Annuity Association of America, Petitioner-Plaintiff, against City of New York, Board of Estimate of the City of New York and Landmarks Preservation Commission of the City of New York, Respondents-Defendants, April 27, 1990, 68 pp., FPL, box 08-L-770.
89. Landmarks Law § 25-301(b), cited in ruling of Supreme Court, New York County, Teachers Insurance and Annuity Association of America, Petitioner-Plaintiff, against City of New York, Board of Estimate of the City of New York and Landmarks Preservation Commission of the City of New York, Respondents-Defendants, October 16, 1990, 4, FPL, box 08-L-649.
90. Ibid., 5.
91. Landmarks Law § 25-302(m), cited in ibid., 6.
92. Landmarks Law § 25-302(1), cited in ibid.
93. Ruling of Supreme Court, New York County, October 16, 1990, 9. Among interiors designated, the judge added court houses to the examples—the Appellate Division, First Department; the New York Supreme Court; and the New York Surrogates Court—as well as theater interiors, and enumerated individual institutions and interior designations (9–10).
94. Ibid., 10.
95. Ibid.
96. Ibid., 12.
97. Ibid., 12.
98. Ibid., 13.
99. Ibid., 14.
100. Ibid.
101. Ibid., 15.
102. Ibid.
103. Ibid.
104. Sullivan, J. P., Carro, Wallach, Smith, JJ. 46076, Teachers Insurance and Annuity Association of America, Petitioner-Plaintiff-Appellant, against The City of New York, Board of Estimate of New York, Landmark Preservation Commission of the City of New York, Respondent-Defendants-Respondents, July 30, 1992, Records of the Office of Facilities and Office Services, FSB, box 134-OF-010. See also Daniel R. Paladino, manuscript note, in Nancy Brownstein Mallery to Paladino, October 16, 1992, Records of the Office of Facilities and Office Services, FSB, box 134-OF-010.
105. Decision of New York Court of Appeals In the Matter of Teachers Insurance and Annuity Association of America, Appellant, v. The City of New York, et al., Respondents. Real Estate Board of New York, Inc.; National Trust for Historic Preservation in the United States; and Municipal Art Society of New York, Inc., *amici curiae,* October 19, 1993, 12, FPL, box 08-L-649. Judith S. Kaye, appointed New York's

chief judge in 1993 by Governor Mario M. Cuomo, became the first woman to occupy that post. She was also the first woman to serve on the court of appeals, which she joined in 1983. Chief Judge Kaye was president of the Conference of Chief Justices, chair-elect of the National Center for State Courts, and a member of the American Law Institute, the American College of Trial Lawyers, and the American Academy of Arts and Sciences. These judgments, each giving the reasons for rejection of the TIAA Appeal, make absorbing reading.

106. See Kathie Riley (legal counsel to the Preservation League of New York State), "NY Courts Uphold Historic Interior Designation," *Preservation New York* 2, no. 2 (Spring 1994): 11.

EPILOGUE.
CHANGING HANDS

1. Robert A. M. Stern views the differences from a postmodern point of view, concerned with the traditional street front rather than with volume and space in three dimensions. He adopts the "building in the plaza" critique leveled then at Le Corbusier. However this theory did not underlie New York high-rise structures, not even Seagram. After 1961, to calculate volume, developers used the formula of Floor Area Ratio (FAR) to establish a ratio between floor area and site area rather than set-back zoning. The new buildings did not rise out of plazas, but open spaces, often leftover spaces that were organized around their buildings in order to be awarded extra volume to add to their towers. Stern compared the old zoning ordinance "with its solid roots in the traditional spacemaking of streets and avenues bounded by walls of buildings filling up the block with near solidity," with the new regulations that "encouraged unmodulated, independently spaced skyscraper tower slabs rising from generously scaled plazas—an 'open' city, a city that was space positive rather than mass positive." Robert A. M. Stern, *New York 1960: Architecture and Urbanism Between the Second World War and the Bicentennial* (New York: Monacelli, 1995), 9.
2. Charles V. Bagli, "Office Tower Is Planned, Without Leases Set," *New York Times*, November 7, 1999.
3. See Carter B. Horsley, "590 Madison Avenue (Formerly the IBM Building)," www.thecityreview.com/ibm.html.
4. Adam R. Rose, quoted by David Samuels in "The Real-Estate Royals: End of Line?" *New York Times Magazine*, August 10, 1997, 38. Rose was a member of the real estate company of Rose Associates, Inc., founded by his uncle. The firm was a conglomerate specializing in the design, construction, and management of high-rise apartments.
5. Ibid. Samuels, "Real-Estate Royals," 39.
6. Ibid., 38.
7. Ibid.
8. Ibid.
9. Stephanie Strom, "Japanese Scrap $2 Billion Stake in Rockefeller," *New York Times*, September 12, 1995.
10. Charles V. Bagli, "A New Owner to Take Over an Old Classic," *New York Times*, November 25, 1997. The building had changed hands in the real estate boom of the 1950s; it was purchased by William Zeckendorf, who was forced to sell in 1957. The government of Abu Dhabi acquired 90 percent ownership in the building in 2008. See Charles V. Bagli, "Abu Dhabi Buys 90 Percent Stake in Chrysler Building," *New York Times*, July 10, 2008.
11. The renovation program, undertaken by the original architectural firm, SOM, included the building's curtain wall and public spaces, as well as repositioning it as a multi-tenant property. A sculpture garden designed by Isamu Noguchi, originally planned for Lever House but never realized, was added at the plaza level.
12. David Dunlap, "Commercial Real Estate; Updating a Skyscraper That Woolworth Built," *New York Times*, February 24, 1999. Dunlap wrote: "That leaves the new owners, the Witkoff Group, Rubin Schron and other investors—with the challenge of leasing a tower clad in medieval frosting to tenants obsessed with the latest technologies."
13. Jayson Blair, "CBS's 'Black Rock' Building Is Said to Be for Sale," *New York Times*, August 30, 2000.
14. Wechsler in Natalie Keith, "Seagram Building Reportedly for Sale," *Real Estate Weekly*, August 30, 2000, http://www.allbusiness.com/management/632566-1.html.
15. Charles V. Bagli, "On Park Avenue, Another Trophy Changes Hands," *New York Times*, October 12, 2000. Bagli's article also appeared that same day under the title "Developers' Bid Wins Seagram Building." Bagli reported that the Port Authority of New York and New Jersey was considering seven bids of up to three billion dollars for a ninety-nine-year lease of the World Trade Center.
16. Charles V. Bagli, "October 8–14; On Sale Now," *New York Times*, October 15, 2000. The sale price in other reports is given as four million dollars less.
17. Bagli, "On Park Avenue, Another Trophy Changes Hands."
18. Ibid.
19. Keith, "Seagram Building Reportedly for Sale."
20. See Appendix 3, "Some Conservation Issues as Remembered by Arvid Klein and Tom Stetz of Pasanella + Klein," in this volume.
21. "TIAA Sells Seagram Building to RFR Holding, LLC," TIAA-CREF press release, December 15, 2000, http://www.prnewswire.com/news-releases/tiaa-sells-seagram-building-to-rfr-holding-llc-76223402.html.
22. "Seagram Building Is Sold," *Real Estate Weekly*, December 20, 2000.
23. Ibid.
24. Elaine Misonzhnik, "Sir Norman Foster in Contract for

Second New York Project," *Real Estate Weekly,* October 19, 2005. The reported price of the YWCA site was given as $31.5 million.

25. The thirty-six-story Hines building at 600 Lexington Avenue, originally named Manhattan Tower, was completed in 1985. Today it advertises itself on the Internet as being, "next door to the renowned Four Seasons Restaurant in the Seagram Building and across from Citicorp Center, Manhattan Tower is conveniently located within a block of a major subway and within walking distance of Grand Central Station." http://www.loopnet.com/Listing/15866301/600-Lexington-Avenue-New-York-NY/.

26. Matthew Grace, "Seagram Switch," *New York Observer,* November 11, 2005.

27. See Carter B. Horsley, "Sir Norman Foster Designs Tower at 610 Lexington Avenue Using Air Rights from Seagram Building," *City Review,* November 22, 2005, http://www.thecityreview.com/lex610.html.

28. PL, quoted by Richard Waite, "Seagram Awaits Foster's Arrival," *Architects' Journal,* February 9, 2006, 10.

29. City Planning Commission, July 2, 2008, http://www.nyc.gov/html/dcp/pdf/cpc/080178.pdf.

30. See Lisa Fickenscher, "Luxury Hotelier Abandons NYC," *Crain's New York Business,* April 30, 2009, http://www.crainsnewyork.com/article/20090430/FREE/904309993; Adam Pincus, "Rosen Faces Foreclosure at Hotel Site," *Real Deal Magazine,* June 19, 2009, http://therealdeal.com/newyork/articles/developer-aby-rosen-faces-144m-foreclosure-suit-at-midtown-hotel; and "The National Bureau of Economic Research Announced Monday That the U.S. Has Been in a Recession since December 2007," http://money.cnn.com/2008/12/01/news/economy/recession/index.htm.

31. As director of the CCA, I was appointed commissioner of the Canadian pavilion, where we presented *Un dictionnaire* by Melvin Charney within the Biennale theme "Cities: Less Aesthetics, More Ethics," June 13–20, 2000.

32. See Phyllis Lambert, ed., *Mies in America* (Montreal: Canadian Centre for Architecture, and New York: Whitney Museum of American Art and Harry N. Abrams, 2001).

33. See John Cassidy, "The Greed Cycle: How the Financial System Encouraged Corporations to Go Crazy," *New Yorker,* September 23, 2002, 64–77. Cassidy, a business journalist, traces the problem to its roots, pointing to how owners of companies prevailed on the individuals they hired to run their companies to serve the interests of the owners, that is the stockholders, by providing executive stock options, thus encouraging the goal of maximizing the value of the firm as it was determined in the stock market, which led to fraud in financial reporting and accounting practices. Cassidy quotes Paul Volcker, former chairman of the Federal Reserve Board: "Corporate greed exploded beyond anything that could have been imagined in 1990. . . . Traditional norms didn't exist [public companies as social organizations with social responsibilities].You had this whole culture where the only sign of worth was how much money you made" (64).

34. For a succinct account, see Alex Berenson, "A New Entertainment Giant: The Seller; The Sun Is Setting on Seagram Empire," *New York Times,* June 20, 2000. See also Nicholas Faith, *The Bronfmans: The Rise and Fall of the House of Seagram* (New York: St. Martin's, 2006), 270–279; and Jo Johnson and Martine Orange, *The Man Who Tried to Buy the World: Jean-Marie Messier and Vivendi Universal* (London: Penguin, 2003). See also reference in Graham D. Taylor, "'From Shirtsleeves to Shirtless': The Bronfman Dynasty and the Seagram Empire," *Business and Economic History On-Line* 4 (2006), 30, http://www.thebhc.org/publications/BEHonline/2006/taylor.pdf.

35. DuPont had been brought in as a white night by Conoco, and Seagram who owned 32 percent of the oil company lost the bidding war but gained 24 percent of DuPont.

36. The best short account of these events is by Taylor, "'From Shirtsleeves to Shirtless.'"

37. PL to Edgar Bronfman, Jr., July 31, 2002, 1–2, FPL, box 08-L-663.

38. Edmund L. Andrews, "International Business; Vivendi Chief Bets on His Ability to Create Media Empire," *New York Times,* June 15, 2000.

39. The sale of the Seagram art collection was minor considering the extent of Vivendi's debts. Vivendi Universal sold Seagram's 2,500-piece collection valued at $15 million in the process of liquidating its $11.7 billion debt. Phillips, de Pury & Luxembourg auctioned off the entire photographs collection in New York on April 25–26, 2003. At the Post-War and Contemporary Art sale at Christie's on May 14, 2003, the greater part of the collection, including the "most valuable" artworks (by artists such as Rothko, Gorky, and Rivers), was sold; prints and tapestries were sold in Christie's Impressionist and Modern Art sale on May 8, 2003; the Latin American works were auctioned by Christie's on May 28–29, 2003; other artifacts, including fine furniture and art objects, were auctioned by Christie's on June 18, 2003; and the European drinking vessels collection was sold in Paris by Artcurial on March 15, 2005.

40. See PL to Jean-François Dubos, June 15, 2003, FPL, box 08-L-753. As Vivendi Universal was to be sold in the marketplace, my letter stated that the company could benefit from a tax deduction by donating *Le Tricorne* to an institution such as MoMA that would maintain the curtain in situ, resulting in a best-of-both-worlds solution that would have economic and social consequences which would reconcile the interests of the company with those of New York: "La portée économique et sociale de ce geste aurait le mérite de satisfaire le meilleur des deux mondes et ainsi concilier les intérêts de Vivendi Universal avec ceux de la ville de New York." The donation of *Le Tricorne* to the New York Land-

marks Conservancy was announced in a press release by both parties on December 14, 2005, "in order to preserve the integrity of a classical building designed by Mies van der Rohe and Philip Johnson." Press release, December 14, 2005, FPL, box 08-L-810. See also "Picasso's *Le Tricorne* to Remain in New York City; Vivendi Universal Donates Picasso Painting to the New York Landmarks Conservancy," *Business Wire*, December 14, 2005.

INDEX

References to illustrations are in *italics*.

Abu Dhabi, as purchaser of Chrysler building, 292*n*10
The Accident (Rivers), 166
Adam, Robert, 129
Adams, Ansel, 278*n*81
Advertising, 4–5, 28, 255*nn*10–11, 255*nn*18–19
Advisory Committee (Seagram), 22–23, 28, 49, 136–37, 258*n*32
AEG Turbine Hall (Berlin 1910), 53
AIA. *See* American Institute of Architects (AIA)
Air conditioning, 55, 59, 60–61, 62, 123, *126,* 263*n*54, 265*n*72
Air rights, 12, 20, 47, 201–6, 217, 235–36, 287*n*101
Alcoholic beverage industry: Distillers Company Limited, 2, 254*n*3; Distillers Corporation Limited, 2, 254*n*3; Distillers Corporation–Seagrams Limited, 2, *3,* 5, 254*n*3; history of wine and spirits depicted in artwork, 166, 278*n*81, 278–79*nn*82–84; negativity toward, 4, 22, 199; New York World's Fair (1939) Distilled Spirits Institute Pavilion, 6, 256*n*25; Prohibition, repeal of, 2–4, 254*n*8; rivalries in, 257*n*3; whisky blends, 4, 214, 288*n*12. *See also* Joseph E. Seagram & Sons, Inc.
Alpine Architektur (Taut), 112, *112*
Altes Museum (Berlin), 51, 83, 130, 132
Aluminum, 35, 55, 62, 63, 143, 263–64*n*60, 275*n*77
American Federation of Arts, 280*n*104
American Institute of Architects (AIA), 67, 176, 198, 236
Americans with Disabilities Act of 1990, 251–52, 288–89*n*32
Amsterdam Commodity Exchange, 9
André Emmerich Gallery, 170
Animals series (Winogrand), 174
Antique City on a Mountain (Schinkel), 131
Apraxine, Pierre, 173, 280*n*99
Architect selection for Seagram building, 28–37; choice of Mies, 35–36, 260*n*80; defining question, 35; Johnson's role, 32–33; Lambert's decision, 35–36; Lambert's letter to SB about proposed design (June 28, 1954), 30–32, *240–47;* names under consideration, 23–29, 260*n*60, 260*n*76; Saarinen's list for, 33–35. *See also* Advisory Committee (Seagram)
The Architects' Collaborative (TAC), 35
Architects' role, ix, x
Architectural Forum: on business strategy of Seagram building, 201, 284*n*52; on innovations of Seagram building, 123–28, *124–27;* on tax assessment on Seagram building, 200, 284*n*49
Architectural Record: on architectural facts of Seagram, 83; on landmark status of Seagram, 209
Architectural Review, article (1950) by Johnson, 129
"Architecture and Technology," Mies article, viii
The Architecture of the Well-Tempered Environment (Banham), 60, 265*n*72
Armour Institute of Technology. *See* Illinois Institute of Technology
Article 26 of lease agreement attached to Deed of Sale, 12, 214–20, 234, 236, 237, 288*n*18, 289–90*n*58

Artwork for Seagram and Four Seasons, 11, 150–93; *l'art de boire* collection, 166, 278–79*nn*82–84; costs, 165; curatorial office, 173, 215; drawings, 178, *178–79;* European and American drinking vessels collection, 171–73, *172–73,* 238, 280*n*96; and landmarking process, 221–22, 221–24, *224–25,* 229, 290*n*66; lithographs and etchings, 169–70, 279*n*90, 279*n*94; paintings, 148, 152, 159, 161–64; photography, 173–78; posters, 170, 171, 279*n*90; sale of, 238, 293*n*39; sculptures, 120–21, 144–45, *140–41, 144–45,* 148, 152–54, *154,* 159, *160,* 181–83, 222–24; silkscreens, 167, 279*n*87; special exhibits on plaza, 181–93, *182–88;* staff related to, 166; stage curtains (see also *Le Tricorne*), 158; tapestries, *143,* 164–65, 166, *167–68,* 169, *170,* 171, 279*nn*85–86; unity with architecture, 165–66
Ash, Carla, 219, 249–50, 280*n*97, 281*nn*127–28, 288–89*n*32, 289*n*35
Ashkenazi, Peter, 227
Assessment. *See* Tax assessment on Seagram building
AT&T building (now Sony, Madison Avenue), 211–12, *213,* 214, 232, 288*n*11
Aubusson tapestries, 165, 171

Baader, Johannes, 271*n*40
Bagli, Charles, 234, 292*n*15
Les Baigneurs (Picasso), 159, *160*
Bailey, George R., 46
Ballets Russes, 85, 154, 158, 277*n*34
Baltz, Lewis, 176
Balzac (Rodin), 171
Banham, Reyner, 60, 113, 265*n*72
Bankers Trust Company, 23–26, 33
Barberry Room, 273–74*n*56
Barcelona Pavilion (1928–29), 7, 8, 51, 56, 61, 106, *108,* 113, 263*n*57
Barnes, Edward Larabee, 211, *213*
Barr, Alfred H., Jr., 32, 122, 129, 158, 277*n*35
Bauhaus, viii, 33, 42, 113, 261*n*7
Baukunst (building art), 9
Baum, Joseph, 138–39, 144, 147, 274*nn*64–65
Bay dimensions, 57, 59, 196, 264*n*61
Beame, Abraham D., 208–9, 214, 287*n*101
Becher, Hilla & Bernd, 174
Beck, Deborah, 227
Beck, Martha, 181, 281*n*116
Beckmann, Max, 277*n*34
Behrens, Peter, 51, 53, 104, 106, 110, 268–69*n*1, 269*nn*13–14, 270*n*20
Bellman, David, 178
Bergdoll, Barry, vii, 103, 106, 130
Berlage, Hendrik Petrus, 9, 130
Berlin: AEG Turbine Hall (1910), 53; Altes Museum, 51, 83, 130, 132; Friedrichstrasse Turmhaus competition (1921), 109–10, *110,* 119, 270*n*35; light festival (1928), 265*n*79; New Guardhouse on Unter den Linden, 114; New National Gallery (Berlin), 270*n*25
Bicentennial photographic campaign on county courthouses, ix, 167, 174–80, *176–77,* 280–81*nn*102–4, 280*n*107

295

Bien, Sylvan, 27, 260n60
Bismarck Monument competition project (1910), 105, *105*, 119
Black Rock (CBS tower), 234
Black Silhouette (Gottlieb), 170
Board of Estimate. *See* New York City Board of Estimate
Board of Estimate of City of New York v. Morris (1989), 291n78
The Bomb, Survival, and You (Severud), 59
Bomb-resistant structures, 59
Bomb shelters, 59, 264–65n71
Borsook, Eve, 8, 33, 262n31, 276n7
Brancusi, Constantin, 152, *153*, 181, 276n8
Braque, Georges, 169–70
Brasserie restaurant, 217, 222, 274n69
Breslin, James, 161
Breuer, Marcel, 32–33, 260n76
Brick bond, 44
Brick Guest House. *See* New Canaan Brick Guest House and Glass House (Johnson)
Brody, Jerome, 81, 136–39, 144
Brokaw Mansion, proposed demolition of, 11, 284n41
Broken Obelisk (Newman), 183, *183*
Bronfman, Edgar M., 137, 181–82, 206–9, 214, 237, 286n79, 286n93, 286–87n96
Bronfman, Edgar Jr., 237
Bronfman, Samuel (SB): on architect choice, 37, 260n80; character of, 7; death of, 206; decision making, slow process of, 23; design preferences of, *38*, 62, 70; life and business career of, 2, 4, 7, 254nn1–2; Mies's ability to translate desires of, 7; motivation for building Seagram, 7, 13, 283–84n38; as NY outsider, 1; photographs of, *14*, *78*, *80*; quality as focus of, 2, 4, 7, 17; restaurant for Seagram building, meeting on, 137; satisfaction with Mies's vision, 50, 68, 71, 262n39
Bronze, *41*, 58, 62–66, 83, *84*, 159, 220, 265–66n84, 266n95; and SB, 38. *See also* Curtain walls
Brown and Blacks in Reds (Rothko), 167, 169, *169*
Browne-Vintners, 278n81
Brownstone Circle (Long), 184, *185*
Bruni, Leonardi, 194
Building Committee (Seagram), 23, 28, 44, *79*, 259n41, 262nn20–21
"Building Identification Prize Contest," 23–26, *24–25*
Building Planning Service Council of National Association of Building Owners and Managers, 46, *46*, 262n25
Buildings for Business and Government (MoMA exhibition 1957), 68, 266n101, 267n108
Bunshaft, Gordon, 70–71
Burgee, John, 205
Byard, Paul, 219, 222, 224, 290n61

Cage, John, *151*
Calder, Alexander, 266n95
Canada: The Foundations of Its Future (Leacock), 4, 81, 255n15, 255n17
Canadian Centre for Architecture (CCA), ix, 10, 151, 285n66, 290n71
Carey, Hugh, 206
Carr, J. Gordon, 267–68n128
Carrier, Willis Haviland, 265n72
Carter, Peter, 208, 287n97
Cassidy, John, 293n33
CBS, 232, 234, 260n78
CCA. *See* Canadian Centre for Architecture (CCA)
Celebrations in City Places: The Seagram Building and Its Plaza (1972), 188–89, *189*
Chapel of St. Hubert at Aix-la-Chapelle, 114
Chicago: apartment houses at 860 and 880 Lakeshore Drive, x, 8, 34, 35, 49, 50, 53–56, *54–55*, 57, 61, 114, 115–16, *116–17*, 264n69, 265n75, 269n6; Commonwealth Promenade Apartments, 62, 263–64n60; as competing site to NYC for a Seagram building, 22; Federal Center, 49, 269n6, 287n97; Mies's emigration to, viii, 1, 8; 900 Esplanade, 53–55, *55*, 62, 66, 263n53, 263–64n60; Promontory, *52*, 53, 263n50. *See also* Illinois Institute of Technology
Chicago Architects Oral History Project, 256n36
Chicago School (photography), 174
Choisy, Auguste, 129
Christmas trees, as New York tradition in Seagram landscaping, 70, 267nn121–22, 288n22, 289n33
Chrysler building: Abu Dhabi's purchase of, 292n10; architecture of, 198; Seagram offices at, 4–6, *5–6*, 13, 59, 255n22, 256n24, 265n73; Speyer's purchase of, 233, 234; Webb & Knapp's purchase of, 257n14
Citibank (Citicorp), 204–5, 211, 212, *212*, 214, 232, 285n64, 287–88n9
The Cities of Canada (exhibition 1953), 5, 81, 255nn18–19
Claflin, Agnes Rindge, 276n7
Classical and Classicism, 60, 114–15, 132, 265n76, 277n32
Coburn, Alvin Langdon, 174
College Art Journal, article by Kelly (1950s), 135
Collins, Peter, 283n21
Composition (Kline), 166
Composition (Miró), 169
Compton, Michael, 161
Concrete vs. steel structures, 51–53
Conoco, 237, 293n35
Construction phase of Seagram, 71–81, 267–68n128; completion and moving in, 81, 261n86; dedication events, 81, 268nn131–32; fence around site, 71; photographs of, 71, *72–79*; steel and concrete, 78; tinted glass installation, 78; topping out, 78
Cooper, Douglas, 158, 276n24
Le Coq (Brancusi), 152, *153*
County courthouses, bicentennial photographic campaign of, ix, 167, 174–80, *176–77*, 280nn102–104, 280n107
Crandall, Lou R.: and assigning search for architect to Lambert, 33; and building costs, 44, 45; on building study ("Project Skytop"), 18; on choice of Mies, 36; on demolition of Montana, 19; on financial analysis for Seagram building, 21–22; at initial SB viewing of model, 50; opposition to SB's consideration of a bank on plaza, 70, 71; in search for architect, 29, 32
Cret, Paul-Philippe, 33
Criticism of Mies, vii, 62, 105
Cross & Brown, 21, 258n27
Crossing the Ohio River from Kentucky (Lyon), 175
Cubism, 157–58, 277n30, 277n32
Cultural role of Seagram, 11–12
Curtain walls: apartment houses at 860 and 880 Lakeshore Drive, 265n75; Commonwealth Promenade, 62; comparative, 59, *60*; development of, 263n43; extrusion technique for, 63, *64*, 65; glass in, 56, 109, 270n35; history of, 50–51, 109, 263n43, 263n46; innovation in Seagram, 9, 123; Lever House, 199, 292n11; Mies's evolution of, 50–53, 263n46; model for Seagram, 39–41, 62; 900 Esplanade, 62; United Nations Headquarters, 199; and water infiltration, 65–66
Cushman, J. Clydesdale, 258n27
Cushman & Wakefield, 19–21, *20–21*, 23, *24–25*, 44, 136, 205, 258n27. *See also* Sheaff, L'Huillier
Cuttoli, Marie, 159, *160*, 164, 165, 171, 278n74, 278n77

Daché, Lilly, 133
Dadaists, 113
Daix, Pierre, 277n30, 277n32
Dal Co, Francesco, 269n1

Damian, Horia, 189

Danforth, George, *51,* 272*nn*75–76

Darnley Bottling Plant (Seagram commission, Scotland, unbuilt), 208, 287*n*97

Das Plakat journal on city landscape, 110

David and Bathsheba (Picasso), 170

Davis, Gordon J., 222

Davis, Stuart, 169

A Day in the Life of the North Front Ledge at Seagram's (film), 180

de Alarcón, Pedro, 156

The Death and Life of Great American Cities (Jacobs), 204

de Kooning, Willem, 184, 278*n*68

Delaunay, Robert, 166

Demonstration Cities and Metropolitan Development Act of 1966, 284*n*54

Denver's Mile High Center, 33, 257*n*14

Der Kristallberg (Taut), *112*

"Der moderne Garten" (Behrens), 104

Der Sturm, 113

Design phase of Seagram, 42–71; "addition of bank" crisis, 70–71; bustle, 47, *48, 86–87;* dimensions of tower, 56–58; duration of, 71; fountains on plaza, 67–70, 266–67*n*105, 267*nn*123–24; Kahn and Jacobs challenge Mies's design, 45–46; Lambert's role, 44–45; mechanical engineering, 59–61; Mies's approach to, 46–47, 55–56, 266*n*85; offices for, 38–39, 47; rapidity of, 49; reaction of SB to, 50, 262*n*39; sketches of Seagram plaza, *40,* 67; structural engineering, 57–59, *58,* 264*nn*65–66. *See also* Models during design phase

Des Plaines, Illinois, Seagram facilities in, 208

Development rights. *See* Air rights

Diaghilev, Sergei, 85, 146, 154, 156, 157, 277*n*34

Diderot, Denis, 166, 170, 278*n*82

Distillers Company Limited, 2, 254*n*3

Distillers Corporation Limited, 2, 254*n*3

Distillers Corporation–Seagrams Limited, ix, 2, *3,* 206, 254*n*3

di Suvero, Mark, 186, *187,* 218–19, 289*n*35

"Doctrine of Conspicuous Waste," 197, 199

Douglas Community (Chicago), 201

Dow, Jim, *177*

Draper and Kramer, Inc., 207

Drawings by Sculptors: Two Decades of Non-Objective Art, 178, 178–79, 238

Drinking vessels collection, European and American, 171–73, *172–73,* 238

Dubuffet, Jean, 186, *186*

Duckett, Edward, 42, *48,* 50, *52*

Dudok, Willem, 8

Dumbarton Oaks museum, 265–66*n*84

Dunlap, David, 292*n*12

Dunn, Alan, *66,* 124, *125*

DuPont (E. I. du Pont de Nemours), 237, 293*n*35

Easter Island head displayed on plaza, 183, 281*n*125

Eggers & Higgins, 29, 260*n*60

Eggleston, William, 174, *175*

Eisenhower, Milton S., 81

E. J. Minskoff Equities, Inc., 233

Elevators, 47, 57–58, *58,* 59, 85, 124, *125,* 264*n*66

El Sombrero de tres picos (de Alarcón), 156

Ely Jacques Kahn, 44–46, *46*

Emery Roth & Sons, *25,* 26, 259*n*47, 259–60*n*59

Endell, August, 109, 270*n*31

Escargot, femme, fleur, étoile (Miró), 169

Esso building (NYC 1947), 26

Evans, Walker, *120,* 174, 189, 281*n*130

Exedral benches, 106, 270*n*23

Fairview Corporation Ltd., 205

Falla, Manuel de, 156, 157, 276*n*24

Farnsworth, Edith, 9

Farnsworth house (1951), 9, 11, 41, 49, 103, 261*n*11, 269*n*6

Feininger, Lyonel, 113

Fine Arts Federation of New York, 198, 283*n*28

First National Bank, 204–5. *See also* Citibank (Citicorp)

Fischel, Victor A., 22, 23, *29,* 29–30, 260*n*68

Fischer, John Hurt, 162

Fischer-Dieskau, Dietrich, 211

Fisher Brothers, 213, 232

Fix, David, *202–4,* 203–4

Fixtures, defined, 224, 290–91*nn*75–76

Flair (1950) on Johnson's Glass House lighting, *133,* 133–34

Flatiron building (NYC), 270–71*n*40

Fleur du Mexique (Léger), 166

Flexner, Carolin A., 266*n*102

Floor area ratio (FAR), 196, 214, 292*n*1

Flying Carpet (Davis), 169

Fontainebleau hotel (Miami Beach), 6

Fordyce & Hamby, 30, 260*n*68

Forster, Kurt, 114

Fortune on SB and House of Seagram, 4, 13, 257*n*3

Forum of the Twelve Caesars (restaurant), 138, 274*n*68

Foster, Norman, 236

Foster, Richard, 42, 44, *46,* 65, 261*n*15

Foster + Partners, *235*

Fountains. *See* Plaza of Seagram building

The Four Seasons: A History of America's Premier Restaurant (Mariani & von Bidder), 81, 139

Four Seasons Restaurant, 138–49, *140–47;* bar, *140–41,* 145, *145;* ceiling, *142,* 142–43, *146, 155;* creation and design of, 41, 85, 136–49, *141–42;* curtains, *98–99, 140,* 143–44, *145,* 275*nn*76–77; Grill Room, 139, *140–41,* 144, *144,* 149, 152, *154, 155,* 223, *224–25;* Johnson's role in designing, 128, 138–49; and landmarking process, 12, 221–28, *224–26,* 291*n*75, 291*nn*80–81; lease, 137–38, 274*n*61; lighting of, 11, 136, 139, *142,* 142–44, 275*n*75; lobby staircase, *143;* mezzanine, Pool Room, 148, *149;* Mies's disinterest in designing, 138; opening of, 81; paintings for, ix, 85, *146–47,* 148, 154, *156–59,* 161–65, *164–65,* 217, 222, 238; plants and trees, *142,* 148–49, 275*n*86; Pool Room, 139, *142,* 147–49, *149, 226,* 275*nn*86–87; restoration since 2009, 275*n*77; restrooms, 126; sculptures, *140–41,* 144–45, *144–45,* 148, *149,* 152–54, *154–55,* 276*n*14; tapestry, 169. *See also* Landmarking process

14 Pictures (Eggleston), 173, *175*

Francé, Raoul H., 109, 270*n*27

Frank, Robert, 174

Franklin Glass Corporation, 66

Frasconi, Antonio, 278–79*n*84

Freeman, Belmont, 275*n*77

Friedrichstrasse Turmhaus competition (Berlin 1921), 109–10, *110,* 119, 270*n*35

Friel, James E., 13, 23, 26, 257*n*2

Friel, Joseph G., 44

Friends of the Upper East Side Historic District, 221

Frost, Robert, 81

Frühlicht (Taut), 109, 113

Fuchs, Michael, 234

Fujikawa, Joseph, 51–53, 56, 256*n*33, 263*n*50, 263*n*54, 263–64*n*60, 269*n*6

Fuller, George A. *See* George A. Fuller Company
Furniture designers (for Seagram) 167, 171, 208, 279n93, 286n95, 286–87n96
The Future of Man symposium (1959), 81–82, 268n132

Gabo, Naum, 32
Gallerias, 287–88nn9–10
Gayle, Margot, 220
General Bronze Corporation, 63, 65
General Realty & Utilities Corporation, 22
George A. Fuller Company, 18–19, *20–21,* 23, 29, 44
Gérmination nocturne (Miró), 170
Gesamtkunstwerk ("total design"), 122, 128, 148, 150
Giedion, Sigfried, 42
Gill, Brendan, 221
Glaeser, Ludwig, 102, 180, 249, 281n111
Glasarchitektur (Scheerbart), 112, 113
Glass: in architectural projects, viii, 109–13, *111,* 271n55; floor-to-ceiling, 55, 106, *107,* 123, *126;* post–World War II buildings with glass walls, 132; and reflection of light, 94, 109–10, 114, 132; size of glass, 55–56; and skin separated from structure, 50–55, 114; tinted glass, 55–56, 66, 79, 113, 263–64n57; transparency, 215, 220–21; window and spandrel insertion, 63–64, *64. See also* Curtain walls
Glass House. *See* New Canaan Brick Guest House and Glass House (Johnson)
Glass House floor lamp, 131, 273n22
Glass Skyscraper (Mies), 109–10, *110–11,* 113–14
Goelet, Robert W., 17
Goethe, 109
Goldberger, Paul, 208
Goldman Sachs, 234
Goldsmith, Myron, 53, 57, 263n51, 264n64, 264n69, 269n6
Granite, 68–69, 83, 85
Grigoriev, S. L., 277n34
Gropius, Walter, 33, 35, 113, 260n76, 260n78, 265n80
Grossman, Sanford, 285n72
Guenette (Heizer), 186, *187*

Hagley Museum and Library (Wilmington, Delaware), 10
Haid, David, 42
Handicapped access, 288–89n32
Handy, John A., Jr., 44, *46*
Harleman, Donald R. F., 266–67n105, 267n123
Harrison, Wallace K., *27,* 258n24, 259n50
Harrison & Abramovitz, 27, 33, 35
Hawe, Thomas P., 207–8
Hawe Report, 207–8, 286n88, 286n91
Hays, K. Michael, 115, 271n65
H- and I-beams (and wide-flange mullions), 51, 53, 62–63, 266n87
Heizer, Michael, 186, *187,* 281n128
Hellman, Geoffrey T., 274n64
Hess, Thomas B., 275n5
Hilberseimer, Ludwig, 113, 118, 265n79
The Hill (Damian), 189
Hines building (NYC), 293n25
Hirondelle d'amour (Miró), *168,* 169
Historic Districts Council, 236
Historic preservation. *See* Landmarking process; Preservation issues
Hitchcock, Henry-Russell, 8, 128–29
Höch, Hannah, 113
Hodgson house (1951), 272n13, 273n37

Hoffman automobile showroom (NYC) designed by Wright, 28, 41, 259–60n59
L'Homme à la pastèque (Léger), 166, *167*
House and Garden article by Kelly (1952), 135
House of Seagram, 2, 4–5, 13, 254nn7–8. *See also* Distillers Company Limited; Distillers Corporation Limited; Distillers Corporation–Seagrams Limited; Joseph E. Seagram & Sons, Inc.
Housing and Urban Development, Department of (HUD), 284n54
Howe, George, 29, 35, 122, 260n60, 260n76
Huxley, Julian, 81
Huxtable, Ada Louise, 200, 222
Hydrodynamics Laboratory at MIT, 67, 266n103, 267n123

IBM Building (Madison Avenue), *213,* 212–13, 214, 232, 287n8
Idzikowski, Stanislas, 154
Illinois Institute of Technology (IIT, formerly Armour Institute of Technology): building design by Mies at, viii, x, 50–51, *51,* 115, *115,* 118; cinematographic conceptual sketches of, 119, *119;* Lambert as architecture student at, 201; Mies as instructor at, viii, 8; structural architecture development of Mies at, x, 114; Summers's construction and development role at, 261n11
Incentive zoning, 11, 195, 199, 231–32
Institute of Fine Arts, New York University, 8
Interior design, 208, 274n68, 286n95, 286–87n96. *See also* Johnson, Philip
International Fund for Monuments, 183
International Style, 27, 176
Ippen, Arthur T., 67, 266–67n105

Jacobs, Jane, 204
Jacobs, Robert Allan, 258n24
James, Henry, 173
Janis, Sidney, 161
Le Jardin (Lurçat), 169
Jaros, Baum & Bolles, 36, 264–65n71
Johnson, Philip: on "addition of bank" crisis, 71; and American art, 171; on architectural challenges, 268n136; architectural education of, 129–30; architectural role of, 8–9, 128–30, 256n32; AT&T building (Madison Avenue), 211–12, *213,* 288n11; on building exterior covering, 58–59; compared to Mies, 4, 131–32; design phase of Seagram, 41–47; Dumbarton Oaks museum design by, 265–66n84; early contacts with Lambert, 32–33, 151; executive offices, furnishings and design by, 166, *167, 167–71,* 169–71, 279n93; fountains and plaza landscape, 67–68, 69, 183; Four Seasons design phase, 138–49; and integration of art and architecture, 150, 152, 164, *172–73;* introducing Mies to America in MoMA exhibition, 8–9, 102, 104; and Lambert's apartment lighting, 136, 273–74n49; landmarking comments of, 220; Mies's influence on, ix, 129–30; offices of Van der Rohe and Johnson, New York, design of, 38–39; partnership with Mies, 36, 122, 266n102; photographs of, *46, 123;* and Picasso curtain, 158–59; and plaza design, 67–69, 267n119; as potential architect choice, 35–36, 261n83; relationship with Mies, 9, 41, 47, 67–68, 122, 128, 131, 134, 256n33, 266n92; and Rothko, 159, 164; Seagram role of, 1, 9, 10–11, 35–36, 41–47, 122–23, 128–30, 223. *See also* Four Seasons Restaurant; Lighting; New Canaan Brick Guest House and Glass House (Johnson)
Johnson Wax Company Complex (1936–39), *37*
Joie de vivre (Delaunay), 166
Jordy, William, 194
Joseph E. Seagram & Sons, Inc.: advertising, 4–5, 28, 255nn10–11, 255nn18–19; diversification of holdings, 237; history of, 2–5, 206,

254n4, 254n8, 255n9; lease with Uris Brothers, 13, 257nn1–2; loss of market, 214, 288n12; NYC offices (pre-Seagram building), 4–6, *5–6*, 13, 255n22, 257n2, 262n35; relocation study (Danbury as possible site), 207–8, 286n88, 286nn91–93; Seagram building advancing reputation of, 283–84n38; seal in cast bronze sculpture, 279n89; Vivendi-Seagram deal, 237–38, 293n39, 293–94n40. *See also* Chrysler building; Seagram building

Kahn, Ely Jacques, 258n24
Kahn, Louis, 32, 35, 201
Kahn and Jacobs, 19–21, *20–21,* 26, 36, 39, 45, 59, 64, 258n24
Kandinsky, Wassily, 42, 261n7
Kaufmann House (1947), 265n80
Kaye, Judith S., 230, 291–92n105
Kefauver Committee, 22, 199, 258n31
Kelly, Richard: background of and influences on, 134–35, 272n5, 272n13; exterior lighting by, 61, *62,* 265n80; Four Seasons Restaurant lighting, 142–43, 145–46, 223; interior lighting, 61, 127, 129, 272n19; Johnson influenced by, 10–11; Johnson office's lighting, 38; New Canaan Glass House's lighting, 131–34
Kennedy, Joseph P., Sr., 18, 257n13
Khokhlova, Olga, 154, 156
Kirstein, Lincoln, 276n7
Klee, Paul, 42, 261n7
Klein, Arvid, 214, 251–53
Kline, Franz, 166
Klutznick, Philip M., 286n87
Koolhaas, Rem, 62
Kornacker, Frank, 57, 264n66, 265n75
Kramer, Fred, 33, 36, 44–46, *46*
Krauss, Rosalind, 120
Krautheimer, Richard, 8

Lambert, Phyllis (née Bronfman): architecture degree of, 201; architectural projects, 201–5, *202–4,* 284n56; art collection and exhibitions at Seagram, role in, 150–52, 159, 165; artistic background of, 1, 7–8, 256n27; CCA role of, 151, 293n31; enforcer of Mies's concept, 45; and European and American drinking vessels collection, 171–73, *172–73;* landmarking role of, 219–20; letter to SB about proposed design (June 28, 1954), 30–32, *240–47;* memories as well as research forming base of book, ix, 10; NYC apartment of, designed by Johnson, 136; photographs of, *ii, 41, 46, 80, 151, 160;* regional and urban planning study of, 201; relationship with father, 8–9; relationship with Mies, 42; search for architect role of, 23–37; stewardship role of, ix
Landhaus und Garten (Muthesius), 103, *104*
Landmarking process: and artwork, 221–24, 229, 290n66; court actions brought by TIAA, 227–30, 289–90n58; exterior of building, 223; and Four Seasons Restaurant, 12, 221–28, *224–26,* 290n75, 291nn80–81; Landmarks Preservation Commission hearings and decisions, 12, 85, 208–9, 215, 219–27; lobby and first-floor interior, 223, 289n70; and plaza, 220–21; testimony during, 220–22, 227, 289n46, 290n47, 291nn80–81; understanding of, 232; waiver of thirty-year requirement, 208, 287n101
Landmarks Preservation Commission, 12, 85, 208–9, 215, 219–30, 236, 284n41. *See also* Landmarking process
Landscape and building, spatial relationship between, 9–10, 12, 67–70, 83, 102–21; Mies's approach in American buildings, 113–21; Mies's approach in European buildings, 106–13; and Scheerbart, 112–13, 114; Schinkel's influence, 105–6, 109; sense of calm, viii, 69, 105, 115; tree selection, 68, 267n113, 267n117

Landscape with Gothic Arcades (Schinkel), 131, *132*
Land-Weber, Ellen, *177*
Language, architecture as, viii, 50, 56
Lapidus, Morris, *5–7,* 6, 10, 255n22
Laudatio Florentinae Urbis (Bruni), 194
Laurence, William L., 81
Le Corbusier, 33, 35, 36, 129, 135, 171, 258n24, 259n50, 292n1
Leacock, Stephen, 4, 255n15
Ledoux, Claude-Nicolas, 129
Léger, Fernand, 166, *167*
Lehman, Herbert H., 266n102
Lescaze, William, 29, 35, 38, 122, 260n60, 265n80
Lever House: air conditioning of, 265n72; bay size, 196, 264n61; curtain wall of, 199, 292n11; footprint of, 196; landmarking of, 289n47; Luckman's involvement with, ix; relationship to Seagram design process, 18, *19,* 20, 35, *60,* 256n26, 264n61; sale of, 234, 236, 292n11; urban influence of, 231; windows in, 66, 199, 263n57
LeWitt, Sol, 167, 279n87
Lexington Avenue property adjoining Seagram building, *202,* 203–6, *235,* 235–36, 284–85n58
Libbey-Owens-Ford, 66, 263n57
Library of Congress, 10, 178, 269n2, 280n107
Liebes, Dorothy, 278n74
Lighting: evolution of, 265n80; exterior's reciprocity with interior's lighting, 134; "focal glow," "ambient luminescence," and "play of brilliants," 135–36, 143–44, *146;* in Four Seasons, 136, 139, *142,* 142–44; Glass House floor lamp, 131, 273n22; influences on, 129–33, 272n13; innovations in, 142, 275n75; and Johnson's contribution, 9, 136–43, 273n49; New Canaan Brick Guest House and Glass House, *129,* 129–32, *131–32;* PAR lamp, 136, 273n48. *See also* Night illumination
Lightolier, 61
Light Up (Smith), 183, *184*
Lincoln Center for the Performing Arts, 205, 275n3
Lind, Frederick J., 44
Lines & Color silkscreens (LeWitt), 167, 279n87
Linn, Karl, 148, 267n113, 267n117
Lipchitz, Jacques, 68
Lippold, Richard, ix, 143–45, *144–45,* 152–54, *154–55,* 165, 222–24, 229, 275n81, 276n14
Lissitzky, El, 109
Long, Richard, 184, *185*
Look building (1949–50), 26
Lord, Martin, 219
Luckman, Charles, ix, 29, 36, 66, 260–61n82
Luminous ceiling, *61,* 61–62, 66, 127, *127,* 265n80
Lunch Poems (O'Hara), 181
Lustig, Elaine, 126
Lynes, Russell, 121
Lyon, Danny, *175*

Macdonald, Nesta, 154
Machine Art (exhibition 1934), 122
Maeght, Aimé, 278n76
Maillol sculptures, 120
Malevich, Kasimir, 113, 129
Manfre, Noel, 280n97
Manley, John, 42, 261n9
Marble, 58, 69, 85, *96–98, 120,* 126. *See also* Travertine
Marca-Relli, Conrad, 170, *171*
Mariani, John, 81, 139, 274n66
Marilyn Wood and the Celebration Group, 188–89, 189

Marrus, Michael, 4, 254*n*1, 254*n*3
Martin, Agnes, 120
Massachusetts Institute of Technology (MIT), design of fountains, 67, 70, 266–67*n*105, 267*n*123
Massine, Léonide, 154, 156, 157, 158
Masson, André, 169–70, 279*n*84
Matter, Herbert, 169, *170*, 278*n*83, 279*n*89
MCA/Universal, 237
McCandless, Stanley, 134–35
McKim, Mead & White, 17, *17*, 49, 85, 116, 200
Mendelsohn, Eric, 26
Mendelsohn, Felix, 265*n*80
Messier, Jean-Marie, 237
Messinger, Ruth, 227
A Method of Lighting the Stage (McCandless), 134
Metropolitan Club (NYC), 13, *15*, 17
Metropolitan Opera, 30, 260*n*68
Michelangelo Buonarotti, 162, *163*
Miesian idiom, viii, 134
Mies in America (2001 exhibition), vii, 11, 237, 238
Mies in Berlin (2001 exhibition), vii, 105, 238
Mies van der Rohe: on architecture and spiritual realm, 8, 83, 90, 256*n*31, 268–69*n*1; archives of, 10; art collecting by, 276*n*12; in Berlin light festival (1928), 265*n*79; on building elements, 90; career of, vii, 10; character of, 7, 44; communication style of, 39, 42, 261*n*2; compared to Lapidus, 6; criticism of, vii, 41–42, 62, 105; design approach of, 9, 46–47, 49, 50, 69, 103–5, 262*n*30, 264*n*66; at design offices in NYC, 39, 43–44; emigration to Chicago, viii, 1, 8; on glass and "light reflections," 94, 110, 113; inventiveness of, 47, 60, 69, 262*n*28; large drawings, use of, 50, 262*n*37; licensing issues in New York, 67, 128, 266*n*102; on lighting, 61, 134, 265*n*79; on organic principle of order, 109; partnership with Johnson, 36, 122, 266*n*102; photographs of, *39*, *41*, *46*, *79–80*, *82*; private library of, 102, 268–69*n*1; and "Project Skytop" studies, 21; prominence of (1920), 7; Seagram building as emblematic of, viii, 56, 85, 102; selection of, 33, 35–36, 260*n*76, 260*n*80; separating structure and enclosure, 50–55; studying steel high-rise buildings, 51–53; tensions with Philip Johnson, 9, 266*n*92; as "thinker," 39, 261*n*1. *See also* Design phase of Seagram; Illinois Institute of Technology, Landscape and building, spatial relationship between
Mies van der Rohe (MoMA exhibition 1947), 8–9, 102, 104
Mies van der Rohe, buildings of: apartment houses at 860 and 880 Lakeshore Drive (1949–52), x, 8, 34, 35, 49, 50, 53–56, *54–55*, 57, 61, 114, 115–16, *116–17*, 264*n*69, 269*n*6; Arts Club (Chicago), 274*n*67; Barcelona Pavilion (1928–29), 7, 8, 51, 56, 61, 106, *108*, 113, 263*n*57; Bismarck Monument competition project (1910), 105, *105*, 119; Commonwealth Promenade, 62, 263–64*n*60; Farnsworth glass house (1951), 9, 11, 41, 49, 103, 261*n*11, 269*n*6; Federal Center (Chicago), 49, 269*n*6, 287*n*97; Friedrichstrasse Turmhaus competition (Berlin 1921), 109–10, *110*, 119, 270*n*35; Glass Skyscraper, 109; New National Gallery (Berlin), 270*n*25; 900 Esplanade (1953–57), 53–55, *55*, 62, 66, 263*n*53, 263–64*n*60; Promontory Apartment Building (1946), *52*, 53, 263*n*50; Resor house (1939), 120, 265–66*n*84; Riehl house (1906–07), 103–5, *104*, 106, 116, 118; Stuttgart Bank (1928), 119; Toronto-Dominion Centre, 49, 205, 269*n*6, 287*n*97; Tugendhat house (Brno 1928–30), 7, 9, 106, *107*, 265–66*n*84, 270*n*23, 271*n*58; Werkbund exhibition *Die Wohnung* (Stuttgart 1927), 8, 61, 271*n*56; Westmount Square (Montreal), 49. *See also* Illinois Institute of Technology
Miller, Herbert McCrae, 7
Miller, Wallis, 273*n*20

Milord la Chamarre (Dubuffet), 186, *186*
Miró, Joan, 133, 165, 167, 169–70, 278*n*77
Mitsubishi, 233
Model Cities Program, 201, 284*n*54
Models during design phase, 39, *41*, *48*, 49, 50, 67, 68, 180, 262*n*36, 266*n*101
Modern Architecture: International Exhibition (1932), 8–9
Modern Design: Art and Architecture (exhibition 1948), 151, *151*, 276*n*7
Moderne Bauformen on Riehl house, 105
Modernism, 8, 29, 130, 180
MoMA. *See* Museum of Modern Art (MoMA)
Montagu, Ashley, 81
Montana Apartments (NYC), 13, *15*, 18–19, 47, 136
Montreal: Beaux-Arts Mount Royal Hotel, 2, 254*n*6; Distillers Corporation–Seagrams Limited offices, 2, *3*, *5*, 254*n*5; Milton-Parc neighborhood condominium, 288*n*14; Place Ville Marie, 205, 257*n*14; Saidye Bronfman Centre, 201, 275*n*75; Westmount Square, 49
Moore, Gene, 267*n*122
Moore, Henry, 68, 181–82
More, Timothy, 198, 282–83*n*20, 283*n*36
Motherwell, Robert, 162
Mount Royal Hotel (Montreal), 2, 254*n*6
Movement in design, 67, 118–20, 217–18
Mozart's Birthday (di Suvero), 218–19, 289*n*36
Muller, Hermann J., 81
Mumford, Lewis, 32, 121, 128, 194
Municipal Arts Society, 227, 236
Municipal Assistance Corporation (MAC), 285*n*77
Muschamp, Herbert, 115
Musée National Picasso (Paris), 157
"Museum for a Small City" (1943), 120
Museum of Modern Art (MoMA): architecture exhibitions, 10, 104, 199; *Buildings for Business and Government* (exhibition 1957), 68, 266*n*101, 267*n*108; Court House prints, exhibition at, 176; Johnson's work at, 1, 8–9, 32, 275*n*85; *Machine Art* (exhibition 1934), 122; *Mies in Berlin* (exhibition 2001), vii, 10, 105, 238; Mies's bequest of drawings to, 10, 256*n*35, 269*n*2; *Mies van der Rohe* (exhibition 1947), 8–9, 102, 104; Rothko exhibition (1961), 163, 278*n*73; Szarkowski exhibition (1977), 176
Muthesius, Hermann, 103, 104, *104*, 269*n*12

Nagy, Moholy, 113
"Nasci" issue of *Merz* (1924), 109
National Association of Counties, 176
National Intercollegiate Arts Conference (Vassar College, 1948), 151, *151*
National Trust for Historic Preservation, 280*n*104
Nature and architecture. *See* Landscape and building, spatial relationship between
Negbaur, Hal K., 213–14, 287–88*n*9
Nervi, Pier Luigi, 264*n*64
Neumann, Dietrich, 265*n*80, 270*n*35, 272*n*5
Neumeyer, Fritz, 112, 269*n*2
Neutra, Richard, 42, 265*n*80
Newarker (restaurant at Newark Airport), 136–38, 274*n*64
New Canaan Brick Guest House and Glass House (Johnson), 9, 10, *123*, 126, 128–32, *129*, *131–33*, 136, 143, 151
New Guardhouse on Unter den Linden (Berlin), 114
Newman, Barnett, 183, *183*
New National Gallery (Berlin), 270*n*25
Newsweek on New York City's decline, 206

New Topographics, 174, 280*n*100

New York City: choice of location for Seagram in, 16–18; financial difficulties of, 206, 232, 285*n*77; Fortune 500 companies located in, 207, 286*n*88; lighting of buildings (1930s), 265*n*80; Midtown Manhattan development, 16, *16*, 195, 232; public space in, 9, 11, 211, 275*n*3; Seagram's impact on, 11. *See also* Joseph E. Seagram & Sons, Inc.; *specific buildings and addresses*

New York City Board of Estimate, 226–27, 291*n*78

New York City Landmarks Preservation Law (1965), 200, 229

New York City Planning Commission, 195, 203, 236, 282*n*3, 287–88*n*9

New Yorker: Mumford review of Seagram (1958), 121, 128; on Seagram Christmas trees with white lights, 70, 267*n*122

New York Herald Tribute: on New York City's decline, 206; on tax assessment on Seagram building, 200

New York Landmarks Conservancy, 236, 293–94*n*40

New York Observer on photo exhibition of Seagram as NYC landmark, 180–81

New York Times: on proposed Pennsylvania Station demolition, 199, 200; on proposed Seagram building, 29, 30; on sale of Seagram building, 210, 234; on Seagram Gallery, 176, 281*n*105 181; on Seagram plaza, 192–93, 281*n*127

New York World's Fair (1939) Distilled Spirits Institute Pavilion, 6, 256*n*25

The Next Hundred Years: A Scientific Symposium (November 22, 1957), 268*n*133

Nichols, Marie, 143

Night illumination, 61–62, *62*, 127, *127, 131, 133*, 265n79

Nixon, Nicholas, *176*

Norman, Gene A., 219–21

Noyes, Charles, 21, 258*n*27

Ockman, Joan, 264–65*n*71

Office of Midtown Planning and Development (OMPD), 202–3, 287*n*101

O'Hara, Frank, 181

Oil company acquisition (Seagram), 23, 237, 293*n*35

Olmec head displayed on plaza, *182*, 182–83

Oud, J. J. P., 8

Pahlmann, William, 138–40, *140–42*, 274*n*68

Palumbo, Peter, 265–66*n*84

Parade (Picasso), 157, 277*n*30, 277*n*34

Parallax, 118–20

Pare, Richard, ix, 12, 174, 176, 179, 280*n*100, 280*nn*102–3; photographs by, *89–101, 114, 144, 156, 172–73, 186*

Park Avenue, 13–14, *16*, 16–18, 26, 236, 257*n*4

Park Avenue Plaza, 214, 232, *232*

PAR lamp, 136, 273*n*48

Pasanella, Giovanni, 220, 221, 236, 286*n*95, 286–87*n*96

Pasanella + Klein, 205, 208, 214, 251–53, 286*n*95

Pavia, Philip, 275*n*5

Pavilion, building type, 11, 71, 116. *See also* Barcelona Pavilion (1928–29)

"Pedestrians' sculpture," 275*n*5

Pei, I. M., 33, 205

Pennsylvania Station, proposed demolition of, 11, 199–200, 284*n*41

Penrose, Roland, 158

Pereira & Luckman, 29, 29–31, 260*n*60

Perls, Klaus G., 158–59

Persius, Ludwig, 130

"Personal Poem" (O'Hara), 181

Personnages avec étoile (Miró), 169, *170*

Petty, Margaret Maile, 265*n*80

Philadelphia Saving Fund Society building (1929–32), 122

"Photographs of American Urban Life" (1973), 173–75

Photography collection, 173–78, *174–175*

Picasso, Pablo: lithographs and etchings by, 169–70; *Parade* (curtain), 157, 277*n*30, 277*n*34; photograph of, *160*; portraits by, 154, 276*n*19; sculptures by, 68, 120, 152, 159, *160*. *See also* Le Tricorne (ballet)

Pier Associates, Inc., Architects and Planners, *202–4*, 203

Place Ville Marie (Montreal), 205, 257*n*14

Placzek, Adolf, 223, 290*nn*70–71

Planning Commission. *See* New York City Planning Commission

Plaza of Seagram building, 66–71, *89–97, 101, 120*; benches, 12, 68, 69, 189, *193*, 216, 236, 270*n*23; Christmas trees as New York tradition, 70, 267*nn*121–22, 288*n*22, 289*n*33; design phase, *40*, 67–68, 70–71, 267*n*117; fountains and landscape, 67–70, *89–91*, 181, 266–67*n*105, 267*n*113, 267*n*124; and landmarking considerations, 220–21; lease terms governing, 217–18; as open space, 189–93; *Open Space Design Criteria* (NYC Planning Commission), 191–92; sculptures for, 152, 181, 276*n*12, 280*n*97; special exhibits, 180–93, *182–88, 248*; and TIAA concerns, 218–19, 289*n*35. *See also* Landscape and building, spatial relationship between

Polk, Willis, 263*n*43

Pollack, Reginald, 279*n*84

Polunin, Vladimir, and Elizabeth Violet, 156–57

Pope, John Russell, 29

Praise for Elohim Adonai (di Suvero), 186, *187*

Preservation issues, 199, 287*n*5. *See also* Landmarking process

Preservation League of New York State, 230

Prestige as tax issue, 196–99, 282–83*n*11, 283*n*36, 284*n*49

Price, Edison, 127, 142–43, 145–46, 275*n*75

Project Skytop study (1952), 18–19, *20–21*, 231, 258*n*28

Promontory Apartment Building (1946), *52*, 53, 263*n*50

Public awareness of architecture in NYC, 11

Public space: and movement, 118–20; in NYC, 9, 11, 211, 275*n*3; open plaza as, 189–93; value of, 199, 201–2

Queen Luise's bedchamber, 130, *130*, 143–44, 273*n*20

RA. *See* Restaurant Associates (RA)

Racquet and Tennis Club (NYC), 17, *17*, 49, 85, *101*, 116, 214, 236, 257*n*10

Raggio, Olga, 172, 279–80*nn*95–96

Real Estate Board of New York, 227, 233

Real Estate Forum on tax assessment on Seagram building, 200

Real estate professionals and families, power of, 233

Reber, G. F., 158, 277*n*34

Reich, Lilly, 61, 271*n*56

Resor house (1939), 120, 265–66*n*84

Restaurant Associates (RA), 136, 138, 274*n*69

Le Rêve (Miró), 169

RFR Holding LLC, 234–36, 279*n*89, 289*n*33

Rice, Dan, 161

Richardson, John, 156–58, 276*n*21

Rideau de scène (Picasso), 157–58

Riehl, Alois, 103

Riehl house (1906–7), 103–5, *104*, 106, 116, 118

Rivers, Larry, 166

Robertson, Jaquelin, 202–3

Roché, H. P., 152, 276*n*9

Rockefeller, Nelson, 276*n*8

Rockefeller Center, 26, 198, 233, 275n3
Rockefeller Guest House (1950), 273n37
Rohatyn, Felix, 285n77
Roque, Jacqueline, 159
Rorimer, James, 279–80n95
Rose, Adam R., 292n4
Rosen, Aby, 234, 235–36, 279n89
Rosenthal, Halina, 289n47
Roth, Emery, 26, 27, 235
Rothko, Mark, 148, 152, 159, 161–64, 165, *164–65,* 167, 169, *169,* 275n85, 277n49, 278n68, 278nn71–73
Rouse & Goldstone, 14, *15,* 257n5
Royal Palace at Orianda, Crimea (1938), 105, *105,* 270n19
Rudolph, Paul, 33
Ruegenberg, Sergius, 110
Russell, Bertrand, 81
Russell, John, 181

Saarinen, Aline Berstein, 33, 35, 260n77
Saarinen, Eero, 33, 35, 137, 234, 260n78
Saidye Bronfman Centre (Montreal), 201, 275n75
St. Cyprian's Day (Marca-Relli), 170, *171*
St. Thomas University, Houston, 164
Sanchez, Frank, 220
Saxe, Edward, 210, 214
SB. *See* Bronfman, Samuel
Scène antique (Picasso), 170
Scheerbart, Paul, 112–13, 114, 271n55, 271n58
Schenley Industries, 257n3
Schinkel, Karl Friedrich: Altes Museum (Berlin), 51, 83, 130, 132; Hall of the Stars in the Palace of the Queen of the Night (Mozart's *Magic Flute*), *146,* 146–47; Hofgärtnerei (Potsdam), 131, 132; influence on Johnson, 129–30, *130, 132,* 134, 149; influence on Mies, ix, 105–6, *105–6,* 109, 114, 131–32, 149, 270n19; Queen Luise's bedroom design, 130, *130,* 143, 273n20; Schloss Charlottenhof (Potsdam), 106, *106,* 116, 270n23, 273n20
Schwengel, Frank R., 30, 206, 262n20
Sculptures, 120–21, 148, 181–89, *182–87;* Lippold, 144–45, *140–41, 144–45,* 152–54, *154–55,* 222–24; Picasso, 159, *160,* 181
Seagram, Calvert, Carstairs building (unbuilt NYC), 6–7, *7,* 256n26
Seagram building: advancing reputation of Seagram business, 283–84n38; bay dimensions, 57, 59, 196, 264n61; building module, 56–57; building plans, 85; bustle, 47, 166; change of ownership to RFR, 12, 234; change of ownership to TIAA, 12, 210, 214–30, 232, 251–53; construction phase, 71–81, *72–79;* corners, 83, *84;* cost of, 21, 44, 45, 61, 64; critical reaction to, 114–115, 121, 128, 194; curatorial office, 173, 215; curtain wall, 9, 32, 39–41, 61, 62, 114; doors, 124, *125;* east wing great rooms, 83, 85, *98–99, 140–41, 224–26,* 268n135; elevators, 47, 57–58, *58,* 59, 85, 124, *125,* 264n66; as emblematic of Mies, viii, 56, 85, 102; executive bathrooms, 122, 124, *126;* executive furniture and offices, 128, *167–71, 170–71, 171,* 279n93, 286n95; as exemplar of prototypical American building type, ix, 9, 211, 231, 235; impact on New York City, 10, 11, 284n52; innovations of, 62, 123–26, 194–95; interest in moving from NYC, 206–7, 286n87; Johnson's role, 1, 9, 10–11, 35–36, 41–47, 122–23, 128–30, 223; land acquisition for, 47; landmarking of, 12, 208–9, 219–30; lease terms upon sale to TIAA, 12, 214–20, 234, 237, 288n14, 288n16, 288n18; lobby, 60, 69, 85, *117,* 136, 169, 216, 223; luminous ceiling, *61,* 61–62, 66, *127, 127,* 265n80; material sensuality of, 83–85; meeting (conference) rooms, 166, *168;* Mies's opinion of, 83; neighborhood changes since 1960s, 236; night-time illumination of, 61–62, *62, 127, 127;* official opening of, 81; and parallax, 120; photographs of, *63, 76–77, 86–87, 89–101, 114, 238–39;* reception rooms, 166–67, 169, *167–70;* relocation of some functions to 800 Third Avenue, 208, 286n95; rental space and rates, 38, 46, 57, 196, 197, 207, 283–84n38, 288n21; and Riehl house, 104; setback and sidewalk, 69, 267n116; skin's relationship to structure, 83, *84,* 114; spatial relationship with landscape, 9–10, 12, 67–70; steps to building, 41; tower dimensions, 56–58; under Vivendi, 237–38, 293–94n40; White Horse Tavern, 278n78. *See also* Air rights; Design phase of Seagram; Johnson, Philip; Landmarking; Mies van der Rohe; Plaza of Seagram building; Tax assessment on Seagram building; Zoning
"Seagram East," 202–3, *203–4*
Seagram Gallery, 11, 12, 167, *169,* 178, 181, *248–50. See also* Artwork for Seagram and Four Seasons
"Seagram Interior Design Guidelines," 208, 286–87nn95–96
The Seagram Plaza: Its Design and Use (1977 exhibition), 102, 180, *180,* 210, 237, 269n3
Selz, Peter, 278n73
Serra, Richard, 178, *178*
Setback and sidewalk of Seagram, 69, 267n116
Setback rules, 194, 196, 236
Seventh International Architecture Biennale (Venice 2000), 237, 293n31
Severud-Elstad-Krueger Associates, 36, 57–59, *58,* 264n66
Severud-Perrone-Sturm-Bandel, *187*
Shainswit, Beatrice J., 228–29
Shangri-La Hotels, 236
Shapiro, Joel, 184, *185*
Sheaff, L'Huillier, 44, 46, *46,* 50, 56, 71, 136, 137, 139, 261–62n16
Shore, Stephen, 176
Sinclair Oil building (1952), 26
Sitwell, Sacheverell, 157, 158
Sixty Years of Living Architecture (Wright exhibition 1952), 28
Skidmore, Owings & Merrill, 18, *19,* 29, 33, 49, 207, 214, 232, *232,* 260n60
Skyscrapers, ix, 8, 28, 54, 57, 65, 109, 110, *111,* 113–14, 270n35, 292n1. *See also specific buildings*
"Skytop" study. *See* Project Skytop study
Slater, Ellis D., 28, 44–46, *46,* 49–50, 262n20
Smith, Barrett, 221, 222
Smith, Neill, 284n49
Smith, Tony, 183–84, *184*
Smithson, Robert, 178, *179*
Snow, Michael, 178, *179*
Soane, John, 129, 150
The Social Life of Small Urban Spaces (Whyte), *191–93,* 192, 281n133
Solomon R. Guggenheim Museum, 28, 152
Somerset Importers, 257n13
"Specialty properties," 196–99
Spence, David Jerome, 2, *3,* 254n5
Speyer, Jerry, 234
Stable Gallery, 170
Stagflation, 206
Standardization, 56
Steel structure, 51–55, 57–58, *58,* 79, 83, 264n65
Steichen Edward, 174
Stern, Robert A. M., 292n1
Stetz, Tom, 251–53, 288–89n32
Steuer, Aaron, 197, 199, 282n16
Stewardship: of modern architecture, 11–12, 211; of Seagram building, ix, 208, 211
Stieglitz, Alfred, 174
Stimmung, 122, 134, 148, 149

Stock Exchange (Chicago), demolition of, 202, 284n57
Stockli, Albert, 138, 274n66
Stoller, Ezra, 86–87, 140, 167, 167–68, 171, 180, 239
The Story of a Winery (Adams photographic exhibition), 278n81
Strand, Paul, 174
The Street Life Project, 190–91
Structural architecture, 113–18, 263–42, 271n61
Structural engineering, 59–61, 264nn65–66
Stubbins, Hugh, 205, 211, 212, 285n68
Stuttgart Bank (1928), 119
Sullivan, Louis, ix, 53
Sullivan & Adler, 202
Summers, Gene: on bronze exterior, 62–64, 266n92, 266n95; and design phase of Seagram, 41, 42–44, 57, 264n66, 266n85; on fountains and plaza landscape, 67–68, 69, 70; on Mies's communication style, 39, 261n2; in Mies's office, 42, 261n11; photograph of, 46
Sweeney, James Johnson, 50, 152
Szarkowski, John, 174, 176

Tapestries, 143, 164–65, 166, 166, 168, 169, 170, 279nn85–86
Tate Modern (London), Rothko Room, 164, 278n71
Taut, Bruno, 109, 110, 112, 112–13, 270n33, 271n45
Tax assessment on Seagram building: consequences of, 11, 12, 284n53; cost basis, 21, 283n21, 283n26; court case, 196–99, 282n16, 283n31, 283n35; public reaction to, 200–201
Tax Commission of the City of New York, 196, 283n26
Teachers Insurance and Annuity Association (TIAA), 12, 214–30, 251–53, 285n72, 288–89n32
Thornton, Gene, 176
375 Park Avenue Restaurant Corporation, 137
Tietz, Bernhard Schring, 270n35
Time on New York City's situation, 206, 211
Time's importance in resolution of concepts, 10
Tishman, David, 22, 258n35
Tishman Speyer, 234
Todd, David, 220, 224
Toronto-Dominion Centre, 49, 205, 269n6, 287n97
Travertine, 85, 92–93, 101, 124–125, 146, 147. See also Marble
Le Tricorne (ballet), curtain (Picasso), ix, 85, 146–47, 147, 154–60, 156–57, 165, 217, 222, 238, 277n30, 293–94n40
Tristis, Antonis, 284n54
Trump Tower, 287n8
Trunk, Anton L., 13, 18, 257n4
Tugendhat house (Brno 1928–30), 7, 9, 106, 107, 265–66n84, 270n23, 271n58

Unilever, 234
United Nations, 27, 29, 35, 60, 199, 231, 257n14, 259n50, 264n61, 265n72
Universal Pictures building (1946–47), 26, 259n44
University of Illinois at Chicago, 10
University of Pennsylvania, student plaza design project, 67
Upper Michigan Avenue Project (Chicago), 207
Urban Design Group of NYC Planning Commission's *Open Space Design Criteria,* 191–92
Urban planning and urban crisis, 206
Uris Brothers, 13, 26, 257nn1–2
Uris building, 27

van Doesburg, Nelly, 166, 279n85
van Doesburg, Theo, 129, 166
Vassar College, 8, 151, 151

Veblen, Thorsten, 197, 199
Venetian blinds, 124, 125
Ventilation, 59, 265n73. See also Air conditioning
Village of Euclid v. Ambler (1926), 282n4
Vivendi-Seagram deal, 237–38, 293n39, 293–94n40
Voisin restaurant, 30, 136, 260n64
von Bidder, Alex, 81, 139, 274n66, 275n77
von Eckardt, Wolf, 176
von Pückler, Carl Friedrich, 129
Voorhees, Walker, Smith & Smith, 29, 196, 260n60

Wagner, Robert, 195, 282n5
Wall Street (Strand), 174
Webb & Knapp, 257n14
Wechsler, Warren, 234
Werkbund exhibition *Die Wohnung* (Stuttgart 1927), 8, 61, 271n56
Westchester County Airport office building (unbuilt), 208
Westmount Square (Montreal), 49
White, Stanford, 15, 17
White Horse Tavern (Seagram building), 278n78
Whitney Museum of American Art, 186. See also *Mies in America*
Whyte, William H., 180, 190–93, 191–93, 217, 281n133, 287–88n9
Wiley house (1953), 273n37
Willkie, H. Frederick, 4
Windows. *See* Glass
Winogrand, Garry, 174
Wirt Dexter building (Chicago 1887), 53
Wohnreform movement, 103
Wood, Marilyn, 188–89, 189
Woolworth building, 234, 292n12
World Trade Center (1973), 57, 59, 264–65n71, 292n15
Wright, Frank Lloyd, 27–28, 33, 35, 37, 41, 109, 259n52, 259n56, 259–60n59, 263n43

Yamasaki, Minoru, 33, 57
YWCA buildings on Lexington Avenue, 203–6, 235, 236, 285n60, 293n24

Zeckendorf, William, 18, 33, 199, 257n14, 292n10
Zoning, 11, 12, 16, 20, 47, 195–96, 231–32, 282n4. See also Air rights; Incentive zoning
Zoning change of 1929, 14, 16–17
Zoning Resolution of 1916 (NYC), 14, 195, 196, 204, 282n4
Zoning Resolution of 1961 (NYC), 23, 85, 189, 195–96, 200, 201, 212, 236, 281n133, 287n8

ILLUSTRATION CREDITS

The photographers and the sources of visual material other than the owners indicated in the captions are as follows. Every effort has been made to supply complete and correct credits; if there are errors and omissions, please contact Yale University Press so that corrections can be made in any subsequent edition.

Frontispiece Fonds Phyllis Lambert, Canadian Centre for Architecture, Montreal. © United Press International.

1 From "Hands Across the Border: Salutations from Montreal," *Seagram Spotlight* 1, no. 9 (August 1937): 7. Seagram Museum Collection, Hagley Museum and Library, Wilmington, Delaware.

2 From Morris Lapidus, *Too Much Is Never Enough* (New York: Rizzoli International, 1996), 116. Reproduced with permission from Alan Lapidus.

3 Library of Congress, Prints and Photographs Division, Gottscho-Schleisner Collection LC-G612-T01–35833 DLC.

4 Fonds Phyllis Lambert, Canadian Centre for Architecture, Montreal. Reproduced with permission from Alan Lapidus.

5 Arthur Schatz/Time & Life Pictures/Getty Images.

6 From *A Monograph of the Works of McKim, Mead & White, 1879–1915* (New York: Arno, 1977), pl. 61 (top).

7 Cover of *Montana Apartments Prospectus* (c. 1913). Fonds Seagram Building, Canadian Centre for Architecture, Montreal.

8 From *Montana Apartments Prospectus* (c. 1913). Fonds Seagram Building, Canadian Centre for Architecture, Montreal.

9 Advertisement by George A. Fuller Company, from "A Special Report on 375 Park Avenue," *New York Times,* April 7, 1957. Reproduced with permission from George A. Fuller Company.

10 Library of Congress, Prints and Photographs Division, Historic American Building Survey, HABS NY, 31-NEYO, 73-1.

11 © G. E. Kidder Smith/Corbis.

12 Collection Seagram Company, Ltd., Hagley Museum and Library, Wilmington, Delaware. Reproduced with permission from George A. Fuller Company and Cushman & Wakefield.

13 Fonds Seagram Building, Canadian Centre for Architecture, Montreal. Reproduced with permission from George A. Fuller Company and Cushman & Wakefield.

14 Fonds Seagram Building, Canadian Centre for Architecture, Montreal. Reproduced with permission from George A. Fuller Company and Cushman & Wakefield.

15 Collection Seagram Company, Ltd., Hagley Museum and Library, Wilmington, Delaware. Reproduced with permission from Cushman & Wakefield.

16 From Robert F. R. Ballard, *Directory of Manhattan Office Buildings* (New York: McGraw-Hill, 1978), 29.

17 From "A Great Debate," *Architectural Forum* 93, no. 5 (November 1950): [102].

18 *New York Herald Tribune,* July 13, 1954. The Queens Borough Public Library, Long Island Division, New York Herald Tribune Photo Morgue.

19 Chicago History Museum: HB-13809-J6, Hedrich-Blessing.

20 From "Frank Lloyd Wright," *Architectural Forum* 94, no. 1 (January 1951): [77].

21 Fonds Phyllis Lambert, Canadian Centre for Architecture, Montreal. © Phyllis Lambert.

22 The Mies van der Rohe Archive, The Museum of Modern Art, New York. Gift of the architect. © MoMA, New York.

23 Canadian Centre for Architecture, Montreal. Gift of Gene Summers to Phyllis Lambert. © Estate of Ludwig Mies van der Rohe/SODRAC (2013).

24 From "The Birth of a Building," *Seagram Spotlight* (October 1955): 29. Fonds Phyllis Lambert, Canadian Centre for Architecture, Montreal.

25 Fonds Phyllis Lambert, Canadian Centre for Architecture, Montreal. © Tommy Weber.

26 Photograph: Fonds Seagram Building, Canadian Centre for Architecture, Montreal. Model: The Museum of Modern Art, New York. Gift of Joseph E. Seagram & Sons, Inc., and Philip Johnson. © 2013 Artists Rights Society (ARS), New York/VG Bild-Kunst, Bonn.

27 The Mies van der Rohe Archive, The Museum of Modern Art, New York. Gift of the architect. © MoMA, New York.

28 Photograph: Chicago History Museum: HB-9522-A, Hedrich-Blessing. Model: The Mies van der Rohe Archive, The Museum of Modern Art, New York.

29 The Mies van der Rohe Archive, The Museum of Modern Art, New York. Gift of the architect. Digital Image © The Museum of Modern Art/Licensed by SCALA/Art Resource, NY.

30 Chicago History Museum: HB-13809-L4, Hedrich-Blessing.

31 Chicago History Museum: HB-13809-J6, Hedrich-Blessing.

32 "A Skyscraper Crammed with Innovations," *Engineering News Record* 158, no. 24 (June 13, 1957): 47. Digital image: McGill University, Schulich Library of Science and Engineering. Reproduced with permission from Severud Associates Consulting Engineers, P.C.

33 Canadian Centre for Architecture, Montreal. © CCA. Reyner Banham, *The Architecture of the Well-Tempered Environment* (Chicago: University of Chicago Press, 1969), 224, 226.

34 From "Seagram Building, New York City," *International Lighting Review* 12, no. 2 (1961): 69.

35 "New Progress in Light," *Architectural Forum* 106, no. 2 (February 1957): 155.

36 © Werner Blaser.

37 "Bronze Gem for Park Avenue," *Copper and Brass Bulletin,* no. 180 (February 1957): detail of p. 4.

38 *Architectural Record* 121, no. 3 (March 1957): 21. Reproduced with permission from the Mary Petty and Alan Dunn Estate at Syracuse University.

39 Fonds Phyllis Lambert, Canadian Centre for Architecture, Montreal.

40 Fonds Phyllis Lambert, Canadian Centre for Architecture, Montreal.

41 Fonds Phyllis Lambert, Canadian Centre for Architecture, Montreal.

42 Fonds Phyllis Lambert, Canadian Centre for Architecture, Montreal.

43 Fonds Phyllis Lambert, Canadian Centre for Architecture, Montreal.

44 Fonds Phyllis Lambert, Canadian Centre for Architecture, Montreal.

45 Fonds Phyllis Lambert, Canadian Centre for Architecture, Montreal.

46 Fonds Phyllis Lambert, Canadian Centre for Architecture, Montreal.

47 Fonds Phyllis Lambert, Canadian Centre for Architecture, Montreal.

48 Fonds Phyllis Lambert, Canadian Centre for Architecture, Montreal.

49 Fonds Phyllis Lambert, Canadian Centre for Architecture, Montreal.

50 Fonds Phyllis Lambert, Canadian Centre for Architecture, Montreal.

51 Bethlehem Steel advertisement, from "A Special Report on 375 Park Avenue," *New York Times,* April 7, 1957. Reproduced with permission from the National Museum of Industrial History.

52 From "Building Construction Starts," *Seagram Spotlight* (April 1956): 23. Seagram Museum Collection, Hagley Museum and Library, Wilmington, Delaware.

53 Frank Scherschel/Time Life Pictures/Getty Images.

54 Frank Scherschel/Time Life Pictures/Getty Images.

55 Fonds Seagram Building, Canadian Centre for Architecture, Montreal. © Tommy Weber.

56 Fonds Seagram Building, Canadian Centre for Architecture, Montreal.

57 "The Seagram Building," *Architectural Record* 124, no. 1 (July 1958): 141. Reprinted with permission from Architectural Record © 2013, The McGraw-Hill Companies.

58 Canadian Centre for Architecture, Montreal. Ezra Stoller © Esto.

59 Canadian Centre for Architecture, Montreal. Ezra Stoller © Esto.

PF 1 Canadian Centre for Architecture, Montreal. © Richard Pare.

PF 2 Canadian Centre for Architecture, Montreal. © Richard Pare.

PF 3 Canadian Centre for Architecture, Montreal. © Richard Pare.

PF 4 Canadian Centre for Architecture, Montreal. © Richard Pare.

PF 5 Canadian Centre for Architecture, Montreal. © Richard Pare.

PF 6 Canadian Centre for Architecture, Montreal. © Richard Pare.

PF 7 Canadian Centre for Architecture, Montreal. © Richard Pare.

PF 8 Canadian Centre for Architecture, Montreal. © Richard Pare.

PF 9 Canadian Centre for Architecture, Montreal. © Richard Pare.

PF 10 Canadian Centre for Architecture, Montreal. © Richard Pare.

PF 11 Canadian Centre for Architecture, Montreal. © Richard Pare.

PF 12 Canadian Centre for Architecture, Montreal. © Richard Pare.

PF 13 Canadian Centre for Architecture, Montreal. © Richard Pare.

PF 14 Canadian Centre for Architecture, Montreal. © Richard Pare.

PF 15 Canadian Centre for Architecture, Montreal. © Richard Pare.

60 Hermann Muthesius, *Landhaus und Garten: Beispiele neuzeitlicher Landhäuser nebst Grundrissen, Innenräumen und Gärten,* 2nd ed. (Munich: F. Bruckmann, 1910), 50–51.

61 The Mies van der Rohe Archive, The Museum of Modern Art, New York. Gift of the architect. Digital Image © The Museum of Modern Art/Licensed by SCALA/Art Resource, NY.

62 Karl Friedrich Schinkel, *Entwürf zu dem Kaiserlichen Palast Orianda in der Krimm: Für die Ausführung erfunden* (Berlin: Verlag von Ernst und Korn, 1873), pl. 1. Canadian Centre for Architecture, Montreal.

63 Karl Friedrich Schinkel, *Sammlung Architektonischer Entwürfe* (Potsdam: F. Riegel, 1852), detail of pl. 1. Canadian Centre for Architecture, Montreal.

64 Archive Daniela Hammer-Tugendhat, Vienna/Austria.

65 From Fritz Neumeyer, *The Artless Word: Mies van der Rohe on the Building Art* (Cambridge, MA: MIT Press, 1991), 191. Reprinted with permission from the MIT Press.

66 The Mies van der Rohe Archive, The Museum of Modern Art, New York. Gift of the architect. Digital Image © The Museum of Modern Art/Licensed by SCALA/Art Resource, NY.

67 Photograph: The Mies van der Rohe Archive, The Museum of Modern Art, New York. Plan: © Estate of Ludwig Mies van der Rohe/SODRAC (2013).

68 The Mies van der Rohe Archive, The Museum of Modern Art, New York. Gift of the architect. Digital Image © The Museum of Modern Art/Licensed by SCALA/Art Resource, NY.

69 The Mies van der Rohe Archive, The Museum of Modern Art, New York. Gift of the architect. Digital Image © The Museum of Modern Art/Licensed by SCALA/Art Resource, NY.

70 The Mies van der Rohe Archive, The Museum of Modern Art, New York. Gift of the architect. Digital Image © The Museum of Modern Art/Licensed by SCALA/Art Resource, NY.

71 From *L'Architecture Vivante*, fall 1925. Photograph: The Mies van der Rohe Archive, The Museum of Modern Art, New York. Model: © Estate of Ludwig Mies van der Rohe/SODRAC (2013).

72 From Bruno Taut, *Alpine Architektur: In 5 Teilen und 30 Zeichnungen des Architekten Bruno Taut* (Hagen i. W.: Erschienen im Folkwang-Verlag, 1919), pl. 7. Canadian Centre for Architecture, Montreal.

73 Canadian Centre for Architecture, Montreal. © Richard Pare.

74 Chicago History Museum: HB-26823-B, Hedrich-Blessing. © Estate of Ludwig Mies van der Rohe/SODRAC (2013).

75 Canadian Centre for Architecture, Montreal. © CCA.

76 Chicago History Museum: HB-13809-K5, Hedrich-Blessing.

77 Canadian Centre for Architecture, Montreal. Ezra Stoller © Esto.

78 Canadian Centre for Architecture, Montreal. © Estate of Ludwig Mies van der Rohe/SODRAC (2013).

79 Canadian Centre for Architecture, Montreal. © Estate of Ludwig Mies van der Rohe/SODRAC (2013).

80 Canadian Centre for Architecture, Montreal. © Estate of Ludwig Mies van der Rohe/SODRAC (2013).

81 Canadian Centre for Architecture, Montreal. © Walker Evans Archive, The Metropolitan Museum of Art.

82 Arnold Newman/Arnold Newman Collection/Getty Images.

83 *Architectural Forum* 109, no. 1 (July 1958): [72]. Photograph by George Cserna: Reproduced with permission from Avery Architectural and Fine Arts Library, Columbia University.

84 *Architectural Record* 124, no. 3 (September 1958): 25. Reproduced with permission from the Mary Petty and Alan Dunn Estate at Syracuse University.

85 *Architectural Forum* 109, no. 1 (July 1958): 73. Photograph by Ezra Stoller: Ezra Stoller © Esto. Photographs by George Cserna: Reproduced with permission from Avery Architectural and Fine Arts Library, Columbia University.

86 *Architectural Forum* 109, no. 1 (July 1958): 74. Photograph by Ezra Stoller: Ezra Stoller © Esto. Photographs by George Cserna: Reproduced with permission from Avery Architectural and Fine Arts Library, Columbia University.

87 *Architectural Forum* 109, no. 1 (July 1958): [75]. Photograph by Ezra Stoller: Ezra Stoller © Esto. Photographs by George Cserna: Reproduced with permission from Avery Architectural and Fine Arts Library, Columbia University. Photograph by Alexandre Georges: © Alexandre Georges.

88 Ezra Stoller © Esto. © Ibram Lassaw.

89 Stiftung Preussische Schlösser und Gärten Berlin-Brandenburg/Jörg P. Anders.

90 From John M. Jacobus, *Philip Johnson* (London: Prentice-Hall; New York: G. Braziller, 1962), [53]. Image reprinted with the permission of George Braziller, Inc. © Alexandre Georges.

91 From "The Current Work of Phillip Johnson." *Zodiac* 8 (1961): [64]. © Alexandre Georges.

92 Stiftung Preussische Schlösser und Gärten Berlin-Brandenburg/Jörg P. Anders.

93 *Flair* 1, no. 1 (February 1950): 68–69. © Mark Faurer. © Successió Miró/SODRAC (2013).

94 Ezra Stoller © Esto. © Richard Lippold/SODRAC (2013).

95 From "The Four Seasons," *Interiors* 119, no. 5 (December 1959): [81]. Reproduced with permission from Richard Reens. © Richard Lippold/SODRAC (2013).

96 From "More Elegance at the House of Seagram," *Architectural Record* 126, no. 5 (November 1959): 202. Digital image: McGill University, Blackader-Lauterman Library of Art and Architecture. Reprinted with permission from Architectural Record © 2013, The McGraw-Hill Companies.

97 From "The Four Seasons: Collaboration for Elegance," *Progressive Architecture* 40, no. 12 (December 1959): [143]. Reproduced with permission from Richard Reens.

98 "The Four Seasons Multipurpose Ceiling," *Progressive Architecture* 41, no. 5 (May 1960): 196.

99 "The Four Seasons Multipurpose Ceiling," *Progressive Architecture* 41, no. 5 (May 1960): 198.

100 From "The Four Seasons," *Interiors* 119, no. 5 (December 1959): [87]. Reproduced with permission from Richard Reens. © Successió Miró/SODRAC (2013).

101 © Richard Pare. © Richard Lippold/SODRAC (2013).

102 From "The Four Seasons," *Interiors* 119, no. 5 (December 1959): [83]. Reproduced with permission from Richard Reens. © Richard Lippold/SODRAC (2013).

103 From "Variable Lighting in Four Seasons Restaurant, New York City," *International Lighting Review* 12, no. 2 (1961): 67.

104 "Decoration Zu Der Oper: Die Zauberflöte Act 1 Scene VI," *Sammlung von Theater-Dekorationen erfunden von Carl Friedrich Schinkel* (Berlin: Ernst und Korn, 1874), pl. 14. Canadian Centre for Architecture, Montreal.

105 Ezra Stoller © Esto. © Picasso Estate/SODRAC (2013). Stage curtain owned by New York Landmarks Conservancy.

106 Fonds Seagram Building, Canadian Centre for Architecture, Montreal. © Robert Walker.

107 Fonds Phyllis Lambert, Canadian Centre for Architecture, Montreal. © Haig W. Shekerjian.

108 Musée National d'Art Moderne, Centre Georges Pompidou, Paris. © CNAC/MNAM/Dist. Réunion des Musées Nationaux/Art Resource, NY. © Estate of Constantin Brancusi/SODRAC (2013).

109 From "The Four Seasons," *Interiors* 119, no. 5 (December 1959): [86]. Reproduced with permission from Richard Reens. © Richard Lippold/SODRAC (2013).

110 *Building Seagram* Research Collection, Canadian Centre for Architecture, Montreal. © Phyllis Lambert. From "Restaurant-Details of Sculpture Ceilings and Moving Picture Screens," Drawing R-29, June 2, 1958, diazotype. Fonds Seagram Building, Canadian Centre for Architecture, Montreal.

111 *Building Seagram* Research Collection, Canadian Centre for Architecture, Montreal. © Phyllis Lambert. From "Restaurant-Details of Sculpture Ceilings and

Moving Picture Screens," Drawing R-29, June 2, 1958, diazotype. Fonds Seagram Building, Canadian Centre for Architecture, Montreal.

112 Fonds Seagram Building, Canadian Centre for Architecture, Montreal. © Richard Pare. © Picasso Estate/SODRAC (2013).

113 Musée Picasso, Paris. © Réunion des Musées Nationaux/Art Resource, NY. © Picasso Estate/SODRAC (2013).

114 Fonds Phyllis Lambert, Canadian Centre for Architecture, Montreal. © André Villers.

115 From Roland Penrose, *The Sculpture of Picasso* (New York: The Museum of Modern Art, 1967), [156]. Reproduced with permission from the Réunion des Musées Nationaux, Paris. © Picasso Estate/SODRAC (2013).

116 Alinari Archives, Florence.

117 *Building Seagram* Research Collection, Canadian Centre for Architecture, Montreal. © Phyllis Lambert. © 2013 Kate Rothko Prizel & Christopher Rothko/SODRAC. Tate London/Art Resource, NY. Collection of Kawamura Memorial DIC Museum of Art. Image courtesy of the National Gallery of Art, Washington.

118 Fonds Seagram Building, Canadian Centre for Architecture, Montreal. Ezra Stoller © Esto. © Estate of Fernand Léger/SODRAC (2013).

119 Fonds Seagram Building, Canadian Centre for Architecture, Montreal.

120 Canadian Centre for Architecture, Montreal. Ezra Stoller © Esto. © Succesió Miró/SODRAC (2013).

121 Canadian Centre for Architecture, Montreal. Ezra Stoller © Esto.

122 Fonds Seagram Building, Canadian Centre for Architecture, Montreal. Ezra Stoller © Esto.

123 Fonds Seagram Building, Canadian Centre for Architecture, Montreal. © Russell Hart. © Succesió Miró/SODRAC (2013). © Herbert Matter, courtesy Staley-Wise Gallery.

124 Fonds Seagram Building, Canadian Centre for Architecture, Montreal. © Russell Hart. © Herbert Matter, courtesy Staley-Wise Gallery.

125 Canadian Centre for Architecture, Montreal. Ezra Stoller © Esto. Conrad Marca-Relli, St. Cyprian's Day © Courtesy Archivio Marca-Relli, Parma.

126 Canadian Centre for Architecture, Montreal. Ezra Stoller © Esto.

127 Canadian Centre for Architecture, Montreal. Ezra Stoller © Esto.

128 Fonds Seagram Building, Canadian Centre for Architecture, Montreal. © Richard Pare.

129 Fonds Seagram Building, Canadian Centre for Architecture, Montreal. © Richard Pare.

130 © Aperture Foundation, Inc., Paul Strand Archive.

131 Courtesy Cheim & Read, New York. © Eggleston Artistic Trust.

132 © Danny Lyon/Magnum Photos.

133 Canadian Centre for Architecture, Montreal. Nicholas Nixon, Seagram County Court House Archives, Library of Congress, LC-S37-NN16-1.

134 Canadian Centre for Architecture, Montreal. Jim Dow, Seagram County Court House Archives, Library of Congress, LC-S37-JD80-1.

135 Fonds Seagram Building, Canadian Centre for Architecture, Montreal. Ellen Land-Weber, Seagram County Court House Archives, Library of Congress, LC-S35-EL47-3.

136 Photograph of study: Fonds Seagram Building, Canadian Centre for Architecture, Montreal. © Richard Serra/SODRAC (2013).

137 Photograph of study: Fonds Seagram Building, Canadian Centre for Architecture, Montreal. © Estate of Robert Smithson/SODRAC, Montreal/VAGA, New York (2013).

138 Photograph of study: Fonds Seagram Building, Canadian Centre for Architecture, Montreal. © Michael Snow.

139 Fonds Seagram Building, Canadian Centre for Architecture, Montreal.

140 Cover of *Progressive Architecture* 46, no. 9 (September 1965). © Architect/Hanley Wood, LLC. © Maude Dorr.

141 Fonds Seagram Building, Canadian Centre for Architecture, Montreal. Fred W. McDarrah/Premium Archive/Getty Images. © The Barnett Newman Foundation, New York/SODRAC, Montreal (2013).

142 Fonds Seagram Building, Canadian Centre for Architecture, Montreal. © Carla Caccamise Ash. © Estate of Tony Smith/SODRAC (2013). Sculpture now held by Hillman Library, University of Pittsburgh.

143 Fonds Seagram Building, Canadian Centre for Architecture, Montreal. © Carla Caccamise Ash. © Estate of Tony Smith/SODRAC (2013). Sculpture now held by Hillman Library, University of Pittsburgh.

144 Public Art Fund. © Estate of Tony Smith/SODRAC (2013). Sculpture now held by Hillman Library, University of Pittsburgh.

145 Fonds Seagram Building, Canadian Centre for Architecture, Montreal. © Carla Caccamise Ash. © Richard Long.

146 Fonds Seagram Building, Canadian Centre for Architecture, Montreal. © Carla Caccamise Ash. © Richard Long.

147 Fonds Seagram Building, Canadian Centre for Architecture, Montreal. Courtesy Paula Cooper Gallery, New York. © Joel Shapiro/SODRAC (2013).

148 Fonds Phyllis Lambert, Canadian Centre for Architecture, Montreal. © Richard Pare. © Estate of Jean Dubuffet/SODRAC (2013).

149 Fonds Phyllis Lambert, Canadian Centre for Architecture, Montreal. © Mark di Suvero. Sculpture now held by Saint Louis Art Museum, funds given by Mr. and Mrs. Norman B. Champ, Jr., 31: 1967.

150 Fonds Seagram Building, Canadian Centre for Architecture, Montreal. Reproduced with permission from Severud Associates Consulting Engineers, P.C.

151 © Michael Heizer, 1979. Sculpture now held by The Metropolitan Museum of Art, Purchase, Christophe de Menil Gift, 1979 (1979.187a-k).

152 Fonds Phyllis Lambert, Canadian Centre for Architecture, Montreal. © Marilyn Wood.

153 Fonds Seagram Building, Canadian Centre for Architecture, Montreal. © Phyllis Lambert.

154 William H. Whyte, *The Social Life of Small Urban Spaces* (Washington, DC: Conservation Foundation, 1980), 23. Reprinted with permission from Project for Public Spaces, Inc.

155 William H. Whyte, *The Social Life of Small Urban Spaces* (Washington, DC: Conservation Foundation, 1980), 33. Reprinted with permission from Project for Public Spaces, Inc.

156 William H. Whyte, *The Social Life of Small Urban Spaces* (Washington, DC: Conservation Foundation, 1980), 48. Reprinted with permission from Project for Public Spaces, Inc.

157 William H. Whyte, *The Social Life of Small Urban Spaces* (Washington, DC: Conservation Foundation, 1980), 50. Reprinted with permission from Project for Public Spaces, Inc.

158 William H. Whyte, *The Social Life of Small Urban Spaces* (Washington, DC: Conservation Foundation, 1980), 60. Reprinted with permission from Project for Public Spaces, Inc.

159 Fonds Phyllis Lambert, Canadian Centre for Architecture, Montreal. © Phyllis Lambert.

160 Fonds Phyllis Lambert, Canadian Centre for Architecture, Montreal. © Phyllis Lambert.

161 Fonds Phyllis Lambert, Canadian Centre for Architecture, Montreal. © Phyllis Lambert.

162 Fonds Phyllis Lambert, Canadian Centre for Architecture, Montreal. © Phyllis Lambert.

163 © Norman McGrath.

164 Courtesy of IBM Archives.

165 © Wolfgang Hoyt/Esto.

166 N.Y.C. Landmarks Preservation Commission, 1989.

167 N.Y.C. Landmarks Preservation Commission, 1989.

168 N.Y.C. Landmarks Preservation Commission, 1989.

169 N.Y.C. Landmarks Preservation Commission, 1989.

170 N.Y.C. Landmarks Preservation Commission, 1989.

171 N.Y.C. Landmarks Preservation Commission, 1989.

172 From "Skidmore, Owings & Merrill, Park Avenue Plaza," *Architecture and Urbanism*, no. 150 (March 1983): [51].

173 © Foster + Partners.

174 Fonds Phyllis Lambert, Canadian Centre for Architecture, Montreal. © Tommy Weber.

175 Ezra Stoller © Esto.